Essentials of Autism Spectrum Disorders

Essentials of Autism Spectrum Disorders

Editor: Draco Oldman

AMERICAN
MEDICAL PUBLISHERS
www.americanmedicalpublishers.com

AMERICAN
MEDICAL PUBLISHERS
www.americanmedicalpublishers.com

Cataloging-in-Publication Data

Essentials of autism spectrum disorders / edited by Draco Oldman.
p. cm.
Includes bibliographical references and index.
ISBN 979-8-88740-101-0
1. Autism spectrum disorders. 2. Developmental disabilities. 3. Autism spectrum disorders--Diagnosis.
4. Autism spectrum disorders--Treatment. 5. Psychiatry. I. Oldman, Draco.
RC553.A88 E87 2023
616.858 82--dc23

American Medical Publishers,
41 Flatbush Avenue,
1st Floor, New York,
NY 11217, USA

ISBN 979-8-88740-101-0 (Hardback)

Contents

Preface

The purpose of the book is to provide a glimpse into the dynamics and to present opinions and studies of some of the scientists engaged in the development of new ideas in the field from very different standpoints. This book will prove useful to students and researchers owing to its high content quality.

Autism spectrum disorder (ASD) refers to a type of disorder that appears in early childhood and is distinguished by qualitative abnormalities in social interactions. The disorder can also be characterized by impaired communication skills and restricted repetitive behaviors, activities and interests. As autism is a spectrum disorder, each autistic individual has a unique set of abilities and difficulties. The manner in which people with autism can think, learn and solve problems can range from severely impaired to highly skilled. Some people with ASD could need a lot of assistance in their daily lives, whereas others may require less assistance and in some circumstances they could even live independently. The behavioral treatments or interventions associated with autism can help both adults and children. These treatments can teach new abilities to adults and children in addressing their underlying weaknesses and reduce their core symptoms. This book elucidates the innovative models around prospective developments with respect to autism spectrum disorders. It will help new researchers by foregrounding their knowledge on this condition.

At the end, I would like to appreciate all the efforts made by the authors in completing their chapters professionally. I express my deepest gratitude to all of them for contributing to this book by sharing their valuable works. A special thanks to my family and friends for their constant support in this journey.

Editor

1

An Overview of the Main Genetic, Epigenetic and Environmental Factors Involved in Autism Spectrum Disorder Focusing on Synaptic Activity

Elena Masini [1,†], Eleonora Loi [1,†], Ana Florencia Vega-Benedetti [1], Marinella Carta [2], Giuseppe Doneddu [3], Roberta Fadda [4] and Patrizia Zavattari [1,*]

1 Department of Biomedical Sciences, Unit of Biology and Genetics, University of Cagliari, 09042 Cagliari, Italy; elena.masini97@gmail.com (E.M.); eleonora.loi@unica.it (E.L.); anaf.vegab@unica.it (A.F.V.-B.)
2 Center for Pervasive Developmental Disorders, Azienda Ospedaliera Brotzu, 09121 Cagliari, Italy; marinellacarta@aob.it
3 Centro per l'Autismo e Disturbi correlati (CADc), Nuovo Centro Fisioterapico Sardo, 09131 Cagliari, Italy; io.donez@gmail.com
4 Department of Pedagogy, Psychology, Philosophy, University of Cagliari, 09123 Cagliari, Italy; robfadda@unica.it
* Correspondence: pzavattari@unica.it
† The authors contributed equally to this work.

Abstract: Autism spectrum disorder (ASD) is a neurodevelopmental disorder that affects social interaction and communication, with restricted interests, activity and behaviors. ASD is highly familial, indicating that genetic background strongly contributes to the development of this condition. However, only a fraction of the total number of genes thought to be associated with the condition have been discovered. Moreover, other factors may play an important role in ASD onset. In fact, it has been shown that parental conditions and in utero and perinatal factors may contribute to ASD etiology. More recently, epigenetic changes, including DNA methylation and micro RNA alterations, have been associated with ASD and proposed as potential biomarkers. This review aims to provide a summary of the literature regarding ASD candidate genes, mainly focusing on synapse formation and functionality and relevant epigenetic and environmental aspects acting in concert to determine ASD onset.

Keywords: autism spectrum disorder; ASD; genetic factors; epigenetic factors; environmental factors; pervasive developmental disorder; post-synaptic density; CNV; SNP; gene fusion

1. Introduction

Autism is a complex syndrome characterized by a range of conditions and symptoms that frame it as a spectrum of disorders (autism spectrum disorder, ASD), including relevant physiological and biochemical ones, whose core symptoms includes social deficits and restrictive/repetitive behaviors. In the 1960s, thanks to the studies of Bernard Rimland, it was understood that ASD is a psychiatric disorder which might be grounded on a combination of genetic and environmental factors. To cope with ASD, it is necessary to achieve positive results through multidisciplinary, biomedical and behavioral therapies. Early diagnosis and intensive therapeutic interventions greatly improve the disease outcomes. In this context, the discovery of new diagnostic methods to detect ASD-related genetic alterations and biomarkers becomes fundamental in order to make an early diagnosis of the disorder.

In this review, we provide an overview of the genetic, epigenetic and environmental factors contributing to ASD pathogenesis.

2. Autism

2.1. Clinical Characteristics of ASD

ASD can be considered as a group of early-onset neuroevolutionary disorders which seem to be at the basis of alterations in brain connectivity, with cascading effects on many neuropsychological functions [1,2]. The The Diagnostic and Statistical Manual of Mental Disorders (DSM-5) (The American Psychiatric Association, APA, Philadelphia, PA, USA, 2013) gives the condition of autism the attribute of "spectrum" and uses criteria derived from diagnostic research assessment tools.

As indicated in the DSM-5 (APA, Philadelphia, PA, USA, 2013), individuals with ASD are characterized by persistent deficits in social communication and social interaction across multiple contexts and by restricted, repetitive patterns of behaviour, interests or activities. Deficiency in social communication and social interaction might appear in the form of deficits in social-emotional reciprocity, in nonverbal communicative behaviours used for social interaction and deficit in developing, maintaining and understanding age-appropriate relationships. As reported in the DSM-5, symptoms could be masked during early development and fully manifest only when social demands exceed limited capacities or may be hidden by learned strategies in later life. The impairments should cause clinically significant damage in social, occupational or other important areas of current functioning.

ASD symptoms should not be better explained by a diagnosis of intellectual disability (ID) or global developmental delay. Intellectual disability and ASD might co-occur.

The DSM-5 proposes differentiations based on commorbidity with intellectual impairment, language impairment, another neurodevelopmental, mental, or behavioral disorder, genetic or medical condition or environmental factors. Furthermore, it is possible to differentiate between different levels of severity according to the level of support required to function in daily contexts. According to this description, it is clear that different clinical variants of ASD exist and should be taken into account for diagnosis and intervention (APA, 2013). A distinction is made between a congenital form of ASD, representing a small percentage of cases in which the symptoms occur shortly after birth and in which the genetic fingerprint is prevalent, and a regressive or acquired form, in which the disorder appears after a period of typical development and it is not characterised by typical and constant genetic abnormalities, although several single nucleotide polymorphisms (SNPs) have been associated with the disease [3,4]. SNPs constitute variations of a single nucleotide in certain DNA traits. SNPs associated with ASD have been identified in genes encoding for proteins involved in different processes, including: cellular detoxification, some neuronal receptors and metabolism of several neurotransmitters and metabolites, in particular those of the metabolic circuits of methylation and transulfuration [5,6].

2.2. Epidemiology

Autism has been considered relatively rare for many years, with a prevalence of less than 1 in 1000 children, while today, the estimated rate is 1 in 160, and it seems likely to increase in the coming years (World Health Organization, Geneva, Switzerland, 2019). In the last decade, the study of ASD genetics has proved to be crucial not only to interpret and explain its phenotypic heterogeneity but also to discover new diagnostic procedures and therapies. It is estimated to-date that hundreds of genes are involved in ASD, resulting in a unified spectrum of different phenotypes, including different language and social deficits with various associated sub-phenotypes [7].

ASD show an unequal distribution based on gender: males have a four times higher risk of developing the disorder than females. A number of hypotheses have been made to interpret this unequal prevalence: in females, a higher dose of genetic "defect" is required than in males, consistent with the hypothesis of the contribution of protective genetic factors in females, because in males, there is only one X chromosome, so when alterations appear, it cannot be compensated by the normality of a second X chromosome. An association between testosterone levels and ASD risk has also been described: males have more frequent inflammatory reactions and use the brain in a more focal way and therefore suffer more from alterations in neuronal development that affect the connection systems between the different areas [8].

Genetic, environmental and developmental factors play a key role in the onset of autism spectrum disorders, as highlighted from many epidemiological studies [9,10]. It is unlikely that a single condition or event plays a major role in the causality of ASD; based on research to date, rather, none of the risk factors identified is a necessary and sufficient condition for ASD. Even for syndromic or secondary autism, which refers to autism with a single defined cause, such as fragile X syndrome and tuberous sclerosis, none of these etiologies are specific to autism because each of them encompasses a variable proportion of individuals with and without autism [11]. At present, ASD appears to have a multifactorial etiology to which developmental (in utero and early childhood), environmental and genetic aspects contribute, in as-yet unknown and different ways. Emerging methodologies in genomics and epigenomics research could be the key to elucidate the mysteries underlying the epidemiology of autism spectrum disorder.

3. Genetic and Epigenetic Factors

The involvement of genetic etiology in ASD was first suggested by a study on twins reported in the 1970s. The genetic heritability of a trait can be estimated by comparing the phenotypic concordance between monozygotic twins (MZ), which have 100% genetic similarity, and dizygotic twins (DZ), who have approximately 50% genetic similarity. The greater the difference between the concordance of MZ twins and DZ twins, the higher the genetic heritability and the contribution of genetics to that trait. The genetic fingerprint was confirmed by the high concordance of autism in monozygotic twins (60–90%) compared to dizygotic twins (5–40%) [12,13].

One of the largest studies to date, involving more than two million children born between 1982 and 2006 in Sweden, concluded that ASD has an inheritability of 45–56% [14]. A study of all twins born in the UK between 1994 and 1996 estimated an inheritability of more than 56% using concordance in MZ (0.77–0.99) compared to DZ (0.22–0.65) twins [13].

Considering all lines of evidence, the genetic heritability of ASD is estimated to play a fundamental role in ASD onset, together with environmental and epigenetic factors. However, despite most of the studies aimed at understanding the etiological basis of ASD having been focused on the genetic component, it has been possible to associate genetic variants to only a relatively small fraction of ASD patients. The problem, known as the "missing heritability issue", is common to most complex genetic diseases. Several hypotheses have been put forward to justify the missing heritability, such as the existence of poorly characterised variants, genotype/genotype interactions, incomplete penetrance, epigenetic factors and genotype/environment interactions [15–17].

In the 1990s, most of the research consisted of candidate gene studies, focusing on a particular gene that might be involved in ASD. From 2005, technologies such as whole-exome sequencing (WES), but also microarrays, have allowed genome-wide studies, leading to the identification of different variations in copy number (CNVs), DNA segments larger than 1 kilobase present in a variable copy number compared to a reference genome and single nucleotide variations (SNVs) in autistic patients, suggesting a highly heterogeneous genetic architecture. CNVs would contribute at about 15% and SNVs at 7% to the causes of ASD. Only a few of these genetic alterations have such complete penetrance that they are associated with ASD in almost every person who carries that variant [18]. On the contrary, genetic alterations with incomplete penetrance, variable expressivity or both are more frequently observed. However, the cause in most ASDs (>75%) remains elusive [18]. Genome-wide association studies (GWAS) have identified several SNPs associated with ASD. The first GWAS study allowed the identification of six polymorphisms, including some localized in *CDH10* and *CDH9*, genes encoding for cadherins, proteins that are important in cell adhesion, as common genetic variants in ASD [19].

However, the fact that several GWASs failed to identify some relevant loci despite the use of genetic data from more than 1000 families affected by autism suggests that the effect of individual common variants is relatively small [20].

On the other hand, WES analysis of affected and unaffected individuals has proven to be a powerful approach that offers new opportunities of sporadic cases studies and has the ability to detect mutations and de novo variants with incomplete penetrance [21]. WES has already led to the identification of over 150 new candidate genes for ASD.

In addition to SNPs, evidence is accumulating that CNVs play an important role in human neuropsychiatric diseases. ASD patients have three to five times more de novo CNVs than other family members and unaffected controls [22,23].

CNVs can influence gene expression, thus contributing to the pathogenesis of the disease through various mechanisms, including gene dosage, gene interruption, position effects, gene fusion and unmasking of recessive alleles or polymorphisms [24].

Screening for CNVs has proven to be a method of choice for identifying genes associated with ASD susceptibility [25]. Although CNVs associated with the disease are usually unique and show a low frequency in the population, they are identified in 8–21% of individuals with ASD and are most likely related to a severe clinical picture [26,27]. In addition, previous studies have indicated that individuals with syndromic ASD and intellectual disability have more pathogenic CNVs than individuals with non-syndromic ASD or ID [26,28].

CNVs may also lead to the generation of chimeric genes. Several studies have investigated whether fusion transcripts may lead to an increased ASD susceptibility. Holt and colleagues identified a fusion transcript involving *MAPKAPK5* and *ACAD10* genes in two ASD probands. However, the fusion transcript was detected at similar rates in both ASD patients and controls and had a premature stop codon, suggesting that it may be degraded by nonsense-mediated decay [29]. Similarly, Pagnamenta et al. identified a *DOCK4-IMMP2L* fusion transcript, likely to be subjected to nonsense-mediated decay in ASD individuals and their unaffected family members [30]. A study conducted on a multiplex family identified a *BST1-CD38* fusion transcript in one ASD proband with asthma, suggesting that it may be related to the more severe phenotype of this patient compared to the other ASD sibling [31]. qRT-PCR analysis showed that the fusion transcript was less expressed compared to the wild-type *BST1* transcript in the lymphoblastoid cell line derived from the proband, while the aberrant protein was not detected in a preliminary Western blot analysis [31]. Recently, our research group identified a microdeletion leading to the formation of an *ELMOD3-SH2D6* chimeric transcript in a multiplex ASD family [32]. *SH2D6* is expressed at extremely low levels in blood cells. On the other hand, the fusion transcript was highly expressed in PMBCs from the two ASD siblings and their unaffected mother carrying the deletion, suggesting that it was not subjected to nonsense-mediated decay. Bioinformatic analysis has shown that the fusion transcript would encode for a chimeric protein with an interrupted domain of ELMOD3 and would not contain the canonical SH2D6 sequence, suggesting an impaired function of the protein [32]. These results suggest a possible contribution of fusion transcripts in the complex ASD phenotype. Therefore, in case of copy number loss, the possible transcript fusion and chimeric protein product should be deeply investigated.

Recent studies have shown that epigenetic factors, including DNA methylation, hystone modifications and microRNAs (miRNAs), could play an important role in predisposition to autism.

We herein provide an overview of the main candidate genes (extensively reviewed in [33]) and epigenetic mechanisms involved in ASD etiology. Figure 1 summarizes some ASD candidate genes and epigenetic factors, belonging to the pathways mainly associated with ASD described in this review.

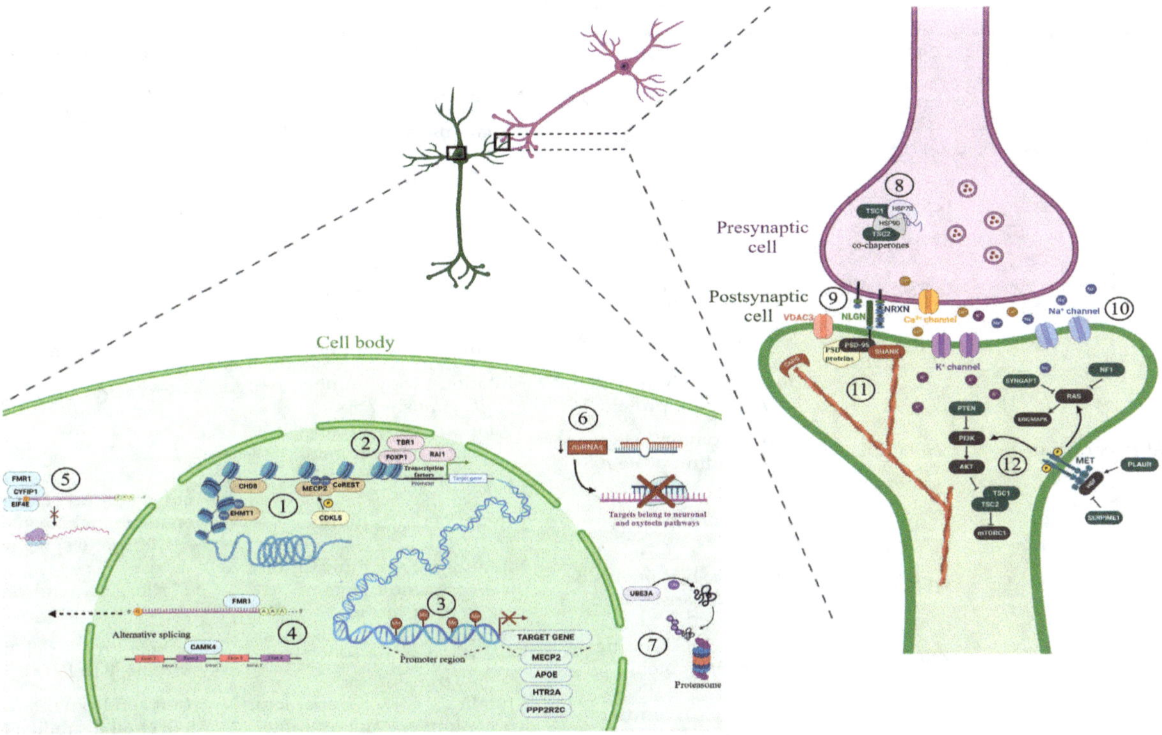

Figure 1. Candidate genes and epigenetic factors representative of the main processes involved in autism spectrum disorder (ASD) development. The illustration shows a synapse between neurons (presynaptic cell in violet and postsynaptic cell in green). On the bottom-left, a cell body of a neuron including different nuclear and cytoplasmic mechanisms involved in ASD. In the nucleus, several processes implicated in gene expression regulation are shown: (**1**) chromatin packaging and factors involved in chromatin remodeling; (**2**) gene transcription regulated by transcription factors; (**3**) DNA methylation at promoter region associated with transcription inhibition of target genes; (**4**) alternative splicing and mRNA export to the cytoplasm. In the cytoplasm, the following mechanisms are shown: (**5**) regulation of protein translation by the CYFIP1-EIF4E-FMR1 complex; (**6**) post-transcriptional regulation by miRNA; (**7**) protein ubiquitination and degradation by proteasome. On the right, the synapse architecture and functionality mechanisms associated with ASD. In the presynaptic cell, (**8**) TSC proteins and co-chaperons. (**9**) The neurexin/neuroligin transsynaptic complex and (**10**) the voltage-gated ion channels are represented. In the postsynaptic cell, (**11**) actin filaments, capping proteins and scaffold proteins; (**12**) some members of PI3K/AKT pathway, RAS signal transduction pathway and MET receptor tyrosine kinase pathway. Chromatin remodelers are indicated in beige, transcription factors in pink, proteins involved in RNA binding and export in light blue, protein ubiquitination in purple, scaffold proteins in red, cell growth and proliferation proteins in green and their related pathway members in grey. A more comprehensive list of ASD candidate genes can be found in Table 1 and along the text. Figure created using BioRender.com images.

3.1. *Relevant Candidate Genes*

Case-control studies on population and animal models have pointed out more than 800 genes associated with autism. The most affected genes in ASD encode for proteins involved in chromatin remodeling and transcriptional regulation, cell proliferation and mostly synaptic architecture and functionality. In this review, we will focus on this last category since our recent studies have also pointed out alterations in these genes fundamental for a proper synaptic function. Table 1 provides a summary of several genes clearly implicated in ASD, included in the SFARI Gene database as high confidence ASD genes (release 26 October 2020, gene.sfari.org) belonging to the other categories. Most of these genes were indicated in the largest exome sequencing study of ASD to date [34], as well as in the list narrowing down the number of amygdala-expressed genes associated to the social pathophysiology of ASD [35].

Table 1. Several relevant ASD candidate genes.

Category	Gene Symbol	Gene Name	Alterations	Associated Syndromes
Chromatin regulators	*ANKRD11*	Ankyrin repeat domain 11	Mutations; copy number loss	KBG syndrome; Cornelia de Lange syndrome
	ARID1B	AT-rich interaction domain 1B	Mutations; copy number loss; copy number gain; translocation	Coffin–Siris syndrome
	ASXL3	ASXL Transcriptional Regulator 3	Mutations	Bainbridge-Ropers syndrome
	ATRX	ATRX Chromatin Remodeler	Mutations; copy number loss	
	AUTS2	Autism susceptibility candidate 2	Mutations; copy number loss; copy number gain; inversion; translocation	
	CHD2	Chromodomain helicase DNA binding protein 2	Mutations; copy number loss	Tourette syndrome
	CHD7	Chromodomain helicase DNA binding protein 7	Mutations; copy number loss; translocation	CHARGE syndrome
	CHD8	Chromodomain helicase DNA binding protein 8	Mutations; copy number loss; copy number gain; translocation	
	CREBBP	CREB-binding protein	Mutations; copy number loss	Rubinstein–Taybi syndrome, Menke-Hennekam syndrome 1, Tourette syndrome
	EHMT1	Euchromatic histone-lysine N-methyltransferase 1	Mutations; copy number loss; copy number gain; translocation	Kleefstra syndrome
	MBD5	Methyl-CpG binding domain protein 5	Mutations; copy number loss; copy number gain; inversion; translocation	2q23.1 microdeletion syndrome, Kleefstra syndrome
	MECP2	Methyl CpG binding protein 2	Mutations; copy number loss; copy number gain; promoter methylation	Rett syndrome, X-linked intellectual disability, MECP2 duplication syndrome
	SETD5	SET domain containing 5	Mutations; copy number loss	
Transcription factors/regulators	*ADNP*	Activity-dependent neuroprotector homeobox	Mutations; copy number loss	Helsmoortel-Van der Aa syndrome
	FOXG1	Forkhead box G1	Mutations; copy number loss; copy number gain; translocation	Rett syndrome, FOXG1 syndrome, West syndrome,
	FOXP1	Forkhead box P1	Mutations; copy number loss; inversion; translocation	
	FOXP2	Forkhead box P2	Mutations; copy number loss; translocation	FOXP2-related speech and language disorder
	MED13L	Mediator complex subunit 13-like	Mutations; copy number loss; copy number gain	
	POGZ	Pogo transposable element with ZNF domain	Mutations; copy number loss; copy number gain	White–Sutton syndrome
	RAI1	Retinoic Acid Induced 1	Mutations; copy number loss; copy number gain	Smith–Magenis syndrome, Potocki–Lupski syndrome
	TBR1	T-box, brain, 1	Mutations; copy number loss	
	TCF4	Transcription factor 4	Mutations; copy number loss; translocation	Pitt–Hopkins syndrome
	ZBTB20	Zinc finger and BTB domain containing 20	Mutations; copy number loss; translocation	3q13.31 microdeletion syndrome, Primrose syndrome,
mRNA binding and trafficking regulator	*FMR1* and its pathways	Fragile X mental retardation 1	Mutations; copy number loss	Fragile X syndrome, Fragile X-associated tremor/ataxia syndrome
Protein degradation	*UBE3A*	Ubiquitin protein ligase E3A	Mutations; copy number gain	Angelman syndrome
Cell growth/proliferation	*DYRK1A*	Dual-specificity tyrosine-(Y)-phosphorylation regulated kinase 1A	Mutations; copy number loss; inversion; translocation	
	NF1	Neurofibromin 1	Mutations; copy number loss	
	PTEN and its pathways	Phosphatase and tensin homolog	Mutations; copy number loss	Cowden syndrome, Macrocephaly/autism syndrome, PTEN hamartoma tumor syndrome
	SYNGAP1	Synaptic Ras GTPase activating protein 1	Mutations; copy number loss; translocation	
	TSC1/TSC2	Tuberous sclerosis 1/2	Mutations	
Protein modification	*CDKL5*	Cyclin-dependent kinase-like 5	Mutations; copy number loss; copy number gain translocation	Rett syndrome, Angelman syndrome

Prepared by the authors with data from gene.sfari.org (release 26 October 2020).

Synaptic Architecture and Functionality

It is not surprising that many candidate ASD genes are involved in synaptic architecture and function, which allows the transmission of information between neurons and between neurons and other cells, such as muscle, sensory and other cells. Many ASD candidate genes are involved in dendritic spine formation. Dendritic spines are small actin-rich protrusions that form the postsynaptic part of most excitatory synapses. Remodeling of actin cytoskeleton is responsible for the changes in the shape and size of dendritic spines and, consequently, to the synaptic functions [36]. Actin regulation mechanisms regulate the formation, maturation and plasticity of dendritic spines and of neuronal processes, such as learning and memory [36]. Abnormalities in the number and shape of dendritic spines have been observed in several neurological disorders, including autism, and contribute to brain dysfunction [37].

Post-synaptic density proteins (PSD), including cell adhesion molecules, scaffold proteins, receptors and cytoskeleton proteins, are fundamental for synaptic transmission and plasticity. Alterations of these proteins have been associated with many neurological disorders, including ASD [38].

- Cell adhesion molecules

Neurexins (NRXN) and neuroligins (NLGN) are transmembrane synaptic proteins that form the neurexin/neuroligin transsynaptic complex, crucial for synaptic function [39]. NLGNs bind to SHANK3 through PSD-95 and other synaptic proteins.

Loss of function NRX1 variants in ASD individuals have been identified in multiple studies [23,40,41]. Studies conducted in animal models knockout (KO) for *NLGN* and *NRXN* family members showed that mice develop ASD-like symptoms and have confirmed their role in synaptic function [42–44].

CNTNAP2, also known as *CASPR2*, encodes for a member of the NRXN family that serves as an adhesion protein, primarily between neuronal and glial cells. CNVs encompassing *CNTNAP2* and resulting in its decreased expression have been described in subjects with ASD [45–47]. The suppression of CNTNAP2 in murine models causes autistic behaviors, such as repetitive behaviors and reduced socialization and communication [48].

- Scaffold proteins

SHANK gene family, including *SHANK1*, *SHANK2* and *SHANK3*, has been suggested as a strong candidate for ASD. SHANK proteins are multi-domain post synaptic density scaffold proteins that connect neurotransmitter receptors, ion channels and other membrane proteins to cytoskeleton actin and signaling proteins. These proteins are important for synapse formation and dendritic spine maturation [49]. Rare deletions of *SHANK2* and de novo variants causing loss of protein function have been identified in individuals with ASD [50]. A microdeletion encompassing *SHANK3* determines Phelan–McDermid syndrome, characterized by intellectual disability, ASD, severe speech disorders and epilepsy [51]. A meta-analysis of SHANK mutations found low frequency of *SHANK1* and *SHANK2* deleterious mutations in contrast to the high frequency of loss of function *SHANK3* mutations in cases with ASD [52].

Our studies led to the identification of another promising ASD candidate gene, *CAPG*. This gene encodes for a member of the gelsolin family of actin-regulatory proteins, important for the remodeling of actin architecture. A microdeletion encompassing the entire *CAPG* gene has been recently described in three completely independent families in the heterozygous [53,54] and homozygous state [55]. Importantly, a reduced CAPG expression, both at transcriptional and protein levels, has been detected in the Sardinian family members carrying the deletion, and reduced *CAPG* mRNA levels have been also observed in an independent cohort of 13 non-Sardinian ASD cases compared to age-matched healthy controls [54].

Several studies have demonstrated the importance of CAPG for the formation of functional synapses. In fact, experiments conducted on cultured hippocampal neurons have demonstrated that capping proteins are present at the branched actin filament network of dendritic spine heads and they are fundamental for dendritic spine development [56,57]. In fact, *CAPG* knock-down led to a decline in spine density and to an increased number of filopodia-like protrusions [56].

- Voltage-gated ion channels

The role of genetic defects of different ion channels in the pathogenesis of ASD is well established. In fact, GWAS, WES and WGS have identified several polymorphisms and rare variants in calcium, sodium and potassium channels in ASD subjects (reviewed in [58]).

Point mutations in *CACNA1C* gene, which encode for L-type voltage-gated Ca^{2+} channel Cav1.2, lead to Timothy syndrome (TS), a disorder affecting multiple organs and characterized by an autistic phenotype [59,60]. L-type channels are mainly expressed in neuronal dendrites and cell bodies and are crucial for the activation of Ca^{2+}-signaling pathways and for neuronal excitability [61]. Defects in CACNA1C prevent the inactivation of the channel and lead to its prolonged opening and consequent increase in Ca^{2+} flux [60,62].

Mutations in other genes encoding for L-type and T-type Ca^{2+} channels, such as *CACNA1D, CACNA1E, CACNA1F* and *CACNA1H*, have been described in ASD [63–67]. Moreover, mutations of *CACNB2*, the gene encoding for the regulatory β2 subunit of CACNA1C, have been found in ASD families [68].

Genetic defects in genes encoding for sodium channels, such as *SCN1A, SCN2A, SCN3A, SCN7A* and *SNC8A*, have been also associated with ASD [69–73]. Voltage-dependent sodium channels are mainly expressed in neurons and glial cells and are fundamental for the initiation and propagation of action potentials. Mutations of SCN1A cause Dravet syndrome, characterized by seizures and frequently manifesting, also, autistic symptoms. A study has shown that *Scn1a+/−* heterozygous KO mice display stereotypical and anxious behaviors other than seizures [74].

Several studies have also shown that mutations in genes encoding for K^+ channels, including *KCNMA1, KCND2, KCNJ10, KCNQ3* and *KCNQ5*, may play a central role in ASD etiology [75–78]. It has been shown that KO of *Fmr1* in mice results in K^+ channel dysregulation and consequent dysregulation of synaptic transmission [79].

Some evidence has shown that voltage-dependent anion channel (VDAC) genes, a class of postsynaptic density genes highly expressed in several brain regions, could be implicated in ASD. In fact, autoantibodies against VDAC proteins have been detected in autistic individuals, suggesting a possible causal role in ASD pathogenesis [80]. Moreover, the beneficial effects observed in ASD patients treated with coenzyme Q, or other agents influencing the transport of electrons, have been attributed to the control of such molecules on the porin channels [81]. Recently, a study conducted by our research group identified a 2-bp frameshift deletion of *VDAC3* in an ASD family [54].

3.2. Epigenetic Factors

There is increasing evidence supporting the possible role of epigenetic aberrations, including DNA methylation alterations and microRNAs, in ASD etiology.

- DNA methylation

Several studies have conducted global methylation analyses in peripheral tissues as well as post-mortem brain tissues from ASD subjects and controls.

Studies conducted on lymphoblastoid cell lines and whole-blood DNA from monozygotic twins discordant for ASD diagnosis and controls identified several differentially methylated regions (DMRs) between discordant MZ twins and between ASD patients and control samples [82,83].

Zhu et al. identified 400 DMRs, enriched at promoters of genes involved in neuronal development, between placentas from children later diagnosed with ASD and those from typically developing controls. Methylation levels of two DMRs, mapping on *CYP2E1* and *IRS2*, were respectively associated with genotype within the DMR and prenatal vitamin use [84].

Conversely, a large epigenome-wide association study, performed on blood-DNA from 796 ASD cases and 858 controls, did not detect any differentially methylated CpG site after correction for multiple testing [85].

Similarly, Siu et al. did not detect any DNA methylation patterns clearly distinguishing heterogenous ASD cases from controls. However, they identified unique DNA methylation signatures for ASD individuals with 16p11.2 deletions or pathogenic variants of *CHD8* [86].

On the other hand, Kimura et al. identified a potential biomarker for adult ASD. The identified CpG site was hypermethylated in whole-blood DNA from ASD patients compared to controls and mapped on the *PPP2R2C* gene, which resulted down-regulated in ASD subjects [87].

Alterations in Alu methylation patterns have been observed in ASD cases sub-grouped based on Autism Diagnostic Interview-Revised scores compared with matched controls [88].

More recently, a genome-wide methylation study was performed on post-mortem tissue samples from different brain regions dissected from ASD subjects and controls. Wide-spread methylation differences, with more pronounced effects in cortical regions compared to cerebellum, were detected between idiopathic ASD cases and controls and in individuals carrying 15q11–13 duplication [89].

Another global methylation study has recently reported that differentially methylated CpG sites identified in ASD cases compared to controls are enriched in pathways converging on mitochondrial metabolism and protein ubiquitination, suggesting a possible role of DNA methylation and mitochondrial dysfunction in ASD [90].

Other studies measuring methylation levels of candidate genes using targeted approaches detected hypermethylation of genes including *APOE* [91] and *HTR2A* [92] and hypomethylation of genes such as *HTR4* [93] in ASD subjects compared to controls.

The functional impact of locus-specific *Mecp2* methylation on ASD onset has been recently demonstrated in vitro and in vivo. *MECP2* is known to be hypermethylated and down-regulated in ASD subjects. The authors of this study employed the CRISPR-dCas9 methylation editing system to induce methylation of the *Mecp2* transcription start site in Neuro-2a cells and in mouse models, resulting in *Mecp2* down-regulation and the acquisition of behavioral changes attributable to an ASD phenotype in mice [94].

- miRNA

Several studies have found that miRNA expression profiles are dysregulated in different matrices, including saliva, blood and brain tissues, from ASD individuals [95].

A study conducted on saliva samples from individuals with and without ASD has identified a panel of four microRNAs differentially expressed between ASD patients and controls [96]. A panel of five salivary miRNAs has shown an accuracy of about 90% in the detection of developmental disorders, including ASD [97].

Down-regulation of miR-6126 has been detected in peripheral blood samples from adult individuals with ASD. The predicted targets of this miRNA belong to neuronal and oxytocin pathways [98]. Similarly, Ozkul et al. identified a consistent decrease and a slight reduction in six microRNAs (miR-19a-3p, miR-361-5p, miR-3613-3p, miR-150-5p, miR-126-3p and miR-499a-5p) in serum samples from ASD children and their unaffected family members compared to healthy controls. This result was replicated in the blood, hypothalamus and sperm of two ASD mouse models [99]. Another study conducted on serum samples identified a panel of three miRNAs (miR-130-3p, miR-181b-5p and miR-320a) showing an area under the curve >0.85 in distinguishing ASD subjects from controls [100].

Studies conducted on knockout (KO) mouse models for some ASD candidate genes, including *Fmr1*, *Mecp2* and *Ube3A*, have observed dysregulation of different miRNAs and evaluated their regulatory role in neuronal context [101–103].

4. Environmental Factors

As mentioned above, several studies investigated the possible role of environmental factors in the etiology of ASD. According to recent studies, up to 40–50% of variance in ASD liability could be determined by environmental factors, such as drugs, toxic exposures, parental age, nutrition, fetal environment and many others [104–106]. However, while for some potential risk factors, there is strong evidence, supported by association studies but also by in vitro and in vivo studies, only weak associations have been described for many others.

Below is reported an overview of the most-studied environmental factors that have been found to potentially contribute to cause ASD (recently reviewed in [107]) (Figure 2).

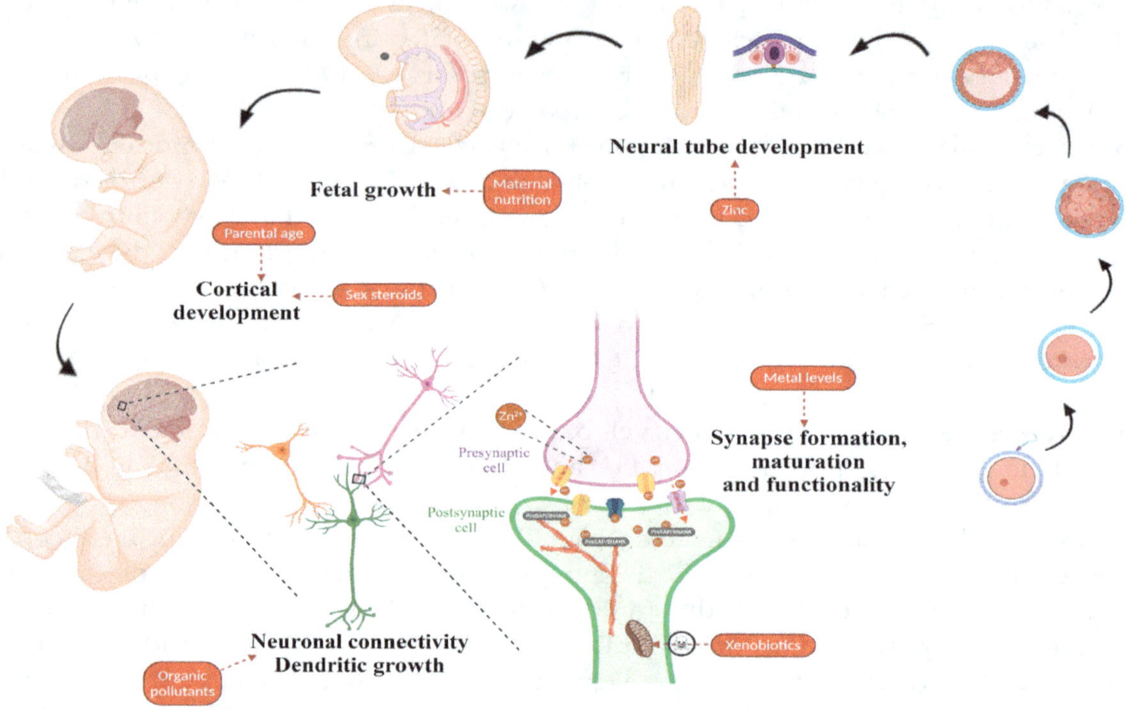

Figure 2. Environmental factors associated with ASD. The illustration indicates the putative impact of environmental factors on embryonic and fetal development with a particular focus on neuronal development and synaptic function. Figure created using BioRender.com images.

Parental age is one of the most established environmental ASD risk factors. In fact, much evidence has correlated advanced paternal age (APA) with the development of bipolar disorder, schizophrenia, ADHD and ASD [108]. A meta-analysis of 27 studies on the association between advanced parental age and ASD showed that a 10-year increase in maternal and paternal age is associated with a 20% higher risk of ASD in children [109]. A study has shown that age-related methylation changes observed in sperm could be related to an increased ASD risk in the offspring [110]. APA has been associated with reduced cortical thickness of the right posterior ventral cingulate cortex in ASD offspring [111]. Experiments conducted in mouse models have confirmed that APA is associated with the development of autism-like symptoms in the offspring [112,113] and with altered cortical morphology in male APA mice [112]. Moreover, behaviors related to ASD have also been observed in the second generation of mice with older grandfathers, suggesting that genetic and epigenetic alterations associated with APA are heritable [113].

Perinatal risk factors are also among the most-studied ASD risk factors and among the most difficult to determine and predict in advance. Two comprehensive meta-analyses examined 60 obstetric factors and found statistically significant associations between ASD risk and umbilical cord complications, injury or trauma at birth, multiple births, maternal hemorrhage, low birth weight, neonatal anemia, genital malformation, ABO or Rh blood group incompatibility and hyperbilirubinemia [114,115]. Another study has described an association between increased risk of autism and different factors, including caesarean section delivery, induced labor, management age less than 36 weeks and fetal distress [116].

Fetal exposure to sex steroids represents a potential risk factor for ASD. In fact, the fetal testosterone theory has been proposed to explain the higher ASD prevalence in males [8]. However, this hypothesis is controversial. In fact, while higher testosterone levels have been reported in ASD women, ASD males display testosterone levels similar to controls [117]. Baron-Cohen and colleagues have supposed that testosterone has effects on brain development during the prenatal masculinization window. The authors detected higher levels of sex steroids and cortisol in the amniotic fluid samples from male autistic patients compared with matched typically developing controls [118]. Recently, the same authors reported an association between fetal estrogen levels, important in synaptogenesis and corticogenesis, and autism risk [119]. Similarly, a study conducted on post-mortem brains detected reduced levels of estrogen receptor beta, aromatase and estrogen coactivators in the frontal gyrus of subjects with ASD compared to controls [120]. Moreover, several SNPs in genes encoding for proteins involved in sex steroid synthesis/transport have been associated with autistic traits [121].

The health condition of the mother has a major impact on the risk of ASD. It appears that maternal nutrition in pregnancy is of fundamental importance as it determines the nutrients available to support fetal growth [122]. Therefore, diets lacking specific nutrients can have adverse effects on fetal development. It has been shown that even short intervals between pregnancies can be harmful, since the body needs time, up to one year after childbirth, to recover acceptable levels of several essential substances [123].

Deficiencies of micronutrients, including vitamins and trace elements, have been associated with an increased risk of ASD. For instance, a Swedish study found that maternal vitamin D deficiency is associated with the risk of ASD with ID in the offspring [124]. Unbalanced levels of vitamins have also been detected in ASD children. Moreover, beneficial effects of vitamin supplementation have been observed in ASD patients [125]. Similarly, altered hair and/or blood concentrations of several trace elements, including chromium, magnesium and zinc, have been found in ASD patients compared with controls [126]. Association between maternal deficiency of microelements and ASD risk has also been reported. For example, iron deficiency, common in pregnant women, was associated with a five-fold increased risk of ASD, especially in the presence of other risk factors [127].

The involvement of altered trace elements concentrations on ASD phenotype is also supported by in vitro and animal studies. The effects on unbalanced metal levels on synapse formation and functionality have been evaluated on hippocampal cultured cells from rat brains, finding that the metal profile of autistic children led to down-regulation of crucial synaptic components, including Shank proteins and NMDA receptor subunits, and reduction of synaptic density. Interestingly, it was observed that zinc supplementation was able to revert the observed alterations [128]. The importance of zinc in ASD is supported by multiple pieces of evidence, including a strong association between low levels of this metal and ASD risk as well as a causative role of zinc deficiency in neuronal defects and development of ASD-related symptoms and "therapeutic" effects of zinc supplementation. In fact, low hair and serum levels of zinc and/or altered Zn/Cu ratio have been detected in children with ASD [129–131]. The effects of zinc deficiency on ASD have been observed in animal models. It has been shown that prenatal zinc deficiency alters social behavior in mice [132]. In vitro and in vivo studies have shown that zinc deficiency at the synaptic level leads to a decrease in ProSAP/Shank family members, a reduction in synaptic density and the development of ASD-related symptoms in mice [133]. In fact, other studies have shown that Zn^{2+} ions, highly abundant at PSD level, influence the recruitment of ProSAP1/Shank2 or ProSAP2/Shank3 for a correct formation and maturation of synapses [134]. The mechanism regulating the abundance of Zn at PSD levels has been hypothesized: Zn is released from pre-synaptic terminals and can translocate into post-synaptic neurons through Zn-permeable channels, including NMDA, and voltage-gated Ca^{2+} and AMPA channels [135]. Notably, a recent study has shown maternal zinc supplementation can prevent ASD-associated deficits in *Shank3* KO mouse models [136]. Recently, Shih et al. have elegantly demonstrated the impact of the crosstalk between genetic and environmental factors in the development of ASD. The authors have shown that KO of *Cttnbp2*, an actin cytoskeleton regulator, leads to a reduction in Zn concentration and expression levels of different synaptic proteins, consequently affecting dendritic spine formation and leading to the development of autism-like behaviors rescued by zinc supplementation [137].

The beneficial effects of zinc supplementation have been also observed in pregnant women, where an increase in zinc intake has been shown to reduce the risk of neural tube defects in the offspring [138].

The association between maternal obesity and risk of ASD in offspring is controversial. A Swedish study described a relationship between maternal BMI and ASD at population level; however, sibling analysis did not reveal any association between elevated maternal BMI and ASD risk [139]. On the other hand, a meta-analysis has shown a 28% and 36% increased risk of ASD in offspring born from overweight and obese mothers, respectively [140], even though there were relatively small numbers of ASD cases within the category of maternal underweight. However, it has also been shown that children born from underweight mothers are also at high risk of ASD [141]. Another study has shown that the combination of maternal obesity and maternal diabetes was associated with an increased risk of ASD and ID [142].

Maternal consumption of substances such as smoke, alcohol and medicines during pregnancy might be a potential risk factor as well. However, the association between smoking and alcohol-use with ASD is rather weak; in fact, two meta-analyses showed no evidence that smoking is a risk factor for ASD [143,144]. Moreover, cohort studies or case-control studies have examined the risk of ASD due to maternal alcohol consumption, indicating that mild to moderate consumption does not pose any risk [145–148].

The safety of medicines during pregnancy is very difficult to establish. In the ASD literature, antidepressant and anticonvulsant drugs have emerged as drugs of potential interest. An example is valproic acid, a drug that has been used to treat epilepsy or as a mood stabilizer in bipolar disorder. Its use during pregnancy leads to congenital malformations, developmental delay and cognitive malfunction [149,150]. Maternal use of selective serotonin uptake inhibitors has been associated with a 50% increase in ASD risk, although maternal psychiatric condition is a confounding factor [151].

An association between maternal diseases and ASD risk has been shown. A meta-analysis limited to case-control studies identified a 62% increased ASD risk among diabetic mothers compared to non-diabetic mothers [152], while a second study found a 74% increase in ASD risk for pregestational diabetes and 43% for gestational diabetes [153].

It has also been shown that maternal viral and bacterial infections are associated with ASD risk [154–156]. Two meta-analyses found that maternal autoimmune diseases are associated with an increased risk of ASD in offspring [157,158]. However, it is not the presence of viruses and bacteria per se to be associated with ASD development, but the immune response they cause, a conclusion supported by research identifying elevated inflammatory markers and antibodies in pregnant women with autistic children [159,160]. This hypothesis is supported by animal studies where maternal immune activation, induced by different immunogens, has been shown to induce post-natal brain dysfunction observable in a phenotype characteristic of ASD and other neurological disorders [161].

It is interesting to note that, although from different perspectives, much evidence points out the importance of maternal immune system condition during fetal development. Several studies have also reported an association between family history of autoimmune diseases and ASD [158,162,163]. It could be speculated that this link could be supported by maternal levels of zinc. In fact, our recent meta-analysis has shown that Zn concentrations in both serum and plasma levels of patients with autoimmunity are significantly lower compared to controls [164]. It is known that Zn plays an important role in the regulation of the immune system and, according to the studies provided above, it plays also an important role in neuronal tube formation.

Finally, exposure to toxic xenobiotics could represent another potential environmental risk factor. Substances such as brominated flame retardants could cause mitochondrial toxicity through a variety of mechanisms, leading to an altered energy balance in the brain [165], an important association with autism since mitochondrial dysfunction has been documented in patients with ASD [166]. Heavy metals can have a negative impact on many body functions by inducing neurological and behavioral damage. A meta-analysis of three case-control studies found a 60% increase in the risk of ASD due to exposure to high levels of inorganic mercury [167]. A recent case-control study found that exposure to organophosphates during pregnancy is associated with a 60% increase in the risk of ASD [168]. This category includes non-persistent organic pollutants, including phthalates and bisphenol A, and persistent organic pollutants, including DDT, PCB and PBDE. A research group found that three out of five studies on phthalate exposure showed a significant association between phthalate exposure and ASD risk [169]. Exposure to PCBs and PBDEs appears to alter calcium-related signal pathways, leading to alterations in dendritic growth and consequent abnormalities in neuronal connectivity, a key feature of ASD [170,171].

Table 2 summarizes several environmental factors associated with ASD described above.

Table 2. Several environmental factors associated with ASD.

Factor	Evidence	References
Parental age	Association studies; meta-analyses; animal studies	[108–113]
Perinatal factors	Meta-analyses	[114–116]
Sex steroids	Association studies	[117–121]
Maternal nutrition	Association studies; meta-analyses; in vitro studies, animal studies	[123–134,136–142]
Fetal exposure to drugs, smoke, alcohol	Association studies; meta-analyses	[143–151]
Maternal diseases	Meta-analyses	[152,153]
Maternal infections	Association studies; meta-analyses; animal studies	[154–161]
Fetal exposure to toxic xenobiotics	Association studies; meta-analyses; in vitro studies; animal studies	[166–171]

5. Conclusions

Given the complexity of the etiology of autism and the increasing prevalence of new confirmed cases of ASD worldwide, there is an urgent need to find effective diagnostic methods and study as many risk factors as possible—not only genetic but also epigenetic and environmental ones—without neglecting also genetic/environmental interactions, where risk factors influence each other.

Author Contributions: Conceptualization, E.L. and P.Z.; bibliographic search, E.M. and E.L.; writing—original draft preparation, E.M., E.L., R.F. and P.Z.; writing—review and editing, all authors; visualization, A.F.V.-B.; supervision, E.L. and P.Z.; funding acquisition, P.Z., M.C., G.D. All authors have read and agreed to the published version of the manuscript.

References

1. Kana, R.K.; Uddin, L.Q.; Ekenet, T.; Echugani, D.; Müller, R.-A. Brain connectivity in autism. *Front. Hum. Neurosci.* **2014**, *8*, 349. [CrossRef] [PubMed]
2. Narzisi, A.; Muratori, F.; Calderoni, S.; Fabbro, F.; Urgesi, C. Neuropsychological Profile in High Functioning Autism Spectrum Disorders. *J. Autism Dev. Disord.* **2012**, *43*, 1895–1909. [CrossRef] [PubMed]
3. Goin-Kochel, R.P.; Myers, B.J. Congenital Versus Regressive Onset of Autism Spectrum Disorders. *Focus Autism Other Dev. Disabil.* **2005**, *20*, 169–179. [CrossRef]
4. Tamouza, R.; Fernell, E.; Eriksson, M.A.; Anderlid, B.; Manier, C.; Mariaselvam, C.M.; Boukouaci, W.; Leboyer, M.; Gillberg, C. HLA Polymorphism in Regressive and Non-Regressive Autism: A Preliminary Study. *Autism Res.* **2019**, *13*, 182–186. [CrossRef]
5. Cohen, J.; Eyu, S.; Efu, Y.; Eli, X. Synaptic proteins and receptors defects in autism spectrum disorders. *Front. Cell. Neurosci.* **2014**, *8*, 276. [CrossRef]
6. James, S.J.; Melnyk, S.; Jernigan, S.; Cleves, M.A.; Halsted, C.H.; Wong, D.H.; Cutler, P.; Bock, K.; Boris, M.; Bradstreet, J.J.; et al. Metabolic endophenotype and related genotypes are associated with oxidative stress in children with autism. *Am. J. Med. Genet. Part B Neuropsychiatr. Genet.* **2006**, *141*, 947–956. [CrossRef] [PubMed]

7. Iossifov, I.; O'Roak, B.J.; Sanders, S.J.; Ronemus, M.; Krumm, N.; Levy, D.; Stessman, H.A.; Witherspoon, K.T.; Vives, L.; Patterson, K.E.; et al. The contribution of de novo coding mutations to autism spectrum disorder. *Nature* **2014**, *515*, 216–221. [CrossRef] [PubMed]
8. Werling, D.M. The role of sex-differential biology in risk for autism spectrum disorder. *Biol. Sex Differ.* **2016**, *7*, 1–18. [CrossRef]
9. Newschaffer, C.J.; Croen, L.A.; Daniels, J.; Giarelli, E.; Grether, J.K.; Levy, S.E.; Mandell, D.S.; Miller, L.A.; Pinto-Martin, J.; Reaven, J.; et al. The Epidemiology of Autism Spectrum Disorders. *Annu. Rev. Public Health* **2007**, *28*, 235–258. [CrossRef] [PubMed]
10. Elsabbagh, M.; Mercure, E.; Hudry, K.; Chandler, S.; Pasco, G.; Charman, T.; Pickles, A.; Baron-Cohen, S.; Bolton, P.; Johnson, M.H. Infant Neural Sensitivity to Dynamic Eye Gaze Is Associated with Later Emerging Autism. *Curr. Biol.* **2012**, *22*, 338–342. [CrossRef] [PubMed]
11. Benvenuto, A.; Moavero, R.; Alessandrelli, R.; Manzi, B.; Curatolo, P. Syndromic autism: Causes and pathogenetic pathways. *World J. Pediatr.* **2009**, *5*, 169–176. [CrossRef] [PubMed]
12. Hu, V.W.; Devlin, C.A.; Debski, J.J. ASD Phenotype—Genotype Associations in Concordant and Discordant Monozygotic and Dizygotic Twins Stratified by Severity of Autistic Traits. *Int. J. Mol. Sci.* **2019**, *20*, 3804. [CrossRef]
13. Colvert, E.; Tick, B.; McEwen, F.; Stewart, C.; Curran, S.R.; Woodhouse, E.; Gillan, N.; Hallett, V.; Lietz, S.; Garnett, T.; et al. Heritability of Autism Spectrum Disorder in a UK Population-Based Twin Sample. *JAMA Psychiatry* **2015**, *72*, 415–423. [CrossRef] [PubMed]
14. Sandin, S.; Lichtenstein, P.; Kuja-Halkola, R.; Larsson, H.; Hultman, C.M.; Reichenberg, A. The Familial Risk of Autism. *JAMA* **2014**, *311*, 1770–1777. [CrossRef]
15. Eichler, E.E.; Flint, J.; Gibson, G.; Kong, A.; Leal, S.M.; Moore, J.H.; Nadeau, J.H. Missing heritability and strategies for finding the underlying causes of complex disease. *Nat. Rev. Genet.* **2010**, *11*, 446–450. [CrossRef]
16. Génin, E. Missing heritability of complex diseases: Case solved? *Hum. Genet.* **2020**, *139*, 103–113. [CrossRef]
17. Wiśniowiecka-Kowalnik, B.; Nowakowska, B.A. Genetics and epigenetics of autism spectrum disorder—Current evidence in the field. *J. Appl. Genet.* **2019**, *60*, 37–47. [CrossRef] [PubMed]
18. Fatemi, S.H. *The Molecular Basis of Autism*; Springer: New York, NY, USA, 2015; ISBN 9781493921904.
19. Wang, K.; Zhang, H.; Ma, D.; Bucan, M.; Glessner, J.T.; Abrahams, B.S.; Salyakina, D.; Imielinski, M.; Bradfield, J.P.; Sleiman, P.M.A.; et al. Common genetic variants on 5p14.1 associate with autism spectrum disorders. *Nature* **2009**, *459*, 528–533. [CrossRef]
20. Anney, R.; Klei, L.; Pinto, D.; Almeida, J.; Bacchelli, E.; Baird, G.; Bolshakova, N.; Bölte, S.; Bolton, P.F.; Bourgeron, T.; et al. Individual common variants exert weak effects on the risk for autism spectrum disorders. *Hum. Mol. Genet.* **2012**, *21*, 4781–4792. [CrossRef]
21. Sener, E.F.; Canatan, H.; Ozkul, Y. Recent Advances in Autism Spectrum Disorders: Applications of Whole Exome Sequencing Technology. *Psychiatry Investig.* **2016**, *13*, 255–264. [CrossRef]
22. Pinto, D.; Pagnamenta, A.T.; Klei, L.; Anney, R.; Merico, D.; Regan, R.; Conroy, J.; Magalhaes, T.R.; Correia, C.; Abrahams, B.S.; et al. Functional impact of global rare copy number variation in autism spectrum disorders. *Nature* **2010**, *466*, 368–372. [CrossRef]
23. Marshall, C.R.; Noor, A.; Vincent, J.B.; Lionel, A.C.; Feuk, L.; Skaug, J.; Shago, M.; Moessner, R.; Pinto, D.; Ren, Y.; et al. Structural Variation of Chromosomes in Autism Spectrum Disorder. *Am. J. Hum. Genet.* **2008**, *82*, 477–488. [CrossRef]
24. Lupski, J.R.; Stankiewicz, P. Genomic Disorders: Molecular Mechanisms for Rearrangements and Conveyed Phenotypes. *PLoS Genet.* **2005**, *1*, e49. [CrossRef] [PubMed]
25. Devlin, B.; Scherer, S.W. Genetic architecture in autism spectrum disorder. *Curr. Opin. Genet. Dev.* **2012**, *22*, 229–237. [CrossRef]
26. Napoli, E.; Russo, S.; Casula, L.; Alesi, V.; Amendola, F.A.; Angioni, A.; Novelli, A.; Valeri, G.; Menghini, D.; Vicari, S. Array-CGH Analysis in a Cohort of Phenotypically Well-Characterized Individuals with "Essential" Autism Spectrum Disorders. *J. Autism Dev. Disord.* **2018**, *48*, 442–449. [CrossRef]
27. Beaudet, A.L. The utility of chromosomal microarray analysis in developmental and behavioral pediatrics. *Child Dev.* **2013**, *84*, 121–132. [CrossRef] [PubMed]

28. Jacquemont, M.-L.; Sanlaville, D.; Redon, R.; Raoul, O.; Cormier-Daire, V.; Lyonnet, S.; Amiel, J.; Le Merrer, M.; Heron, D.; De Blois, M.-C.; et al. Array-based comparative genomic hybridisation identifies high frequency of cryptic chromosomal rearrangements in patients with syndromic autism spectrum disorders. *J. Med. Genet.* **2006**, *43*, 843–849. [CrossRef]
29. Holt, R.; Sykes, N.H.; Conceição, I.; Cazier, J.-B.; Anney, R.J.; Oliveira, G.G.; Gallagher, L.; Vicente, A.M.; Monaco, A.P.; Pagnamenta, A.T. CNVs leading to fusion transcripts in individuals with autism spectrum disorder. *Eur. J. Hum. Genet.* **2012**, *20*, 1141–1147. [CrossRef]
30. Pagnamenta, A.T.; Bacchelli, E.; De Jonge, M.V.; Mirza, G.; Scerri, T.S.; Minopoli, F.; Chiocchetti, A.; Ludwig, K.U.; Hoffmann, P.; Paracchini, S.; et al. Characterization of a Family with Rare Deletions in CNTNAP5 and DOCK4 Suggests Novel Risk Loci for Autism and Dyslexia. *Biol. Psychiatry* **2010**, *68*, 320–328. [CrossRef]
31. Ceroni, F.; Sagar, A.; Simpson, N.H.; Gawthrope, A.J.; Newbury, D.F.; Pinto, D.; Francis, S.M.; Tessman, D.C.; Cook, E.H.; Monaco, A.P.; et al. A Deletion Involving CD 38 and BST 1 Results in a Fusion Transcript in a Patient With Autism and Asthma. *Autism Res.* **2014**, *7*, 254–263. [CrossRef]
32. Loi, E.; Moi, L.; Blois, S.; Bacchelli, E.; Benedetti, A.F.V.; Cameli, C.; Fadda, R.; Maestrini, E.; Carta, M.; Doneddu, G.; et al. ELMOD3—SH2D6 gene fusion as a possible co-star actor in autism spectrum disorder scenario. *J. Cell. Mol. Med.* **2019**, *24*, 2064–2069. [CrossRef] [PubMed]
33. Yin, J.; Schaaf, C.P. Autism genetics—An overview. *Prenat. Diagn.* **2016**, *37*, 14–30. [CrossRef]
34. Satterstrom, F.K.; Kosmicki, J.A.; Wang, J.; Breen, M.S.; De Rubeis, S.; An, J.-Y.; Peng, M.; Collins, R.; Grove, J.; Klei, L.; et al. Large-Scale Exome Sequencing Study Implicates Both Developmental and Functional Changes in the Neurobiology of Autism. *Cell* **2020**, *180*, 568–584.e23. [CrossRef]
35. Herrero, M.J.; Velmeshev, D.; Hernandez-Pineda, D.; Sethi, S.; Sorrells, S.; Banerjee, P.; Sullivan, C.; Gupta, A.R.; Kriegstein, A.R.; Corbin, J.G. Identification of amygdala-expressed genes associated with autism spectrum disorder. *Mol. Autism* **2020**, *11*, 1–14. [CrossRef] [PubMed]
36. Hotulainen, P.; Hoogenraad, C. Actin in dendritic spines: Connecting dynamics to function. *J. Cell Biol.* **2010**, *189*, 619–629. [CrossRef]
37. Van Spronsen, M.; Hoogenraad, C.C. Synapse Pathology in Psychiatric and Neurologic Disease. *Curr. Neurol. Neurosci. Rep.* **2010**, *10*, 207–214. [CrossRef]
38. Kaizuka, T.; Takumi, T. Postsynaptic density proteins and their involvement in neurodevelopmental disorders. *J. Biochem.* **2018**, *163*, 447–455. [CrossRef]
39. Südhof, T.C. Neuroligins and neurexins link synaptic function to cognitive disease. *Nature* **2008**, *455*, 903–911. [CrossRef] [PubMed]
40. Kim, H.-G.; Kishikawa, S.; Higgins, A.W.; Seong, I.-S.; Donovan, D.J.; Shen, Y.; Lally, E.; Weiss, L.A.; Najm, J.; Kutsche, K.; et al. Disruption of Neurexin 1 Associated with Autism Spectrum Disorder. *Am. J. Hum. Genet.* **2008**, *82*, 199–207. [CrossRef]
41. Schaaf, C.P.; Boone, P.M.; Sampath, S.; Williams, C.; Bader, P.I.; Mueller, J.M.; Shchelochkov, O.A.; Brown, C.W.; Crawford, H.P.; Phalen, J.A.; et al. Phenotypic spectrum and genotype–phenotype correlations of NRXN1 exon deletions. *Eur. J. Hum. Genet.* **2012**, *20*, 1240–1247. [CrossRef]
42. Radyushkin, K.; Hammerschmidt, K.; Boretius, S.; Varoqueaux, F.; El-Kordi, A.; Ronnenberg, A.; Winter, D.; Frahm, J.; Fischer, J.; Brose, N.; et al. Neuroligin-3-deficient mice: Model of a monogenic heritable form of autism with an olfactory deficit. *Genes Brain Behav.* **2009**, *8*, 416–425. [CrossRef]
43. Liang, J.; Xu, W.; Hsu, Y.-T.; Yee, A.X.; Chen, L.; Südhof, T.C. Conditional neuroligin-2 knockout in adult medial prefrontal cortex links chronic changes in synaptic inhibition to cognitive impairments. *Mol. Psychiatry* **2015**, *20*, 850–859. [CrossRef] [PubMed]
44. Pak, C.; Danko, T.; Zhang, Y.; Aoto, J.; Anderson, G.R.; Maxeiner, S.; Yi, F.; Wernig, M.; Südhof, T.C. Human Neuropsychiatric Disease Modeling using Conditional Deletion Reveals Synaptic Transmission Defects Caused by Heterozygous Mutations in NRXN1. *Cell Stem Cell* **2015**, *17*, 316–328. [CrossRef]
45. Arking, D.E.; Cutler, D.J.; Brune, C.W.; Teslovich, T.M.; West, K.; Ikeda, M.; Rea, A.; Guy, M.; Lin, S.; Cook, E.H.; et al. A Common Genetic Variant in the Neurexin Superfamily Member CNTNAP2 Increases Familial Risk of Autism. *Am. J. Hum. Genet.* **2008**, *82*, 160–164. [CrossRef] [PubMed]

46. Alarcón, M.; Abrahams, B.S.; Stone, J.L.; Duvall, J.A.; Perederiy, J.V.; Bomar, J.M.; Sebat, J.; Wigler, M.; Martin, C.L.; Ledbetter, D.H.; et al. Linkage, Association, and Gene-Expression Analyses Identify CNTNAP2 as an Autism-Susceptibility Gene. *Am. J. Hum. Genet.* **2008**, *82*, 150–159. [CrossRef] [PubMed]
47. Nord, A.S.; Network, S.P.; Roeb, W.; Dickel, D.E.; Walsh, T.; Kusenda, M.; O'Connor, K.L.; Malhotra, D.; McCarthy, S.E.; Stray, S.M.; et al. Reduced transcript expression of genes affected by inherited and de novo CNVs in autism. *Eur. J. Hum. Genet.* **2011**, *19*, 727–731. [CrossRef]
48. Peñagarikano, O.; Abrahams, B.S.; Herman, E.I.; Winden, K.D.; Gdalyahu, A.; Dong, H.; Sonnenblick, L.I.; Gruver, R.; Almajano, J.; Bragin, A.; et al. Absence of CNTNAP2 Leads to Epilepsy, Neuronal Migration Abnormalities, and Core Autism-Related Deficits. *Cell* **2011**, *147*, 235–246. [CrossRef]
49. Kreienkamp, H.-J. Scaffolding Proteins at the Postsynaptic Density: Shank as the Architectural Framework. In *Protein-Protein Interactions as New Drug Targets*; Springer: Berlin, Germany, 2008; Volume 186, pp. 365–380.
50. Berkel, S.; Marshall, C.; Weiss, B.; Howe, J.; Roeth, R.; Moog, U.; Endris, V.; Roberts, W.; Szatmari, P.; Pinto, D.; et al. Mutations in the SHANK2 synaptic scaffolding gene in autism spectrum disorder and mental retardation. *Nat. Genet.* **2010**, *42*, 489–491. [CrossRef]
51. Jiang, Y.-H.; Ehlers, M.D. Modeling Autism by SHANK Gene Mutations in Mice. *Neuron* **2013**, *78*, 8–27. [CrossRef]
52. Leblond, C.S.; Nava, C.; Polge, A.; Gauthier, J.; Huguet, G.; Lumbroso, S.; Giuliano, F.; Stordeur, C.; Depienne, C.; Mouzat, K.; et al. Meta-analysis of SHANK Mutations in Autism Spectrum Disorders: A Gradient of Severity in Cognitive Impairments. *PLoS Genet.* **2014**, *10*, e1004580. [CrossRef]
53. Pinto, D.; Delaby, E.; Merico, D.; Barbosa, M.; Merikangas, A.; Klei, L.; Thiruvahindrapuram, B.; Xu, X.; Ziman, R.; Wang, Z.; et al. Convergence of Genes and Cellular Pathways Dysregulated in Autism Spectrum Disorders. *Am. J. Hum. Genet.* **2014**, *94*, 677–694. [CrossRef]
54. Bacchelli, E.; Loi, E.; Cameli, C.; Moi, L.; Vega-Benedetti, A.F.; Blois, S.; Fadda, A.; Bonora, E.; Mattu, S.; Fadda, R.; et al. Analysis of a Sardinian Multiplex Family with Autism Spectrum Disorder Points to Post-Synaptic Density Gene Variants and Identifies CAPG as a Functionally Relevant Candidate Gene. *J. Clin. Med.* **2019**, *8*, 212. [CrossRef]
55. Lahbib, S.; Leblond, C.S.; Hamza, M.; Regnault, B.; Lemée, L.; Mathieu, A.; Jaouadi, H.; Mkaouar, R.; Ben Youssef-Turki, I.; Belhadj, A.; et al. Homozygous 2p11.2 deletion supports the implication of ELMOD3 in hearing loss and reveals the potential association of CAPG with ASD/ID etiology. *J. Appl. Genet.* **2018**, *60*, 49–56. [CrossRef]
56. Fan, Y.; Tang, X.; Vitriol, E.A.; Chen, G.; Zheng, J.Q. Actin capping protein is required for dendritic spine development and synapse formation. *J. Neurosci.* **2011**, *31*, 10228–11033. [CrossRef] [PubMed]
57. Korobova, F.; Svitkina, T.M. Molecular Architecture of Synaptic Actin Cytoskeleton in Hippocampal Neurons Reveals a Mechanism of Dendritic Spine Morphogenesis. *Mol. Biol. Cell* **2010**, *21*, 165–176. [CrossRef]
58. Schmunk, G.; Gargus, J.J. Channelopathy pathogenesis in autism spectrum disorders. *Front. Genet.* **2013**, *4*, 222. [CrossRef]
59. Despang, P.; Salamon, S.; Breitenkamp, A.F.; Kuzmenkina, E.; Herzig, S.; Matthes, J. Autism-associated mutations in the CaVβ2 calcium-channel subunit increase Ba2+-currents and lead to differential modulation by the RGK-protein Gem. *Neurobiol. Dis.* **2020**, *136*, 104721. [CrossRef]
60. Splawski, I.; Timothy, K.W.; Sharpe, L.M.; Decher, N.; Kumar, P.; Bloise, R.; Napolitano, C.; Schwartz, P.J.; Joseph, R.M.; Condouris, K.; et al. CaV1.2 Calcium Channel Dysfunction Causes a Multisystem Disorder Including Arrhythmia and Autism. *Cell* **2004**, *119*, 19–31. [CrossRef]
61. Catterall, W.A.; Perez-Reyes, E.; Snutch, T.P.; Striessnig, J. International Union of Pharmacology. XLVIII. Nomenclature and Structure-Function Relationships of Voltage-Gated Calcium Channels. *Pharmacol. Rev.* **2005**, *57*, 411–425. [CrossRef]
62. Barrett, C.F.; Tsien, R.W. The Timothy syndrome mutation differentially affects voltage- and calcium-dependent inactivation of CaV1.2 L-type calcium channels. *Proc. Natl. Acad. Sci. USA* **2008**, *105*, 2157–2162. [CrossRef]
63. Hemara-Wahanui, A.; Berjukow, S.; Hope, C.I.; Dearden, P.K.; Wu, S.-B.; Wilson-Wheeler, J.; Sharp, D.M.; Lundon-Treweek, P.; Clover, G.M.; Hoda, J.-C.; et al. A CACNA1F mutation identified in an X-linked retinal disorder shifts the voltage dependence of Cav1.4 channel activation. *Proc. Natl. Acad. Sci. USA* **2005**, *102*, 7553–7558. [CrossRef]

64. Pinggera, A.; Lieb, A.; Benedetti, B.; Lampert, M.; Monteleone, S.; Liedl, K.R.; Tuluc, P.; Striessnig, J. CACNA1D De Novo Mutations in Autism Spectrum Disorders Activate Cav1.3 L-Type Calcium Channels. *Biol. Psychiatry* **2015**, *77*, 816–822. [CrossRef]
65. Pinggera, A.; Mackenroth, L.; Rump, A.; Schallner, J.; Beleggia, F.; Wollnik, B.; Striessnig, J. New gain-of-function mutation shows CACNA1D as recurrently mutated gene in autism spectrum disorders and epilepsy. *Hum. Mol. Genet.* **2017**, *26*, 2923–2932. [CrossRef]
66. Boczek, N.J.; Miller, E.M.; Ye, D.; Nesterenko, V.V.; Tester, D.J.; Antzelevitch, C.; Czosek, R.J.; Ackerman, M.J.; Ware, S.M. Novel Timothy syndrome mutation leading to increase in CACNA1C window current. *Heart Rhythm* **2015**, *12*, 211–219. [CrossRef]
67. Splawski, I.; Yoo, D.S.; Stotz, S.C.; Cherry, A.; Clapham, D.E.; Keating, M.T. CACNA1HMutations in Autism Spectrum Disorders. *J. Biol. Chem.* **2006**, *281*, 22085–22091. [CrossRef]
68. Breitenkamp, A.F.S.; Matthes, J.; Nass, R.D.; Sinzig, J.; Lehmkuhl, G.; Nürnberg, P.; Herzig, S. Rare Mutations of CACNB2 Found in Autism Spectrum Disease-Affected Families Alter Calcium Channel Function. *PLoS ONE* **2014**, *9*, e95579. [CrossRef]
69. Morrow, E.M.; Yoo, S.-Y.; Flavell, S.W.; Kim, T.-K.; Lin, Y.; Hill, R.S.; Mukaddes, N.M.; Balkhy, S.; Gascon, G.; Hashmi, A.; et al. Identifying Autism Loci and Genes by Tracing Recent Shared Ancestry. *Science* **2008**, *321*, 218–223. [CrossRef]
70. Veeramah, K.R.; O'Brien, J.E.; Meisler, M.H.; Cheng, X.; Dib-Hajj, S.D.; Waxman, S.G.; Talwar, D.; Girirajan, S.; Eichler, E.E.; Restifo, L.L.; et al. De Novo Pathogenic SCN8A Mutation Identified by Whole-Genome Sequencing of a Family Quartet Affected by Infantile Epileptic Encephalopathy and SUDEP. *Am. J. Hum. Genet.* **2012**, *90*, 502–510. [CrossRef]
71. Chen, C.-P.; Lin, S.-P.; Chern, S.-R.; Chen, Y.-J.; Tsai, F.-J.; Wu, P.-C.; Wang, W. Array-CGH detection of a de novo 2.8 Mb deletion in 2q24.2→q24.3 in a girl with autistic features and developmental delay. *Eur. J. Med. Genet.* **2010**, *53*, 217–220. [CrossRef]
72. Sanders, S.J.; Murtha, M.T.; Gupta, A.R.; Murdoch, J.D.; Raubeson, M.J.; Willsey, A.J.; Ercan-Sencicek, A.G.; DiLullo, N.M.; Parikshak, N.N.; Stein, J.L.; et al. De novo mutations revealed by whole-exome sequencing are strongly associated with autism. *Nature* **2012**, *485*, 237–241. [CrossRef] [PubMed]
73. Weiss, L.A.; Escayg, A.; Kearney, J.A.; Trudeau, M.; Macdonald, B.T.; Mori, M.; Reichert, J.; Buxbaum, J.D.; Meisler, M.H. Sodium channels SCN1A, SCN2A and SCN3A in familial autism. *Mol. Psychiatry* **2003**, *8*, 186–194. [CrossRef]
74. Han, S.; Tai, C.; Westenbroek, R.E.; Yu, F.H.; Cheah, C.S.; Potter, G.B.; Rubenstein, J.L.; Scheuer, T.; De La Iglesia, H.O.; Catterall, W.A. Autistic-like behaviour in Scn1a+/− mice and rescue by enhanced GABA-mediated neurotransmission. *Nature* **2012**, *489*, 385–390. [CrossRef]
75. Gilling, M.; Rasmussen, H.B.; Calloe, K.; Sequeira, A.F.; Baretto, M.; Oliveira, G.; Almeida, J.; Lauritsen, M.B.; Ullmann, R.; Boonen, S.E.; et al. Dysfunction of the Heteromeric KV7.3/KV7.5 Potassium Channel is Associated with Autism Spectrum Disorders. *Front. Genet.* **2013**, *4*, 54. [CrossRef]
76. Gross, C.; Yao, X.; Pong, D.L.; Jeromin, A.; Bassell, G.J. Fragile X Mental Retardation Protein Regulates Protein Expression and mRNA Translation of the Potassium Channel Kv4.2. *J. Neurosci.* **2011**, *31*, 5693–5698. [CrossRef]
77. Sicca, F.; Imbrici, P.; D'Adamo, M.C.; Moro, F.; Bonatti, F.; Brovedani, P.; Grottesi, A.; Guerrini, R.; Masi, G.; Santorelli, F.M.; et al. Autism with Seizures and Intellectual Disability: Possible Causative Role of Gain-of-function of the Inwardly-Rectifying K+ Channel Kir4.1. *Neurobiol. Dis.* **2011**, *43*, 239–247. [CrossRef]
78. Laumonnier, F.; Eroger, S.; Guérin, P.; Molinari, F.; M'Rad, R.; Cahard, D.; Belhadj, A.; Halayem, M.; Persico, A.M.; Elia, M.; et al. Association of a Functional Deficit of the BKCa Channel, a Synaptic Regulator of Neuronal Excitability, With Autism and Mental Retardation. *Am. J. Psychiatry* **2006**, *163*, 1622. [CrossRef]
79. Deng, P.Y.; Rotman, Z.; Blundon, J.A.; Cho, Y.; Cui, J.; Cavalli, V.; Zakharenko, S.S.; Klyachko, V.A. FMRP Regulates Neurotransmitter Release and Synaptic Information Transmission by Modulating Action Potential Duration via BK Channels. *Neuron* **2013**, *77*, 696–711. [CrossRef]
80. Gonzalez–Gronow, M.; Cuchacovich, M.; Francos, R.; Cuchacovich, S.; Fernandez, M.D.P.; Blanco, A.; Bowers, E.V.; Kaczowka, S.; Pizzo, S.V. Antibodies against the voltage-dependent anion channel (VDAC) and its protective ligand hexokinase-I in children with autism. *J. Neuroimmunol.* **2010**, *227*, 153–161. [CrossRef]
81. Gvozdjáková, A.; Löw, H.; Sun, I.; Navas, P.; Crane, F.L. Plasma membrane coenzyme Q: Evidence for a role in autism. *Biol. Targets Ther.* **2014**, *8*, 199. [CrossRef]

82. Wong, C.C.Y.; Meaburn, E.L.; Ronald, A.; Price, T.S.; Jeffries, A.R.; Schalkwyk, L.C.; Plomin, R.; Mill, J. Methylomic analysis of monozygotic twins discordant for autism spectrum disorder and related behavioural traits. *Mol. Psychiatry* **2013**, *19*, 495–503. [CrossRef]
83. Nguyen, A.; Rauch, T.A.; Pfeifer, G.P.; Hu, V.W. Global methylation profiling of lymphoblastoid cell lines reveals epigenetic contributions to autism spectrum disorders and a novel autism candidate gene, RORA, whose protein product is reduced in autistic brain. *FASEB J.* **2010**, *24*, 3036–3051. [CrossRef]
84. Zhu, Y.; Mordaunt, C.E.; Yasui, D.H.; Marathe, R.; Coulson, R.L.; Dunaway, K.; Jianu, J.M.; Walker, C.K.; Ozonoff, S.; Hertz-Picciotto, I.; et al. Placental DNA methylation levels at CYP2E1 and IRS2 are associated with child outcome in a prospective autism study. *Hum. Mol. Genet.* **2019**, *28*, 2659–2674. [CrossRef]
85. Andrews, S.V.; Sheppard, B.; Windham, G.C.; Schieve, L.A.; Schendel, D.E.; Croen, L.E.; Chopra, P.; Alisch, R.S.; Newschaffer, C.J.; Warren, S.T.; et al. Case-control meta-analysis of blood DNA methylation and autism spectrum disorder. *Mol. Autism* **2018**, *9*, 40. [CrossRef]
86. Siu, M.T.; Butcher, D.T.; Turinsky, A.L.; Cytrynbaum, C.; Stavropoulos, D.J.; Walker, S.; Caluseriu, O.; Carter, M.; Lou, Y.; Nicolson, R.; et al. Functional DNA methylation signatures for autism spectrum disorder genomic risk loci: 16p11.2 deletions and CHD8 variants. *Clin. Epigenetics* **2019**, *11*, 1–19. [CrossRef]
87. Kimura, R.; Nakata, M.; Funabiki, Y.; Suzuki, S.; Awaya, T.; Murai, T.; Hagiwara, M. An epigenetic biomarker for adult high-functioning autism spectrum disorder. *Sci. Rep.* **2019**, *9*, 13662–13667. [CrossRef] [PubMed]
88. Saeliw, T.; Tangsuwansri, C.; Thongkorn, S.; Chonchaiya, W.; Suphapeetiporn, K.; Mutirangura, A.; Tencomnao, T.; Hu, V.W.; Sarachana, T. Integrated genome-wide Alu methylation and transcriptome profiling analyses reveal novel epigenetic regulatory networks associated with autism spectrum disorder. *Mol. Autism* **2018**, *9*, 27. [CrossRef]
89. Wong, C.C.Y.; Smith, R.G.; Hannon, E.; Ramaswami, G.; Parikshak, N.N.; Assary, E.; Troakes, C.; Poschmann, J.; Schalkwyk, L.C.; Sun, W.; et al. Genome-wide DNA methylation profiling identifies convergent molecular signatures associated with idiopathic and syndromic autism in post-mortem human brain tissue. *Hum. Mol. Genet.* **2019**, *28*, 2201–2211. [CrossRef]
90. Stathopoulos, S.; Gaujoux, R.; Lindeque, Z.; Mahony, C.; Van Der Colff, R.; Van Der Westhuizen, F.; O'Ryan, C. DNA Methylation Associated with Mitochondrial Dysfunction in a South African Autism Spectrum Disorder Cohort. *Autism Res.* **2020**, *13*, 1079–1093. [CrossRef]
91. Hu, Z.; Yang, Y.; Zhao, Y.; Yu, H.; Ying, X.; Zhou, D.; Zhong, J.; Zheng, Z.; Liu, J.; Pan, R.; et al. APOE hypermethylation is associated with autism spectrum disorder in a Chinese population. *Exp. Ther. Med.* **2018**, *15*, 4749–4754. [CrossRef]
92. Hranilović, D.; Blažević, S.; Stefulj, J.; Zill, P. DNA Methylation Analysis of HTR2A Regulatory Region in Leukocytes of Autistic Subjects. *Autism Res.* **2015**, *9*, 204–209. [CrossRef]
93. Hu, Z.; Ying, X.; Huang, L.; Zhao, Y.; Zhou, D.; Liu, J.; Zhong, J.; Huang, T.; Zhang, W.; Cheng, F.; et al. Association of human serotonin receptor 4 promoter methylation with autism spectrum disorder. *Medicine* **2020**, *99*, e18838. [CrossRef]
94. Lu, Z.; Liu, Z.; Mao, W.; Wang, X.; Zheng, X.; Chen, S.; Cao, B.; Huang, S.; Zhang, X.; Zhou, T.; et al. Locus-specific DNA methylation of Mecp2 promoter leads to autism-like phenotypes in mice. *Cell Death Dis.* **2020**, *11*, 85. [CrossRef]
95. Hicks, S.D.; Middleton, F.A. A Comparative Review of microRNA Expression Patterns in Autism Spectrum Disorder. *Front. Psychiatry* **2016**, *7*, 176. [CrossRef]
96. Hicks, S.D.; Carpenter, R.L.; Wagner, K.E.; Pauley, R.; Barros, M.; Tierney-Aves, C.; Barns, S.; Greene, C.D.; Middleton, F.A. Saliva MicroRNA Differentiates Children with Autism from Peers with Typical and Atypical Development. *J. Am. Acad. Child. Adolesc. Psychiatry* **2020**, *59*, 296–308. [CrossRef]
97. Sehovic, E.; Spahic, L.; Smajlovic-Skenderagic, L.; Pistoljevic, N.; Dzanko, E.; Hajdarpasic, A. Identification of developmental disorders including autism spectrum disorder using salivary miRNAs in children from Bosnia and Herzegovina. *PLoS ONE* **2020**, *15*, e0232351. [CrossRef]
98. Hagiwara, M.; Kimura, R.; Funabiki, Y.; Awaya, T.; Murai, T.; Hagiwara, M. MicroRNA profiling in adults with high-functioning autism spectrum disorder. *Mol. Brain* **2019**, *12*, 82–84. [CrossRef]
99. Ozkul, Y.; Taheri, S.; Bayram, K.K.; Sener, E.F.; Mehmetbeyoglu, E.; Öztop, D.B.; Aybuga, F.; Tufan, E.; Bayram, A.; Dolu, N.; et al. A heritable profile of six miRNAs in autistic patients and mouse models. *Sci. Rep.* **2020**, *10*, 1–14. [CrossRef]

100. Vasu, M.M.; Anitha, A.; Thanseem, I.; Suzuki, K.; Yamada, K.; Takahashi, T.; Wakuda, T.; Iwata, K.; Tsujii, M.; Sugiyama, T.; et al. Serum microRNA profiles in children with autism. *Mol. Autism* **2014**, *5*, 40. [CrossRef]
101. Vatsa, N.; Kumar, V.; Singh, B.K.; Kumar, S.S.; Sharma, A.; Jana, N.R. Down-Regulation of miRNA-708 Promotes Aberrant Calcium Signaling by Targeting Neuronatin in a Mouse Model of Angelman Syndrome. *Front. Mol. Neurosci.* **2019**, *12*, 35. [CrossRef]
102. Urdinguio, R.G.; Fernández, A.F.; López-Nieva, P.; Rossi, S.; Huertas, D.; Kulis, M.; Liu, C.-G.; Croce, C.M.; Calin, G.A.; Esteller, M. Disrupted microRNA expression caused by Mecp2 loss in a mouse model of Rett syndrome. *Epigenetics* **2010**, *5*, 656–663. [CrossRef]
103. Edbauer, D.; Neilson, J.R.; Foster, K.A.; Wang, C.-F.; Seeburg, D.P.; Batterton, M.N.; Tada, T.; Dolan, B.M.; Sharp, P.A.; Sheng, M. Regulation of Synaptic Structure and Function by FMRP-Associated MicroRNAs miR-125b and miR-132. *Neuron* **2010**, *65*, 373–384. [CrossRef]
104. Gaugler, T.; Klei, L.; Sanders, S.J.; Bodea, C.A.; Goldberg, A.P.; Lee, A.B.; Mahajan, M.C.; Manaa, D.; Pawitan, Y.; Reichert, J.G.; et al. Most genetic risk for autism resides with common variation. *Nat. Genet.* **2014**, *46*, 881–885. [CrossRef]
105. Deng, W.; Zou, X.; Deng, H.; Li, J.; Tang, C.; Wang, X.; Guo, X. The Relationship Among Genetic Heritability, Environmental Effects, and Autism Spectrum Disorders. *J. Child Neurol.* **2015**, *30*, 1794–1799. [CrossRef]
106. Edelson, L.R.; Saudino, K.J. Genetic and environmental influences on autistic-like behaviors in 2-year-old twins. *Behav. Genet.* **2009**, *39*, 255–264. [CrossRef]
107. Bölte, S.; Girdler, S.; Marschik, P.B. The contribution of environmental exposure to the etiology of autism spectrum disorder. *Cell. Mol. Life Sci.* **2019**, *76*, 1275–1297. [CrossRef]
108. Janecka, M.; Mill, J.; Basson, M.A.; Goriely, A.; Spiers, H.; Reichenberg, A.; Schalkwyk, L.; Fernandes, C. Advanced paternal age effects in neurodevelopmental disorders—Review of potential underlying mechanisms. *Transl. Psychiatry* **2017**, *7*, e1019. [CrossRef]
109. Wu, S.; Wu, F.; Ding, Y.; Hou, J.; Bi, J.; Zhang, Z. Advanced parental age and autism risk in children: A systematic review and meta-analysis. *Acta Psychiatr. Scand.* **2016**, *135*, 29–41. [CrossRef]
110. Atsem, S.; Reichenbach, J.; Potabattula, R.; Dittrich, M.; Nava, C.; Depienne, C.; Böhm, L.; Rost, S.; Hahn, T.; Schorsch, M.; et al. Paternal age effects on spermFOXK1andKCNA7methylation and transmission into the next generation. *Hum. Mol. Genet.* **2016**, *25*, 4996–5005. [CrossRef]
111. Kojima, M.; Yassin, W.; Owada, K.; Aoki, Y.; Kuwabara, H.; Natsubori, T.; Iwashiro, N.; Gonoi, W.; Takao, H.; Kasai, K.; et al. Neuroanatomical Correlates of Advanced Paternal and Maternal Age at Birth in Autism Spectrum Disorder. *Cereb. Cortex* **2018**, *29*, 2524–2532. [CrossRef]
112. Foldi, C.J.; Eyles, D.; McGrath, J.J.; Burne, T.H.J. Advanced paternal age is associated with alterations in discrete behavioural domains and cortical neuroanatomy of C57BL/6J mice. *Eur. J. Neurosci.* **2010**, *31*, 556–564. [CrossRef] [PubMed]
113. Sampino, S.; Juszczak, G.R.; Zacchini, F.; Swiergiel, A.H.; Modlinski, J.A.; Loi, P.; Ptak, G. Grand-paternal age and the development of autism-like symptoms in mice progeny. *Transl. Psychiatry* **2014**, *4*, e386. [CrossRef]
114. Gardener, H.; Spiegelman, D.; Buka, S.L. Prenatal risk factors for autism: Comprehensive meta-analysis. *Br. J. Psychiatry* **2009**, *195*, 7–14. [CrossRef]
115. Gardener, H.; Spiegelman, D.; Buka, S.L. Perinatal and Neonatal Risk Factors for Autism: A Comprehensive Meta-analysis. *Pediatrics* **2011**, *128*, 344–355. [CrossRef]
116. Wang, C.; Geng, H.; Liu, W.; Zhang, G. Prenatal, perinatal, and postnatal factors associated with autism. *Medicine* **2017**, *96*, e6696. [CrossRef]
117. Bejerot, S.; Eriksson, J.M.; Bonde, S.; Carlström, K.; Humble, M.B.; Eriksson, E. The extreme male brain revisited: Gender coherence in adults with autism spectrum disorder. *Br. J. Psychiatry* **2012**, *201*, 116–123. [CrossRef]
118. Baron-Cohen, S.; Auyeung, B.; Nørgaard-Pedersen, B.; Hougaard, D.M.; Abdallah, M.W.; Melgaard, L.; Cohen, A.S.; Chakrabarti, B.; Ruta, L.; Lombardo, M.V. Elevated fetal steroidogenic activity in autism. *Mol. Psychiatry* **2015**, *20*, 369–376. [CrossRef]
119. Baron-Cohen, S.; Tsompanidis, A.; Auyeung, B.; Nørgaard-Pedersen, B.; Hougaard, D.M.; Abdallah, M.; Cohen, A.; Pohl, A. Foetal oestrogens and autism. *Mol. Psychiatry* **2020**, *25*, 2970–2978. [CrossRef] [PubMed]
120. Crider, A.; Thakkar, R.; Ahmed, A.O.; Pillai, A. Dysregulation of estrogen receptor beta (ERβ), aromatase (CYP19A1), and ER co-activators in the middle frontal gyrus of autism spectrum disorder subjects. *Mol. Autism* **2014**, *5*, 46. [CrossRef]

121. Chakrabarti, B.; Dudbridge, F.; Kent, L.; Wheelwright, S.; Hill-Cawthorne, G.; Allison, C.; Banerjee-Basu, S.; Baron-Cohen, S. Genes related to sex steroids, neural growth, and social-emotional behavior are associated with autistic traits, empathy, and Asperger syndrome. *Autism Res.* **2009**, *2*, 157–177. [CrossRef]
122. Jackson, A.A.; Robinson, S.M. Dietary guidelines for pregnancy: A review of current evidence. *Public Health Nutr.* **2001**, *4*, 625–630. [CrossRef]
123. Van Eijsden, M.; Smits, L.J.M.; Van Der Wal, M.F.; Bonsel, G.J. Association between short interpregnancy intervals and term birth weight: The role of folate depletion. *Am. J. Clin. Nutr.* **2008**, *88*, 147–153. [CrossRef] [PubMed]
124. Magnusson, C.; Kosidou, K.; Dalman, C.; Lundberg, M.; Lee, B.K.; Rai, D.; Karlsson, H.; Gardner, R.; Arver, S. Maternal vitamin D deficiency and the risk of autism spectrum disorders: Population-based study. *BJPsych Open* **2016**, *2*, 170–172. [CrossRef]
125. Robea, M.; Luca, A.-C.; Ciobica, A. Relationship between Vitamin Deficiencies and Co-Occurring Symptoms in Autism Spectrum Disorder. *Medicine* **2020**, *56*, 245. [CrossRef]
126. Saghazadeh, A.; Ahangari, N.; Hendi, K.; Saleh, F.; Rezaei, N. Status of essential elements in autism spectrum disorder: Systematic review and meta-analysis. *Rev. Neurosci.* **2017**, *28*, 783–809. [CrossRef]
127. Schmidt, R.J.; Tancredi, D.J.; Krakowiak, P.; Hansen, R.L.; Ozonoff, S. Maternal Intake of Supplemental Iron and Risk of Autism Spectrum Disorder. *Am. J. Epidemiol.* **2014**, *180*, 890–900. [CrossRef]
128. Hagmeyer, S.; Mangus, K.; Boeckers, T.M.; Grabrucker, A.M. Effects of Trace Metal Profiles Characteristic for Autism on Synapses in Cultured Neurons. *Neural Plast.* **2015**, *2015*, 1–16. [CrossRef]
129. Goyal, D.K.; Neil, J.R.; Simmons, S.D.; Mansab, F.; Benjamin, S.; Pitfield, V.; Boulet, S.; Miyan, J.A. Zinc Deficiency in Autism: A Controlled Study. *Insights Biomed.* **2019**, *4*, 4. [CrossRef]
130. Yasuda, H.; Yoshida, K.; Yasuda, Y.; Tsutsui, T. Infantile zinc deficiency: Association with autism spectrum disorders. *Sci. Rep.* **2011**, *1*, 129. [CrossRef]
131. Li, S.-O.; Wang, J.-L.; Bjørklund, G.; Zhao, W.-N.; Yin, C.-H. Serum copper and zinc levels in individuals with autism spectrum disorders. *NeuroReport* **2014**, *25*, 1216–1220. [CrossRef]
132. Grabrucker, S.; Boeckers, T.M.; Grabrucker, A.M. Gender Dependent Evaluation of Autism like Behavior in Mice Exposed to Prenatal Zinc Deficiency. *Front. Behav. Neurosci.* **2016**, *10*, 37. [CrossRef]
133. Grabrucker, S.; Jannetti, L.; Eckert, M.; Gaub, S.; Chhabra, R.; Pfaender, S.; Mangus, K.; Reddy, P.P.; Rankovic, V.; Schmeisser, M.J.; et al. Zinc deficiency dysregulates the synaptic ProSAP/Shank scaffold and might contribute to autism spectrum disorders. *Brain* **2013**, *137*, 137–152. [CrossRef] [PubMed]
134. Grabrucker, A.M.; Knight, M.J.; Proepper, C.; Bockmann, J.; Joubert, M.; Rowan, M.; Nienhaus, G.U.; Garner, C.C.; Bowie, J.U.; Kreutz, M.R.; et al. Concerted action of zinc and ProSAP/Shank in synaptogenesis and synapse maturation. *EMBO J.* **2011**, *30*, 569–581. [CrossRef]
135. Frederickson, C.J.; Koh, J.-Y.; Bush, A.I. The neurobiology of zinc in health and disease. *Nat. Rev. Neurosci.* **2005**, *6*, 449–462. [CrossRef] [PubMed]
136. Vyas, Y.; Lee, K.; Jung, Y.; Montgomery, J.M. Influence of maternal zinc supplementation on the development of autism-associated behavioural and synaptic deficits in offspring Shank3-knockout mice. *Mol. Brain* **2020**, *13*, 1–18. [CrossRef]
137. Shih, P.-Y.; Hsieh, B.-Y.; Lin, M.-H.; Huang, T.-N.; Tsai, C.-Y.; Pong, W.-L.; Lee, S.-P.; Hsueh, Y.-P. CTTNBP2 Controls Synaptic Expression of Zinc-Related Autism-Associated Proteins and Regulates Synapse Formation and Autism-like Behaviors. *Cell Rep.* **2020**, *31*, 107700. [CrossRef]
138. Velie, E.M.; Block, G.; Shaw, G.M.; Samuels, S.J.; Schaffer, D.M.; Kulldorff, M. Maternal supplemental and dietary zinc intake and the occurrence of neural tube defects in California. *Am. J. Epidemiol.* **1999**, *150*, 605–616. [CrossRef]
139. Gardner, R.M.; Lee, B.K.; Magnusson, C.; Rai, D.; Frisell, T.; Karlsson, H.; Idring, S.; Dalman, C. Maternal body mass index during early pregnancy, gestational weight gain, and risk of autism spectrum disorders: Results from a Swedish total population and discordant sibling study. *Int. J. Epidemiol.* **2015**, *44*, 870–883. [CrossRef]
140. Wang, Y.; Tang, S.; Xu, S.; Weng, S.; Liu, Z. Maternal Body Mass Index and Risk of Autism Spectrum Disorders in Offspring: A Meta-analysis. *Sci. Rep.* **2016**, *6*, 34248. [CrossRef] [PubMed]
141. Getz, K.D.; Anderka, M.T.; Werler, M.M.; Jick, S.S. Maternal Pre-pregnancy Body Mass Index and Autism Spectrum Disorder among Offspring: A Population-Based Case-Control Study. *Paediatr. Périnat. Epidemiol.* **2016**, *30*, 479–487. [CrossRef]

142. Li, M.; Fallin, M.D.; Riley, A.; Landa, R.; Walker, S.O.; Silverstein, M.; Caruso, D.; Pearson, C.; Kiang, S.; Dahm, J.L.; et al. The Association of Maternal Obesity and Diabetes with Autism and Other Developmental Disabilities. *Pediatrics* **2016**, *137*, e20152206. [CrossRef]
143. Tang, S.; Wang, Y.; Gong, X.; Wang, G.-H. A Meta-Analysis of Maternal Smoking during Pregnancy and Autism Spectrum Disorder Risk in Offspring. *Int. J. Environ. Res. Public Health* **2015**, *12*, 10418–10431. [CrossRef]
144. Rosen, B.N.; Lee, B.K.; Lee, N.L.; Yang, Y.; Burstyn, I. Maternal Smoking and Autism Spectrum Disorder: A Meta-analysis. *J. Autism Dev. Disord.* **2014**, *45*, 1689–1698. [CrossRef]
145. Visser, J.C.; Rommelse, N.; Vink, L.; Schrieken, M.; Oosterling, I.J.; Van Der Gaag, R.J.; Buitelaar, J.K. Narrowly Versus Broadly Defined Autism Spectrum Disorders: Differences in Pre- and Perinatal Risk Factors. *J. Autism Dev. Disord.* **2012**, *43*, 1505–1516. [CrossRef]
146. Perrone-McGovern, K.; Simon-Dack, S.; Niccolai, L. Prenatal and Perinatal Factors Related to Autism, IQ, and Adaptive Functioning. *J. Genet. Psychol.* **2015**, *176*, 1–10. [CrossRef]
147. Eliasen, M.H.; Tolstrup, J.S.; Andersen, A.-M.N.; Gronbaek, M.; Olsen, J.; Strandberg-Larsen, K.; Grønbæk, M. Prenatal alcohol exposure and autistic spectrum disorders—A population-based prospective study of 80 552 children and their mothers. *Int. J. Epidemiol.* **2010**, *39*, 1074–1081. [CrossRef] [PubMed]
148. Gallagher, C.; McCarthy, F.P.; Ryan, R.M.; Khashan, A.S. Maternal Alcohol Consumption during Pregnancy and the Risk of Autism Spectrum Disorders in Offspring: A Retrospective Analysis of the Millennium Cohort Study. *J. Autism Dev. Disord.* **2018**, *48*, 3773–3782. [CrossRef]
149. Meador, K.J. Effects of in Utero Antiepileptic Drug Exposure. *Epilepsy Curr.* **2008**, *8*, 143–147. [CrossRef] [PubMed]
150. Veroniki, A.A.; Cogo, E.; Rios, P.; Straus, S.E.; Finkelstein, Y.; Kealey, R.; Reynen, E.; Soobiah, C.; Thavorn, K.; Hutton, B.; et al. Comparative safety of anti-epileptic drugs during pregnancy: A systematic review and network meta-analysis of congenital malformations and prenatal outcomes. *BMC Med.* **2017**, *15*, 1–20. [CrossRef]
151. Kobayashi, T.; Matsuyama, T.; Takeuchi, M.; Ito, S. Autism spectrum disorder and prenatal exposure to selective serotonin reuptake inhibitors: A systematic review and meta-analysis. *Reprod. Toxicol.* **2016**, *65*, 170–178. [CrossRef]
152. Wan, H.; Zhang, C.; Li, H.; Luan, S.; Liu, C. Association of maternal diabetes with autism spectrum disorders in offspring. *Medicine* **2018**, *97*, e9438. [CrossRef] [PubMed]
153. Xu, G.; Jing, J.; Bowers, K.; Liu, B.; Bao, W. Maternal diabetes and the risk of autism spectrum disorders in the offspring: A systematic review and meta-analysis. *J. Autism Dev. Disord.* **2014**, *44*, 766–775. [CrossRef]
154. Jiang, H.-Y.; Xu, L.-L.; Shao, L.; Xia, R.-M.; Yu, Z.-H.; Ling, Z.; Yang, F.; Deng, M.; Ruan, B. Maternal infection during pregnancy and risk of autism spectrum disorders: A systematic review and meta-analysis. *Brain Behav. Immun.* **2016**, *58*, 165–172. [CrossRef]
155. Zerbo, O.; Qian, Y.; Yoshida, C.; Grether, J.K.; Van De Water, J.; Croen, L.A. Maternal Infection during Pregnancy and Autism Spectrum Disorders. *J. Autism Dev. Disord.* **2015**, *45*, 4015–4025. [CrossRef]
156. Atladóttir, H.Ó.; Thorsen, P.; Østergaard, L.; Schendel, D.E.; Lemcke, S.; Abdallah, M.; Parner, E.T. Maternal Infection Requiring Hospitalization During Pregnancy and Autism Spectrum Disorders. *J. Autism Dev. Disord.* **2010**, *40*, 1423–1430. [CrossRef]
157. Chen, S.-W.; Zhong, X.-S.; Jiang, L.-N.; Zheng, X.-Y.; Xiong, Y.-Q.; Ma, S.-J.; Qiu, M.; Huo, S.-T.; Ge, J.; Chen, Q. Maternal autoimmune diseases and the risk of autism spectrum disorders in offspring: A systematic review and meta-analysis. *Behav. Brain Res.* **2016**, *296*, 61–69. [CrossRef]
158. Wu, S.; Ding, Y.; Wu, F.; Li, R.; Xie, G.; Hou, J.; Mao, P. Family history of autoimmune diseases is associated with an increased risk of autism in children: A systematic review and meta-analysis. *Neurosci. Biobehav. Rev.* **2015**, *55*, 322–332. [CrossRef]
159. Brown, A.S.; Sourander, A.; Hinkka-Yli-Salomäki, S.; McKeague, I.W.; Sundvall, J.; Surcel, H.-M. Elevated maternal C-reactive protein and autism in a national birth cohort. *Mol. Psychiatry* **2013**, *19*, 259–264. [CrossRef]
160. Brown, A.S.; Surcel, H.-M.; Hinkka-Yli-Salomäki, S.; Cheslack-Postava, K.; Bao, Y.; Sourander, A. Maternal thyroid autoantibody and elevated risk of autism in a national birth cohort. *Prog. Neuro-Psychopharmacol. Biol. Psychiatry* **2015**, *57*, 86–92. [CrossRef]

161. Meyer, U.; Feldon, J.; Fatemi, S.H. In-vivo rodent models for the experimental investigation of prenatal immune activation effects in neurodevelopmental brain disorders. *Neurosci. Biobehav. Rev.* **2009**, *33*, 1061–1079. [CrossRef]
162. Comi, A.M.; Zimmerman, A.W.; Frye, V.H.; Law, P.A.; Peeden, J.N. Familial Clustering of Autoimmune Disorders and Evaluation of Medical Risk Factors in Autism. *J. Child Neurol.* **1999**, *14*, 388–394. [CrossRef]
163. Atladóttir, H.O.; Pedersen, M.G.; Thorsen, P.; Mortensen, P.B.; Deleuran, B.; Eaton, W.W.; Parner, E.T.; Sutton, R.M.; Niles, D.; Nysaether, J.; et al. Association of Family History of Autoimmune Diseases and Autism Spectrum Disorders. *Pediatrics* **2009**, *124*, 687–694. [CrossRef]
164. Sanna, A.; Firinu, D.; Zavattari, P.; Valera, P. Zinc Status and Autoimmunity: A Systematic Review and Meta-Analysis. *Nutrients* **2018**, *10*, 68. [CrossRef] [PubMed]
165. Napoli, E.; Hung, C.; Wong, S.; Giulivi, C. Toxicity of the Flame-Retardant BDE-49 on Brain Mitochondria and Neuronal Progenitor Striatal Cells Enhanced by a PTEN-Deficient Background. *Toxicol. Sci.* **2013**, *132*, 196–210. [CrossRef]
166. Rossignol, D.A.; Frye, R.E. Mitochondrial dysfunction in autism spectrum disorders: A systematic review and meta-analysis. *Mol. Psychiatry* **2012**, *17*, 290–314. [CrossRef]
167. Yoshimasu, K.; Kiyohara, C.; Takemura, S.; Nakai, K. A meta-analysis of the evidence on the impact of prenatal and early infancy exposures to mercury on autism and attention deficit/hyperactivity disorder in the childhood. *NeuroToxicology* **2014**, *44*, 121–131. [CrossRef]
168. Shelton, J.F.; Geraghty, E.M.; Tancredi, D.; Delwiche, L.D.; Schmidt, R.J.; Ritz, B.; Hansen, R.L.; Hertz-Picciotto, I. Neurodevelopmental Disorders and Prenatal Residential Proximity to Agricultural Pesticides: The CHARGE Study. *Environ. Health Perspect.* **2014**, *122*, 1103–1109. [CrossRef]
169. Jeddi, M.Z.; Janani, L.; Memari, A.H.; Akhondzadeh, S.; Yunesian, M. The role of phthalate esters in autism development: A systematic review. *Environ. Res.* **2016**, *151*, 493–504. [CrossRef]
170. Dingemans, M.M.; Berg, M.V.D.; Westerink, R.H.S. Neurotoxicity of Brominated Flame Retardants: (In)direct Effects of Parent and Hydroxylated Polybrominated Diphenyl Ethers on the (Developing) Nervous System. *Environ. Health Perspect.* **2011**, *119*, 900–907. [CrossRef]
171. Wayman, G.A.; Bose, D.D.; Yang, N.; Lesiak, A.; Bruun, N.; Impey, S.; LeDoux, V.; Pessah, I.N.; Lein, P.J. PCB-95 Modulates the Calcium-Dependent Signaling Pathway Responsible for Activity-Dependent Dendritic Growth. *Environ. Health Perspect.* **2012**, *120*, 1003–1009. [CrossRef]

2

Pharmacogenetics Informed Decision Making in Adolescent Psychiatric Treatment

Teri Smith *, Susan Sharp, Ann M. Manzardo and Merlin G. Butler

Department of Psychiatry and Behavioral Sciences, University of Kansas Medical Center, 3901 Rainbow Boulevard, Kansas City, Kansas 66160, USA; ssharp@kumc.edu (S.S.); amanzardo@kumc.edu (A.M.); mbutler4@kumc.edu (M.G.B.)

* Author to whom correspondence should be addressed; tsmith2@kumc.edu

Academic Editor: Kenji Hashimoto

Abstract: Advances made in genetic testing and tools applied to pharmacogenetics are increasingly being used to inform clinicians in fields such as oncology, hematology, diabetes (endocrinology), cardiology and expanding into psychiatry by examining the influences of genetics on drug efficacy and metabolism. We present a clinical case example of an adolescent male with anxiety, attention deficit hyperactivity disorder (ADHD) and autism spectrum disorder who did not tolerate numerous medications and dosages over several years in attempts to manage his symptoms. Pharmacogenetics testing was performed and DNA results on this individual elucidated the potential pitfalls in medication use because of specific pharmacodynamic and pharmacokinetic differences specifically involving polymorphisms of genes in the cytochrome p450 enzyme system. Future studies and reports are needed to further illustrate and determine the type of individualized medicine approach required to treat individuals based on their specific gene patterns. Growing evidence supports this biological approach for standard of care in psychiatry.

Keywords: pharmacogenetics; cytochrome p450 enzymes; psychotropic medications; psychiatry; behavior; autism; clinical case

1. Introduction

Pharmacogenetics is the field of study that examines the influence of genetics on drug efficacy and tolerability often based on the cytochrome p450 enzymes involved in drug metabolism encoded by a large family of protein-coding genes [1]. Cytochrome p450 (CYP450) enzymes are present in most bodily tissues primarily positioned within the inner mitochondrial membrane or endoplasmic reticulum of cells. They are perhaps best known for their function in the metabolism of potentially toxic compounds including metabolic byproducts (e.g., bilirubin) and drugs but play an important role in the biosynthesis and metabolism of lipids, steroids, including hormones, and select vitamins [1]. PharmacoGENETICS can be discriminated from the related field of "PharmacoGENOMICS" which considers the broader influences of inheritance on gene products, expression and function outside the limited scope of the cytochrome p450 enzyme system, primarily found in the liver. Natural variation in sensitivity and action of cytochrome p450 enzymes contributes to variations in drug response and side effect profiles of direct relevance to medical management of drug therapy. For example, about one in every 15 individuals show an exaggerated response to standard doses of beta blockers, a class of medications commonly prescribed for hypertension and metabolized by the CYP450 enzyme system and when disturbed leads to side effects [2,3].

CYP450 enzymes are encoded by genes with the wild-type allele occurring in most individuals; however, an extensive or normal metabolizer receives two copies of the wild-type allele. The presence of other allele variants usually indicates reduced or no CYP450 enzyme activity. Individuals with two copies of a variant allele of one of the genes encoding a CYP450 enzyme are considered poor metabolizers while individuals with one wild-type allele and one variant allele have significantly reduced enzymatic activity. Individuals who inherit multiple copies of the wild-type allele are generally extensive metabolizers or ultrametabolizers and degrade drugs quickly [2,3].

Despite the relatively large number and broad function of the cytochrome p450 enzyme superfamily with over 50 members, 90 percent of all drugs are metabolized by just six different enzymes (CYP1A2, CYP3A5, CYP2C19, CYP2D6, CYP3A4 and CYP3A5) which significantly limit the number of genetic targets needed for screening and enhancing clinical utility [2]. Clinical testing platforms tailored for medical specialties are now available and typically provide interpretive services for treatment and dosage recommendations based upon the genetic testing results. Interpretive insight is particularly important for clinicians and hospitals that may be unfamiliar or apprehensive about the application of novel technologies in diagnosis and treatment in changing medical practice.

Pharmacogenetics have been used successfully to optimize treatment in cardiology, diabetes, and oncology [4,5], and has been particularly helpful for psychiatric medications which account for 20% of the 121 pharmacogenetic markers currently recognized by the US Food and Drug Administration [6]. Pharmacogenetics testing typically targets single nucleotide polymorphisms (SNPs) of the top six CYP450 enzyme genes which are now utilized in many areas of medicine including psychiatry for drug selection and adjustment to improve efficacy and reduce medication adverse events [7]. Potential financial and personal costs of adverse drug events, including deaths, and effectiveness in treatment and reducing psychiatric costs may be helped by providing better informed decision making when prescribing psychotropic drugs as outlined in a recent report by Durham [8]. The American Medical Association has made similar suggestions regarding how pharmacogenetics can reduce healthcare costs by decreasing the number of adverse drug reactions and number of medications used by patients to yield more effective therapies [9]. The following detailed clinical case history and report is presented as an example of how pharmacogenetics and the practice of psychiatry can interface now and in the future. In this case, pharmacogenetics testing provided more comprehensive and informed psychiatric care decision-making and evaluation as well as therapeutic outcomes beneficial for the patient and immediate family.

2. Results and Discussion

2.1. Clinical Case Report

Our 12-year-old Caucasian male was first evaluated by his current psychiatrist in April 2010 after years of seeking care from other psychiatrists and psychotherapists during his childhood due to disruptive behaviors. His history included psychiatric hospitalization for 2 days while on fluoxetine at 10 years of age and occupational therapy for sensory issues at 12 years of age. He had received a variety of treatments from psychotherapists. His past diagnoses included Attention Deficit Hyperactivity Disorder (ADHD), combined type, since 7 years of age, Anxiety Disorder-Not Otherwise Specified (NOS), learning problems, Obsessive Compulsive Disorder, chronic bed-wetting at a younger age, Pervasive Developmental Disorder-NOS (Autism Spectrum Disorder), Sensory Integration Disorder and drug induced mania. He reported no drug allergies, food sensitivities or intolerances.

Many different psychotropic medications had been prescribed, many of which were not tolerated or helpful. At the time of his initial evaluation, he was taking oxcarbazepine (total 375 mg), lamotrigine (175 mg), fluvoxamine (75 mg) and risperidone (0.5 mg) which were of limited to no benefit in controlling his behavior. He had experienced irritability, tantrums, impulsivity, distractibility, fidgetiness and obsessive thoughts without rituals, rigidity to change, sensory sensitivities and oppositional behaviors for much of his life. He slept well and had a normal diet. Over the next two years (2010–2012), he was prescribed atomoxetine (18 mg) and stimulants (dexamfetamine (30–60 mg), dextroamphetamine (15 mg). Risperidone was replaced with aripiprazole (5–10 mg). In February 2011 his laboratory findings showed a normal hematogram, a normal comprehensive metabolic panel, normal thyroid studies and normal fasting lipid levels. A fluoxetine (5–15 mg) trial showed minimal benefit, and he did not tolerate doses higher than 15 mg. Citalopram 10 mg was added in April 2012.

He was evaluated at 14 years of age by a clinical geneticist on our team (MGB). His height was 159 cm (15%), weight was 53.8 kg (50%) and head circumference was 53.1 cm (5%). He was non-dysmorphic and no single gene disorder was identified. The family history was positive for obsessive compulsive disorder, anxiety, irritability and anger control problems, ADHD, learning problems, heart problems, bipolar disorder, stuttering and drug and alcohol addiction. A chromosomal microarray test was normal without recognized deletions or duplications in the genome. Additional laboratory studies showed a normal comprehensive metabolic panel, hematogram, cortisol (morning), C-reactive protein, insulin (fasting), somatomedin C, but his total testosterone levels were low (80 ng/dL with reference range 270–1070 ng/dL). An X-ray bone age study showed delayed bone development. A referral was then made to an endocrinologist who prescribed testosterone cypionate injections (200 mg/mL). He was also taking over the counter (OTC) supplements, fish oil and lactobacillus probiotics at this time along with OTC flaxseed oil and ω-3 fatty acids. Veema liquid vitamins were added in January 2012. All OTC supplements were given as suggested by label. There was no perceived benefit from aripiprazole (2.5 mg) and it was discontinued. He then experienced trouble sleeping with irritability and reportedly visualized shadows. Aripiprazole (2.5 mg) was again prescribed and citalopram was increased to 15 mg. Psychotherapy was suggested, but he became more hyperactive, irritable, and angry. Aripiprazole was decreased to 2 mg while citalopram was decreased to 10 mg and testosterone injections continued. In April 2013, aripiprazole was decreased to 1 mg and hypnotherapy with relaxation techniques were offered but with only small positive effects. Aripiprazole was then discontinued. He began to take OTC amino acid supplements, salmon oil, melatonin for sleep and Empower Plus Vitamin with mineral supplements as suggested by label. He was taking 10 mg of citalopram prescribed by his psychiatrist but began to experience a crawling sensation of his skin. A low dose of diphenhydramine was suggested. His mother was advised to discuss with the pharmacist the use of OTC supplements and their possible side effects.

By June 2013, he was having frequent panic attacks and tactile sensory sensitivities which often triggered explosive episodes. His citalopram was reduced to 7.5 mg and buspirone was considered as a possible next step for pharmacotherapy. By August 2013, he was off all medications other than Empower Plus Vitamins and experienced increased symptoms of inattention and anxiety about school. He was sleeping better, but became stressed prior to attending school and wearing street clothes. He saw a new psychotherapist in August 2013 at 15 years of age for constructive methods to deal with his anxiety and sensory issues. He was a high school sophomore who did well academically (A's and B's). He participated in cross country and swimming but experienced anger dysregulation at home. Wearing street clothes bothered him extremely causing mood irritability by the time he arrived home from school.

He reported taking the following prescription medications in the past: Fluvoxamine (25–100mg), divalproex (125 mg), clonidine (0.5 mg), guanfacine (1 mg), sertraline (25 mg), aripiprazole (2–10 mg), oxcarbazepine (375 mg), risperidone (0.5 mg), lamotrigine (175 mg), lisdexamfetamine (30–60 mg), dextroamphetamine (15 mg), citalopram (10 mg), fluoxetine (5–15 mg), atomoxetine (18 mg), quetiapine (50 mg), imipramine (25 mg), testosterone, and alprazolam (0.5 mg). He felt hopelessness at times and did not understand why this was happening to him. He was polite and had a supportive family. He was socially awkward and friendships were limited. He had problems transitioning from one activity to another. At this point, his mother was giving him OTC supplements including amino acids, salmon oil, Empower vitamins, inositol when anxious, vitamin D3, choline, and probiotics as suggested by label.

At 15 years of age, he continued to have frequent "melt-downs" in the morning and could not tolerate tactile sensory stimulation. He had anxiety attacks during which he screamed and protested loudly. He became shaky, hot, and sweaty. He did not eat well or sleep normally. On September 30, 2013 escitalopram (5 mg) was prescribed and he immediately recorded less anxiety and his sensory issues improved. He requested an increase in dosage of escitalopram immediately because of the positive effect. He then began to use coping skills more efficiently such as mindfulness, listening to music, and deep breathing as well as behavioral strategies for coping with his symptoms. At about this time, he contracted a sinus infection and was using Zyrtec and escitalopram. His anger problems became much worse and his sensory problems increased. His therapist consulted with an occupational therapist in October 2013 and he began to use exercise and joint compressions along with other behavioral strategies to decrease sensory sensitivities. The patient's parents observed when the patient recently used OTC Nyquil Cold Medicine which contains acetaminophen, dextromethorphan and doxylamine succinate that it not only helped his cold symptoms, but his anxiety, sensory sensitivities, and other related behavioral problems lessened. When he discontinued this OTC medication, his anxiety, panic, and nail picking behaviors increased. Pharmacogenetics testing was then suggested due to his multiple episodes of behavioral problems that were not controlled over time with the use of several different medications and dosages.

Over time, escitalopram continued to help his anxiety, but sensory issues were still present. Escitalopram was increased to 10 mg on October 28, 2013 and behavioral improvement was notable with many days without melt-downs. Over the following few months he was dealing better with wearing specific clothing (e.g., long pants) and with transitions. He was better motivated to improve his grades from Bs to As and his overall school performance. He began to wear dress clothes (usually he would wear only soft, loose clothing). He wanted to socialize more by making new friends and to improve his social skills. ADHD symptoms lessened while on the increased level of escitalopram. He felt he could now take charge of his own self-soothing but could think through issues *versus* over-reacting to trivial frustrations. His social life improved and escitalopram was increased to 20 mg in June 2014. The family saw a correlation between inadequate eating and sleeping and the patient's over-reactions. They devised a plan to remind him to eat regularly and to encourage him to obtain sufficient sleep. His sensory issues improved and he was much kinder to others. He now had a job and was able to tolerate wearing rough-textured fabric pants and a T-shirt. He excelled at work and was given a promotion.

2.2. *Pharmacogenetics*

The DNA-based pharmacogenetics Genecept assay testing (Genomind, Chalfont, PA, USA) examines polymorphisms from 10 separate genes with three genes encoding cytochrome p450 enzymes related to medication metabolism (*CYP2D6*, *CYP2C19*, *CYP3A4*) and 7 additional genes consisting of neurotransmitter receptors (*5HT2C*, *DRD2*) and transporters (*SLC6A4*), enzymes (*COMT*, *MTHFR*) and ion channel function (*CACNA1C*, *ANK3*) involved with pharmacodynamics of drug activity and interaction. The three liver cytochrome p450 enzymes selected are major metabolizers of psychiatric medications and their gene variants are determined to have clinically relevant impacts on drug interaction and metabolism in the clinical setting. The assay contains a C/C gene variation of a serotonin receptor [5-hyroxytryptamine receptor 2C (5HT2C)] that has been associated with increased weight gain with atypical antipsychotic therapy [10–14]. The *SLC6A4* gene codes for a presynaptic serotonin transporter protein (SERT) responsible for serotonin reuptake and targeted by most selective serotonin reuptake inhibitors (SSRIs). The *SLC6A4* gene product can produce a long (L) and short (S) length variant with different clinical significance. Possession of two S variants is associated with a poor or slow response to SSRIs or with adverse events [10,15].

The DRD2 receptor is a target of most neuroleptics which act to block signaling of the neurotransmitter dopamine. The *DRD2* variant selected (-141C Ins/Del) is a variation in the promoter region of the gene that reduces *DRD2* gene expression and responsiveness along with potential adverse events when using atypical antipsychotic medications. The *COMT* gene codes for catechol-*O*-methyl-transferase which is an enzyme responsible for the majority of dopamine metabolism. Dopamine is critical for memory, judgment, attention, and other executive functions and strongly linked to multiple neuropsychiatric disorders [16]. A valine (Val) to methionine (Met) amino acid substitution is produced by a polymorphism at codon 158 due to a nucleotide G to A transition which results in approximately 40% reduction in COMT enzymatic activity [17]. The Val/Val substitution leads to elevated enzyme activity causing increased dopamine degradation (producing low dopamine) while the Met/Met substitution produces a 3 fold reduction in enzyme activity and reduced dopamine metabolism relative to Val/Val [18]. The Val/Val substitution is associated with a hypodopaminergic state and lower executive function and implicated in susceptibility to schizophrenia, panic disorder and anorexia nervosa.

A methylenetetrahydrofolate reductase (*MTHFR*) C/T gene variation has been shown to slow the conversion of folate or folic acid to methylfolate, a precursor to serotonin, norepinephrine, and dopamine synthesis. This variant impacts monoamine and catecholamine production [19–26] and associated with depression. L-methylfolate has shown efficacy as an adjunctive therapy in individuals with Selective Serotonin Reuptake Inhibitor resistant major depression [21–25]. The MTHFR enzyme metabolizes homocysteine and if not broken down effectively, can build up in the blood stream and lead to health concerns related to cardiovascular disease [26].

Molecular transport and regulation of intracellular calcium levels are important in neurological development and function with pathology linked to numerous neuropsychiatric disorders including depression, schizophrenia and bipolar disorder [27]. A variant (G to A) of the α-1C subunit of the L-type voltage gated calcium channel gene (*CACNA1C*) influences the threshold for activation and duration of channel opening leading to excessive calcium influx into the cell and neuronal hypersensitivity to activating stimuli [27]. The variation predicts poor clinical response to current pharmacotherapy. Another ion channel function related gene is Ankyrin-G (ANK3) which encodes a protein located at the nodes of Ranvier and neurons responsible for the generation of action potentials. It is important for the function and maintenance of voltage dependent sodium channels. Modest evidence links a common T to G transition with schizophrenia in this specific ankyrin gene family member [27].

2.3. DNA-based Pharmacogenetic Results

The Genecept assay results identified in our clinical case involved three known significant variations in the 10 genes tested which impact on several pharmacologic substrates (see Table 1). Our clinical case was found to have a *5HT2C* C/C gene variation of a serotonin receptor which is associated with satiety signaling in the hypothalamus and hence, serotonin has a potent satiety signal function and thus 5HT2C antagonism can lead to increased food intake [10–14]. Although the weight of our clinical case was within normal limits, this finding suggested that caution be used when prescribing atypical antipsychotics such as risperidone. Our clinical case also showed a *MTHFR* C/T gene variation that suggested reduced enzymatic activity associated with a reduced conversion of folic acid to methylfolate. As methylfolate is a precursor to serotonin, norepinephrine, and dopamine, this gene variant would indicate a possible reduced production of these peptides [19–26].

Variants of *MTHFR* have been related to increased risk for depression and L-methylfolate has shown efficacy as an adjunctive therapy. It was recommended that our clinical case should take folic acid supplements or L-methylfolate to help in the conversion of homocysteine and health concerns related to cardiovascular disease [26]. Interestingly, there was a maternal family history of heart disease that may be associated with this gene variation and homocysteine levels.

Table 1. Pharmacologic substrates, inhibitors and inducers of cytochrome P450 (CYP2D6) of relevant psychotropic drugs.

Substrate	Inhibitors	Inducers
Acetaminophen	Amiodarone	Dexamethasone
Amphetamine-Dextroamphetamine	Bupropion	Rifampin
Aripiprazole	Celecoxib	
Atomoxetine	Chlorpheniramine	
Clonidine	Chlorpromazine	
Codeine *	**Citalopram**	
Dextromethorphan	Clozapine	
Duloxetine	Cocaine	
Fluoxetine	Desipramine	
Fluvoxamine	**Diphenhydramine**	
Haloperidol	Duloxetine	
Iloperidone	**Fluoxetine**	
Methadone	Halofantrine	
Methamphetamine	Haloperidol	
Mirtazapine	Hydroxychloroquine	
Nefazodone	Imatinib	
Olanzapine	**Imipramine**	
Paroxetine	Levomepromazine	
Phenothiazines	Methadone	
Risperidone *	Metoclopramide	
Sertraline	Mibefradil	
Tricyclic antidepressants (TCAs)	Moclobemide	
Tramadol	Nelfinavir	
Venlafaxine *	Norfluoxetine	
Vortioxetine	Paroxetine	
	Perphenazine	
	Quinidine	
	Ranitidine	
	Ritonavir	
	Sertraline	
	Terbinafine	
	Thioridazine	
	Tranylcypromine	

Phenothiazines include: Chlorpromazine, fluphenazine, perphenazine, promethazine, thioridazine; tricyclic antidepressants include: Amitriptyline, amoxapine, clomipramine, desipramine, doxepin, imipramine, nortriptyline, protriptyline, trimipramine; * Metabolized to active compound; ω-3 fatty acids can inhibit CYP2D6 activity at high doses [28]; Compounds prescribed for our clinical case are indicated in **bold**. Table revised from literature supplied by Genomind, LLC (www.genomind.com).

Additionally, our clinical case had *CYP2D6*4/*5* gene allele variation that indicated significant reduction in enzyme activity. The *4 variation represents a G to A transition at the first nucleotide of exon 4 of one allele while the *5 variation represents a deletion of the second allele [29]. This is likely to put the patient at risk for significantly reduced hepatic degradation of targeted drugs and higher plasma levels of drugs that are typically processed by this enzyme thereby increasing the risk for drug interactions and reduced effectiveness of medications such as risperidone [13,30–53]. Caution should be used when prescribing medications that require this enzyme for metabolic break down. It would be important to avoid prescribing any inhibitors of CYP2D6, as well, which includes other medications that may lower further the enzymatic activity. On the other hand, inducers of CYP2D6 would increase the metabolic activity of CYP2D6. Table 1 lists psychotropic drugs known to be processed by CYP2D6, as well as inhibitors and inducers of this enzyme activity [54,55].

Many drugs prescribed for our patient (aripiprazole, dextroamphetamine, fluoxetine, fluvoxamine) were dependent on normal CYP2D6 enzyme activity and metabolism for degradation while other drugs such as risperidone require conversion to a therapeutic agent using this enzyme. Disruption of CYP2D6 function may partially or completely explain problems experienced by our clinical case when using these drugs. Some of the medications used were also inhibitors of CYP2D6 (e.g., citalopram, sertraline) which are expected to further suppress the reduced activity (see Table 2). Also, dextomethoraphan (DM) is an ingredient found in Nyquil Cold Medicine and used as a cough suppressant. It is a non-psychotropic medication substrate of CYP2D6 and excreted by the kidneys. It has a half-life of 2 to 4 h (for those with extensive (normal) metabolism) but 24 h for those individuals categorized as poor metabolizers (as found in our clinical case). Directions for use of Nyquil Cold Medication are not to exceed 4 doses in 24 h and with this recommended dosage, the amount of DM would be expected to be increased in the blood stream in those with poor metabolism. DM acts as an NMDA receptor antagonist at high doses and produces dissociative states similar to what is seen by other dissociative anesthetics such as ketamine and phencyclidine. When exceeding label-specified maximum dosages, dextromethorphan can thus act as a dissociative hallucinogen including visual field disturbances, distorted bodily perception and excitement.

Table 2. Pharmacogenetic test results with drug interactions from our clinical case.

Pharmacogenetic Target	Variant Functional Impact	Compounds Prescribed
CYP2D6	Poor cytochrome p450 metabolism	Acetaminophen, Aripiprazole, Atomoxetine, Citalopram, Dextroamphetamine, Dextromethorphan, Fluoxetine, Fluvoxamine, Risperidone *, Sertraline
5HT2C	Reduced affinity for serotonin	Fluoxetine, Fluvoamine, Sertraline
MTHFR	Reduced activity (low monoamine and catecholamine production)	Methyl/folate-related agents (vitamins)

* Metabolized to active compound.

As a slow or poor metabolizer, our clinical case would likely experience an increased prolonged sedative effect which was noted by his parents during the time he was using Nyquil Cold Medication [56,57]. Of interest, escitalopram is not dependent on CYP2D6 for metabolism but is dependent on both CYP3A4 and CYP2C19 [53], different p450 enzymes which were found to be normal by gene polymorphism testing in our clinical case. Ultimately, escitalopram, which was prescribed, was found to be the most effective medication to date for treating his behavioral problems and supported by his pharmacogenetic testing results.

3. Experimental Section

Saliva was collected from our patient in June 2014 when he was 16 years of age. DNA was isolated from saliva samples and sent for pharmacogenetics Genecept DNA-based assay commercially available from Genomind (Chalfont, PA, USA). The Genecept assay examines polymorphisms of selected genes for CYP450 hepatic enzymes which metabolize drugs as well as other genes related to neurotransmitters, their function, receptors and enzymes implicated in psychiatric disorders, and responsiveness to psychiatric medications. The list includes ten separate genes encoding cytochrome p450 enzymes with three related to the metabolism of pharmaceutical agents commonly used in psychiatry (*CYP2D6, CYP2C19, CYP3A4*) and seven additional genes encoding neurotransmitter receptors (*5HT2C, DRD2*), transporters (*SLC6A4*), enzymes (*COMT, MTHFR*) and ion channel function (*CACNA1C, ANK3*) involved in pharmacodynamic aspects of psychiatric medications.

4. Conclusions

It is clear in this clinical case that certain recommendations for care could be made due to pharmacogenetic findings. An approach would be to select a different class or drug that has a similar function but metabolized by a different CYP450 enzyme. The dosage or frequency of drug of administration of the specific medication could be adjusted to account for the metabolic disturbance (poor or ultrametabolizer). One should also consider other prescribed drugs or over the counter that may induce or inhibit the specific CYP450 enzyme (Table 1 shows a list of medications/agents that either induce or inhibit CYP2D6 activity). For example, eicosapentaenoic acid (EPA) is an ω-3 fatty acid and acts as an inhibitor of CYP2D6 [28] at higher doses as are antihistamines such as diphenhydramine [58]. Dietary considerations, such as the addition of folic acid or methyl group donor compound can decrease homocysteine blood levels and thus lower the negative impact from the *MTHFR* gene variant seen in our clinical case.

In summary, the history of our clinical case illustrates how pharmacogenetics and psychiatry can potentially interface to provide more informed decision making regarding use of psychotropic medications. Pharmacogenetics testing is new to the field of psychiatry and in similar situations may appear to be more humane and likely save years of personal distress associated with trial and error drug prescription without taking into consideration an individual's specific drug metabolism pattern. It would also likely be more cost effective to prescribe psychotropic medications with the more informed decision making provided by this type of genetic testing. The cost of testing (approximately $400) is low when compared to the financial costs of many other treatments utilized by this clinical case over several years. The current report involving only one clinical case is limited in generalizability and more clinical reports are needed to help guide treatment for providers. However, if similar experiences and clinical case studies are found then pharmacogenetic testing should become standard of care in mental health treatment and decision making when using psychotropic medications. Sharing these experiences would be encouraged by the authors.

Acknowledgments: We thank the family of the patient whose case history is presented in this paper. We acknowledge the support from the NICHD (HD02528) grant. The authors thank Carla Meister for manuscript preparation.

Author Contributions: Teri Smith and Merlin G. Butler conceived this study; Teri Smith, Susan Sharp, Ann Manzardo and Merlin G. Butler analyzed data and wrote the manuscript; Susan Sharp, Teri Smith and Merlin G. Butler evaluated the clinical information; and Teri Smith, Susan Sharp, Ann Manzardo and Merlin G. Butler reviewed the literature and contributed to the content of the manuscript.

References

1. Lee, J.W.; Aminkeng, F.; Bhavsar, A.P.; Shaw, K.; Carleton, B.C.; Hayden, M.R.; Ross, C.J. The emerging era of pharmacogenomics: Current successes, future potential, and challenges. *Clin. Genet.* **2014**, *86*, 21–28. [CrossRef] [PubMed]
2. Lynch, T.; Price, A. The effect of cytochrome p450 metabolism on drug response, interactions, and adverse effects. *Am Fam Physician* **2007**, *76*, 391–396. [PubMed]
3. Yang, X.; Zhang, B.; Molony, C.; Chudin, E.; Hao, K.; Zhu, J.; Gaedigk, A.; Suver, C.; Zhong, H.; Leeder, J.S.; *et al.* Systematic genetic and genomic analysis of cytochrome p450 enzyme activities in human liver. *Genome Res.* **2010**, *20*, 1020–1036. [CrossRef] [PubMed]
4. Weng, L.; Zhang, L.; Peng, Y.; Huang, R.S. Pharmacogenetics and pharmacogenomics: A bridge to individualized cancer therapy. *Pharmacogenomics* **2013**, *14*, 315–324. [CrossRef] [PubMed]
5. Toomula, N.; Hima Bindu, K.; Sathish Kumar, D.; Kumar, A. Pharmacogenomics—Personalized treatment of cancer, diabetes and cardiovascular diseases. *J. Pharmacogenomics Pharmacoproteomics* **2011**, *2*, 107.
6. Hamilton, S.P. The promise of psychiatric pharmacogenomics. *Biol. Psychiatry* **2015**, *77*, 29–35. [CrossRef] [PubMed]
7. Zandi, P.P.; Judy, J.T. The promise and reality of pharmacogenetics in psychiatry. *Psychiatr. Clin. N. Am.* **2010**, *33*, 181–224. [CrossRef]
8. Durham, D. Utilizing Pharmacogenetics in psychiarty: The time has come. *Mol. Diagn. Ther.* **2014**, *18*, 117–119. [CrossRef] [PubMed]
9. American Medical Association website resource. Available online: http://www.ama-assn.org/ama/pub/physician-resources/medical-science/genetics-molecular-medicine/current-topics/pharmacogenomics.page (accessed on 19 December 2014).
10. Reynolds, G.P.; Zhang, Z.J.; Zhang, X.B. Association of antipsychitic drug-induced weight gain with a 5-HT2C receptor gene polymorphism. *Lancet* **2002**, *359*, 2086–2087. [CrossRef] [PubMed]

11. Mulder, H.; Franke, B.; van der-Beek vander, A.A.; Arends, J.; Wilmink, F.W.; Scheffer, H.; Egberts, A.C. The association between HTR2C gene polymorphisms and the metabolic syndrome in patients with schizophrenia. *J. Clin. Psychopharmacol.* **2007**, *27*, 338–343. [CrossRef] [PubMed]
12. Reynolds, G.P. Pharmacogenetic aspects of antipsychotic drug-induced weight gain—A critical review. *Clin. Psychopharmacol. Neurosci.* **2012**, *10*, 71–77. [CrossRef] [PubMed]
13. Altar, C.A.; Hornberger, J.; Shewade, A.; Cruz, V.; Garrison, J.; Mrazek, D. Clinical validity of cytochrome P450 metabolism and serotonin gene variants in psychiatric pharmacotherapy. *Int. Rev. Psychiatry* **2013**, *25*, 509–533. [CrossRef] [PubMed]
14. Reynolds, G.P.; Hill, M.J.; Kirk, S.L. The 5HT2C receptor and antipsychotic induced weight grain–mechanisms and genetics. *J. Psychopharmacol.* **2006**, *20*, 15–18. [CrossRef] [PubMed]
15. Serretti, A.; Kato, M.; de Ronchi, D.; Kinoshita, T. Meta-analysis of serotonin transporter gene promoter polymorphism (5-HTTLPR) association with selective serotonin reuptake inhibitor efficacy in depressed patients. *Mol. Psychiatry* **2007**, *12*, 247–257. [PubMed]
16. Cohen, B.M.; Carlezon, W.A., Jr. Can't get enough of that dopamine. *Am. J. Psychiatry* **2007**, *164*, 543–546. [CrossRef] [PubMed]
17. Sim, S.C.; Kacevska, M.; Ingelman-Sundberg, M. Pharmacogenomics of drug-metabolizing enzymes: A recent update on clinical implications and endogenous effects. *Pharmacogenomics J.* **2013**, *13*, 1–11. [CrossRef] [PubMed]
18. Lachman, H.M.; Papolos, D.F.; Saito, T.; Yu, Y.M.; Szumlanski, C.L.; Weinshilboum, R.M. Human catechol-*O*-methyltransferase pharmacogenetics: Description of a functional polymorphism and its potential application to neuropsychiatric disorders. *Pharmacogenetics* **1996**, *6*, 243–250. [CrossRef] [PubMed]
19. Heisler, L.K; Zhou, L.; Bajwa, P.; Hsu, J.; Tecott, L.H. Serotonin 5HT2C receptors regulate anxiety-like behavior. *Genes Brain Behav.* **2007**, *6*, 491–496. [CrossRef] [PubMed]
20. Alex, K.D.; Yavanian, G.J.; McFarlane, H.G.; Pluto, C.P.; Pehak, E.A. Modulation of dopamine release by striatal 5-HT2C receptors. *Synapse* **2007**, *55*, 242–251. [CrossRef]
21. Stahl, S.M. L-methylfolate: A vitamin for your monoamines. *J. Clin. Psychiatry* **2008**, *69*, 1352–1353. [CrossRef] [PubMed]
22. Gilbody, S.; Lewis, S.; Lightfoot, T. Methylenetetrahydrofolate reductase (MTHFR) genetic polymorphisms and psychiatric disorders: A huge review. *Am. J. Epidemiol.* **2007**, *165*, 1–13. [CrossRef] [PubMed]
23. Wu, Y.L.; Ding, X.X.; Sun, Y.H.; Chen, J.; Zhao, X.; Jiang, Y.H.; Lv, X.L.; Wu, Z.Q. Association between MTHFR C677T polymorphism and depression: An updated meta-analysis of 26 studies. *Prog. Neuropsychopharmacol. Biol. Psychiatry* **2013**, *46*, 78–85. [CrossRef] [PubMed]
24. Ginsberg, L.D.; Oubre, A.Y.; Daoud, Y.A. L-methylfolate plus SSRI or SNRI from treatment initiation compared to SSRI or SNRI monotherapy in a major depressive episode. *Innov. Clin. Neurosci.* **2011**, *8*, 19–28. [PubMed]
25. Papkostas, G.I.; Shelton, R.C.; Zajecka, J.M.; Etemad, B.; Rickels, K.; Clain, A.; Baer, L.; Dalton, E.D.; Sacco, G.R.; Shoenfeld, D.; *et al.* L-methylfolate as adjunctive therapy for SSRI-resistant major depression: Results of two randomized, double-blind, parallel-sequential trials. *Am. J. Psychiatry* **2012**, *169*, 1267–1274. [CrossRef] [PubMed]
26. Frosst, P.; Blom, H.J.; Milos, R.; Goyette, P.; Sheppard, C.A.; Matthews, R.G.; Boers, G.J.; den Heijer, M.; Kluijtmans, L.A.; van den Heuvel, L.P.; *et al.* A candidate genetic risk factor for vascular disease: A common mutation in methylenetetrahydrofolate reductase. *Nat. Genet.* **1995**, *10*, 111–113. [CrossRef] [PubMed]
27. Yoshimizu, T.; Pan, J.Q.; Mungenast, A.E.; Madison, J.M.; Su, S.; Ketterman, J.; Ongur, D.; McPhie, D.; Cohen, B.; Perlis, R.; *et al.* Functional implications of a psychiatric risk variant within CACNA1C in induced human neurons. *Mol. Psychiatry.* **2014**. [CrossRef]
28. Yao, H.T.; Chang, Y.W.; Lan, S.J.; Chen, C.T.; Hsu, J.T.; Yeh, T.K. The inhibitory effect of polyunsaturated fatty acids on human CYP enzymes. *Life Sci.* **2006**, *79*, 2432–2440. [CrossRef] [PubMed]
29. Gough, A.C.; Miles, J.S.; Spurr, N.K.; Moss, J.E.; Gaedigk, A.; Eichelbaum, M.; Wolf, C.R. Identification of the primary gene defect at the cytochrome p450 CYP2D locus. *Nature* **1990**, *347*, 773–776. [CrossRef] [PubMed]
30. Nichols, A.I.; Focht, K.; Jiang, Q.; Preskorn, S.H.; Kane, C.P. Pharmacokinetics of venlafaxine extended release 75 mg and desvenlafaxine 50 mg in healthy CYP2D6 extensive and poor metabolizers: A randomized, open-label, two-period, parallel-group, crossover study. *Clin. Drug Investig.* **2011**, *48*, 155–167. [CrossRef]

31. Zhou, S.F. Polymorphism of human cytochrome P450 2D6 and its clinical significance: Part I. *Clin. Pharmacokinet.* **2009**, *48*, 689–723. [CrossRef] [PubMed]
32. Grasmader, K.; Verwohlt, P.L.; Rietschel, M.; Dragicevic, A.; Muller, M.; Hiemke, C.; Freymann, N.; Zobel, A.; Maier, W.; Rao, M.L. Impact of polymorphism of human cytochrome-450 isoenzymes 2C9, 2C19, and 2D6 on plasma concentrations and clinical effects of antidepressants in a naturalistic clinical setting. *Eur. J. Clin. Pharmacol.* **2004**, *60*, 329–336. [PubMed]
33. Zhou, S.F. Polymorphism of human cytochrome P450 2D6 and its clinical significance: Part II. *Clin. Pharmacokinet.* **2009**, *48*, 761–804. [CrossRef] [PubMed]
34. Samer, C.F.; Lorenzini, K.I.; Rollason, V.; Daali, Y.; Desmeules, J.A. Applications of CYP450 testing in the clinical setting. *Mol. Diagn. Ther.* **2013**, *17*, 165–184. [CrossRef] [PubMed]
35. Haertter, S. Recent examples on the clinical relevance of the CYP2D6 polymorphism and endogenous functionality of CYP2D6. *Drug Metab. Drug Interact.* **2013**, *28*, 209–216. [CrossRef]
36. De Leon, J.; Susce, M.T.; Pan, R.M.; Fairchild, M.; Koch, W.H.; Wedlund, P.J. The CYP2D6 poor metabolizer phenotype may be associated with risperidone adverse drug reactions and discontinuation. *J. Clin. Psychiatry* **2005**, *66*, 15–27. [CrossRef] [PubMed]
37. Wantanabe, J.; Suzuki, Y.; Fukui, N.; Sugai, T.; Ono, S.; Inoue, Y.; Someya, T. Dose-dependent effect of the CYP2D6 genotype on the steady-state fluvoxamine concentration. *Ther. Drug Monit.* **2008**, *30*, 705–708. [CrossRef] [PubMed]
38. Whyte, E.M.; Romkes, M.; Mulsant, B.H.; Kirshne, M.A.; Begley, A.E.; Reynolds, C.F., III; Pollock, B.G. CYP2D6 genotype and venlafaxine-XR concentrations in depressed elderly. *Int. J. Geriatr. Psychiatry* **2006**, *21*, 542–549. [CrossRef] [PubMed]
39. Lobello, K.W.; Preskorn, S.H.; Guico-Pabia, C.J.; Jiang, Q.; Paul, J.; Nichols, A.L.; Patroneva, A.; Ninan, P.T. Cytochrome P450 2D6 predicts antidepressant efficacy of venlafaxine: A secondary analysis of 4 studies in major depressive disorder. *J. Clin. Psychiatry* **2010**, *71*, 1482–1487. [CrossRef] [PubMed]
40. Van der Weide, J.; van Baalen-Benedek, E.H.; Kootstra-Ros, J.E. Matabloic ratios of psychotropics as indications of cytochrome P450 2D6/2C19 genotype. *Ther. Drug Monit.* **2005**, *27*, 478–483. [CrossRef] [PubMed]
41. Sauer, J.M.; Ring, B.J.; Witcher, J.W. Clinical pharmacokinetics of atomoxetine. *Clin. Pharmacokinet.* **2005**, *44*, 571–590. [CrossRef] [PubMed]
42. Wu, A.H. Drug metabolizing enzyme activities *versus* genetic variances for drug of clinical pharmacogenomics relevance. *Clin. Proteomics* **2011**, *8*, 12. [CrossRef] [PubMed]
43. Desmarais, J.R.; Looper, K.J. Interactions between tamoxifen and antidepressants via cytochrome P450 2D6. *J. Clin. Psychiatry* **2009**, *70*, 1688–1697. [CrossRef] [PubMed]
44. Anzenbacher, P.; Anzenbacherova, E. Cytochromes P450 and metabolism of xenobiotics. *Cell Mol. Life Sci.* **2001**, *58*, 737–747. [CrossRef] [PubMed]
45. Mannheimer, B.; von Bahr, C.; Pettersson, H.; Eliasson, E. Impact of multiple inhibitors or substrates of cytochrome P450 on plasma risperidone levels in patients on polypharmacy. *Ther. Drug Monit.* **2008**, *30*, 565–569. [CrossRef] [PubMed]
46. Jeppesen, U.; Gram, L.F.; Vistisen, K.; Loft, S.; Poulsen, H.E.; Brosen, K. Dose-dependent inhibition of CYP1A2, CYP2C19 and CYP2D6 by citalopram, fluoxetine, fluvoxamine and paroxetine. *Eur. J. Clin. Pharmacol.* **1996**, *51*, 73–78. [CrossRef] [PubMed]
47. DeLeon, J.; Armstrong, S.C.; Cozza, K.L. The dosing of atypical antipsychotics. *Psychosomatics* **2005**, *46*, 262–273.
48. DeLeon, J. Psychopharmacology: Atypical antipsychotic dosing: The effect of co-medication with anticonvulsants. *Psychiatr. Serv.* **2004**, *55*, 125–128. [CrossRef] [PubMed]
49. Sistonen, J.; Sajantila, A.; Lao, O.; Corander, J.; Barbujani, G.; Fuselli, S. CYP2D6 worldwide genetic variation shows high frequency of altered activity variants and no continental structure. *Pharmacogenet. Genomics* **2007**, *17*, 93–101. [PubMed]
50. Gaedigk, A.; Gotschall, R.R.; Forbes, N.S.; Simon, S.D.; Kearns, G.L.; Leeder, J.S. Optimization of cytochrome P4502D6 (CYP2D6) phenotype assignment using a genotyping algorithm based on allele frequency data. *Pharmacogenetics* **1999**, *9*, 669–682. [CrossRef] [PubMed]
51. Swen, J.J.; Nijenhuis, M.; de Boer, A.; Grandia, L.; Maitland-van der Zee, A.H.; Mulder, H.; Rongen, G.A.; van Schaik, R.H.; Schalekamp, T.; Touw, D.J.; *et al.* Pharmacogenetics: From bench to byte—An update of guidelines. *Clin. Pharmacol. Ther.* **2011**, *89*, 662–673. [CrossRef] [PubMed]

52. Pratt, V.M.; Zehnbauer, B.; Wilson, J.A.; Baak, R.; Babic, N.; Bettinotti, M.; Buller, A.; Butz, K.; Campbell, M.; Civalier, C.; *et al.* Characterization of 107 genomic DNA reference materials for CYP2D6, CYP2C19, CYP2C9, VKORC1, and UGT1A1: A GeT-RM and Association for Molecular Pathology collaborative project. *J. Mol. Diagn.* **2010**, *12*, 835–846. [CrossRef] [PubMed]
53. Huezo-Diaz, P.L.; Perroud, N.; Spencer, E.P.; Smith, R.; Sim, S.; Virding, S.; Uher, R.; Gunasinghe, C.; Gray, J.; Campbell, D.; Hauser, J.; *et al.* CYP2C19 genotype predicts steady state escitalopram concentration in GENDEP. *J. Psychopharmacol.* **2012**, *26*, 398–407. [CrossRef] [PubMed]
54. Genomind Literature Review, Version 3.0. Available online: http://www.geneceptassay.com/Content/LitReview/GNOMD_Lit_Review_LATEST.pdf (accessed 9 December 2014).
55. Genomind Assay Report (Sample). Available online: https://www.genomind.com/wp-content/uploads/2014/09/Sample-10-Gene-Report-Jul-2014-Lit-Sum-V-3.01.pdf (accessed 10 December 2014).
56. Zawertailo, L.A.; Kaplan, H.L.; Busto, U.E.; Tyndale, R.F.; Sellers, E.M. Psychotropic effects of dextromethorphan are altered by the CYP2D6 polymorphism: A pilot study. *J. Clin. Psychopharmacol.* **1998**, *18*, 332–337. [CrossRef] [PubMed]
57. Manap, R.A.; Wright, C.E.; Gregory, A.; Rostami-Hodjegan, A.; Meller, S.T.; Kelm, G.R.; Lennard, M.S.; Tucker, G.T.; Morice, A.H. The antitussive effect of dextromethorphan in relation to CYP2D6 activity. *Br. J. Clin. Pharmacol.* **1999**, *48*, 382–387. [CrossRef] [PubMed]
58. Hamelin, B.A.; Bouayad, A.; Methot, J.; Jobin, J.; Desgagnes, P.; Poirier, P.; Allaire, J.; Dumesnil, J.; Turgeon, J. Significant interaction between the nonprescription antihistamine diphenhydramine and the CYP2D6 substrate metoprolol in healthy men with high or low CYP2D6 activity. *Clin. Pharmaco. Ther.* **2000**, *67*, 466–477. [CrossRef]

3

Psychosocial and Behavioral Impact of COVID-19 in Autism Spectrum Disorder

Marco Colizzi [1,2,3,*], Elena Sironi [3], Federico Antonini [3], Marco Luigi Ciceri [3], Chiara Bovo [4] and Leonardo Zoccante [3]

1 Section of Psychiatry, Department of Neurosciences, Biomedicine and Movement Sciences, University of Verona, 37134 Verona, Italy
2 Department of Psychosis Studies, Institute of Psychiatry, Psychology and Neuroscience, King's College London, London SE5 8AF, UK
3 Child and Adolescent Neuropsychiatry Unit, Maternal-Child Integrated Care Department, Integrated University Hospital of Verona, 37126 Verona, Italy; sironi.elena@yahoo.it (E.S.); fede187ant@gmail.com (F.A.); marcoluigi.ciceri@aovr.veneto.it (M.L.C.); leonardo.zoccante@aovr.veneto.it (L.Z.)
4 Medical Direction, Integrated University Hospital of Verona, 37126 Verona, Italy; direzione.sanitaria@aovr.veneto.it
* Correspondence: marco.colizzi@univr.it

Abstract: The 2019 coronavirus disease (COVID-19) outbreak could result in higher levels of psychological distress, especially among people suffering from pre-existing mental health conditions. Young individuals with autism spectrum disorders (ASD) are particularly at risk due to their vulnerability to unpredictable and complex changes. This study aimed to investigate the impact of the COVID-19 pandemic on ASD individuals, whether any pre-pandemic sociodemographic or clinical characteristics would predict a negative outcome, and to narratively characterize their needs. Parents and guardians of ASD individuals filled out an online survey consisting of 40 questions investigating socio-demographic and clinical characteristics of their children, impact of the COVID-19 outbreak on their wellbeing and needs to deal with the emergency. Data were available on 527 survey participants. The COVID-19 emergency resulted in a challenging period for 93.9% of families, increased difficulties in managing daily activities, especially free time (78.1%) and structured activities (75.7%), and, respectively, 35.5% and 41.5% of children presenting with more intense and more frequent behavior problems. Behavior problems predating the COVID-19 outbreak predicted a higher risk of more intense (odds ratio (OR) = 2.16, 95% confidence interval (CI) 1.42–3.29) and more frequent (OR = 1.67, 95% CI 1.13–2.48) disruptive behavior. Even though ASD children were receiving different types of support, also requiring specialist (19.1%) or emergency (1.5%) interventions in a relatively low proportion of cases, a number of needs emerged, including receiving more healthcare support (47.4%), especially in-home support (29.9%), as well as interventions to tackle a potentially disruptive quarantine (16.8%). The COVID-19 outbreak has undoubtedly resulted in increased difficulties among ASD individuals.

Keywords: coronavirus; 2019-nCoV; neurodevelopment; child and adolescent psychiatry; mental health prevention

---

1. Introduction

After the Severe Acute Respiratory Syndrome (SARS) Coronavirus outbreak of 2002–2003, the International Health Regulations (IHR) of the World Health Organization (WHO), which had been first adopted in 1969, were revised in 2005 to extend their scope to any public health risk that might affect human health, irrespective of the source. Emphasis was put on the risk that the increasing international travel and trade could facilitate the international spread of disease, requiring a coordinated international response. Since the 2005 IHR adoption, the WHO has formally declared six Public Health Emergencies of International Concern (PHEIC), the latter of which, the 2019 coronavirus disease (COVID-19), is still ongoing [1]. COVID-19 is caused by a newly identified coronavirus which can induce SARS in man (SARS-CoV-2), as a consequence of a probable zoonotic spillover [2], firstly reported in Central China in December 2019 [3]. Due to person-to-person transmission, it has rapidly spread in Europe [4], with northern Italy becoming Europe's epicenter [5], and USA [6]. As of 1 May 2020, over 3 million cases have been reported worldwide, affecting more than 200 countries.

Since the beginning of the pandemic, most clinical and research efforts have been allocated to advance our understanding of the virus properties and pathogenic armory in order to treat the infection and protect from it [7]. However, according to some research evidence, the COVID-19 pandemic is also unraveling a potential gap in mental health services during emergencies [8]. In particular, the COVID-19 outbreak would result in higher levels of psychological distress among the general population [8] as well as a higher risk or symptom exacerbation among people suffering from a pre-existing mental health condition [9], possibly triggered by concerns about its rapid escalation and global spread [1] as a deadly threat [10]. Furthermore, alarming media reports may unintendedly amplify fear reactions [11], with potential detrimental consequences for people susceptible to negative emotional states. Importantly, the pandemic has required unprecedented measures by national governments including imposing quarantine to citizens [12]. The experience of being quarantined may be negative, as evidence suggests a wide range of long-lasting mental health problems in a substantial proportion of individuals [13]. While there is no strong evidence that any particular demographic factors carry a higher risk of poor psychological outcome following the obligation of home quarantine [13], a pre-existing psychiatric history seems to predict a worse outcome [14] and a higher need for support during quarantine [13].

Among vulnerable populations, young individuals with autism spectrum disorders (ASD) are of particular concern for the impact that the COVID-19 outbreak may have on their wellbeing as well as the specific support they may need to preserve their mental health through the pandemic [15]. ASD are a group of conditions characterized by social communication problems, difficulties with reciprocal social interactions, and unusual patterns of repetitive behavior [16]. Such features are associated with a preference for highly predictable environments, whereas ASD individuals may feel stressed, anxious or confused if unpredictable or complex changes occur [17]. The COVID-19 outbreak has undoubtedly led to a quick-paced and rapidly shifting social situation which may increase ASD individuals' difficulties.

The purpose of this study was threefold. The main aim was to rapidly investigate the impact of the COVID-19 outbreak on ASD individuals through an online parent survey carried in Northern Italy, one of the European regions mostly affected [5]. Due to the ASD individuals' difficulty to deal with the unexpected, a mainly unfavorable psychosocial and behavioral outcome was hypothesized. A further aim was to investigate whether any pre-pandemic sociodemographic or clinical characteristics would predict a negative impact of the pandemic on ASD individuals' wellbeing. Based on previous evidence [13,14], psychological problems predating the emergency were hypothesized to predict a poor outcome. Finally, the survey served to characterize the needs of ASD individuals and their families from a narrative perspective, by collecting the parents' perceptions, as a first step to improving their quality of health care.

2. Materials and Methods

2.1. Research Design

Google Forms was used to create an online parent survey to be shared through the dissemination of a hyperlink. The survey was available online from the 6 April to the 20 April 2020. All participants provided electronic informed consent that contained information about the purpose of the study, procedures, benefits of participating, voluntary participation, and contact information of the researchers.

The survey was part of a larger study which was approved by the research ethics committee at the Integrated University Hospital of Verona (CESC 2242 and CESC 2243).

2.2. *Participants*

Parents and guardians of individuals with an ASD diagnosis were asked by healthcare professionals affiliated with the Veneto Autism Spectrum Disorder Regional Centre at the Integrated University Hospital of Verona to fill out the online survey. Autism advocacy and family support networks were additionally used to distribute and directly encourage survey participation. Children' ASD diagnosis was self-reported.

2.3. *Instrument*

The parent survey was developed by a focus group of physicians, psychologists, and child life specialists, also taking the advice from parents of children with ASD. The survey consisted of 40 questions (18 multiple choice questions, 20 yes/no questions, and 2 open-response questions) in 3 categories: (i) ASD individuals' socio-demographic and clinical characteristics, (ii) impact of the COVID-19 outbreak on their wellbeing, and (iii) needs to deal with the emergency. Participants were allowed to select only 1 item for each multiple-choice question.

2.4. *Analyses*

The final raw data were downloaded from Google Forms into a Microsoft Excel file for analysis using SPSS software (Version 26.0; IBM Corp, Armonk, NY, USA). Descriptive statistics were used to provide baseline information concerning survey participants' ASD children. Then, multiple logistic regressions were performed to investigate whether any ASD individuals' socio-demographic or clinical characteristics would predict a greater frequency and intensity of behavior problems following the COVID-19 outbreak.

The open-response questions did not have a scoring system. The needs identified by the survey responses were gathered with the intent of informing healthcare professionals in their assessment and management of individuals with an ASD diagnosis during the ongoing COVID-19 emergency. Two authors independently evaluated such answers and pooled them into categories (e.g., healthcare, social, financial needs, etc.). In the rare instances of discrepant category attribution, consensus was reached through discussion with a third senior clinical researcher.

The survey was not intended to formally assess severity of ASD among participants' children.

3. Results

A total of 529 respondents participated in the survey. As 2 participants did not answer any questions at all, a total of 527 participants were included in the study. Across the 38 closed questions, survey participants provided 18,738 answers, while 373 answers were missing (<2%). Further, 34 answers and 1 missing item were deemed inconsistent (<0.2%) and excluded from the final analyses.

3.1. *Socio-Demographic and Clinical Characteristics*

The mean age of participants' children was 13 years (SD = 8.1). Almost all of them were from the Veneto region (99.4%) and the large majority were living in married or cohabiting couple families (88.2%). Most children had at least 1 sibling (71.6%), and one out every 10 siblings had a neurodevelopmental disorder (NDD) diagnosis (10.2%). Most children were receiving private therapy (66.2%) and most parents were members of autism advocacy and family support networks (67.1%) (Table 1).

Table 1. Socio-demographic and clinical characteristics.

	M	(SD)
Age (years)	13	8.1
	N	(%)
Veneto Region Province		
Belluno	41	7.8
Padova	88	16.8
Rovigo	26	5
Treviso	40	7.6
Venezia	73	13.9
Verona	149	28.4
Vicenza	105	20
Other Region	3	0.6
Missing	2	
Parenting couple situation		
Married/Cohabiting	463	88.2
Separated	31	5.9
Single parent	31	5.9
Missing	2	
Only child		
No	374	71.6
Yes	148	28.4
Missing	2	
Number of siblings *		
1	290	77.5
2	65	17.4
3	15	4
4	3	0.8
5	1	0,3
Missing	0	
Siblings diagnosed with NDD (ASD, ADHD, etc.) *		
No	336	89.8
Yes	38	10.2
Missing	0	
Child receiving private therapy		
No	175	33.8
Yes	342	66.2
Missing	4	
Membership in Autism advocacy/family support networks		
No	172	32.9
Yes	351	67.1
Missing	4	

Table 1. *Cont.*

	M	(SD)
Child's language level		
Fluent speech	174	33.1
Phrase speech	146	27.8
No phrase speech	205	39
Missing	2	
The child was presenting with behavior problems from before COVID-19		
No	251	48.5
Yes	266	51.5
Missing	6	
Pharmacological treatment for behavior problems **		
No	152	57.8
Yes	111	42.2
Missing	3	
Comorbid medical conditions		
No	377	72.2
Yes	145	27.8
Missing	5	

* Of those reporting siblings; ** Of those reporting behavior problems from before COVID-19; NDD, Neurodevelopment disorder; ASD, Autism spectrum disorder; ADHD, Attention Deficit Hyperactivity Disorder.

Only one every three children had a fluent language (33.1%). About half of the entire sample was presenting with behavior problems from before the outbreak of COVID-19 (51.5%); among those, 42.2% were receiving pharmacological treatment. At least 1 comorbid medical condition was reported in 27.8% of ASD individuals, with neuromotor and gastrointestinal conditions and allergies and food sensitivity being the conditions most frequently reported (Table 1 and Supplementary Table S1).

3.2. Psychosocial and Behavioral Impact of the Emergency Outbreak

COVID-19 positivity was reported among 1.3% of nuclear family members and 4.4% of extended family members, with bereavement occurring in 2.3% of cases. Approximately one out of four parents stopped working due the emergency outbreak (26.1% of mothers and 27.5% of fathers). The large majority of them evaluated the current period of change and restrictions as challenging or very challenging (93.9%) and more challenging than before the emergency outbreak (77%) (Table 2).

Following the emergency outbreak, a proportion of parents reported support from the Local Healthcare Services (27.7%), with the large majority of them reporting both direct (70.1%; e.g., calls, videocalls) and indirect (84%; e.g., text messages, homework assignments) school support as well as support from the private therapist (73.3%). For each type of support, an only slightly lower proportion of parents considered it from sufficiently useful to very useful during the ongoing emergency (Table 2).

A proportion of parents reported difficulties in managing their child's meals (23%), autonomies (31%), free time (78.1%), and structured activities (75.7%). For each activity, an almost overlapping proportion of parents reported such activity as more difficult than before the emergency outbreak. Overall, compared to before the emergency outbreak, behavior problems were reported being more intense (35.5%) and more frequent (41.5%) in a substantial proportion of ASD individuals. Due to the onset of behavior problems, an emergency contact with the child's Neuropsychiatrist was required in 19.1% of cases, while an access to the Accident and Emergency (A&E) happened in 1.5% of cases (Table 2).

Table 2. Psychosocial and behavioral impact of the emergency outbreak.

	N	(%)
COVID-19 positivity among nuclear family members		
No	519	98.7
Yes	7	1.3
Missing	1	
COVID-19 positivity among extended family members		
No	500	95.6
Yes	23	4.4
Missing	4	
Bereavement due to COVID-19		
No	514	97.7
Yes	12	2.3
Missing	1	
Mother's current working situation		
Regularly commuting to work	92	17.6
Smart working	98	18.7
Not working because of COVID-19	137	26.1
Not working since before COVID-19	197	37.6
Missing	3	
Father's current working situation		
Regularly commuting to work	212	42
Smart working	104	20.6
Not working because of COVID-19	139	27.5
Not working since before COVID-19	50	9.9
Missing	22	
Judgement on this period of change and restrictions		
Very challenging	284	54
Challenging	210	39.9
Not challenging	32	6.1
Missing	1	
Judgement on this period of change and restrictions as compared to before COVID-19		
More challenging	405	77
Equally challenging	86	16.3
Less challenging	35	6.7
Missing	1	
Support by Local Healthcare Services since COVID-19		
Daily contacts	7	1.4
Weekly contacts	98	19.4
Twice weekly contacts	35	6.9
No contact	366	72.3

Table 2. *Cont.*

	N	(%)
Missing	21	
Usefulness of support by Local Healthcare Services during COVID-19		
Very useful	10	2.2
Useful	28	6.1
Sufficiently useful	65	14.1
Not very useful	93	20.1
Not useful	266	57.6
Missing	65	
Direct school support since COVID-19		
Daily contacts	110	22.5
Weekly contacts	157	32.2
Twice weekly contacts	75	15.4
No contact	146	29.9
Missing	39	
Indirect school support since COVID-19		
Daily contacts	138	28.7
Weekly contacts	159	33.1
Twice weekly contacts	106	22.1
No contact	77	16
Missing	47	
Usefulness of school support during COVID-19		
Very useful	60	12.9
Useful	113	24.4
Sufficiently useful	116	25
Not very useful	93	20
Not useful	82	17.7
Missing	63	
Private therapist support since COVID-19		
Daily contacts	43	12.6
Weekly contacts	148	43.4
Twice weekly contacts	59	17.3
No contact	91	26.7
Missing	1	
Usefulness of private therapist during COVID-19		
Very useful	65	19.6
Useful	80	24.1
Sufficiently useful	64	19.3
Not very useful	50	15.1
Not useful	73	22

Table 2. *Cont.*

	N	(%)
Missing	10	
Difficulties in managing the child's meals since COVID-19		
No	404	77
Yes	121	23
Missing	2	
Greater difficulties in managing the child's meals as compared to before COVID-19		
No	378	71.9
Yes	148	28.1
Missing	1	
Difficulties in managing the child's autonomies since COVID-19		
No	361	69
Yes	162	31
Missing	4	
Greater difficulties in managing the child's autonomies as compared to before COVID-19		
No	372	71
Yes	152	29
Missing	3	
Difficulties in managing the child's free time since COVID-19		
No	115	21.9
Yes	411	78.1
Missing	1	
Greater difficulties in managing the child's free time as compared to before COVID-19		
No	97	18.4
Yes	429	81.6
Missing	1	
Difficulties in managing the child's structured activities since COVID-19		
No	126	24.3
Yes	393	75.7
Missing	8	
Greater difficulties in managing the child's structured activities as compared to before COVID-19		
No	123	23.8
Yes	394	76.2
Missing	10	
Intensity of the child's behavior problems as compared to before COVID-19		
More intense	183	35.5
Equally intense	264	51.3

Table 2. *Cont.*

	N	(%)
Less intense	68	13.2
Missing	12	
Frequency of the child's behavior problems as compared to before COVID-19		
More frequent	216	41.5
Equally frequent	229	44
Less frequent	76	14.6
Missing	6	
Contacts with the child's Neuropsychiatrist due to behavioral problems since COVID-19		
No	424	80.9
Yes	100	19.1
Missing	3	
Access to A&E for child's behavioral problems since COVID-19		
No	514	98.5
Yes	8	1.5
Missing	5	

3.3. Predictors of Emergency Outbreak Negative Impact on Wellbeing

A multiple logistic regression tested for an effect of (i) behavior problems predating the emergency (yes/no), (ii) age, (iii) language (fluent/non-fluent), (iv) being an only child (yes/no) as a proxy of greater social isolation in quarantine, (v) medical comorbidity (yes/no), (vi) parenting couple situation (married or cohabiting/separated or single parent), (vii) support by Local Healthcare Services since COVID-19 (yes/no), (viii) direct school support since COVID-19 (yes/no), (ix) indirect school support since COVID-19 (yes/no), (x) private therapist support since COVID-19 (yes/no or no private therapist from before COVID-19) on the intensity of the behavior problems following the emergency outbreak (more intense/equally or less intense). The logistic regression model was statistically significant, χ^2 (10, N = 440) = 32.338, $p < 0.001$. ASD individuals with preexisting behavior problems were 2.16 times more likely to exhibit more intense behavior problems that those without preexisting behavior problems. Increasing age and living with a separated or single parent were associated with a reduction in the likelihood of exhibiting more intense behavior problems, while not receiving indirect school support during the emergency tended to be associated with an increased likelihood of exhibiting more intense behavior problems (Table 3).

A further multiple logistic regression tested for the effect of (i) behavior problems predating the emergency (yes/no), (ii) age, (iii) language (fluent/non-fluent), (iv) being an only child (yes/no), (v) medical comorbidity (yes/no), (vi) parenting couple situation (married or cohabiting/separated or single parent), (vii) support by Local Healthcare Services since COVID-19 (yes/no), (viii) direct school support since COVID-19 (yes/no), (ix) indirect school support since COVID-19 (yes/no), (x) private therapist support since COVID-19 (yes/no or no private therapist from before COVID-19) on the frequency of the behavior problems following the emergency outbreak (more frequent/equally or less frequent). The logistic regression model was statistically significant, χ^2 (10, N = 444) = 18.502, $p = 0.047$. ASD individuals with preexisting behavior problems were 1.67 times more likely to exhibit more frequent behavior problems that those without preexisting behavior problems (Table 4).

Table 3. Predictors of emergency outbreak negative impact on intensity of behavior problems.

	B	S.E.	Wald Chi-Square	*p*-Value	OR	95% CI
Age	−0.037	0.019	3.981	0.046	0.963	0.929–0.999
Behavior problems predating COVID-19	0.770	0.215	12.869	<0.001	2.160	1.418–3.291
Non-fluent language	0.352	0.243	2.100	0.147	1.422	0.883–2.290
Medical comorbidity	0.317	0.241	1.726	0.189	1.372	0.856–2.201
Only child	0.286	0.233	1.507	0.220	1.331	0.843–2.102
Separated/single parent	−0.778	0.383	4.127	0.042	0.459	0.217–0.973
No support from Local Health Service	0.050	0.241	0.043	0.836	1.051	0.656–1.685
No direct support from school	−0.127	0.255	0.247	0.619	0.881	0.534–1.453
No indirect support from school	0.605	0.322	3.540	0.060	1.831	0.975–3.439
No support from private therapist	−0.073	0.214	0.118	0.732	0.929	0.610–1.414

Note: OR, odds ratio; CI, confidence interval.

Table 4. Predictors of emergency outbreak negative impact on frequency of behavior problems.

	B	S.E.	Wald Chi-Square	*p*-Value	OR	95% CI
Age	−0.024	0.018	1.841	0.175	0.976	0.943–1.011
Behavior problems predating COVID-19	0.513	0.201	6.509	0.011	1.670	1.126–2.477
Non-fluent language	0.304	0.226	1.800	0.180	1.355	0.869–2.111
Medical comorbidity	0.221	0.229	0.933	0.334	1.248	0.796–1.954
Only child	−0.004	0.224	0.000	0.984	0.996	0.642–1.544
Separated/ single parent	−0.229	0.329	0.486	0.486	0.795	0.417–1.515
No support from Local Health Service	−0.312	0.227	1.888	0.169	0.732	0.469–1.142
No direct support from school	−0.334	0.246	1.849	0.174	0.716	0.442–1.159
No indirect support from school	0.406	0.312	1.694	0.193	1.501	0.814–2.769
No support from private therapist	−0.137	0.203	0.455	0.500	0.872	0.586–1.298

Note: OR, odds ratio; CI, confidence interval.

3.4. *Needs to Deal with the Emergency: A Narrative Perspective*

Out of 527 survey participants, 406 parents (77%) reported at least one need to the open-response question about what could be of help do deal with the ongoing emergency. Ten of them reported more than one need (4 participants reported 2 needs, 6 participants reported 3 needs), for a total of 422 responses. The most commonly reported need was for in-home healthcare support (29.9%), followed by center-based healthcare support (10.4%), loosening quarantine restrictions (9.7%), ending lockdown (7.1%), and in-hospital healthcare support (7.1%; Table 5).

Table 5. Responses to the open-response question about what could be of help do deal with the ongoing emergency.

	N	%
In-home healthcare support	126	29.9
Center-based healthcare support	44	10.4
Loosening quarantine restrictions	41	9.7
Ending lockdown	30	7.1
In-hospital healthcare support	30	7.1

Table 5. *Cont.*

	N	%
Increase school support	29	6.9
Help setting a daily schedule	21	5
"Nothing"	20	4.7
"Don't know"	14	3.3
Parent support	13	3.1
Peer relationship	12	2.8
Structured physical activity	9	2.1
Community support	9	2.1
Financial family support	8	1.9
Work support	6	1.4
Spiritual and religious reflections	4	0.9
Information technology support	3	0.7
Pharmacological support	3	0.7

4. Discussion

To our knowledge, this is the first study which systematically explored the impact of the COVID-19 outbreak in a population of individuals suffering from an autism spectrum disorder (ASD). Results from this parent survey indicate that the large majority of parents of ASD individuals consider the period of change and restrictions that has followed the onset of the emergency as challenging and requiring more commitment than before. Most support was delivered by school services, followed by private therapists and local healthcare services. Consistent with previous reports of executive functioning deficits making ASD individuals more vulnerable to routine disruption [18], an elevated number of parents reported difficulties in managing their children's daily activities, especially in terms of free time and structured activities. Despite requiring specialist intervention in a relatively small proportion of cases, and almost never ending in hospital emergency assessments, behavior problems worsened in more than one third of ASD individuals.

In line with previous evidence that pre-existing psychological difficulties seem to be the only clear predictor of poorer mental health outcomes following respiratory syndromes [14] and quarantine [13], the most relevant finding of this survey is that ASD individuals with behavior problems predating the COVID-19 outbreak are twice as likely to experience more intense and more frequent behavior problems since the beginning of the emergency. As independent evidence supports decreasing symptom levels from childhood to young adulthood in ASD, especially in verbally fluent individuals [19], we also tested whether the age and language level of survey participants' children with ASD would predict a worsening of the behavior problems. Results suggest that older age may play a protective role with regards to the emergency-induced intensification of behavior problems, while the effect of language failed to reach statistical significance. Furthermore, despite social isolation and mental health problems may co-occur in childhood [20], as well as medical conditions and ASD [21], being an only child, as a proxy of greater social isolation, and comorbid medical conditions did not predict a poorer outcome in terms of more intense or more frequent behavior problems following the COVID-19 outbreak and the implementation of restrictive measures and quarantine. Interestingly, living with a separated or single parent was associated with a better outcome in terms of intensity of behavior problems. Despite being counterintuitive, such a finding may reflect a more simplified parent–child interaction which could be effective in preventing the deterioration of the child's wellbeing during quarantine and restrictions. Future studies would need to clarify this issue. Furthermore, it is important to highlight that such evidence does not necessarily apply to other social contexts. Finally, ASD individuals not receiving school support since the COVID-19 outbreak tended to express more intense behavior problems, suggesting the importance of maintaining contact with the school during the emergency.

The last scope of this study was to narratively collect the parents' perceived needs through the emergency by offering an open-response question at the end of the survey. About half of the participants reported needing support from healthcare services, especially in-home services. Interestingly, almost one every five parents reported that loosening restrictions or ending the lockdown would be of help.

Outbreaks of emerging infections such as COVID-19 can elicit strong fear reactions and preoccupations with downstream effects on physical and mental health, especially in vulnerable individuals [22]. Moreover, such negative impacts on health could be worsened by the experience of being quarantined [13]. Autism is no exception. Even though it is a complex genetic disorder, the effect of the environment in shaping the behavioral phenotype should not be underestimated. In fact, a high emotional climate, such as that resulting from the COVID-19 emergency outbreak, has been associated with increased levels of maladaptive behavior in ASD over time [23]. Furthermore, families of individuals with ASD have been reported to experience greater stress than families whose children suffer from other disabilities [24,25], making a compelling case for the implementation of youth-oriented mental health prevention and early intervention strategies [26,27]. Evidence supports the effectiveness of such interventions in mitigating disabilities and even improving skills among young individuals with ASD [28].

Surveys performed during previous Public Health Emergencies of International Concern (PHEIC) have provided timely data to inform best practices in responding to the emergency [29]. Similarly, the online survey presented here has proved to be a powerful data collection tool, benefiting from the strengths that have been associated to this type of instrument such as having a large sample size, fast response times, timely data processing, and low costs [30]. Moreover, thanks to the solid infrastructure of autism advocacy and family support networks, we were able to mitigate the risk of poor response rates and improve sample representativeness, collecting data from over five hundred ASD individuals and their families in a catchment area (the Veneto Region) of about 5 million people. However, the findings of this study have to be seen in light of some limitations. In particular, in spite of the aforementioned advantages, the survey suffered from the lack of a standardized assessment of clinical features such as language and behavior problems. Such aspects may limit the comparability of outcomes among different studies as well as internal comparisons in any follow-up assessments. Furthermore, despite collecting information on children's language and behavior problems predating the emergency as a proxy of their baseline cognitive and adaptive functioning, due to its nature, the online survey did not allow investigating such aspects through a standard method such as psychometric tests. Furthermore, information on the gender of ASD children was not available through the online survey. Even though the main aim of the study was not to investigate gender differences in response to the COVID-19 outbreak in ASD, we acknowledge the limitation.

In conclusion, the present survey indicates that the ongoing COVID-19 emergency has resulted in a challenging period for most ASD individuals and their families, with increased difficulties in managing daily activities and at least one in every three children presenting with more frequent or more intense behavior problems. Children with behavior problems predating the COVID-19 outbreak were found to be particularly at risk to present with more intense and more frequent disruptive behavior. Even though ASD children were receiving different types of support, also requiring specialist or emergency interventions in a relatively low proportion of cases, a number of needs emerged, including receiving more healthcare support, especially from in-home services, as well as interventions to tackle a potentially disruptive quarantine.

Author Contributions: Conceptualization, M.C., E.S., F.A., M.L.C., C.B., and L.Z.; methodology, M.C., E.S., F.A., M.L.C., and L.Z.; validation, M.C., C.B. and L.Z.; formal analysis, M.C., E.S., and L.Z.; investigation, M.C., E.S., F.A., M.L.C., and L.Z.; resources, M.C., E.S., F.A., M.L.C., C.B., and L.Z.; data curation, M.C., E.S., and L.Z.; writing—original draft preparation, M.C.; writing—review and editing, M.C., E.S., F.A., M.L.C., C.B., and L.Z.; visualization, M.C., E.S., F.A., M.L.C., C.B., and L.Z.; supervision, L.Z.; project administration, C.B. and L.Z. All authors have read and agreed to the published version of the manuscript.

Acknowledgments: The authors would like to thank the survey participants and their families for their cooperation and commitment as well as acknowledge infrastructure from the Integrated University Hospital of Verona and the University of Verona.

References

1. Cucinotta, D.; Vanelli, M. WHO Declares COVID-19 a Pandemic. *Acta Biomed.* **2020**, *91*, 157–160. [CrossRef]
2. Lu, R.; Zhao, X.; Li, J.; Niu, P.; Yang, B.; Wu, H.; Wang, W.; Song, H.; Huang, B.; Zhu, N.; et al. Genomic characterisation and epidemiology of 2019 novel coronavirus: Implications for virus origins and receptor binding. *Lancet* **2020**, *395*, 565–574. [CrossRef]
3. Li, Q.; Guan, X.; Wu, P.; Wang, X.; Zhou, L.; Tong, Y.; Ren, R.; Leung, K.S.M.; Lau, E.H.Y.; Wong, J.Y.; et al. Early Transmission Dynamics in Wuhan, China, of Novel Coronavirus-Infected Pneumonia. *N. Engl. J. Med.* **2020**, *382*, 1199–1207. [CrossRef] [PubMed]
4. Rothe, C.; Schunk, M.; Sothmann, P.; Bretzel, G.; Froeschl, G.; Wallrauch, C.; Zimmer, T.; Thiel, V.; Janke, C.; Guggemos, W.; et al. Transmission of 2019-nCoV Infection from an Asymptomatic Contact in Germany. *N. Engl. J. Med.* **2020**, *382*, 970–971. [CrossRef] [PubMed]
5. Gagliano, A.; Villani, P.G.; Cò, F.M.; Paglia, S.; Bisagni, P.A.G.; Perotti, G.M.; Storti, E.; Lombardo, M. 2019-ncov's epidemic in middle province of northern Italy: Impact, logistic & strategy in the first line hospital. *Disaster Med. Public Health Prep.* **2020**, 1–15. [CrossRef]
6. Ghinai, I.; McPherson, T.; Hunter, J.; Kirking, H.; Christiansen, D.; Joshi, K.; Rubin, R.; Morales-Estrada, S.; Black, S.; Pacilli, M.; et al. First known person-to-person transmission of severe acute respiratory syndrome coronavirus 2 (SARS-CoV-2) in the USA. *Lancet* **2020**, *395*, 1137–1144. [CrossRef]
7. Berger, Z.D.; Evans, N.G.; Phelan, A.L.; Silverman, R.D. Covid-19: Control measures must be equitable and inclusive. *BMJ* **2020**, *368*, m1141. [CrossRef]
8. Lima, C.K.T.; Carvalho, P.M.M.; Lima, I.A.A.S.; Nunes, J.V.A.O.; Saraiva, J.S.; de Souza, R.I.; da Silva, C.G.L.; Neto, M.L.R. The emotional impact of Coronavirus 2019-nCoV (new Coronavirus disease). *Psychiatry Res.* **2020**, *287*, 112915. [CrossRef]
9. Yao, H.; Chen, J.H.; Xu, Y.F. Patients with mental health disorders in the COVID-19 epidemic. *Lancet Psychiatry* **2020**, *7*, e21. [CrossRef]
10. Onder, G.; Rezza, G.; Brusaferro, S. Case-Fatality Rate and Characteristics of Patients Dying in Relation to COVID-19 in Italy. *JAMA* **2020**. [CrossRef]
11. Garfin, D.R.; Silver, R.C.; Holman, E.A. The novel coronavirus (COVID-2019) outbreak: Amplification of public health consequences by media exposure. *Health Psychol.* **2020**. [CrossRef] [PubMed]
12. Wilder-Smith, A.; Freedman, D.O. Isolation, quarantine, social distancing and community containment: Pivotal role for old-style public health measures in the novel coronavirus (2019-nCoV) outbreak. *J. Travel Med.* **2020**, *27*. [CrossRef] [PubMed]
13. Brooks, S.K.; Webster, R.K.; Smith, L.E.; Woodland, L.; Wessely, S.; Greenberg, N.; Rubin, G.J. The psychological impact of quarantine and how to reduce it: Rapid review of the evidence. *Lancet* **2020**, *395*, 912–920. [CrossRef]
14. Jeong, H.; Yim, H.W.; Song, Y.J.; Ki, M.; Min, J.A.; Cho, J.; Chae, J.H. Mental health status of people isolated due to Middle East Respiratory Syndrome. *Epidemiol. Health* **2016**, *38*, e2016048. [CrossRef] [PubMed]
15. Narzisi, A. Handle the Autism Spectrum Condition During Coronavirus (COVID-19). *Brain Sci.* **2020**, *10*, 207. [CrossRef] [PubMed]
16. American Psychiatric Publishing. *Diagnostic and Statistical Manual of Mental Disorders*; APA: Arlington, VA, USA, 2013.
17. Baron-Cohen, S. The hyper-systemizing, assortative mating theory of autism. *Prog. Neuropsychopharmacol. Biol. Psychiatry* **2006**, *30*, 865–872. [CrossRef]

18. Narzisi, A.; Muratori, F.; Calderoni, S.; Fabbro, F.; Urgesi, C. Neuropsychological Profile in High Functioning Autism Spectrum Disorders. *J. Autism Dev. Disord.* **2013**, *43*, 1895–1909. [CrossRef]
19. Bal, V.H.; Kim, S.H.; Fok, M.; Lord, C. Autism spectrum disorder symptoms from ages 2 to 19 years: Implications for diagnosing adolescents and young adults. *Autism Res.* **2019**, *12*, 89–99. [CrossRef]
20. Matthews, T.; Danese, A.; Wertz, J.; Ambler, A.; Kelly, M.; Diver, A.; Caspi, A.; Moffitt, T.E.; Arseneault, L. Social isolation and mental health at primary and secondary school entry: A longitudinal cohort study. *J. Am. Acad. Child Adolesc. Psychiatry* **2015**, *54*, 225–232. [CrossRef]
21. Tye, C.; Runicles, A.; Whitehouse, A.; Alvares, G. Characterizing the Interplay Between Autism Spectrum Disorder and Comorbid Medical Conditions: An Integrative Review. *Front. Psychiatry* **2019**, *9*. [CrossRef]
22. Colizzi, M.; Bortoletto, R.; Silvestri, M.; Mondini, F.; Puttini, E.; Cainelli, C.; Gaudino, R.; Ruggeri, M.; Zoccante, L. Medically unexplained symptoms in the times of Covid-19 pandemic: A case-report. *Brain Behav. Immun. Health* **2020**, 100073. [CrossRef] [PubMed]
23. Greenberg, J.; Seltzer, M.; Hong, J.; Orsmond, G. Bidirectional effects of expressed emotion and behavior problems and symptoms in adolescents and adults with autism. *Am. J. Ment. Retard.* **2006**, *111*, 229–249. [CrossRef]
24. Seltzer, M.; Krauss, M. Quality of life of adults with mental retardation/developmental disabilities who live with family. *Ment. Retard. Dev. Disabil. Res. Rev.* **2001**, *7*, 105–114. [CrossRef] [PubMed]
25. Drogomyretska, K.; Fox, R.; Colbert, D. Brief Report: Stress and Perceived Social Support in Parents of Children with ASD. *J. Autism Dev. Disord.* **2020**. [CrossRef]
26. Colizzi, M.; Lasalvia, A.; Ruggeri, M. Prevention and early intervention in youth mental health: Is it time for a multidisciplinary and trans-diagnostic model for care? *Int. J. Ment. Health Syst.* **2020**, *14*. [CrossRef]
27. Vivanti, G.; Kasari, C.; Green, J.; Mandell, D.; Maye, M.; Hudry, K. Implementing and evaluating early intervention for children with autism: Where are the gaps and what should we do? *Autism Res.* **2018**, *11*, 16–23. [CrossRef]
28. French, L.; Kennedy, E. Annual Research Review: Early intervention for infants and young children with, or at-risk of, autism spectrum disorder: A systematic review. *J. Child Psychol. Psychiatry* **2018**, *59*, 444–456. [CrossRef]
29. Abir, M.; Moore, M.; Chamberlin, M.; Koenig, K.; Hirshon, J.; Singh, C.; Schneider, S.; Cantrill, S. Using Timely Survey-Based Information Networks to Collect Data on Best Practices for Public Health Emergency Preparedness and Response: Illustrative Case From the American College of Emergency Physicians' Ebola Surveys. *Disaster Med. Public Health Prep.* **2016**, *10*, 681–690. [CrossRef]
30. Evans, J.; Mathur, A. The value of online surveys: A look back and a look ahead. *Internet Res.* **2018**, *28*, 854–887. [CrossRef]

4

Variability of Creatine Metabolism Genes in Children with Autism Spectrum Disorder

Jessie M. Cameron [1], Valeriy Levandovskiy [1], Wendy Roberts [2,3], Evdokia Anagnostou [2,3], Stephen Scherer [1,4,5], Alvin Loh [2,6] and Andreas Schulze [1,2,7,*]

1. Genetics and Genome Biology, Peter Gilgan Center for Research and Learning, Toronto, ON M5G 0A4, Canada; jessie.cameron@sickkids.ca (J.M.C.); Valeriy.Levandovskiy@sickkids.ca (V.L.); Stephen.Scherer@sickkids.ca (S.S.)
2. Department of Paediatrics, University of Toronto, Toronto, ON M5S 1A1, Canada; wendy.roberts@sickkids.ca (W.R.); Evdokia.Anagnostou@sickkids.ca (E.A.); Alvin.Loh@SurreyPlace.on.ca (A.L.)
3. Holland Bloorview Kids Rehabilitation Hospital, 150 Kigour Rd, Toronto, ON M4G 1R8, Canada
4. The Centre for Applied Genomics and Genetics and Genome Biology, the Hospital for Sick Children, Toronto, ON M5G 1X8, Canada
5. McLaughlin Centre and Department of Molecular Genetics, 686 Bay Street, 13th Floor, Peter Gilgan Center for Research and Learning, Toronto, ON M5G 0A4, Canada
6. Surrey Place Center, 2 Surrey Place, Toronto, ON M5S 2C2, Canada
7. Department of Biochemistry, University of Toronto, Toronto, ON M5S 1A8, Canada

* Correspondence: andreas.schulze@sickkids.ca

Abstract: Creatine deficiency syndrome (CDS) comprises three separate enzyme deficiencies with overlapping clinical presentations: arginine:glycine amidinotransferase (*GATM* gene, glycine amidinotransferase), guanidinoacetate methyltransferase (*GAMT* gene), and creatine transporter deficiency (*SLC6A8* gene, solute carrier family 6 member 8). CDS presents with developmental delays/regression, intellectual disability, speech and language impairment, autistic behaviour, epileptic seizures, treatment-refractory epilepsy, and extrapyramidal movement disorders; symptoms that are also evident in children with autism. The objective of the study was to test the hypothesis that genetic variability in creatine metabolism genes is associated with autism. We sequenced *GATM*, *GAMT* and *SLC6A8* genes in 166 patients with autism (coding sequence, introns and adjacent untranslated regions). A total of 29, 16 and 25 variants were identified in each gene, respectively. Four variants were novel in *GATM*, and 5 in *SLC6A8* (not present in the 1000 Genomes, Exome Sequencing Project (ESP) or Exome Aggregation Consortium (ExAC) databases). A single variant in each gene was identified as non-synonymous, and computationally predicted to be potentially damaging. Nine variants in *GATM* were shown to have a lower minor allele frequency (MAF) in the autism population than in the 1000 Genomes database, specifically in the East Asian population (Fisher's exact test). Two variants also had lower MAFs in the European population. In summary, there were no apparent associations of variants in *GAMT* and *SLC6A8* genes with autism. The data implying there could be a lower association of some specific *GATM* gene variants with autism is an observation that would need to be corroborated in a larger group of autism patients, and with sub-populations of Asian ethnicities. Overall, our findings suggest that the genetic variability of creatine synthesis/transport is unlikely to play a part in the pathogenesis of autism spectrum disorder (ASD) in children.

Keywords: autism spectrum disorder; creatine deficiency syndrome; *glycine amidinotransferase*; *guanidinoacetate methyltransferase*; *solute carrier family 6 member 8*; genetic variability

---

1. Introduction

Autism spectrum disorder (ASD) can be present in children with inborn errors of metabolism, the latter having a prevalence of 1 in every 800 live births [1]. Less than 5% of ASD cases can be attributed to routinely-screened-for inborn errors of metabolism [2,3]. Creatine deficiency syndrome (CDS) is an inherited metabolic disorder that is not included in routine newborn screening panels or in standard ASD diagnostic work up. The presence of autistic symptoms in patients with CDS suggests that genes in the creatine metabolic pathway may play a part in the neurobiology of ASD and may represent a treatable cause of ASD [4]. We recently ascertained the prevalence of CDS in children with non-syndromic autism in a large, prospective, multicentre study by screening for creatine metabolites in urine and sequencing *GAMT*, *GATM* and *SLC6A8* genes (glycine amidinotransferase, guanidinoacetate methyltransferase and solute carrier family 6 member 8) for pathogenic mutations (443 children with ASD). The estimated prevalence of CDS was less than 7 in 1000 and there was no obvious correlation between pathogenic CDS gene mutations and ASD, Therefore, the chances of a child with ASD having a CDS were very low [5].

In the study presented here, we investigate the association of autism with non-CDS disease causing variants in the three creatine metabolism genes. Whereas non-synonymous nucleotide changes resulting in amino acid changes are likely to result in pathogenic mutations, synonymous changes that do not alter the amino acid are often attributable to polymorphisms. It has been shown that single nucleotide polymorphisms (SNPs) can explain up to 40% of the variance in liability to ASD [6,7]; thus common genetic polymorphisms can be a major risk factor for autism.

The clinical presentation of CDS is characterized by developmental delays and cognitive decline, intellectual disability, impaired speech and language, autistic behaviour, epileptic seizure activity, treatment-refractory epilepsy, and extrapyramidal movement disorders [8–11]. Significant behavioural, social and communication challenges seen in ASD can be caused by neurodevelopmental disabilities of complex aetiology. The symptoms in patients with CDS and those with ASD can overlap.

In patients with CDS, the impaired synthesis or transport of creatine leads to depletion of creatine/phosphocreatine in the brain. The creatine–phosphocreatine system plays an essential role in cellular energy homeostasis in the central nervous system. This system acts as a temporal and spatial energy buffer, energy transducer and general regulator of cellular energetics [12]. Creatine has been shown to act as a neuroprotective agent [13]; it protects rat hippocampal neurons against glutamate and amyloid beta peptide toxicity [14]; it seems to function as a potent natural survival and neuroprotective factor for γ-aminobutyric acid (GABA)-ergic neurons in a model for Huntington disease [15] and of dopaminergic neurons in a model for Parkinson's disease [16]. In two studies, creatine supplementation was convincingly shown to improve concentration [17], as well as short-term memory and learning [18] in healthy human subjects. Due to these protective functions of creatine the deficiency of creatine could play a part in the neurobiology of ASD.

CDS includes three separate deficiencies: arginine:glycine amidinotransferase (AGAT), guanidinoacetate methyltransferase (GAMT), and creatine transporter (CrT) [4,8,19]. AGAT and GAMT deficiencies are autosomal recessive inherited biosynthesis defects of creatine. The AGAT gene (NCBI Gene ID 2628, official nomenclature: *GATM*) located on chromosome 15q15.3 is 16.8 Kb in size and contains nine exons, which encode 424 amino acids. The *GAMT* gene (Gene ID 2593) located on chromosome 19p13.3 is 4.46 Kb in size and has six exons encoding 237 amino acids. Dysfunction of the CrT leads to impaired intra-cellular creatine uptake and has X-linked inheritance. The CrT gene (Gene ID 6535, *SLC6A8*) located on Xq28 spans 8.4 Kb and consists of 13 exons encoding 635 amino acids [4]. To date, there are 6, 29, and 88 pathogenic mutations described throughout the *GATM*, *GAMT*, and *SLC6A8* genes, respectively [20]. The common denominator of all these diseases is the virtually complete absence of creatine and phosphocreatine in the brain that can be assessed with in vivo magnetic resonance spectroscopy (MRS). The diagnosis can be made in spot urine determining the concentration of creatine and guanidinoacetate normalized for creatinine, in 24-h urine measuring the excretion of creatine, guanidinoacetate, and creatinine, and by measuring the concentration of these metabolites in blood [4,21,22]. Among CDS, GAMT deficiency, while presenting as a spectrum from mild to severe, has the most severe phenotype that includes severe intellectual deficits. Treatment-refractory epilepsy and extrapyramidal movement disorders are exclusively seen in GAMT patients [4,8,10,23,24]. The few AGAT-deficient patients described so far seem to have a less severe presentation with developmental delays and impaired communication and social contact. Mild seizures have been reported in only some of the cases [9,25,26]. Males with X-linked CrT deficiency present with impairments of speech and language and may have a seizure disorder. They usually show behavioural abnormalities and develop intellectual disability. While most of the female carriers have a normal appearance, some may have mild learning difficulties. Treatment with supplementation of creatine can fully (AGAT) or partly (GAMT) replenish brain creatine and attenuate the clinical course in AGAT and GAMT-deficient patients. In contrast, creatine supplementation has no effect on brain creatine and the clinical course in male CrT patients [4]. There is an even gender distribution in GAMT [10] and likely in AGAT deficiencies, whereas predominantly males are affected with the CrT defect. The latter is an X-linked condition and female carriers are mostly asymptomatic [8].

Because of the overlap of symptoms between CDS and ASD and because of the potential role of the creatine-phosphocreatine homeostasis in autism, we hypothesize that comparing the ASD population to the general population may reveal an altered frequency of genetic variants in the three CDS genes (*GATM*, *GAMT* and *SLC6A8*) that are associated with autism.

2. Results

A total of 166 subjects enrolled in the study, with 71 from the prospective group enrolled in Toronto and 95 from the Genome Canada study sample. Of these, 32 were females, and 134 were males. Ethnicities were described as European "EUR", Asian "ASN", African "AFR" or Admixed/Unknown, "MIX/UNK" (Supplementary Table S1).

2.1. Novel/Rare Variants Observed in CDS Genes in ASD Patients

Sequence data was compared with NCBI reference genes, and genetic variations were compared to three variation databases: the 1000 Genomes phase 3 dataset, the National Heart, Lung and Blood Institute Grand Opportunity Exome Sequencing Project (NHLBI GO ESP) and the Exome Aggregation Consortium (ExAC). A number of variants were identified, some of which are novel (not in the variant databases) or rare (present at allele frequencies less than 1% or 0.01) (Tables 1–3, Figures 1–3).

2.1.1. *GATM* Gene Variants

A total of 29 variants were identified, of which four were present in coding regions (Figure 1, Table 1). Of these, two were rare variants: one was synonymous and one was non-synonymous. Synonymous variants are presumed to not have any potential pathogenicity, unless they are likely to affect splicing. The non-synonymous variant (c.700G > C, p.Asp234His) was not present in 1000 Genomes or ESP, but was present in the ExAC database at a minor allele frequency of 0.00001651 (2/121104 chromosomes, mixed ethnic population) (Table 1). The variant was identified as heterozygous in one individual in the ASD population, resulting in a minor allele frequency (MAF) of 0.003 (1/332 chromosomes). Computational software (SIFT [27], PolyPhen-2 [28] and MutationTaster [29]) all predict this variant to be damaging, and therefore pathogenic if homozygous (Table 1). Further functional testing would be needed to confirm the true pathogenicity of this variant.

Table 1. Summary of *GATM* (glycine amidinotransferase) gene sequencing results. Variants identified in the autisim spectrum disorder (ASD) population are noted, and minor allele frequency (MAF) calculated. MAF of variants present in 1000 Genomes, Exome Sequencing Project (ESP) and Exome Aggregation Consortium (ExAC) databases are shown for comparison. [1] Total number of samples = 166 (332 alleles); [2] MAF = minor allele frequency; the number of alleles in which variant was found/total number of alleles; [3] MAC = minor allele count; the number of times the minor allele was observed in the sample population of chromosomes; [4] Polymorphic variant: (>0.01 MAF in one database); [5] Rare variant: ≤0.01 MAF in at least one published database; [6] Novel variant: Not present in any published database; coding sequence (exons) are in bold. SNP: single nucleotide polymorphism; UTR: untranslated region; and SIFT: 'sorting tolerant from intolerant' algorithm.

		Autism Population (n = 166, Alleles = 332 [1])				Databases			
GATM Exon/Intron	DNA Change/Protein Change	SNP ID	Homozygous/ Heterozygous Change [1]	Number of Observed Alleles	MAF [2]	1000 Genomes (Phase 3) MAF, MAC [3])	ESP Report (July 2013) MAF, MAC	ExAC (January 2015) MAF, MAC	Comments
5UTR	c. − 200C > T	rs7164139	Homo: 20 Hetero: 78	118	0.355	0.444 2223/5008	x	0.5533 83/150	polymorphic variant [4]
5UTR	c. − 140C > T	rs533626184	Hetero: 1	1	0.003	0.0022 11/5008	x	x	rare variant
5UTR	c. − 30T > G	rs8024550	Hetero: 5	5	0.015	0.144 720/5008	0.073 651/8926	0.07742 155/2002	polymorphic variant
intron 1	c.70 − 77C > T	rs12437887	Homo: 20 Hetero: 76	116	0.349	0.443 2221/5008	x	x	polymorphic variant
intron 1	c.70 − 38G > T	rs12437840	Homo: 23 Hetero: 73	119	0.358	0.443 2219/5008	0.270 3509/12992	0.3827 24153/63112	polymorphic variant
exon 2	**c.282G > A p.=**	**rs141223762**	**Hetero: 1**	**1**	**0.003**	**NA**	**0.000154 2/12992**	**0.0001153 14/121390**	**rare variant [5]**
intron 2	c.289 − 76T > C	rs540536879	Hetero: 3	3	0.009	0.000998 5/5008	x	x	rare variant
intron 2	c.289 − 34T > C	rs74009633	Hetero: 1	1	0.003	0.0096 48/5008	0.005 65/12982	0.001947 193/99144	rare variant
intron 2	c.289 − 24G > A	rs145644806	Hetero: 1	1	0.003	0.0002 1/5008	0.000154 2/12988	x	rare variant
exon 3	**c.330A > T p.Q110H**	**rs1288775**	**Homo: 29 Hetero: 74**	**132**	**0.398**	**0.619 3098/5008**	**0.435 5651/12992**	**0.581 70416/121104**	**polymorphic variant**
intron 3	c.485-11_dupT		Homo: 1	2	0.006	x	x	x	novel variant [6]
exon 5	**c.700G > C**		**Hetero: 1**	**1**	**0.003**	**NA**	**x**	**0.00001651**	**rare variant**

Table 1. *Cont.*

			Autism Population (n = 166, Alleles = 332 [1])			Databases			
GATM Exon/Intron	DNA Change/Protein Change	SNP ID	Homozygous/ Heterozygous Change [1]	Number of Observed Alleles	MAF [2]	1000 Genomes (Phase 3) MAF, MAC [3])	ESP Report (July 2013) MAF, MAC	ExAC (January 2015) MAF, MAC	Comments
	p.D234H							**2/121104**	**SIFT: deleterious (score: 0); PolyPhen-2: probably damaging (score: 0.986); MutationTaster: disease-causing (p-value: 1.0)**
intron 5	c.813 + 46C > G	rs150282769	Hetero: 1	1	0.003	0.0002 1/5008	0.000847 11/12992	0.0004 46/118404	rare variant
intron 6	c.978 + 43T > C		Hetero: 1	1	0.003	x	x	x	novel variant
intron 6	c.979 − 316A > G	rs9972405	Homo: 1 Hetero: 38	40	0.120	0.0998 500/5008	x	x	polymorphic variant
intron 6	c.979-49_979-51delTAA	rs200176845	Homo: 1	2	0.006	0.0100 50/5008	0.0137 171/12480	0.00228 248/108652	rare variant
intron 6	c.979 − 39T > C		Hetero: 1	1	0.003	x	x	x	novel variant
intron 7	c.1043 − 254A > G	rs57369693	Homo: 1 Hetero: 38	40	0.120	0.0998 500/5008	x	x	polymorphic variant
intron 8	c.1159 + 39A > G	rs113129788	Hetero: 1	1	0.003	0.0002 1/5008	x	0.000019 2/105236	rare variant
intron 8	c.1160 − 46C > T	rs201589362	Hetero: 2	2	0.006	0.0002 1/5008		0.00006987 7/100180	rare variant
exon 9	**c.1252T > C p.=**	**rs1145086**	**Homo: 46 Hetero: 80**	**172**	**0.518**	**0.2823 1414/5008**	**0.534 6937/12992**	**0.5329 64562/121146**	**polymorphic variant**
3UTR	c.*27C > G	rs200143728	Hetero: 1	1	0.003	NA	x	0.0004716 56/118754	rare variant
3UTR	c.*125G > A	rs143689218	Hetero: 2	2	0.006	0.0086 43/5008	x	x	rare variant
3UTR	c.*411G > A		Hetero: 1	1	0.003	x	x	x	novel variant
3UTR	c.*600A > G	rs1049503	Homo: 23 Hetero: 74	120	0.361	0.4507 2257/5008	x	x	polymorphic variant
3UTR	c.*715T > C	rs1049508	Homo: 27 Hetero: 69	123	0.370	0.618 3094/5008	x	x	polymorphic variant
3UTR	c.*734_*735insCA	rs35410548	Homo: 46 Hetero: 79	171	0.515	0.718 3594/5008	x	x	polymorphic variant
3UTR	c.*913G > A	rs17618637	Hetero: 10	10	0.030	0.0553 277/5008	x	x	polymorphic variant
3UTR	c.*940C > T	rs1049518	Homo: 54	108	0.325	0.718 3594/5008	x	x	polymorphic variant

Table 2. Summary of guanidinoacetate methyltransferase (*GAMT*) gene sequencing results. Variants identified in the ASD population are noted, and minor allele frequency (MAF) calculated. MAF of variants present in 1000 Genomes, ESP and Exome Aggregation Consortium (ExAC) databases are shown for comparison. [1] Total number of samples = 166 (332 alleles); [2] MAF = minor allele frequency; the number of alleles in which variant was found/total number of alleles; [3] MAC = minor allele count; the number of times the minor allele was observed in the sample population of chromosomes; [4] Polymorphic variant: (>0.01 MAF in one database); [5] Rare variant: ≤0.01 MAF in at least one published database; coding sequence (exons) are in bold; and dbSNP: Single Nucleotide Polymorphism database.

			Autism Population (n = 166, Alleles = 332 [1])			Databases			
GAMT Exon/Intron	DNA Change/Protein Change	SNP ID	Homozygous/ Heterozygous Change [1]	Number of Observed Alleles	MAF [2]	1000 Genomes (Phase 3) MAF, MAC [3]	ESP Report (July 2013) MAF, MAC	ExAC (January 2015) MAF, MAC	Comments
intron 1	c.182 − 173G > A	rs112975707	Hetero: 6	6	0.018	0.0491 246/5008	x	x	polymorphic variant [4]
exon 2	**c.227C > T**	**rs150338273**	**Hetero: 2**	**2**	**0.006**	**NA**	**0.000616**	**0.000411**	**rare variant [5]**
	p.S76L						**8/12984**	**29/70554**	**SIFT: deleterious (score: 0.03); PolyPhen-2: possibly damaging (score: 0.66); MutationTaster: disease-causing (p-value: 0.986)**
intron 2	c.327 + 69T > G	rs266808	Hetero: 4	4	0.012	0.0451 226/5008	x	x	polymorphic variant
exon 3	**c.348G > A p.=**	**rs117884619**	**Hetero: 1**	**1**	**0.003**	**0.0104 52/5008**	x	**0.003969 431/108600**	**rare variant, benign allele in dbSNP**
intron 3	c.391 + 47A > G	rs73515058	Hetero: 12	12	0.036	0.0865 433/5008	0.0852 1106/12988	0.06853 5944/86734	polymorphic variant
intron 4	c.460 − 31G > A	rs55776826	Homo: 2 Hetero: 41	45	0.136	0.1132 567/5008	0.153 1989/13006	0.1294 15585/120422	polymorphic variant
intron 5	c.571 − 60C > T	rs266809	Homo: 1 Hetero: 6	8	0.024	0.0731 366/5008			polymorphic variant
intron 5	c.571 − 6G > A	rs2074899	Hetero: 22	22	0.066	0.1088 545/5008	0.02 265/13000	0.06984 8254/118186	polymorphic variant
exon 6	**c.626C > T p.T209M**	**rs17851582**	**Hetero: 23**	**23**	**0.069**	**0.0365 183/5008**	**0.071 926/13004**	**0.07554 8958/118584**	**polymorphic variant**
3UTR	c.*146A > G	rs659455	Homo: 1 Hetero: 5	7	0.021	0.0765 383/5008	x	x	polymorphic variant
3UTR	c.*151T > C	rs659460	Homo: 1 Hetero: 5	7	0.021	0.0761 381/5008	x	x	polymorphic variant
3UTR	c.*276C > T	rs266810	Homo: 1 Hetero: 5	7	0.021	0.0761 381/5008	x	x	polymorphic variant
3UTR	c.*311C > G	rs266811	Homo: 1 Hetero: 5	7	0.021	0.0761 381/5008	x	x	polymorphic variant
3UTR	c.*369C > A	rs75762821	Hetero: 3	3	0.009	0.006 28/5008	x	x	rare variant
3UTR	c.*388C > T	rs266812	Homo: 1 Hetero: 5	7	0.021	0.0757 379/5008	x	x	polymorphic variant
3UTR	c.*406A > G	rs266813	Homo: 2 Hetero: 15	19	0.057	0.274 1372/5008	x	x	polymorphic variant

Table 3. Summary of solute carrier family 6 member 8 (*SLC6A8*) gene sequencing results. Variants identified in the ASD population are noted, and minor allele frequency (MAF) calculated. MAF of variants present in 1000 Genomes, ESP and Exome Aggregation Consortium ExAC databases are shown for comparison. [1] Total number of samples = 166 (134 males, 32 females, 198 alleles); [2] MAF = minor allele frequency; the number of alleles in which variant was found/total number of alleles; [3] MAC = minor allele count; the number of times the minor allele was observed in the sample population of chromosomes; [4] Polymorphic variant: (>0.01 MAF in one database); [5] Rare variant: ≤0.01 MAF in at least one published database; and [6] Novel variant: Not present in any published database; coding sequence (exons) are in bold.

			Autism Pop (n = 166, Alleles = 198 [1])			Databases			
SLC6A8 Exon/Intron	DNA Change/Protein Change	SNP ID	Homozygous/ Heterozygous Change [1]	No. Observed Alleles	MAF [2]	1000 Genomes (Phase 3) MAF, MAC [3]	ESP Report (July 2013) MAF, MAC	ExAC (January 2015) MAF, MAC	Comments
5UTR	c. − 5 A > G	rs384573	Homo: 166	196	1.000	NA	x	1 6172/6172	polymorphic variant [4]
intron 1	c.262 + 26T > C	rs192387453	Homo: 25M Hetero: 6F	31	0.158	0.151 570/3775	0.121 1249/10352	0.1084 5029/46406	polymorphic variant
intron 1	c.263 − 95G > A		Homo: 1M	1	0.005	x	x	x	novel variant [6]
intron 2	c.394 + 88G > A	rs6643763	Homo: 21M Hetero: 7F	28	0.143	0.102 385/3775	x	x	polymorphic variant
intron 2	c.394 + 108G > A		Homo: 1M	1	0.005	x	x	x	novel variant
exon 5	**c.813C > T** **p.=**	**rs138064933**	**Homo: 1M**	**1**	**0.005**	**0.001** **2/3775**	**0.0027** **29/10561**	**0.003346** **280/83683**	**rare variant [5]**
intron 5	c.913 − 40T > C	rs187505163	Homo: 1M	1	0.005	0.009 34/3775	0.014 148/10563	0.003969 339/85417	rare variant
intron 6	c.1016 + 41dupTGCCC	rs371888321	Homo: 1M	1	0.005	x	x	x	novel variant
intron 6	c.1016 + 56del TGCCC		Homo: 1M	1	0.005	x	x	x	novel variant
intron 7	c.1141 + 18G > A	rs187400676	Hetero: 1F	1	0.005	0.006 22/3775	0.000284 3/10563	0.004194 365/87034	rare variant
intron 7	c.1141 + 37G > A	rs2071028	Homo: 20M Hetero: 4F	24	0.122	0.153 576/3775	0.127 1341/10563	0.1014 8811/86854	polymorphic variant
intron 7	c.1141 + 87A > G	rs41302172	Homo: 25 (21M + 4F) Hetero: 3F	32	0.163	0.101 383/3775	x	x	polymorphic variant
intron 7	c.1142 − 130C > T	rs141015652	Homo: 3M	3	0.015	0.021 81/3775	x	x	polymorphic variant
intron 7	c.1142 − 69G > A		Homo: 1M	1	0.005	x	x	x	novel variant
intron 7	c.1142 − 35G > A	rs201555047	Homo: 1M Hetero: 1F	2	0.010	0.006 21/3775	0.00396 39/9845	0.008994 117/13009	rare variant
exon 8	**c.1162G > A**	**rs374163604**	**Homo: 1M**	**1**	**0.005**	**0.0003**	**0.0002886**	**0.00007051**	**rare variant**

Table 3. *Cont.*

			Autism Pop (n = 166, Alleles = 198 [1])			Databases			
SLC6A8 Exon/Intron	DNA Change/Protein Change	SNP ID	Homozygous/ Heterozygous Change [1]	No. Observed Alleles	MAF [2]	1000 Genomes (Phase 3) MAF, MAC [3]	ESP Report (July 2013) MAF, MAC	ExAC (January 2015) MAF, MAC	Comments
	p.A388T					**1/3775**	**3/10394**	**1/14182**	**SIFT: deleterious (score: 0.02); PolyPhen-2: probably damaging (score: 0.969); MutationTaster: disease-causing (p-value: 1.0)**
intron 8	c.1255 − 44delG	rs34035058	Homo: 1M	1	0.005	NA	0.000688 7/10180	0.0002874 18/62628	rare variant
intron 8	c.1255 − 31C > T	rs193175235	Homo: 2M	2	0.010	0.011 42/3775	0.00559 59/10560	0.004952 378/76334	rare variant
intron 9	c.1392 + 31T > C	rs183780161	Homo: 1M	1	0.005	0.003 10/3775	0.00578 61/10556	0.001411 123/87147	rare variant
intron 10	c.1495 + 38C > T	rs200729826	Homo: 2M	2	0.010	0.021 78/3775	0.0000947 1/10562	0.00997 858/86058	rare variant
intron 10	c.1496 − 17G > A	rs375265267	Homo: 1M	1	0.005	NA	0.000189 2/10563	0.0000347 3/86591	rare variant
intron 10	c.1496 − 8C > T	rs376038235	Hetero: 1F	1	0.005	0.002 9/3775	x	0.001025 89/86861	rare variant
intron 11	c.1596 + 21G > A	rs73633747	Homo: 1M	1	0.005	0.019 70/3775	0.0186 194/10422	0.005616 445/79237	rare variant
intron 12	c.1768 − 3C > T	rs150207268	Hetero: 1F	1	0.005	0.002 9/3775	0.00398 42/10554	0.006573 254/38642	rare variant
3UTR	c.*207G > C	rs6571290	Homo: 21M Hetero: 7F	28	0.143	0.194 731/3775	x	x	polymorphic variant

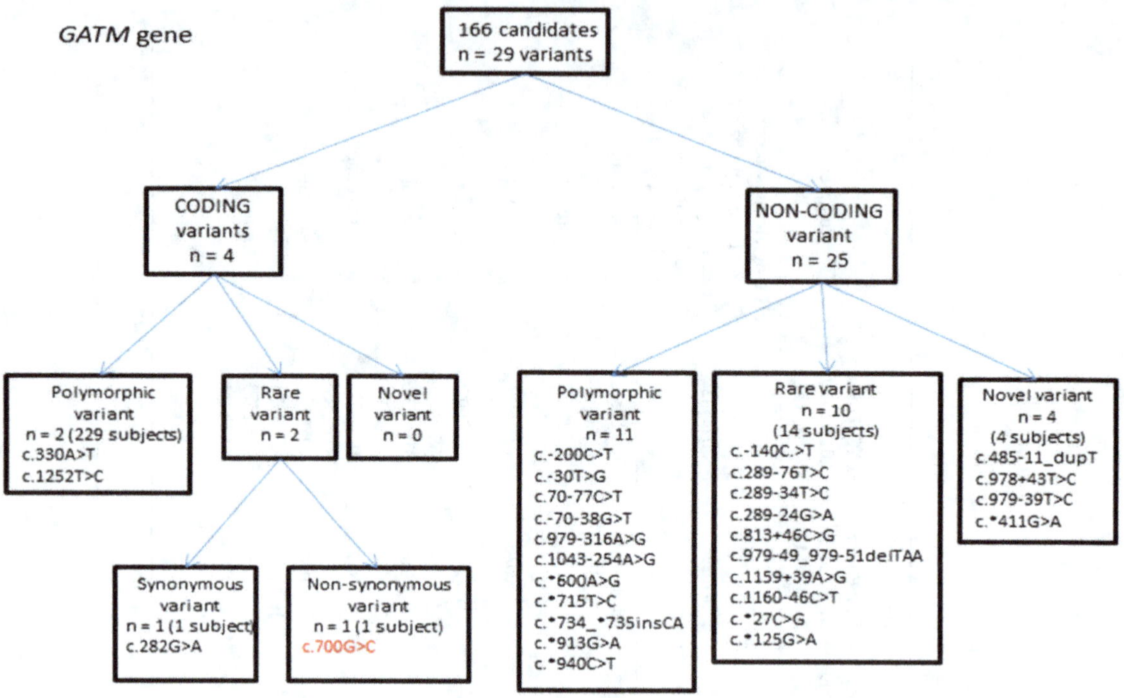

Figure 1. Flowchart summarizing variants identified in the glycine amidinotransferase (*GATM*) gene.

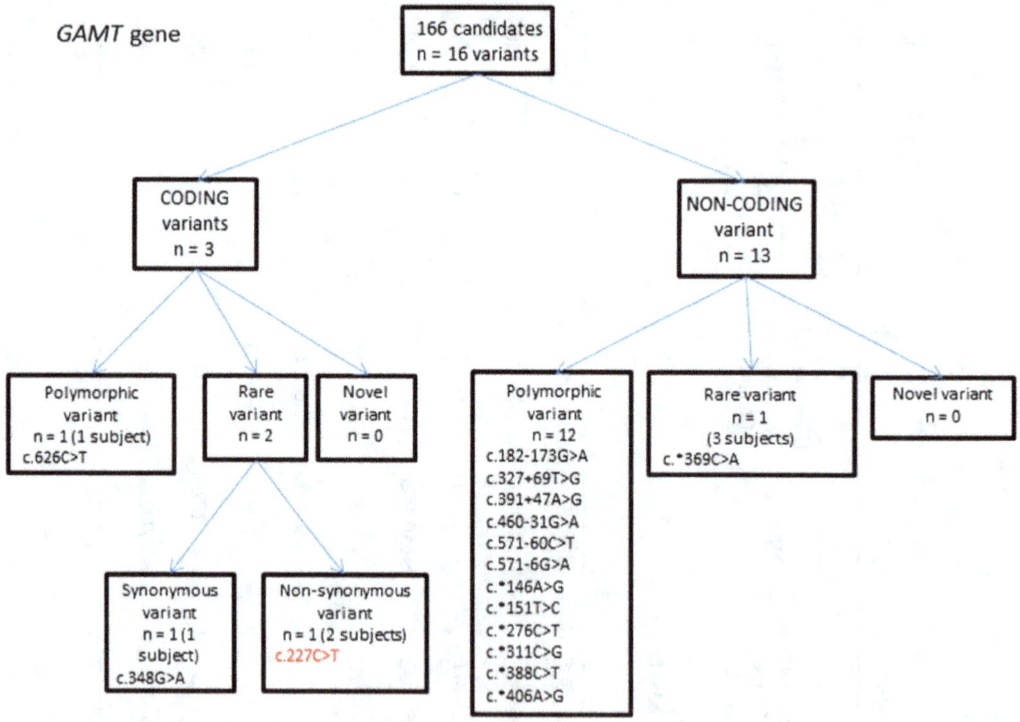

Figure 2. Flowchart summarizing variants identified in the guanidinoacetate methyltransferase (*GAMT*) gene.

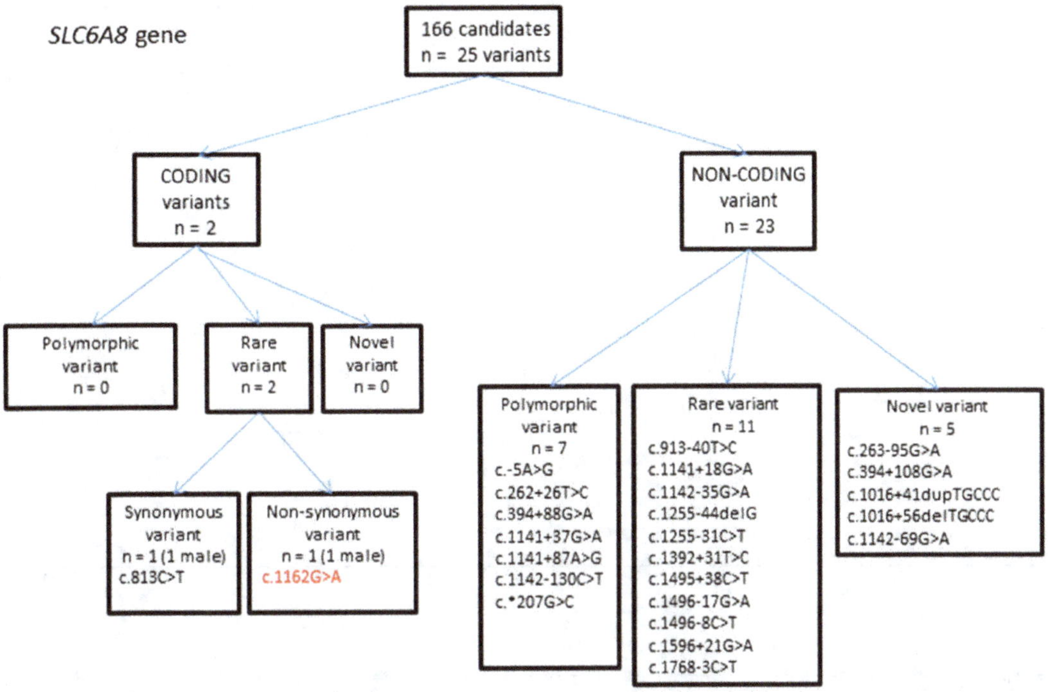

Figure 3. Flowchart summarizing variants identified in the solute carrier family 6 member 8 (*SLC6A8*) gene.

There were several differences seen in the MAFs calculated for *GATM* variants identified in the ASD patient group compared to those from ethnic populations in 1000 Genomes database (European, East Asian, African and Mixed/Unknown) (Supplementary Table S2). Figure 4 shows the p-values from the Fisher's exact test (plotted as -log (p)) and the variants identified. Fifteen of these differences were initially found to be significant (Fisher's exact test, $p = 0.01$), and after running the Benjamini–Hochberg procedure, 11 of these values remained above the threshold of significance. Nine of these values represented a significant difference between the allele frequencies seen in our autism population and the East Asian population of the 1000 Genomes database: SNPs rs7164139 (c. − 200C > T, $p = 0.000005$), rs12437887 (c.70 − 77C > T, $p = 0.00002$), rs12437840 (c.70 − 38G > T, $p = 0.00002$), rs1288775 (c.330A > T, $p = 0.000037$), rs1145086(c.1252T > C, $p = 0.000114$), rs1049503 (c.*600A > G, $p = 0.0003$), rs1049508 (c.*715T > C, $p = 0.000037$), rs35410548 (c.*734_*735insCA, $p = 0.000499$) and rs1049518 (c.*940C > T, $p = 0$), Figure 4). All nine variants had a significantly lower MAF than the 1000 Genomes East Asian population database (Supplementary Table S2). It is possible that some of these SNPs could be inherited as a single haplotype (adjacent SNPs that are inherited together). To further investigate these nine variants, we compared the data from our Asian population with the 1000 Genomes South Asian population (Table 4). This data suggested that none of the variants were significantly different.

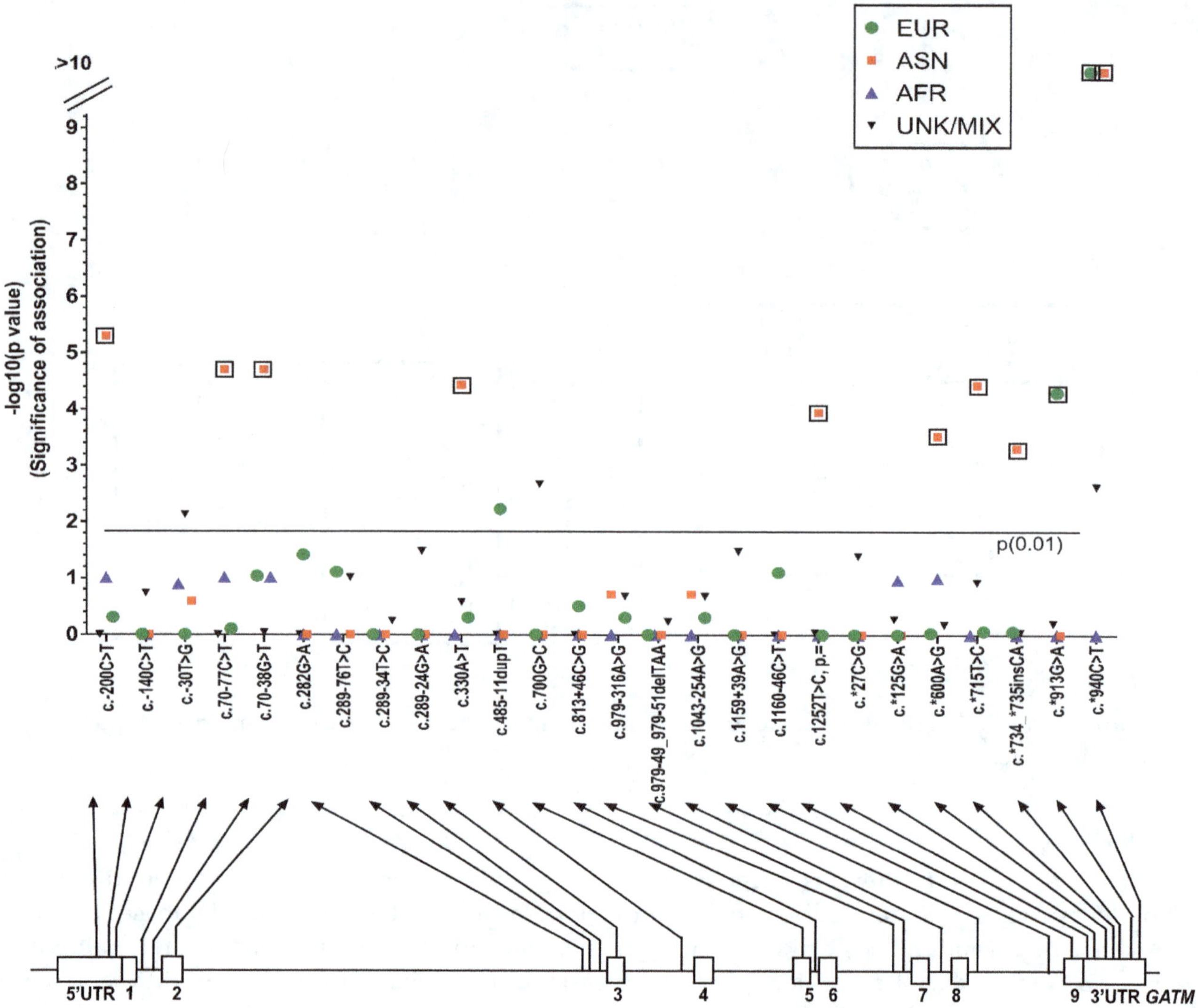

Figure 4. Manhattan plot showing the *p*-values from the Fisher's exact test (significance of association, plotted as -log (*p*)) for each SNP sequenced on the glycine amidinotransferase (*GATM*) gene. *p*-values are shown for European, East Asian, African, and Unknown/Admixed populations. The nominal statistical threshold for $p = 0.01$ is shown, and *p*-values that are still significant after running the Benjamin–Hochburg procedure are indicated with boxes. The location of each SNP is shown on the *GATM* gene below the x-axis. EUR: European; ASN: East Asian; AFR: African; and UNK/MIX: unknown/admixed populations.

Two variants in the European cohort show significant variation from the 1000 Genomes European database population: rs17618637 (c.*913G > A, $p = 0.00005$) and rs1049518 (c.*940C > T, $p = 0$) both in the 3′UTR (untranslated region) of the *GATM* gene. Both had lower MAFs than in the database (Supplementary Table S2).

Table 4. Summary of glycine amidinotransferase (*GATM*) gene variants that showed significance when compared to East Asian population, with additional data from 1000 Genomes South Asian population. [1] Total number of autism cohort Asian samples = 17 (n = 34 alleles); [2] Number of minor alleles seen in population; [3] Number of major alleles seen in the population; [4] Minor allele frequency; the number of alleles in which variant was found/total number of alleles.

GATM (AGAT) DNA Change/Protein Change	SNP ID	ASN n = 34 [1]			East ASN (1000 Genomes Phase 3) n = 1008			Fisher's Exact Test ASN	South ASN (1000 Genomes Phase 3) n = 978			Fisher's Exact Test ASN
		Minor [2]	Major [3]	MAF [4]	Minor	Major	MAF		Minor	Major	MAF	
c. − 200C > T	rs7164139	15	19	0.441	811	197	0.805	0.000005	351	627	0.359	0.365138
c.70 − 77C > T	rs12437887	16	18	0.471	813	195	0.807	0.00002	351	627	0.359	0.205191
c.70 − 38G > T	rs12437840	16	18	0.471	813	195	0.807	0.00002	351	627	0.359	0.205191
c.330A > T, p.Q110H	rs1288775	17	17	0.500	825	183	0.818	0.000037	451	527	0.461	0.727522
c.1252T > C, p.=	rs1145086	22	12	0.647	906	102	0.899	0.000114	621	357	0.635	1
c.*600A > G	rs1049503	18	16	0.529	813	195	0.807	0.0003	384	594	0.393	0.112623
c.*715T > C	rs1049508	17	17	0.500	825	183	0.818	0.000037	451	527	0.461	0.727522
c.*734_*735insCA	rs35410548	23	11	0.676	906	102	0.899	0.000499	621	357	0.635	0.718426
c.*940C > T	rs1049518	18	16	0.529	906	102	0.899	0	621	357	0.635	0.21126

2.1.2. *GAMT* Gene Variants

A total of 16 variants were identified, of which three were in coding regions (Figure 2, Table 2). Two of these were rare variants, and one of these was non-synonymous. This variant (c.227C > T), observed in a heterozygous state in two individuals, had an MAF of 0.000616 in the ESP database (8/12984 chromosomes) and 0.000411 in the ExAC database (29/70554 chromosomes) (Table 2). In our ASD population, the variant was observed in 2/332 chromosomes, resulting in an MAF of 0.006. SIFT, PolyPhen-2 and MutationTaster all predicted the variant to be damaging (Table 2).

There were some differences seen in the MAFs calculated for *GAMT* variants identified in the ASD patient group compared to those from ethnic populations in the 1000 Genomes database (Supplementary Table S3). Figure 5 shows the *p*-values from Fisher's exact test (plotted as $-\log(p)$) and the variants identified. Only three of these differences were significant (Fisher's exact test, $p = 0.01$), and after running the Benjamini–Hochberg procedure only one of these remained significant (r266813).

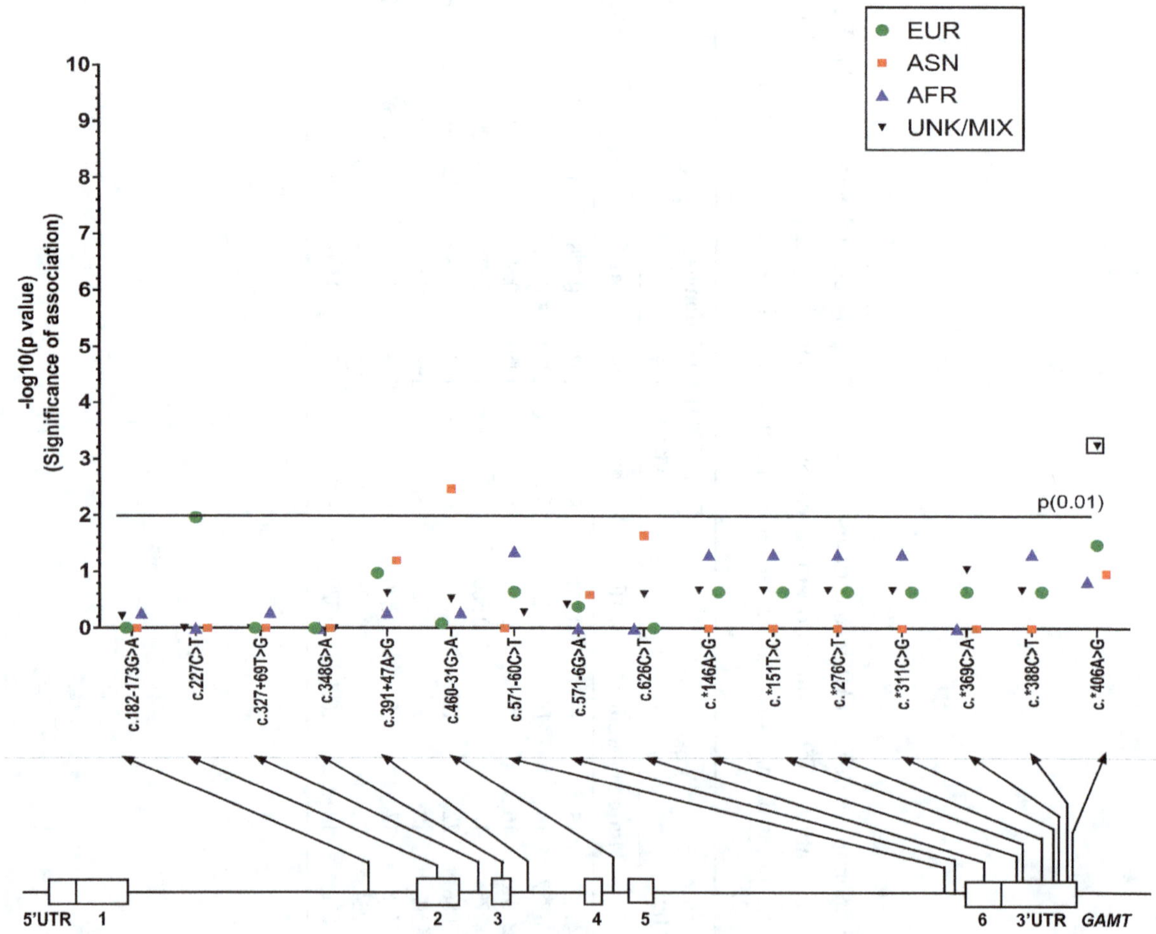

Figure 5. Manhattan plot showing the *p*-values from Fisher's exact test (significance of association, plotted as -log (*p*)) for each SNP sequenced on the guanidinoacetate methyltransferase (*GAMT*) gene. *p*-values are shown for European, East Asian, African, and Unknown/Admixed populations. The nominal statistical threshold for $p = 0.01$ is shown, and *p*-values that are still significant after running the Benjamin–Hochburg procedure are indicated with boxes. The location of each SNP is shown on the *GAMT* gene below the x-axis. EUR: European; ASN: East Asian; AFR: African; UNK/MIX: Unknown/Admixed populations.

2.1.3. *SLC6A8* Gene Variants

In total 25 variants were identified, of which two were in coding regions (Figure 3, Table 3). Of these, one resulted in a rare, non-synonymous coding change in exon 8: c.1162G > A. This was identified as hemizygous in a male individual, which would imply the variant would cause disease if found to be pathogenic, since the *SLC6A8* gene is on the X chromosome. The MAF was 0.005 (1/198 alleles), and allele frequencies for the 1000 Genomes, ESP and ExAC databases were 0.0003 (1/3775 alleles), 0.0002886 (3/10394 alleles) and 0.00007051 (1/14182 alleles) respectively. SIFT, PolyPhen-2 and MutationTaster all suggest the variant is damaging, and if so, the variant could potentially be disease causing. However, the variant is listed in the Leiden Open Variation Database v2 [30] and is shown by one study to be benign. The variant was identified in a patient with mental retardation, but fibroblasts from the patient were confirmed to have normal creatine uptake. The variant was seen in 2/1900 patients with mental retardation [31]. Two more rare variants were also identified as non-pathogenic by other studies: c.813C > T, a synonymous variant in exon 5 [32], and c.1142 − 35G > A in intron 7, as well as several of the non-coding polymorphic variants [33].

There were some differences seen in the MAFs calculated for *SLC6A8* variants identified in the ASD patient group compared to those from ethnic populations in 1000 Genomes database (Supplementary Table S4). Figure 6 shows the p-values from Fisher's exact test (plotted as -log (p)) and the variants identified. Only three of these differences were significant (Fisher's exact test, p = 0.01), but after running the Benjamini–Hochberg procedure, these values fell below the threshold of significance.

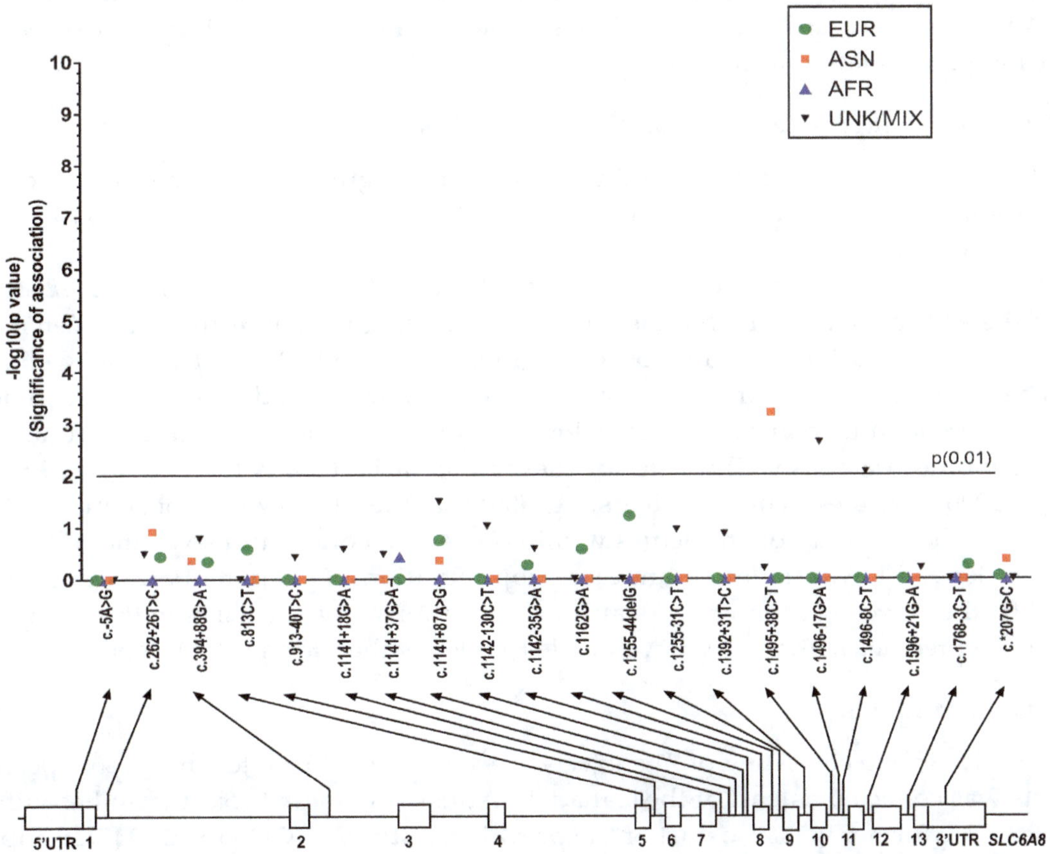

Figure 6. Manhattan plot showing the p-values from Fisher's exact test (significance of association, plotted as -log (p)) for each SNP sequenced on the solute carrier family 6 member 8 (*SLC6A8*) gene. p-values are shown for European, East Asian, African, and Unknown/Admixed populations. The nominal statistical threshold for p = 0.01 is shown. The location of each SNP is shown on the *SLC6A8* gene below the x-axis. EUR: European; ASN: East Asian; AFR: African; UNK/MIX: Unknown/Admixed populations.

3. Discussion

Three rare, non-synonymous genetic variants were identified in coding regions in *GATM, GAMT* and *SLC6A8* genes in four individuals with ASD. The variants were heterozygous in *GATM* and *GAMT*, implying possible carrier status for a pathogenic mutation; and hemizygous for *SLC6A8* in a single male, suggesting creatine transporter deficiency if the variant is proven pathogenic. All three variants were predicted as being damaging using SIFT, PolyPhen-2 and MutationTaster. No creatine transporter defect had been demonstrated in males with the hemizygous *SLC6A8* c.1162G > A variant. This variant was subsequently proven to be benign, based on its presence in two patients with mental retardation and no creatine transporter defect [31]. The variants in *GATM* and *GAMT* can only be proven as truly pathogenic if functional studies are performed. No homozygous or compound-heterozygous variants classified as "damaging" were identified in the ASD population, suggesting the prevalence of CDS in autism patients in our sample is zero. We have recently published another study confirming the prevalence to be zero, as no cases of CDS were identified in 443 children with ASD (screening of patients was done using both metabolic and molecular methods) [5]. Schiff et al. [34] screened urine from 203 children with non-syndromic autism and found none to be affected with CDS. The only other genetic screen was carried out by Newmeyer et al [35]. They screened 100 males with ASD for mutations in the *SLC6A8* gene, and reported one affected child. However, this male patient had the c.1162G > A variant. He was later further investigated and had a normal urine creatine/creatinine ratio, suggesting the variant was benign.

Statistical Differences between MAFs in CDS Genes in ASD and the General Population

Fisher's exact test was used to determine the statistical significance of any differences identified in the allele frequencies of the autism cohort compared to the 1000 Genomes database (divided into four population groups).

There were some differences seen in the MAFs calculated for *GATM, GAMT* and *SLC6A8* variants identified in the ASD patient group, but the only statistically significant results were seen in the *GATM* gene. These included variants in non-coding regions (3′ and 5′UTRs, introns) as well as changes in exons. The Asian autism cohort was compared to the East Asian data in 1000 Genomes initially. Nine variants were identified at a statistically lower frequency in our Asian autism cohort compared to the 1000 Genomes database. The data for these nine variants was then compared to the South Asian data in 1000 Genomes, which further suggested that the MAFs were not significantly different. We do not know the diversity of ethnicities within our Asian cohort and so cannot determine if our population is skewed towards one or another subpopulation. This potentially interesting finding would need further investigation with Asian subpopulations. Two variants in the European autism cohort also presented at a statistically lower allele frequency than in the 1000 Genomes database.

4. Materials and Methods

A prospective group consisting of 71 subjects was enrolled in Toronto, and a retrospective sample of 95 subjects was collected as part of the Canadian Autism Genome Project (families with only one autistic child). The former was also part of the prevalence study of CDS in ASD [5]. Supplementary Table S1 shows the cohort divided by ethnicity and sex.

Participants received a diagnosis of ASD from clinician experts based on diagnostic and statistical manual of mental disorders, 4th edition (DSM-IV) criteria for ASD (autism, Asperger's, or pervasive developmental disorder—not otherwise specified (PDD-NOS)) with the diagnosis confirmed by the autism diagnostic observation schedule (ADOS-G) [36]. An additional group of children with moderate to severe ASD eligible for a publicly-funded Intensive Behavioural Intervention Therapy program for children with ASD was recruited. Children included from this subgroup also underwent assessment by clinician experts, however, rather than the ADOS, their assessment included observation with the Childhood Autism Rating Scale (CARS) [37] and the DSM-IV checklist. Individuals were excluded if they had Rett syndrome, Childhood disintegrative disorder, severe bilateral visual impairment, or severe bilateral hearing impairment.

4.1. Study Design and Measurement

To investigate the genetic variability in genes involved in creatine metabolism in children with ASD, Sanger-based DNA sequencing chemistry was used (ABI-3730) to sequence the three genes, *GATM* (AGAT), *GAMT*, and *SLC6A8* (CrT). The entire gene was sequenced including 3′ and 5′UTRs, coding regions and flanking intronic segments. Examination of raw sequence data was completed manually for missense, nonsense, or small insertion/deletion events, by aligning sequences with NCBI reference genes. Genetic variations were compared to sequence data in Alamut (Alamut Visual version 2.6, Interactive Biosoftware, Rouen, France) and three variation databases: the 1000 Genomes phase 3 dataset [38], Exome Sequencing Project [39] and the Exome Aggregation Consortium [40]. Fisher's exact test was used to calculate "goodness-of-fit" between the allele frequencies in published databases (primarily the 1000 Genomes phase 3 dataset and the autistic patient population, based on ethnicity. If ethnicity was not known, or admixed, then allele frequencies were compared to the combined allele frequency for all ethnicities. Significant variation between allele frequencies for the two populations was noted when $p < 0.01$.

To reduce the false discovery rate, and help reduce type 1 errors (false positives) we applied the Benjamini–Hochberg procedure. The variants for each ethnic population for each gene (excluding the novel variants) were ranked in ascending *p*-values. Each individual *p*-value's Benjamini–Hochberg critical value was calculated using the formula (i/m)Q (with i = the individual *p*-value's rank; m = total number of tests; and Q = the false discovery rate (0.01)). The highest *p*-value that was also smaller than the critical value was noted, and that value and all values with lower *p*-values were considered significant. These variants are identified on the Manhattan plots.

4.2. Molecular Genetics

DNA was prepared from blood or lymphoblasts; PCR products were amplified using the primers listed in Supplementary Table S5, and sequenced by TCAG (Toronto Center of Applied Genomics, Toronto, ON, Canada). *GATM* gDNA was amplified using Herculase II Fusion Taq polymerase (Agilent Tech., Mississauga, ON, Canada). *GAMT* gDNA was amplified using Hotstar Taq polymerase (Qiagen, Toronto, ON, Canada). In some cases, a second nested amplification was carried out on the first PCR product; some of these primers had a GC clamp at their 5′ end. *SLC6A8* was amplified using Herculase II Fusion Taq polymerase, Hotstar Taq polymerase or TaKaRa La Taq polymerase (Takara Bio Inc., Shiga, Japan). Some of these primers had an M13 clamp at their 5′ end (G. Salomons, personal communication).

4.3. Ethics, Consent and Permissions

The study was approved by the Research Ethics Boards of The Hospital of Sick Children, Surrey Place Center, and Holland Bloorview Kids Rehabilitation. Subjects enrolled in the study after parents completed written informed consent.

5. Conclusions

We hypothesized that genetic variability (polymorphisms) in the three genes associated with CDS could impact the health of children and result in an autistic phenotype. This hypothesis was suggested by the fact that rare variants have been shown to have a cumulative effect, contributing to ASD risk (narrow sense heritability); and that CSD and ASD have overlapping phenotypes suggesting some similar disease mechanisms.

Our findings suggest there could be a lower association of some specific *GATM* gene variants in Asians and Europeans with autism compared to the 1000 Genomes database (East Asian population and all Europeans), observations that would need to be corroborated in a larger group of autism patients in which ethnic sub-populations are known. Variants in *GATM* have not been associated with autism previously, nor has the chromosomal region of 15q21.1. There are no genes overlapping *GATM* that have been associated with autism.

By sequencing the three CSD genes, the findings demonstrate that genetic variability in genes of biosynthesis (AGAT and GAMT) and transport of creatine (CrT) is unlikely to play a part in the pathogenesis of ASD in children. Through this work, we have corroborated results determined in our prior prevalence study in which none of the 443 children with ASD was found to be affected with CDS [5]. Both studies taken together suggest that, despite the possibility that there is a shared feature that might cause the separate but similar ASD and CDS autistic symptoms, we should look elsewhere for causation of ASD.

Acknowledgments: This project was supported by the Health Resources and Services Administration (HRSA) of the U.S. Department of Health and Human Services (HHS) under cooperative agreement UA3 MC11054—Autism Intervention Research Network on Physical Health. This information or content and conclusions are those of the author and should not be construed as the official position or policy of, nor should any endorsements be inferred from the HRSA, HHS or the U.S. Government. This work was conducted through the Autism Speaks Autism Treatment Network serving as the Autism Intervention Research Network on Physical Health.

Author Contributions: Andreas Schulze designed the study, carried out data collection, data analysis, drafted and revised the manuscript. Andreas Schulze is the principal investigator in this project. Jessie M. Cameron wrote the manuscript and carried out data analysis. Valeriy Levandovskiy carried out laboratory analyses, participated in data analysis and revised the manuscript. Wendy Roberts, Evdokia Anagnostou, Stephen Scherer, and Alvin Loh contributed to study conceptualization, data collection, data analysis and revised the manuscript. All authors reviewed the article and approved its publication.

Abbreviations

ADOS-G	Autism Diagnostic Observation Schedule
AGAT	Arginine:glycine Amidinotransferase
ASD	Autism Spectrum Disorder
bp	Base Pair
CDS	Creatine Deficiency Syndrome
CARS	Childhood Autism Rating Scale
CrT	Creatine Transporter
ExAC	Exome Aggregation Consortium
GAMT	Guanidinoacetate Methyltransferase
MAC	Minor allele Count
MAF	Minor allele Frequency
NHLBI GO ESP	National Heart, Lung and Blood Institute Grand Opportunity Exome Sequencing Project
PDD-NOS	Pervasive Developmental Disorder–Not Otherwise Specified
SNP	Single Nucleotide Polymorphism
UTR	Untranslated Region

References

1. Pampols, T. Inherited metabolic rare disease. *Adv. Exp. Med. Biol.* **2010**, *686*, 397–431. [PubMed]
2. Ververi, A.; Vargiami, E.; Papadopoulou, V.; Tryfonas, D.; Zafeiriou, D.I. Clinical and laboratory data in a sample of Greek children with autism spectrum disorders. *J. Autism Dev. Disord.* **2012**, *42*, 1470–1476. [CrossRef] [PubMed]
3. Manzi, B.; Loizzo, A.L.; Giana, G.; Curatolo, P. Autism and metabolic diseases. *J. Child Neurol.* **2008**, *23*, 307–314. [CrossRef] [PubMed]
4. Schulze, A. Creatine deficiency syndromes. *Mol. Cell. Biochem.* **2003**, *244*, 143–150. [CrossRef] [PubMed]

5. Schulze, A.; Bauman, M.; Tsai, A.C.; Reynolds, A.; Roberts, W.; Anagnostou, E.; Cameron, J.; Nozzolillo, A.A.; Chen, S.; Kyriakopoulou, L.; et al. Prevalence of Creatine Deficiency Syndromes in Children with Nonsyndromic Autism. *Pediatrics* **2016**, *137*, 1–9. [CrossRef] [PubMed]
6. Gaugler, T.; Klei, L.; Sanders, S.J.; Bodea, C.A.; Goldberg, A.P.; Lee, A.B.; Mahajan, M.; Manaa, D.; Pawitan, Y.; Reichert, J.; et al. Most genetic risk for autism resides with common variation. *Nat. Genet.* **2014**, *46*, 881–885. [CrossRef] [PubMed]
7. Klei, L.; Sanders, S.J.; Murtha, M.T.; Hus, V.; Lowe, J.K.; Willsey, A.J.; Moreno-De-Luca, D.; Yu, T.W.; Fombonne, E.; Geschwind, D.; et al. Common genetic variants, acting additively, are a major source of risk for autism. *Mol. Autism* **2012**, *3*. [CrossRef] [PubMed]
8. Schulze, A. Creatine deficiency syndromes. *Handb. Clin. Neurol.* **2013**, *113*, 1837–1843. [PubMed]
9. Leuzzi, V.; Mastrangelo, M.; Battini, R.; Cioni, G. Inborn errors of creatine metabolism and epilepsy. *Epilepsia* **2013**, *54*, 217–227. [CrossRef] [PubMed]
10. Stockler-Ipsiroglu, S.; van Karnebeek, C.; Longo, N.; Korenke, G.C.; Mercimek-Mahmutoglu, S.; Marquart, I.; Barshop, B.; Grolik, C.; Schlune, A.; Angle, B.; et al. Guanidinoacetate methyltransferase (*GAMT*) deficiency: Outcomes in 48 individuals and recommendations for diagnosis, treatment and monitoring. *Mol. Genet. Metab.* **2014**, *111*, 16–25. [CrossRef] [PubMed]
11. Van de Kamp, J.M.; Betsalel, O.T.; Mercimek-Mahmutoglu, S.; Abulhoul, L.; Grunewald, S.; Anselm, I.; Azzouz, H.; Bratkovic, D.; de Brouwer, A.; Hamel, B.; et al. Phenotype and genotype in 101 males with X-linked creatine transporter deficiency. *J. Med. Genet.* **2013**, *50*, 463–472. [CrossRef] [PubMed]
12. Wallimann, T.; Wyss, M.; Brdiczka, D.; Nicolay, K.; Eppenberger, H.M. Intracellular compartmentation, structure and function of creatine kinase isoenzymes in tissues with high and fluctuating energy demands: The 'phosphocreatine circuit' for cellular energy homeostasis. *Biochem. J.* **1992**, *281*, 21–40. [CrossRef] [PubMed]
13. Almeida, L.S.; Salomons, G.S.; Hogenboom, F.; Jakobs, C.; Schoffelmeer, A.N. Exocytotic release of creatine in rat brain. *Synapse* **2006**, *60*, 118–123. [CrossRef] [PubMed]
14. Brewer, G.J.; Wallimann, T.W. Protective effect of the energy precursor creatine against toxicity of glutamate and beta-amyloid in rat hippocampal neurons. *J. Neurochem.* **2000**, *74*, 1968–1978. [CrossRef] [PubMed]
15. Andres, R.H.; Ducray, A.D.; Huber, A.W.; Perez-Bouza, A.; Krebs, S.H.; Schlattner, U.; Seiler, R.W.; Wallimann, T.; Widmer, H.R. Effects of creatine treatment on survival and differentiation of GABA-ergic neurons in cultured striatal tissue. *J. Neurochem.* **2005**, *95*, 33–45. [CrossRef] [PubMed]
16. Andres, R.H.; Huber, A.W.; Schlattner, U.; Perez-Bouza, A.; Krebs, S.H.; Seiler, R.W.; Wallimann, T.; Widmer, H.R. Effects of creatine treatment on the survival of dopaminergic neurons in cultured fetal ventral mesencephalic tissue. *Neuroscience* **2005**, *133*, 701–713. [CrossRef] [PubMed]
17. Watanabe, A.; Kato, N.; Kato, T. Effects of creatine on mental fatigue and cerebral hemoglobin oxygenation. *Neurosci. Res.* **2002**, *42*, 279–285. [CrossRef]
18. Rae, C.; Digney, A.L.; McEwan, S.R.; Bates, T.C. Oral creatine monohydrate supplementation improves brain performance: A double-blind, placebo-controlled, cross-over trial. *Proc. Biol. Sci.* **2003**, *270*, 2147–2150. [CrossRef] [PubMed]
19. Stromberger, C.; Bodamer, O.A.; Stockler-Ipsiroglu, S. Clinical characteristics and diagnostic clues in inborn errors of creatine metabolism. *J. Inherit. Metab. Dis.* **2003**, *26*, 299–308. [CrossRef] [PubMed]
20. Comeaux, M.S.; Wang, J.; Wang, G.; Kleppe, S.; Zhang, V.W.; Schmitt, E.S.; Craigen, W.J.; Renaud, D.; Sun, Q.; Wong, L.J. Biochemical, molecular, and clinical diagnoses of patients with cerebral creatine deficiency syndromes. *Mol. Genet. Metab.* **2013**, *109*, 260–268. [CrossRef] [PubMed]
21. Stöckler, S.; Holzbach, U.; Hanefeld, F.; Marquardt, I.; Helms, G.; Requart, M.; Hanicke, W.; Frahm, J. Creatine deficiency in the brain: A new, treatable inborn error of metabolism. *Pediatr. Res.* **1994**, *36*, 409–413. [CrossRef] [PubMed]
22. Schulze, A.; Hess, T.; Wevers, R.; Mayatepek, E.; Bachert, P.; Marescau, B.; Knopp, M.V.; De Deyn, P.P.; Bremer, H.J.; Rating, D. Creatine deficiency syndrome caused by guanidinoacetate methyltransferase deficiency: Diagnostic tools for a new inborn error of metabolism. *J. Pediatr.* **1997**, *131*, 626–631. [CrossRef]
23. Mercimek-Mahmutoglu, S.; Stoeckler-Ipsiroglu, S.; Adami, A.; Appleton, R.; Araujo, H.C.; Duran, M.; Ensenauer, R.; Fernandez-Alvarez, E.; Garcia, P.; Grolik, C.; et al. GAMT deficiency: Features, treatment, and outcome in an inborn error of creatine synthesis. *Neurology* **2006**, *67*, 480–484. [CrossRef] [PubMed]

24. Gordon, N. Guanidinoacetate methyltransferase deficiency (GAMT). *Brain Dev.* **2009**, *32*, 79–81. [CrossRef] [PubMed]
25. Battini, R.; Leuzzi, V.; Carducci, C.; Tosetti, M.; Bianchi, M.C.; Item, C.B.; Stockler-Ipsiroglu, S.; Cioni, G. Creatine depletion in a new case with AGAT deficiency: Clinical and genetic study in a large pedigree. *Mol. Genet. Metab.* **2002**, *77*, 326–331. [CrossRef]
26. Nouioua, S.; Cheillan, D.; Zaouidi, S.; Salomons, G.S.; Amedjout, N.; Kessaci, F.; Boulahdour, N.; Hamadouche, T.; Tazir, M. Creatine deficiency syndrome. A treatable myopathy due to arginine-glycine amidinotransferase (AGAT) deficiency. *Neuromuscul. Disord.* **2013**, *23*, 670–674. [CrossRef] [PubMed]
27. Ng, P.C.; Henikoff, S. Predicting deleterious amino acid substitutions. *Genome Res.* **2001**, *11*, 863–874. [CrossRef] [PubMed]
28. Adzhubei, I.A.; Schmidt, S.; Peshkin, L.; Ramensky, V.E.; Gerasimova, A.; Bork, P.; Kondrashov, A.S.; Sunyaev, S.R. A method and server for predicting damaging missense mutations. *Nat. Methods* **2010**, *7*, 248–249. [CrossRef] [PubMed]
29. Schwarz, J.M.; Cooper, D.N.; Schuelke, M.; Seelow, D. MutationTaster2: Mutation prediction for the deep-sequencing age. *Nat. Methods* **2014**, *11*, 361–362. [CrossRef] [PubMed]
30. Fokkema, I.F.; Taschner, P.E.; Schaafsma, G.C.; Celli, J.; Laros, J.F.; den Dunnen, J.T. LOVD v.2.0: The next generation in gene variant databases. *Hum. Mutat.* **2011**, *32*, 557–563. [CrossRef] [PubMed]
31. Betsalel, O.T.; Rosenberg, E.H.; Almeida, L.S.; Kleefstra, T.; Schwartz, C.E.; Valayannopoulos, V.; Abdul-Rahman, O.; Poplawski, N.; Vilarinho, L.; Wolf, P.; et al. Characterization of novel SLC6A8 variants with the use of splice-site analysis tools and implementation of a newly developed LOVD database. *Eur. J. Hum. Genet.* **2011**, *19*, 56–63. [CrossRef] [PubMed]
32. Clark, A.J.; Rosenberg, E.H.; Almeida, L.S.; Wood, T.C.; Jakobs, C.; Stevenson, R.E.; Schwartz, C.E.; Salomons, G.S. X-linked creatine transporter (SLC6A8) mutations in about 1% of males with mental retardation of unknown etiology. *Hum. Genet.* **2006**, *119*, 604–610. [CrossRef] [PubMed]
33. Rosenberg, E.H.; Almeida, L.S.; Kleefstra, T.; de Grauw, R.S.; Yntema, H.G.; Bahi, N.; Moraine, C.; Ropers, H.H.; Fryns, J.P.; Degrauw, T.J.; et al. High prevalence of SLC6A8 deficiency in X-linked mental retardation. *Am. J. Hum. Genet.* **2004**, *75*, 97–105. [CrossRef] [PubMed]
34. Schiff, M.; Benoist, J.F.; Aissaoui, S.; Boepsflug-Tanguy, O.; Mouren, M.C.; de Baulny, H.O.; Delorme, R. Should metabolic diseases be systematically screened in nonsyndromic autism spectrum disorders? *PLoS ONE* **2011**, *6*, e21932. [CrossRef]
35. Newmeyer, A.; deGrauw, T.; Clark, J.; Chuck, G.; Salomons, G. Screening of male patients with autism spectrum disorder for creatine transporter deficiency. *Neuropediatrics* **2007**, *38*, 310–312. [CrossRef] [PubMed]
36. Lord, C.; Risi, S.; Lambrecht, L.; Cook, E.H., Jr.; Leventhal, B.L.; DiLavore, P.C.; Pickles, A.; Rutter, M. The autism diagnostic observation schedule-generic: A standard measure of social and communication deficits associated with the spectrum of autism. *J. Autism Dev. Disord.* **2000**, *30*, 205–223. [CrossRef] [PubMed]
37. Schopler, E.; Reichler, R.J.; DeVellis, R.F.; Daly, K. Toward objective classification of childhood autism: Childhood Autism Rating Scale (CARS). *J. Autism Dev. Disord.* **1980**, *10*, 91–103. [CrossRef] [PubMed]
38. The International Genome Sample Resource (IGSR). 1000 Genomes Phase 3 Dataset. Available online: http://www.1000genomes.org (accessed on 20 May 2015).
39. National Heart Lung and Blood Institute (NHLBI). Exome Sequencing Project (ESP). Available online: http://evs.gs.washington.edu/EVS/ (accessed on 20 May 2015).
40. Exome Aggregation Consortium (ExAC). ExAC Browser (Beta). Available online: http://exac.broadinstitute.org/ (accessed on 20 May 2015).

5

Disentangling Restrictive and Repetitive Behaviors and Social Impairments in Children and Adolescents with Gilles de la Tourette Syndrome and Autism Spectrum Disorder

Mariangela Gulisano [1,*], Rita Barone [1], Salvatore Alaimo [2], Alfredo Ferro [2], Alfredo Pulvirenti [2], Lara Cirnigliaro [1], Selena Di Silvestre [1], Serena Martellino [1], Nicoletta Maugeri [1], Maria Chiara Milana [1], Miriam Scerbo [1] and Renata Rizzo [1]

[1] Child and Adolescent Psychiatric Section, Department of Clinical and Experimental Medicine, Catania University, Via Santa Sofia 78, 95123 Catania, Italy; rbarone@unict.it (R.B.); laracirnigliaro92@gmail.com (L.C.); selena_disilvestre@yahoo.it (S.D.S.); serena.martellino@live.it (S.M.); nico_maugeri@hotmail.it (N.M.); mariachiara.milana@gmail.com (M.C.M.); mimiscerbo@gmail.com (M.S.); rerizzo@unict.it (R.R.)

[2] Bioinformatics Unit, Department of Clinical and Experimental Medicine, Catania University, Viale Andrea Doria 6, 95125 Catania, Italy; alaimos@gmail.com (S.A.); ferro@dmi.unict.it (A.F.); apulvirenti@dmi.unict.it (A.P.)

* Correspondence: mariangelagulisano@gmail.com

Abstract: Gilles de la Tourette syndrome (GTS) and autism spectrum disorder (ASD) are two neurodevelopmental disorders with male predominance, frequently comorbid, that share clinical and behavioral features. The incidence of ASD in patients affected by GTS was reported to be between 2.9% and 22.8%. We hypothesized that higher ASD rates among children affected by GTS previously reported may be due to difficulty in discriminating GTS sub-phenotypes from ASD, and the higher scores in the restrictive and repetitive behaviors in particular may represent at least a "false comorbidity". We studied a large population of 720 children and adolescents affected by GTS (n = 400) and ASD (n = 320), recruited from a single center. Patients were all assessed with The Yale Global Tic Severity Rating Scale (YGTSS), The Autism Diagnostic Observation Schedule (ADOS), The Autism Diagnostic Interview Revised (ADI-R), The Children's Yale–Brown Obsessive–Compulsive Scale (CY-BOCS), and The Children's Yale–Brown Obsessive–Compulsive Scale for autism spectrum disorder (CY-BOCS ASD). Our results showed statistically significant differences in ADOS scores for social aspects between GTS with comorbid attention deficit hyperactivity disorder (ADHD) and obsessive–compulsive disorder (OCD) sub-phenotypes and ASD. No differences were present when we compared GTS with comorbid ASD sub-phenotype to ASD, while repetitive and restrictive behavior scores in ASD did not present statistical differences in the comparison with GTS and comorbid OCD and ASD sub-phenotypes. We also showed that CY-BOCS ASD could be a useful instrument to correctly identify OCD from ASD symptoms.

Keywords: autism spectrum disorder; Gilles de la Tourette; obsession; compulsion; social behavior; social impairment

1. Introduction

Autism spectrum disorder (ASD) is a neurodevelopmental disorder with an onset in early childhood characterized by persistent deficits in social communication and social interaction across multiple contexts alongside restricted and repetitive patterns of behavior and interests or activities [1].

Social problems are the most characteristic and persistent components of the behavioral phenotype. Autism is 4.5 times more common in males than in females. The prevalence of ASD is approximately 1% in the general population [2].

Gilles de la Tourette syndrome (GTS) is a neurodevelopmental disorder characterized by motor tics and at least one vocal tic that occurs for more than 1 year, with an age of onset before 18 years [1]. It is also characterized by male predominance. In addition to sharing some symptomatology and sexual dysmorphism, these disorders are commonly comorbid [3].

This comorbidity might partly reflect common etiological mechanisms in children and adolescents affected by GTS, and the strong heritability of both ASD and GTS implies genetic etiology [4]; the Brainstorm consortium (2018) reported shared heritability in both disorders [5]. However, another study examining the shared genetic etiology through analysis of heritability among brain phenotypes found common genetic variation across a number of neuropsychological disorders and proposed a specific relationship between GTS and ASD [6]. A large body of literature has convincingly shown that many similarities are present in genetic factors, functional and structural brain characteristics, and cognitive profiles. In particular, recent studies have found similar overlapping alterations of functional connectivity in ASD and GTS patients [7]. Compulsive attachment to routines and stereotypical behaviors in ASD are associated with changes in the corticostriatal circuitry especially involving the caudate [8]. Likewise, compulsions observed in obsessive–compulsive disorder (OCD) were shown to be associated with alteration of the orbitofrontal circuitry and caudate nucleus dysfunction [9].

The incidence of ASD in patients affected by GTS was reported to be between 2.9% and 4.9% in two clinical populations, using DSM-5 criteria for the diagnoses of both GTS and ASD [10,11]. The first study [10] analyzed the data of 3500 patients from the Tourette Syndrome International Database Consortium Registry that comprised 83 active sites, while the second reported a small group (35 patients) of Iranian children and adolescents aged 6–18 years [11].

More recently Huisman-van Dijk et al. and Darrow et al. [12,13] studied two large clinical cohorts of GTS patients and their family members using two screening instruments, the Autism Quotient and the Social Responsiveness Scale (SRS), to characterize ASD symptoms and reported a higher incidence of "probable" ASD between 20% and 22.8%.

Social communication and interaction challenges as well as the presence of functionally disabling restricted repetitive behaviors are characteristic of ASD. Symptoms such as obsessions, compulsive behaviors, echolalia and palilalia are common in both conditions [14].

Repetitive behaviors are observed in as many as 65% of patients with GTS and can be classified as "tic-like" or OCD-like symptoms according to clinical phenomenology [15]. Repetitive behaviors in ASD typically overlap with phenomena in GTS. It may be challenging to distinguish phenomenological characteristics of ASD from GTS. In clinical practice, medical professionals often struggle to define which disorder best describes the child's symptoms.

Our hypothesis is that higher ASD rates among children affected by GTS reported by Darrow et al. [13] and Huiss Van Dick et al. [12] may be due to the difficulty in discriminating complex tics and OCD symptoms from ASD symptoms, and the higher scores in the repetitive behaviors in particular may represent at least a "false comorbidity".

The primary aim of this study was to disentangle repetitive behavior features and social impairment in two large populations from a single center, GTS patients compared to ASD patients. Specifically, we aimed to determine whether features related to autism as measured by ADOS subscales and CY-BOCS differ for GTS sub-phenotype patients in relation to ASD.

2. Materials and Methods

2.1. Patient Selection

Participants were recruited from a larger database on clinical and molecular features of GTS and ASD that was assembled over a twenty-year period and is still being updated.

Participants in the present study were 720 children and adolescents with a primary diagnosis of GTS or ASD, according to DSM-5 criteria (APA 2013), recruited from January 2016 to February 2019 at the outpatient clinic of the Child and Adolescent Neuropsychiatry Unit at Catania University Hospital. We excluded patients who showed 1) evidence of primary psychiatric disorders different from GTS or ASD and 2) severe neurological or physical impairments or who were minimally verbal.

2.2. *Procedures*

The study was approved by the local Ethics Committee. Investigations were carried out as part of the routine clinical care of the patients in accordance with the ethical standards laid down in the 1964 Declaration of Helsinki and its later amendments (Helsinki Declaration 1975, revision 2013). All parents gave written informed consent, and the subjects assented when possible. All patients underwent physical examination and blood and urine analyses to rule out systemic diseases (e.g., inherited metabolic disorders). Diagnoses of GTS and comorbid disorders and ASD were performed according to DSM5 criteria, and neuropsychological evaluation was carried out by an expert team of child and adolescent neurologists, supervised by R.R., M.G., and R.B.

2.3. *Measures*

All parents participated in a medical history interview to determine prenatal, perinatal, and psychosocial risk factors as well as socio-economic status. Before inclusion in the study, all patients were screened with the Schedule for affective disorders and Schizophrenia for School age children—present and lifetime (Kiddie-SADS-PL) to rule out primary psychiatric disorders considered as criteria of exclusion. The Kiddie-SADS-PL is a semi-structured interview tool developed by Kauffman et al. (1997) that can be used in children and adolescents aged between 6–18 years [16]. This evaluation includes fundamental diagnosis of various psychiatric disorders. All patients underwent neuropsychological evaluation for GTS and related comorbidities.

2.3.1. Tics

To assess tic disorders, the National Hospital Interview Schedule for GTS (NHIS) [17], a semi-structured interview was used to diagnose GTS and its associated conditions, behaviors, and relevant family history. The Yale Global Tic Severity Rating Scale (YGTSS) [18] is an 11-item clinician rated interview that is able to evaluate motor and phonic tic severity considering the number, frequency, and impairments that tics are able to provoke in the patient. The score of the YGTSS ranges from 0 to 100, including the impairment section. Higher scores indicate greater severity of symptoms and impairment.

2.3.2. Obsessive–Compulsive Disorder

To evaluate OCD, the Children's Yale–Brown Obsessive–Compulsive Scale (CY-BOCS) [19] and the ASD CY-BOCS [20] were used. The CY-BOCS is a semi-structured interview conducted principally with parents, even if patients are encouraged to participate. This interview is able to assess the severity of obsessive–compulsive symptoms in children. The total score of CY-BOCS ranges between 0 and 40. It is possible to evaluate an obsession and a compulsion score separately. Higher scores indicate greater severity of symptoms and impairment.

2.3.3. Autism Spectrum Disorder

The Autism Diagnostic Observation Schedule (ADOS) [21] was used for ASD diagnosis. The ADOS is a standardized evaluation scale that is considered the gold standard for the diagnosis of ASD. It is structured in four domains of exploration (A), social interaction (B), imagination (C), and repetitive and stereotyped behaviors (D). Items are scored from 0 to 3 on the basis of severity (3: more severe).

The ADOS provides a total score and partial scores related to Social Affect (SA) and Restricted, Repetitive Behavior (RRB).

The Autism Diagnostic Interview Revised (ADI-R) [22] is a structured interview conducted with the parents/guardians. Its purpose is to investigate the same areas of ADOS based on the judgment of parents/guardians with respect to their children's symptoms. Items are scored from 0 to 3 on the basis of severity (3: more severe).

The Children Yale Brown Obsessive–Compulsive Scale for Autism Spectrum Disorder is a semi-structured interview conducted with patients and parents that was developed after CY-BOCS by Schahill et al. (2014) to detect the differences between obsession and compulsion in OCD and repetitive and restrictive behaviors, interests, and stereotypes in ASD [20]. For this purpose, the scale is structured with a Symptom Checklist (behavior present or absent) and five sub-schedules (Time Spent, Interference, Distress, Resistance, and Control). Each item ranges from 0 (not present) to 4 (severe), and the total score is between 0 and 20. The interview includes a symptom checklist of possible repetitive behaviors grouped into eight categories (e.g., washing rituals, checking behaviors). Each category allows the interviewer to describe "other" behaviors presumed relevant to that overall category. The severity of each item is anchored to the past week and scored from 0 (not present) to 4 (severe) for a total score of 0 to 20 [20].

2.4. Statistical Analysis

Clinical covariates were identified within each psycho-diagnostic class that might be able to detect affected subjects and their comorbidities from healthy individuals. Analyzed psycho-diagnostic classes included ADI-R, ADOS, YGTSS, CY-BOCS, and CY-BOCS ASD.

The identification of class-specific clinical covariates, which have statistically different values, is a fundamental process to identify common elements among different conditions and to stratify affected subjects according to comorbidities. For this purpose, we employed the R software suite to perform statistical analyses using a two-sided t-test or ANOVA and to build a risk classification model based on C-Tree Induction [23].

Risk models were developed with the use of decision-tree induction from class-labeled training records, i.e., the training set was composed of records in which one attribute was the class label (or dependent variable), and the remaining attributes were the predictor variables; the individual records were the tuples for which the class label was known.

The aim of this analysis was the objective identification of the classification power of evaluation metrics used in the context of Gilles de la Tourette syndrome and the assessment of a joint model to distinguish between pure GTS, GTS plus comorbidities, and ASD. For this purpose, the usage of a classification model is crucial to study the predictive power of a set of diagnostic metrics. The classification, starting from the characteristics (in our case the independent variables are those reported in Table 1), named predictor variables, of the examined subjects, aims to infer a set of rules allowing the prediction of covariate values, named class labels (or dependent variables). Each node of the tree analyzes a covariate by computing an optimal binary split. The goodness of the split is supported by a two-sample statistical test based on a permutation analysis.

In our study the objective was to distinguish six different classes: GTS, GTS + OCD, GTS + attention deficit hyperactivity disorder (ADHD), GTS + OCD + ADHD, GTS + ASD, and ASD.

The performance of the classification model was analyzed, randomly splitting the data in the training set (2/3 of the records) and the testing Set (1/3 of the records); this partition was repeated 100 times, and the classification accuracy was taken as the average of each accuracy measurement. All differences were considered statistically significant at a 5% probability level.

Table 1. Demographic and clinical features.

	GTS (pt 400)	ASD (pt 320)
M/F	274/62	196/37
Mean age	11.4 (± 3.1)	11.1 (± 3.5)
IQ		
TIQ	91.7 (± 17.9)	77.2 (± 24.4)
PIQ	91.61 (± 18.0)	79.1 (± 24)
VIQ	92.87 (± 18.5)	77.7 (± 25.1)
YGTSS	19.54 (± 9.4)	1.4 (± 2.6)
CY-BOCS	15.61 (± 10.9)	13,9 (± 11,3)
CY-BOCS ASD	6.2 (± 4.4)	17 (± 3.2)

GTS: Gilles de la Tourette Syndrome; ASD: Autism Spectrum Disorder; CY-BOCS: Children Yale Brown Obsessive–Compulsive Scale; CY-BOCS ASD: Children Yale Brown Obsessive–Compulsive Scale for Autism Spectrum Disorder; YGTSS: Yale Global Tic Severity Scale; TIQ: Total Intelligence Quotient; PIQ: Performance Intelligence Quotient; VIQ: Verbal Intelligence Quotient.

3. Results

We recruited a clinical cohort of 720 patients aged 6–18 years, mean age 11.3 (±3.3) years. Of this cohort, 400 subjects were affected by GTS. They were 274 males and 62 females, with a mean age of 11.4 (±3.1) years. Patients with ASD ($n = 320$) included 196 males and 37 females, with a mean age of 11.1 (±3.5). Demographic and clinical characteristics of the study samples are reported in Table 1. The GTS clinical cohort had a significantly higher mean IQ (91.7 ± 17.9) than that of the ASD patients (77.2 ± 24.4) (Table 1).

Nearly all subjects with GTS presented at least one comorbidity. The results of the neuropsychological evaluation enabled assessment of GTS clinical sub-phenotypes distributed as follows: GTS only (15.5%), GTS + ADHD (32%), GTS + OCD (33.5%), GTS + ADHD + OCD (10.25%), and GTS + ASD (8.9%). GTS sub-phenotypes were compared to the ASD clinical group.

3.1. *Yale Global Tic Severity Rating Scale*

GTS patients presented a mean YGTSS total score of 19.5 (±9.4). The YGTSS score in the GTS clinical sub-phenotypes was as follows: pure GTS, 16.1 (±7); GTS+ADHD, 19.1 (±1); GTS+OCD, 22.2 (±9.7); GTS + ADHD + OCD, 25.9 (±9); and GTS + ASD, 11.7 (±3.2). The ASD group presented a mean YGTSS of 2.3 (±1.8). Statistically significant differences were observed in the comparisons of YGTSS scores between the GTS sub-phenotypes and ASD clinical cohort ($p < 0.001$) (see Figure 1 and Table 2).

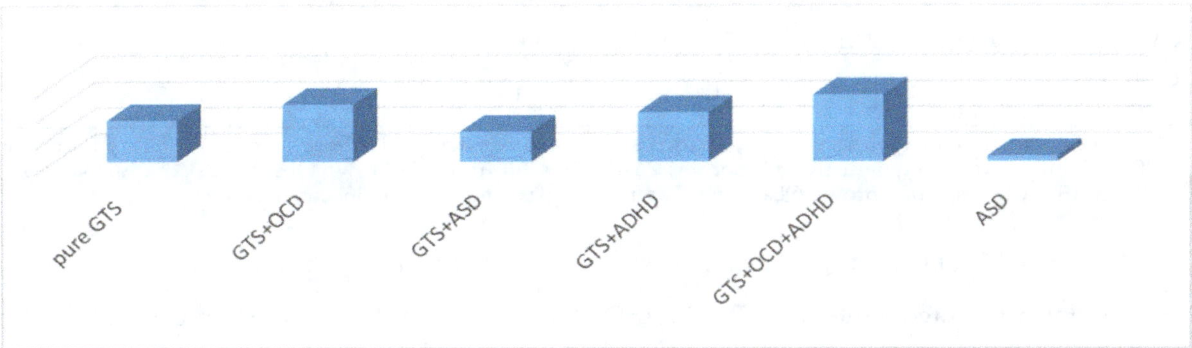

Figure 1. YGTSS score between clinical groups. GTS: Gilles de la Tourette Syndrome; ASD: Autism Spectrum Disorder; OCD: Obsessive–Compulsive Disorder; ADHD: Attention Deficit Hyperactivity Disorder; YGTSS: Yale Global Tic Severity Scale.

Table 2. Comparison between mean YGTSS values in each sub-phenotype and statistical significance.

	GTS Only	GTS + OCD	GTS + ASD	GTS + ADHD	GTS + OCD + ADHD	ASD	*p*-Value
YGTSS	16.1 (±7)	22.2 (±9.7)	11.7 (3.2)	19.1 (±1)	25.9 (±9.6)	2.3 (±108)	0.0005

GTS: Gilles de la Tourette Syndrome; ASD: Autism Spectrum Disorder; OCD: Obsessive–Compulsive Disorder; ADHD: Attention Deficit Hyperactivity Disorder; YGTSS: Yale Global Tic Severity Scale.

3.2. Children's Yale–Brown Obsessive–Compulsive Scale

GTS patients presented a mean CY-BOCS of 15.6 (±1). With regard to GTS clinical sub-phenotypes, the following mean CY-BOCS scores were computed: pure GTS, 7.6 (±6); GTS + ADHD, 9.9 (±7.8); GTS + OCD, 23.5 (±8.3); GTS + ADHD + OCD, 27.1 (±1); and GTS + ASD, 12.1 (±6.1). ASD patients presented a mean CY-BOCS score of 17.9 (±3.1) (Figure 2, Table 3).

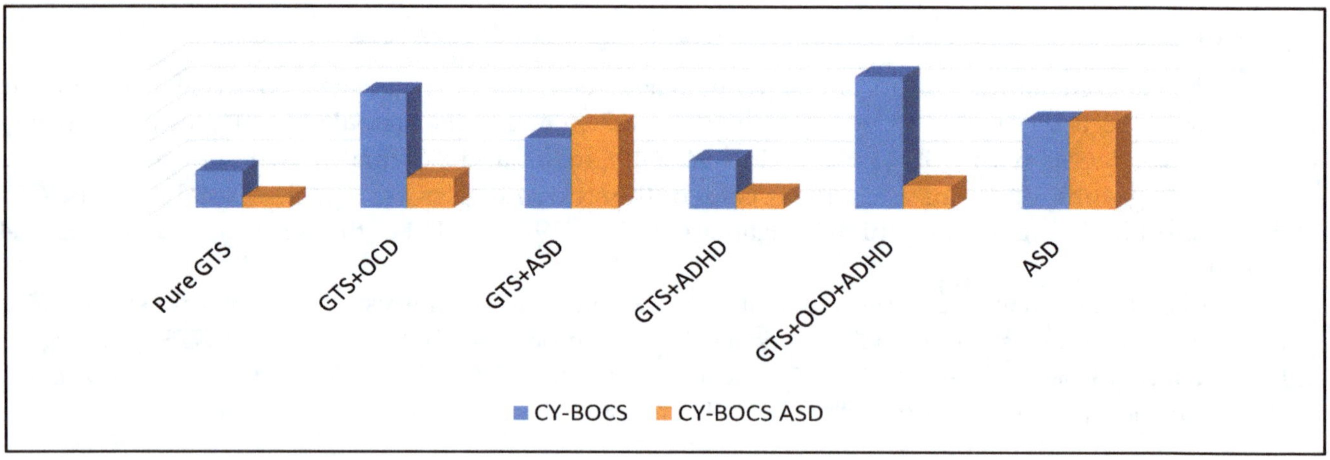

Figure 2. Comparison between CY-BOCS and CY-BOCS ASD scores between clinical groups. GTS: Gilles de la Tourette Syndrome; ASD: Autism Spectrum Disorder; OCD: Obsessive–Compulsive Disorder; ADHD: Attention Deficit Hyperactivity Disorder; CY-BOCS: Children Yale Brown Obsessive–Compulsive Scale; CY-BOCS ASD: Children Yale Brown Obsessive–Compulsive Scale for Autism Spectrum Disorder.

Table 3. Comparison between mean values of measures in each sub-phenotype and statistical significance.

	Pure GTS	GTS + OCD	GTS + ASD	GTS + ADHD	GTS + OCD + ADHD	ASD	*p*-Value
CY-BOCS	7.6 (±6)	23.5 (±8.3)	14.4 (9.3)	9.9 (±7.8)	27.1 (±1)	17.9 ± 3.1	0.0005
CY-BOCS ASD	2.2 (±1.9)	6.2 (±4.4)	17.1 (4.1)	3 (±1.9)	4.8 (±2.1)	18.1 ± 3.2	0.0005

GTS: Gilles de la Tourette Syndrome; ASD: Autism Spectrum Disorder; OCD: Obsessive–Compulsive Disorder; ADHD: Attention Deficit Hyperactivity Disorder; CY-BOCS: Children Yale Brown Obsessive–Compulsive Scale; CY-BOCS ASD: Children Yale Brown Obsessive–Compulsive Scale for Autism Spectrum Disorder.

3.3. Children's Yale–Brown Obsessive–Compulsive Scale: Autism Spectrum Disorder

GTS patients presented a mean CY-BOCS ASD of 6.2 (±4.4). In detail, GTS clinical sub-phenotypes presented the following mean scores: pure GTS, 2.2 (±1.9); GTS + ADHD, 2.9 (±1.9); GTS + OCD, 6.2 (±4.4); GTS + ADHD + OCD, 3.1 (±2.1); and GTS + ASD, 17.9 (±2.9). ASD patients presented a mean CY-BOCS ASD score of 18.1 (±3.2) (Figure 2, Table 3).

Figure 3 shows a decision tree. Among all the inferred models, we showed the one built as a function of the CY-BOCS ASD variable. Each internal node of the tree represents a statistical test (on such a variable, the two departing branches split the data according to the most discriminant threshold). These analyses revealed that when the score of CY-BOCS ASD was lower than 1, the analyses were able to detect GTS only, whereas when the CY-BOCS ASD score was higher than 14, the more represented clinical group was that with pure ASD, followed by GTS+ASD. However, the overall accuracy of the model is 46,35%, which means that this variable is not reliable for detection of GTS + comorbidities when its value is between 1 and 14.

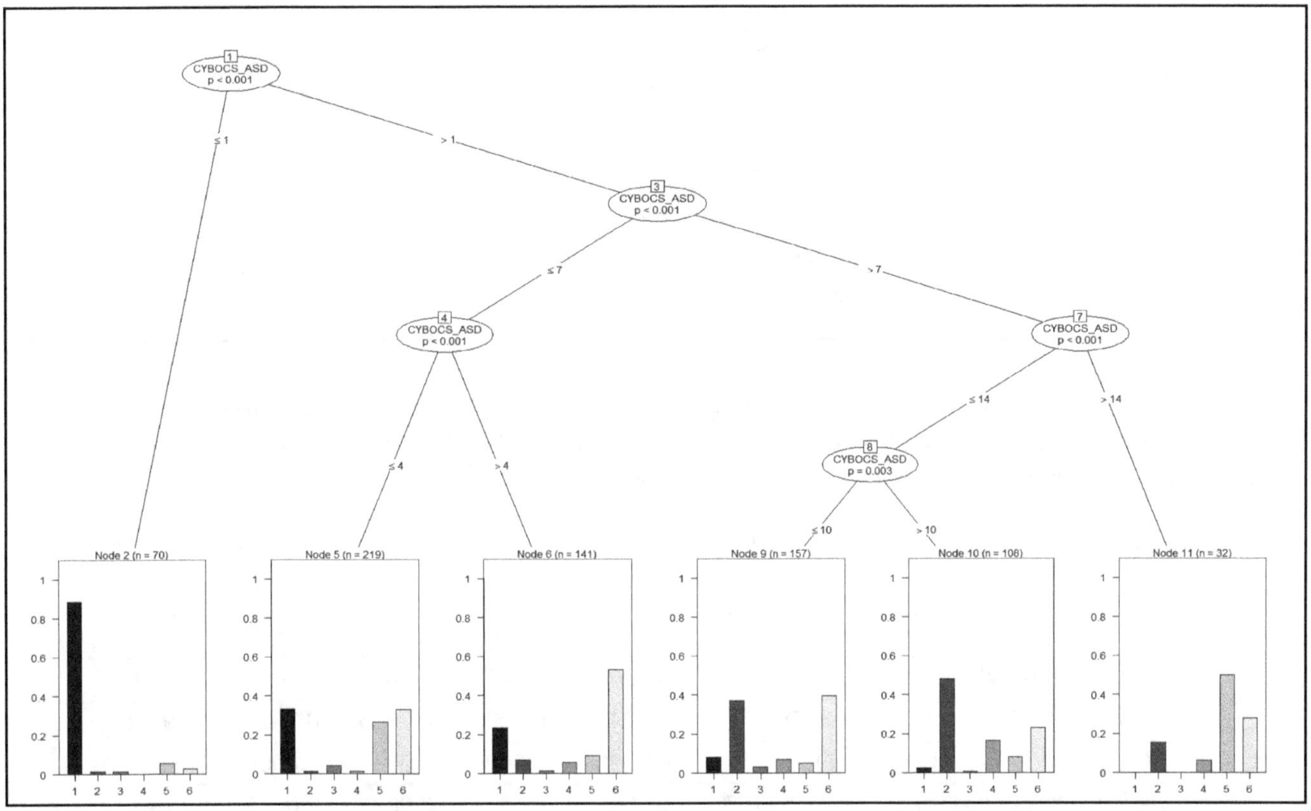

Figure 3. Decision tree. Clinical groups: 1: pure GTS; 2: GTS+ OCD; 3: GTS + ADHD; 4: GTS + ADHD + OCD + OCD; 5: GTS + ASD; 6 ASD.

3.4. Autism Diagnostic Observation Schedule

For all ADOS scales, ASD and GTS + ASD presented scores that fulfilled the diagnosis of ASD. No significant differences in scores were observed between these groups. In contrast, GTS presented significantly lower mean scores in ADOS scales compared to those of ASD and GTS + ASD.

With regard to ADOS-SA "Social Interaction", "Imagination", and "Communication, Language, and Behavior", the GTS sub-phenotypes always presented significantly lower scores than ASD and GTS + ASD sub-phenotypes. When ADOS-RR subscale scores of "restricted and repetitive behaviors" from the GTS sub-phenotype were analyzed in detail, different results related to the compared groups in each ADOS subscale were computed. In particular, no significant differences were detected when comparing GTS sub-phenotypes and ASD as follows: GTS + ASD vs. GTS + OCD in D3 (repetitive and stereotyped behavior) and D4 (compulsions); GTS + ASD vs. GTS + OCD + ADHD in D4 (compulsion); ASD vs. GTS + OCD in D1 (unusual interests), D3 (repetitive and stereotyped behavior), and D4 (compulsions) (Figure 4 and Table 4).

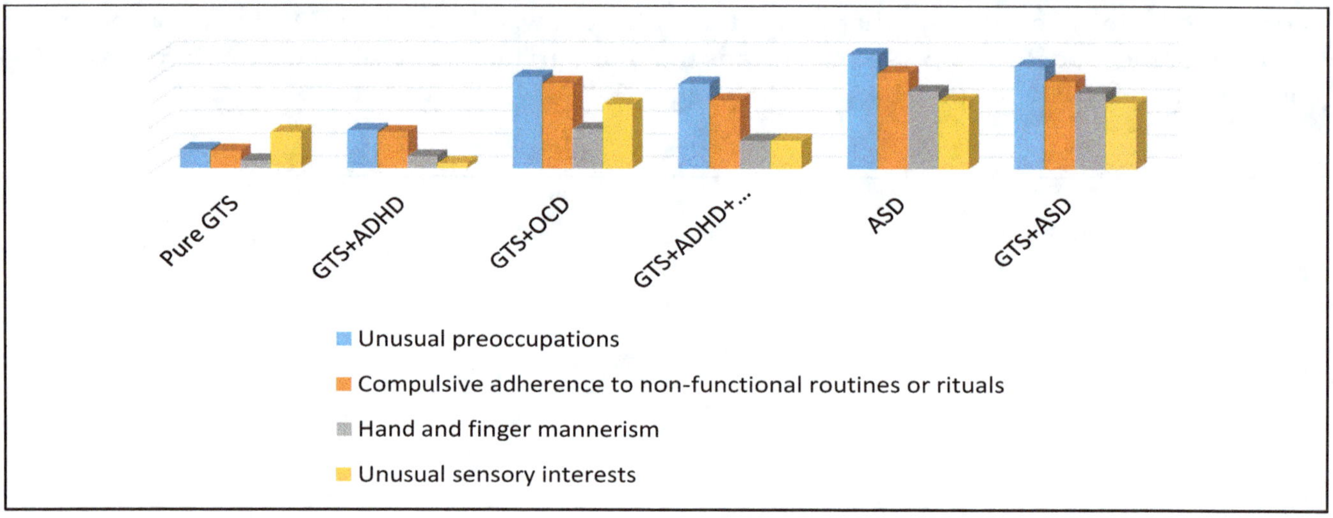

Figure 4. ADOS (D scale) restricted and repetitive behaviors: comparison between clinical sub-phenotypes. GTS: Gilles de la Tourette Syndrome; ASD: Autism Spectrum Disorder; OCD: Obsessive–Compulsive Disorder; ADHD: Attention Deficit Hyperactivity Disorder.

Table 4. ADOS Restricted and repetitive behaviors (D Scale): statistical significance in comparison with clinical sub-phenotypes.

	D. Total	D1	D2	D3	D4
"GTS + ASD" vs. "Pure GTS"	0.0005	0.0005	0.0005	0.0005	0.0005
"GTS + ASD" vs. "GTS + OCD"	0.0045	0.0205	0.0005	0.3828	0.9716
"GTS + ASD" vs. "GTS + ADHD"	0.0051	0.0095	0.0061	0.0065	0.0051
"GTS + ASD" vs. "GTS + OCD + ADHD"	0.0002	0.0071	0.0005	0.0005	0.7991
"ASD" vs. "Pure GTS"	0.0005	0.0005	0.0005	0.0005	0.0061
"ASD" vs. "GTS + OCD"	0.0065	0.1287	0.0005	0.6742	0.7789
"ASD" vs. "GTS + ADHD"	0.0005	0.0005	0.0054	0.0067	0.0065
"ASD" vs. "GTS + OCD + ADHD"	0.0005	0.0005	0.0005	0.0005	0.0005

GTS: Gilles de la Tourette Syndrome; ASD: Autism Spectrum Disorder; OCD: Obsessive–Compulsive Disorder; ADHD: Attention Deficit Hyperactivity Disorder. D1: unusual interests; D2: hand mannerisms and complex mannerisms; D3: repetitive and stereotyped behavior items; D4: compulsions. * represents a statistically significant p-value <0.05.

3.5. Autism Diagnostic Interview Revised

For all ADI-R scales, ASD and GTS + ASD presented scores that fulfilled the diagnosis of ASD. No significant differences in ADI-R scores were found between these groups. Pure GTS ADI-R scores did not fulfill the diagnosis of ASD and were significantly lower compared to those of ASD and GTS + ASD. Regarding the ADI-R scale "Restricted and Repetitive Behaviors" (C scale), no significant differences were detected when comparing GTS sub-groups and ASD as follows: GTS + ASD vs. GTS + OCD in C1 (unusual preoccupations), C2 (rituals), C3 (mannerism), and C4 (unusual interests); GTS + OCD vs. ASD in C2 (rituals) (Figure 5 and Table 5).

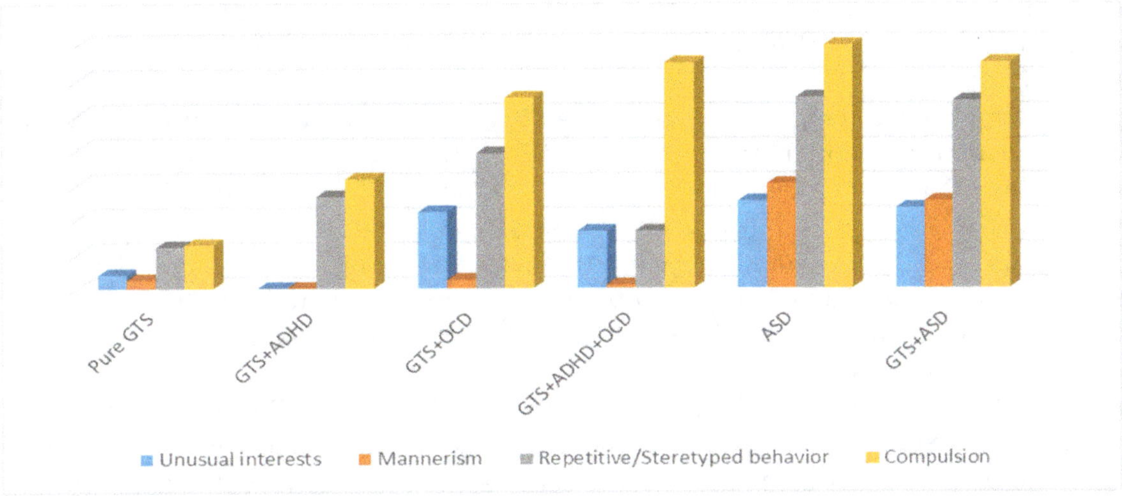

Figure 5. ADI-R, Restricted and Repetitive Behaviors (C Scale): comparison between clinical sub-phenotypes.

Table 5. ADI Restricted and repetitive behaviors (C): comparison between GTS clinical sub-phenotypes.

	C Total	C1	C2	C3	C4
"GTS + ASD" vs. "Pure GTS"	0.0005	0.0005	0.0005	0.0005	0.0005
"GTS + ASD" vs. "GTS + OCD"	0.0155	0.7586	0.4183	0.1235	0.0956
"GTS + ASD" vs. "GTS + ADHD"	0.0005	0.0005	0.0335	0.0005	0.0005
"GTS + ASD" vs. "GTS + OCD + ADHD"	0.0335	0.1924	0.1639	0.001	0.0205
"ASD" vs. "Pure GTS"	0.0005	0.0005	0.0005	0.0005	0.0005
"ASD" vs. "GTS + OCD"	0.0032	0.0038	0.2365	0.0042	0.0005
"ASD" vs. "GTS + ADHD"	0.0005	0.0005	0.0005	0.0005	0.0005
"ASD" vs. "GTS + OCD + ADHD"	0.0005	0.0005	0.0005	0.0005	0.0005

C1: unusual preoccupations; C2: compulsive adherence to non-functional routines or rituals; C3: hand and finger mannerisms; C4: unusual sensory interests; GTS: Gilles de la Tourette Syndrome; ASD: Autism Spectrum Disorder; OCD: Obsessive–Compulsive Disorder; ADHD: Attention Deficit Hyperactivity Disorder. * represents a statistically significant $p < 0.05$.

4. Discussion

Along with a deficit in social communication and interaction, restricted and repetitive behaviors constitute the defining core features of ASD; however, GTS also shares RRB and social communication and interaction problems with ASD.

In this study, we explored the prevalence and pattern of ASD symptoms in relation to GTS and other comorbid disorders, comparing the two distinct cohorts of individuals affected by GTS and ASD. We systematically assessed a large sample of children and adolescents affected by GTS and compared them to an ASD group of children and adolescents with verbal capacity.

As our primary hypothesis was that the higher percentage of ASD in GTS recently reported by other authors [12,13] showed a false comorbidity due to overlap between symptoms that were in common in both conditions, the study examined the degree to which the gold standard instruments for autism diagnosis, the ADI-R and ADOS, disentangle restrictive and repetitive behaviors and social impairment in children and adolescents affected by GTS and ASD and verify the hypothesis that, in particular, the presence of GTS + OCD and related symptoms could mimic ASD symptoms. The patients were also assessed by CY-BOCS and CY-BOCS ASD to investigate the overlap between ASD symptoms and GTS in affected individuals.

The results supported these hypotheses by indicating that higher ASD rates reported in other samples may be due to the confounding of tic or OCD symptoms for ASD or vice versa. In our samples of children and adolescents, 8.9% of patients affected by GTS presented comorbid ASD, in contrast with the incidences of 20% and 28% reported by Darrow et al. and Huisman-van Dijk et al., respectively [12,13].

In particular, when we compared ADOS and ADI-R with GTS and ASD, for ADOS scores, we did not observe any significant differences between GTS + ASD and GTS + OCD in D3 (repetitive and stereotyped behavior) and D4 (compulsions); GTS + ASD and GTS + OCD + ADHD in D4 (compulsion); or ASD and GTS + OCD in D1 (unusual interests), D3 (repetitive and stereotyped behavior), and D4 (compulsions). When examining ADI-R, no significant differences were detected between GTS + ASD and GTS + OCD in C1 (unusual preoccupations), C2 (rituals), C3 (mannerism), and C4 (unusual interests); GTS + ASD and GTS + OCD + ADHD in C1 (unusual preoccupations); and GTS + OCD and ASD in C2 (rituals).

Darrow et al. (2017) studied 535 GTS patients and used the Social Responsiveness Scale Second Edition (SRS) as a measure of ASD symptoms. The SRS contains five treatment subscales including the following domains: social awareness, social cognition, social communication (SC), social interaction (SCI), and restricted interests and repetitive behaviors (RRB).

When they examined the relationship between SRS total score and GTS sub-phenotypes, there were significant differences in SRS scores among the different classes. The highest SRS scores were found in the two classes that endorsed OCD symptoms (GTS + OCD + ADHD, OCD symmetry). These two classes had significantly higher SC and RRB scores than the other classes.

Our findings show that GTS + OCD and GTS + ASD sub-phenotypes were in line with this work; however, they reported a higher percentage (23%) of GTS-affected participants that met the cut-off criteria for probable ASD (83% of whom also met criteria for OCD). In our opinion this is because, as stated in previous studies, children [24] with mood and anxiety disorders have elevated rates of ASD based on SRS cut-off criteria, suggesting that some of the elevation in SRS scores may reflect underlying psychiatric impairment rather than being specific to ASD.

The fact that scores for the RRB subscales were higher for individuals who had OCD symptoms suggests that these SRS subscales may in fact be tapping into common repetitive behaviors in individuals with GTS and/or OCD that could be confused with stereotypies seen in ASD [13]

This is also supported by Huisman-van Dijk et al. (2016) in their significant paper, where items measuring repetitive behaviors in autism were loaded into a factor with OCD related items rather than into a factor with social communication items. Interestingly, the autism factor including lack of social skills as well as non-functional child routines, attention switching problems, and lack of investigation was not related to any of the tic or OCD symptom factors. This autism dimension might be etiologically distinct from the second factor characterized by repetitive behaviors [12].

In our study, the differences between GTS + OCD, GTS + ASD, and ASD samples were significant except in the ADOS and ADI-R domains of restrictive and repetitive behaviors.

More recently, Eapen et al. [25] in a sample of 203 participants, 44 with GTS and 26 with ASD compared to the general sample of 133 with a mean age of 18.17 years, examined the occurrence of autism related features measured by the Social Communication Questionnaire (SCQ) focusing on areas of overlap and differences.

They found that the GTS sample had significantly higher mean SCQ scores than the general population but generally lower scores than the ASD sample. The group differences in mean SCQ scores between GTS and ASD samples were significant except in the domain of RRB.

Eapen et al. suggested that symptom overlap may represent a true overlap through a shared phenotype or that the overlap may be a phenocopy where the clinical symptoms, for example, complex tics and related obsessive–compulsive symptoms of GTS, may mimic ASD symptoms and vice versa where stereotypic and repetitive behaviors characteristic of ASD may mimic GTS. In their study on the domain level, they found a close concordance between the two disorders on restricted and repetitive behaviors and less on social communication.

These results are in line with our study. ADOS differences between GTS clinical sub-phenotypes and ASD were significant in social interaction, imagination, and communication language and behavior; when RRB was analyzed, there were no significant differences.

However, restricted and repetitive behaviors are some of the major impairments shown in ASD and GTS. Having a measure that disentangles these two domains easily in a clinical setting is important for the clinicians who may use it as a basis for their treatment recommendations. We also assessed our clinical sample with CY-BOCS and CY-BOCS ASD.

CY-BOCS had the unique ability to detect symptomatology that differed from ASD characteristics, whereas other measures assessing obsessive–compulsive symptoms did not [26].

Several original CY-BOCS checklist items are nevertheless irrelevant for children with ASD. However, the results of this study provide an incremental refinement for measuring repetitive behavior in children and adolescents with GTS and ASD. Nonetheless, certain repetitive behaviors in children with ASD may have been overlooked due to sample characteristics of children with verbal capacity and normal or mild intellectual disability. Lower-functioning or non-verbal children were more likely to engage in hand and finger stereotypy and object manipulation. With regard to obsession and compulsion measured with CY-BOCS, no significant differences were detected in the comparison of scores in ASD, GTS + OCD, and GTS + ASD patients in our sample.

CY-BOCS ASD results provided a reliable and valid measure of repetitive behavior in youths with ASD and underscored differences in repetitive behavior in ASD compared to GTS [20]. With CY-BOCS ASD, no significant differences were found between GTS + ASD and ASD groups. The score obtained in the GTS + OCD, compared to the ASD group and GTS +ASD, was significantly lower. The clinical implications of these findings are important for clinicians who may use the CY-BOCS ASD as a diagnostic tool. The CY-BOCS ASD yields a total score based on the impact of the symptoms present rather than subscale scores. The results suggest that the CY-BOCS ASD is a valid and reliable measure of repetitive behavior in youths with ASD [27]. It is easy to use in a clinical setting, and clinicians may use it as a basis for their treatment recommendations.

Limitations

The principal limitation of our study is that our Tourette Clinic is a tertiary level center. For this reason, we assessed and followed complicated cases that may have not been representative of the general population affected. The different sex distribution is a limitation of this sample because we analyzed two disorders with a high prevalence in males. Finally, another limitation was related to GTS sub-phenotype analysis and the comparison of GTS sub-phenotypes with ASD without comorbidities.

5. Conclusions

To conclude, the similarities largely contained within the RRS domain rather than across the RRS and social communication domains support our hypothesis that higher ASD rates among children affected by GTS may make it difficult to discriminate between specific features of GTS and ASD, contributing to the representation of a false comorbidity.

However, another possibility exists that certain symptoms may be duplicated due to environmental or other factors rather than due to a common genetic basis. The similarities could be due to a phenocopy rather than phenotypic overlap as suggested by Eapen et al. [25].

Genetic studies together with clinical task-based RMN functional studies could contribute to a better understanding of the underlying mechanism involved in the etiology of ASD and GTS and could be critical in obtaining better treatments.

Compared to their peers with GTS but not ASD, children with GTS and ASD have greater treatment needs (that are either unmet needs or treatment usage). This finding aligns with previous literature focused on children with ASD, which found high rates of service needs, particularly among children diagnosed with co-occurring conditions [28].

When symptoms are not correctly managed, more severe psychopathology may develop, alongside poorer interpersonal, school, family, and cognitive functioning and life outcomes among this population relative to that of controls. The possibility of individualizing symptoms to treat (e.g., compulsions, rituals, and repetitive behaviors) could improve the children's quality of life and, consequently, other social aspects of their life. To our knowledge, this is the first study on a large unique cohort that analyzed symptoms that could mimic diagnosis. ADOS and ADI-R are the gold standard scales for diagnosis, and they are always able to individualize diagnosis. However, it might be helpful to define differences that could individualize treatment and help clinicians in the management of specific patients with GTS and comorbid OCD. In line with previous research [20], we suggest refining ASD diagnosis by using CY-BOSC ASD to better distinguish repetitive behaviors from compulsion and rituals.

Author Contributions: Conceptualization, M.G. and R.R.; Data curation, M.G., R.B., L.C., S.D.S., S.M. and N.M.; Formal analysis, A.F. and A.P.; Investigation, M.C.M. and M.S.; Project administration, R.R.; Software, S.A., A.F. and A.P.; Writing—original draft, R.R.; Writing—review and editing, R.R., M.G. and R.B. All authors have read and agreed to the published version of the manuscript.

Acknowledgments: This study was funded by the 2016/2018 Research Plan of the University of Catania, Department of Clinical and Experimental Medicine.

References

1. American-Psychiatric-Association. *Diagnostic and Statistical Manual of Mental Disorders*; American Psychiatric Publishing: Washington, DC, USA, 2013.
2. Lord, C.; Elsabbagh, M.; Baird, G.; Veenstra-Vanderweele, J. Autism spectrum disorder. *Lancet* **2018**, *392*, 508–520. [CrossRef]
3. Rapanelli, M.; Frick, L.M.; Pittenger, C. The role of interneurons in autism and Tourette syndrome. *Trends Neurosci.* **2017**, *40*, 397–407. [CrossRef] [PubMed]
4. State, M.W. The genetics of child psychiatric disorders: Focus on autism and Tourette syndrome. *Neuron* **2010**, *68*, 254–269. [CrossRef]
5. Benedicto, C.F. Analysis of shared heritability in common disorder of the brain in The Brainstorm Consortium. *Science* **2018**, *22*, 360.
6. Antilla, V.; Bullik-Sullivan, B.; Finucane, H.K. Analysus of shared heritability in common disorders of the brain. *BioRxiv* **2016**. [CrossRef]
7. Worbe, Y.; Marrakchi-Kacem, L.; Lecomte, S.; Valabregue, R.; Poupon, F.; Guevara, P.; Tucholka, A.; Mangin, J.F.; Vidailhet, M.; Lehericy, S.; et al. Altered structural connectivity of cortico-striato-pallido-thalamic networks in Gilles de la Tourette syndrome. *Brain* **2015**, *138*, 472–482. [CrossRef]
8. Langen, M.; Durston, S.; Kas, M.J.; Van Engeland, H.; Staal, W.G. The neurobiology of repetitive behavior: ... and men. *Neurosci. Biobehav. Rev.* **2011**, *35*, 356–365. [CrossRef]
9. Markarian, Y.; Larson, M.J.; Aldea, M.A.; Baldwin, S.A.; Good, D.; Berkeljon, A.; Murphy, T.K.; Storch, E.A.; McKay, D. Multiple pathways to functional impairment in obsessive-compulsive disorder. *Clin. Psychol. Rev.* **2010**, *30*, 78–88. [CrossRef]
10. Burd, L.; Li, Q.; Kerbeshian, J.; Klug, M.G.; Freeman, R.D. Tourette syndrome and comorbid pervasive developmental disorders. *J. Child Neurol.* **2009**, *24*, 170–175. [CrossRef]
11. Ghanizadeh, A.; Mosallaei, S. Psychiatric disorder and behavioral problems in children and adolescents with Tourette syndrome. *Brain Develop.* **2009**, *31*, 15–19. [CrossRef]
12. Huisman-van Dijk, H.M.; Schoot, R.V.; Rijkeboer, M.M.; Mathews, C.A.; Cath, D.C. The relationship between tics, OC, ADHD and autism symptoms: A cross- disorder symptom analysis in Gilles de la Tourette syndrome patients and family-members. *Psych. Res.* **2016**, *237*, 138–146. [CrossRef]
13. Darrow, S.M.; Grados, M.; Sandor, P.; Hirschtritt, M.E.; Illmann, C.; Osiecki, L.; Dion, Y.; King, R.; Pauls, D.; Budman, C.L.; et al. Autism spectrum symptoms in a Tourette syndrome sample. *J. Am. Acad. Child Adolesc. Psychiatry* **2017**, *56*, 610–617. [CrossRef] [PubMed]

14. Rizzo, R.; Gulisano, M.; Domini, C.N.; Ferro, M.C.; Curatolo, P. The relationship between autism spectrum disorder and tourette syndrome in childhood: An overview of shared characteristics. *J. Pediatr. Neurol.* **2017**, *15*, 115–122.
15. Worbe, Y.; Gerardin, E.; Hartmann, A.; Valabrégue, R.; Chupin, M.; Tremblay, L.; Vidailhet, M.; Colliot, O.; Lehéricy, S. Distinct structural changes underpin clinical phenotypes in patients with Gilles de la Tourette syndrome. *Brain* **2010**, *133*, 3649–3660. [CrossRef] [PubMed]
16. Kaufman, J.; Birmaher, B.; Brent, D.; Rao, U.; Flynn, C.; Moreci, P.; Williamson, D.; Ryan, N. Schedule for affective disorders and schizophrenia for school-age children-present and lifetime version (K-SADS-PL): Initial reliability and validity data. *J. Am. Acad. Child Adolesc. Psychiatry* **1997**, *36*, 980–988. [CrossRef]
17. Robertson, M.; Eapen, V. The National Hospital Interview Schedule for the assessment of Gilles de la Tourette syndrome. *Int. J. Methods Psychiatr. Res.* **1996**, *6*, 203–226. [CrossRef]
18. Leckman, J.F.; Riddle, M.A.; Hardin, M.T.; Ort, S.I.; Swartz, K.L.; Stevenson, J.; Cohen, D.J. The yale global tic severity scale: Initial testing of a clinician-rated scale of tic severity. *J. Am. Acad. Child Adolesc. Psychiatry* **1989**, *28*, 566–573. [CrossRef]
19. Scahill, L.; Riddle, M.A.; McSwiggin-Hardin, M.; Ort, S.I.; King, R.A.; Goodman, W.K.; Cicchetti, D.; Leckman, J.F. Children's Yale-Brown Obsessive Compulsive Scale: Reliability and validity. *J. Am. Acad. Child Adolesc. Psychiatry* **1997**, *36*, 844–852. [CrossRef]
20. Scahill, L.; Specht, M.; Page, C. The prevalence of tic disorders and clinical characteristics in children. *J. Obs. Compuls. Relat. Disord.* **2014**, *3*, 394–400. [CrossRef]
21. Lord, C.; Risi, S.; Lambrecht, L.; Cook, E.H., Jr.; Leventhal, B.L.; DiLavore, P.C.; Pickles, A.; Rutter, M. The autism diagnostic observation schedule-generic: A standard measure of social and communication deficits associated with the spectrum of autism. *J. Autism Dev. Disord.* **2000**, *30*, 205–223. [CrossRef]
22. Kim, S.H.; Lord, C. New autism diagnostic interview-revised algorithms for toddlers and young preschoolers from 12 to 47 months of age. *J. Autism Dev. Disord.* **2012**, *42*, 82–93. [CrossRef] [PubMed]
23. Hothorn, T.; Hornik, K.; Zeileis, A. Unbiased recursive partitioning: A conditional inference framework. *J. Comput. Graph. Stat.* **2006**, *15*, 651–674. [CrossRef]
24. Pine, D.S.; Guyer, A.E.; Goldwin, M.; Towbin, K.A. Autism spectrum disorder scale scores in pediatric mood and anxiety disorders. *Child Adolesc Psychiatry* **2008**, *47*, 652–661. [CrossRef] [PubMed]
25. Eapen, V.; McPherson, S.; Karlov, L.; Nicholls, L.; Črnčec, R.; Mulligan, A. Social communication deficits and restricted repetitive behavior symptoms in Tourette syndrome. *Neuropsychiatr. Dis. Treat.* **2019**, *15*, 2151–2160. [CrossRef]
26. Wu, M.S.; McGuire, J.F.; Arnold, E.B.; Lewin, A.B.; Murphy, T.K.; Storch, E.A. Psychometric properties of the Children's Yale-Brown Obsessive Compulsive Scale in youth with autism spectrum disorders and obsessive-compulsive symptoms. *Child Psychiatry Hum. Dev.* **2014**, *45*, 201–211. [CrossRef] [PubMed]
27. Scahill, L.; McDougle, C.J.; Williams, S.K.; Dimitropoulos, A.; Aman, M.G.; McCracken, J.T.; TIERNEY, E.; Arnold, L.E.; Cronin, P.; Grados, P.; et al. Children's Yale-Brown Obsessive Compulsive Scale modified for pervasive developmental disorders. *J. Am. Acad. Child Adolesc. Psychiatry* **2006**, *45*, 1114–1123. [CrossRef] [PubMed]
28. Zablotsky, B.; Black, L.I.; Maenner, M.J.; Schieve, L.A.; Blumberg, S.J. Estimated prevalence of autism and other developmental disabilities following questionnaire changes in the 2014 National Health Interview Survey. *Natl. Health Stat. Rep.* **2015**, *13*, 1–20.

6

Whole Exome Sequencing for a Patient with Rubinstein-Taybi Syndrome Reveals *de Novo* Variants besides an Overt *CREBBP* Mutation

Hee Jeong Yoo [1,2,†], Kyung Kim [3,4,7,†], In Hyang Kim [1], Seong-Hwan Rho [5], Jong-Eun Park [1], Ki Young Lee [4,7,‡], Soon Ae Kim [6], Byung Yoon Choi [2,8] and Namshin Kim [3,*]

1 Department of Psychiatry, Seoul National University Hospital, Seongnam, Gyeonggi 463-707, Korea; hjyoo@snu.ac.kr (H.J.Y.); iambabyvox@snu.ac.kr (I.H.K.); bulls18@snu.ac.kr (J.-E.P.)
2 Department of Psychiatry, Seoul National University, College of Medicine, Seoul 110-744, Korea; twinwif2@snu.ac.kr
3 Epigenomics Research Center, Genome Institute, Korea Research Institute of Bioscience and Biotechnology, Daejeon 305-806, Korea; kkyung412@gmail.com
4 Department of Biomedical Informatics, Ajou University, School of Medicine, Suwon 443-749, Korea; kiylee@ajou.ac.kr
5 Simulacre Modeling Group, Seoul 140-897, Korea; shrho@simulacre.re.kr
6 Department of Pharmacology, Eulji University College of Medicine, Daejeon 301-746, Korea; sakim@eulji.ac.kr
7 Department of Biomedical Science, Ajou University Graduate School of Medicine, Suwon 443-749, Korea
8 Department of Otolaryngology, Seoul National University Hospital, Seongnam, Gyeonggi 463-707, Korea
* Author to whom correspondence should be addressed; n@rna.kr/deepreds@kribb.re.kr
† These authors contributed equally to this work.
‡ Deceased.

Academic Editor: Merlin G. Butler

Abstract: Rubinstein-Taybi syndrome (RSTS) is a rare condition with a prevalence of 1 in 125,000–720,000 births and characterized by clinical features that include facial, dental, and limb dysmorphology and growth retardation. Most cases of RSTS occur sporadically and are caused by *de novo* mutations. Cytogenetic or molecular abnormalities are detected in only 55% of RSTS cases. Previous genetic studies have yielded inconsistent results due to the variety of methods used for genetic analysis. The purpose of this study was to use whole exome sequencing (WES) to evaluate the genetic causes of RSTS in a young girl presenting with an Autism phenotype. We used the Autism diagnostic observation schedule (ADOS) and Autism diagnostic interview revised (ADI-R) to confirm her diagnosis of Autism. In addition, various questionnaires were used to evaluate other psychiatric features. We used WES to analyze the DNA sequences of the patient and her parents and to search for *de novo* variants. The patient showed all the typical features of Autism, WES revealed a *de novo* frameshift mutation in *CREBBP* and *de novo* sequence variants in *TNC* and *IGFALS* genes. Mutations in the *CREBBP* gene have been extensively reported in RSTS patients, while potential missense mutations in *TNC* and *IGFALS* genes have not previously been associated with RSTS. The *TNC* and *IGFALS* genes are involved in central nervous system development and growth. It is possible for patients with RSTS to have additional *de novo* variants that could account for previously unexplained phenotypes.

Keywords: Rubinstein-Taybi syndrome (RSTS); Autism spectrum disorder (ASD); *de novo* variants; Tenascin C (*TNC*) gene; insulin-like growth factor-binding protein; acid labile subunit (*IGFALS*) gene; CREB (cAMP response element binding protein) binding protein (*CREBBP*) gene

1. Introduction

Rubinstein-Taybi syndrome (RSTS, OMIM 180849, 613684), also known as the broad thumb-hallux syndrome, is a rare condition with a prevalence of 1 in 125,000–720,000 births [1,2]. The syndrome is characterized by a group of well-defined clinical features including characteristic facial, dental, and limb dysmorphology, and growth retardation [3]. RSTS can also affect multiple internal organs including the heart, kidney, eyes, ears, and skin [4]. Patients are known to have an increased risk of developing non-cancerous and cancerous tumors, leukemia, and lymphoma [5]. Mental retardation and learning difficulties are other typical findings of RSTS. The average IQ of the patients is 35–50, although cognitive functioning outside this range has also been documented [6].

The diagnosis of RSTS is essentially a clinical diagnosis based on the features described above [7]. Most RSTS cases are sporadic and are caused by *de novo* mutations [8]. Cytogenetic or molecular abnormalities can be detected in only 55% of patients with RSTS [9]. Missense/non-sense mutations in genes encoding the CREB-binding protein (*CREBBP*) or the E1A-binding protein (*EP300*) are the most common, although micro-deletions in chromosome 16p13.3 and other rare mutations have also been reported as genetic causes of this condition [8,10–15]. Nevertheless, genetic analyses for identifying mutations in RSTS have often yielded inconsistent results, probably because of inadequacies in the methods used for the analyses, and many mutations remain unconfirmed. Previous studies examining genetic mutations in RSTS have mainly used fluorescence *in situ* hybridization (FISH) [16,17] or comparative genomic hybridization (CGH) array analyses [14]. Whole genome or exome sequencing (WES) methods have rarely been used. The purpose of this study was to use WES to evaluate the genetic causes of RSTS in a young girl presenting with RSTS and Autism spectrum disorder (ASD).

2. Results

2.1. Physical Characteristics

The typical dysmorphic features of RSTS were observed in the patient's face and mouth: Microcephaly (head circumference of 32 cm (approximately 3rd to 5th percentile) at birth and 47.8 cm (below the 3rd percentile) at her current age (6.75 years), highly arched eyebrows, long eyelashes, downward-slanting palpebral fissures, a broad nasal bridge, a beaked nose with the nasal septum extending well below the alae, a pouting lower lip, mild micrognathia, and dental crowding.

The patient had big toes that were short and broad, and mild clinodactyly of the fifth digits of both hands. The second, third, and fourth digits of the right hand had short distal phalanges, and the third and fourth digits of the left hand had broad distal phalanges. She also had a curly toe on the fourth digit of both feet and hallux valgus in the right foot. X-ray radiographs showed bilateral pes varus deformities and bilateral big-toe soft tissue thickening. There were abnormal accessory physes on the side of the distal phalanx, as well as other abnormalities in the physes of the big toes of both feet. Hand X-ray radiographs showed delayed carpal bone ossification in both hands and prominent thickening of the soft tissue of all fingers.

Marked growth retardation and poor weight gain were prominent in this patient from birth until her latest evaluation. Her height was 106.3 cm (below the 3rd percentile) and her weight was 17.2 kg (3rd percentile). A videofluoroscopic swallowing study revealed difficulty in swallowing. Furthermore, serum prealbumin and zinc levels were low. Other physical findings in the patient included anomalies of the eye (congenital cataract and nasolacrimal duct obstruction) and skin (pilomatrixoma on the left periauricular area, hypertrichosis on the forehead, anterior chest, and back, as well as nevus depigmentosus on the right calf). Gross hematuria had previously been found at five years of age, although a kidney ultrasound examination showed no abnormal findings. Results of cardiac evaluation were within normal limits. The characteristic physical features and growth curve of the patient are shown in Figure 1.

2.2. Neuropsychiatric and Behavioral Features

The patient showed pronounced developmental delay with no meaningful vocabulary. She also showed moderate mental retardation with a full-scale intelligence quotient (IQ) score of 37 on the Korean Wechsler Preschool and Primary Scale for Intelligence (K-WPPSI) and a score of 45 on the Leiter International Performance Scale. Her adaptive functioning level was equivalent to a child of approximately 3–5 years of age. She had shown the typical behavioral characteristics of Autism from early infancy, including abnormalities in communication and social interaction, along with repetitive behavior and restricted interests. Her scores surpassed the diagnostic thresholds on all categories of both the ADOS and ADI-R. She presented the distinctive mannerism of repetitively waving her hand whenever emotionally disturbed. Scores for other questionnaires also supported the diagnosis of Autism including a score of 15 on the social communication questionnaire (SCQ) and a score of 113 on the social component of the social responsiveness scale (SRS). Further behavioral characteristics included marked hyperactivity, short attention span, withdrawal, and poor motor coordination. Frequent snoring was reported, although the possibility of obstructive sleep apnea was deemed low. Brain magnetic resonance imaging (MRI) showed mild pachygyria. Electroencephalogram (EEG) showed intermittent diffuse high-amplitude semirhythmic 1–1.5-Hz delta activity and one episode of diffuse 1.5-Hz rhythmic, synchronous bifrontal δ/ζ activity lasting up to 20 s.

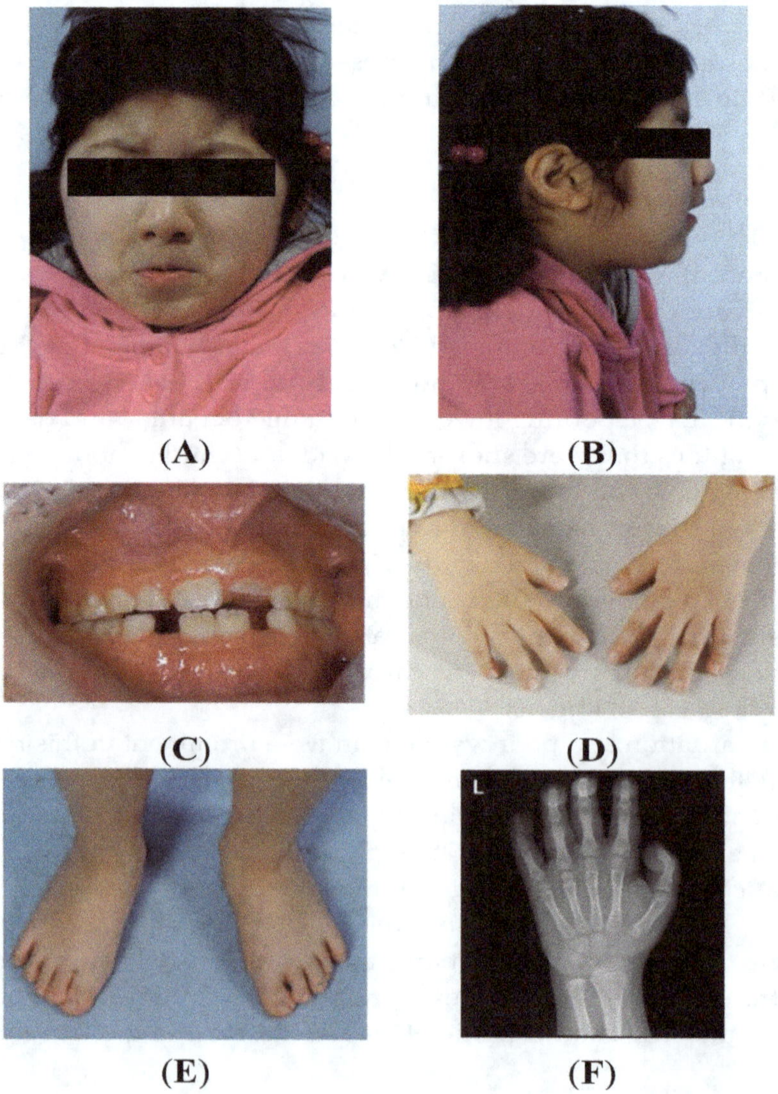

Figure 1. *Cont.*

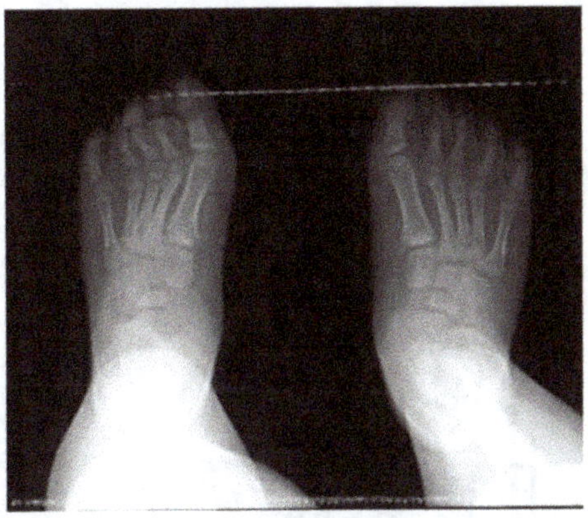

(G)

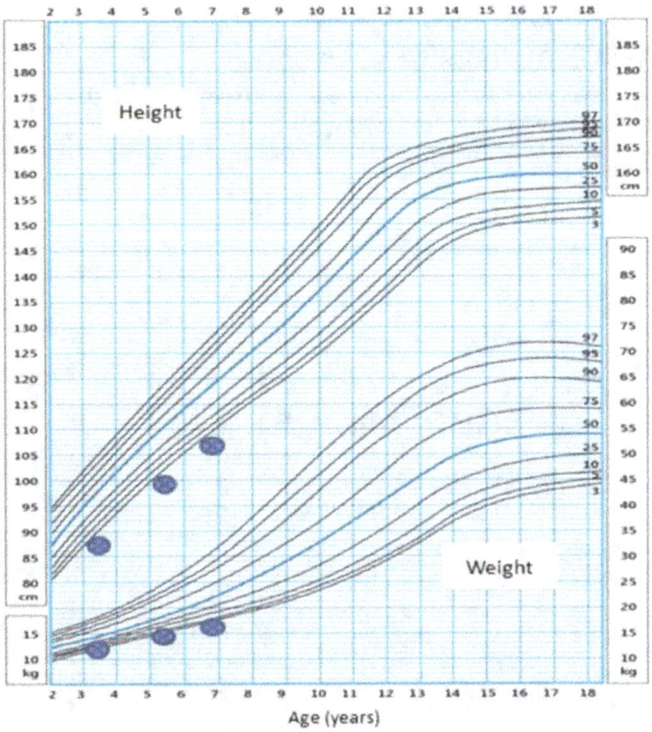

(H)

Figure 1. Physical characteristics of the proband. Patient's eyes are covered for reasons of confidentiality. Typical facial dysmorphic features can be observed in (**A**,**B**), including highly arched eyebrows, a broad nasal bridge, beaked nose with the nasal septum extending well below the alae, a pouting lower lip, and mild micrognathia. Dental crowding is shown in (**C**); The hand and feet abnormalities are shown in (**D**,**E**), showing short and broad big toes and thumbs, as well as mild clinodactyly on the 5th digit of both hands. The 2nd, 3rd, 4th digits of the right hand had short distal phalanges and the 3rd, 4th digits of the left hand had broad distal phalanges. The X-ray of the left hand shows delayed carpal bone ossification and prominent thickening of the soft tissue of all fingers (**F**); The X-ray of the feet shows bilateral pes varus deformities and abnormalities in the physes of big toe metatarsal bones (**G**); Growth curve (**H**) shows marked growth retardation in the proband (blue dot) superimposed on the normal growth curve of Korean girls of age 2 to 18 (black line). The growth curve shows the height and weight changes of the patient over time. These values never exceeded the third percentile since birth. Data for normal growth curve came from the Korea Center for Disease Control and Prevention.

2.3. *Genetic Variants*

Cytogenetic analyses showed normal karyotypes in the proband and both parents. Using in-depth statistics, we obtained a mean read-depth coverage of 120× over the targeted exome. Each exome contained more than 120,000 total variant calls. An average of 111 million individual paired-end reads of 100 bp were aligned to the human reference genome. More than 94% of targeted exon regions were covered with at least 10× depth, which is sufficient for variant discovery.

We found three *de novo* variants after filtering for all common variants in the dbSNP (except clinically associated variants) and an in-house control database comprising normal healthy individuals. We performed a visual inspection of read alignments using the Integrative Genomics Viewer (IGV) browser, and then removed "Benign" and "Likely Benign" variants after classification. A summary of the detected variants is described in Table S1.

Three *de novo* variants were validated by Sanger sequencing: a frameshift mutation in *CREBBP* (c.2199delG), and missense mutations in *TNC* (c.323G > A) and *IGFALS* (c.1415C > T). The results of family sequencing analyses are shown in Figure 2 and the properties of the *de novo* variants are summarized in Table 1 and Figure 2. The genetic variants of the proband and both parents are shown in Figure 3.

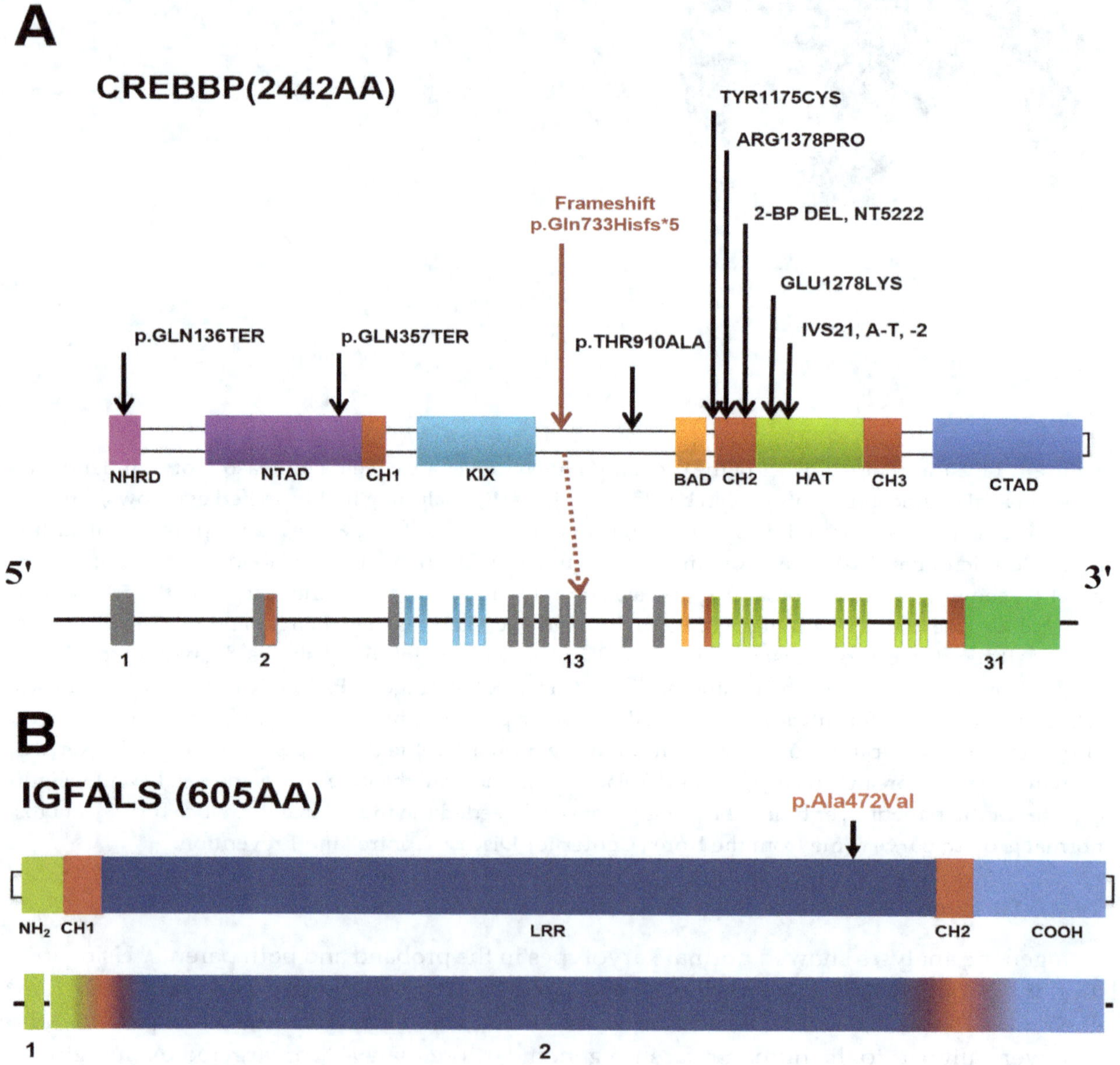

Figure 2. *Cont.*

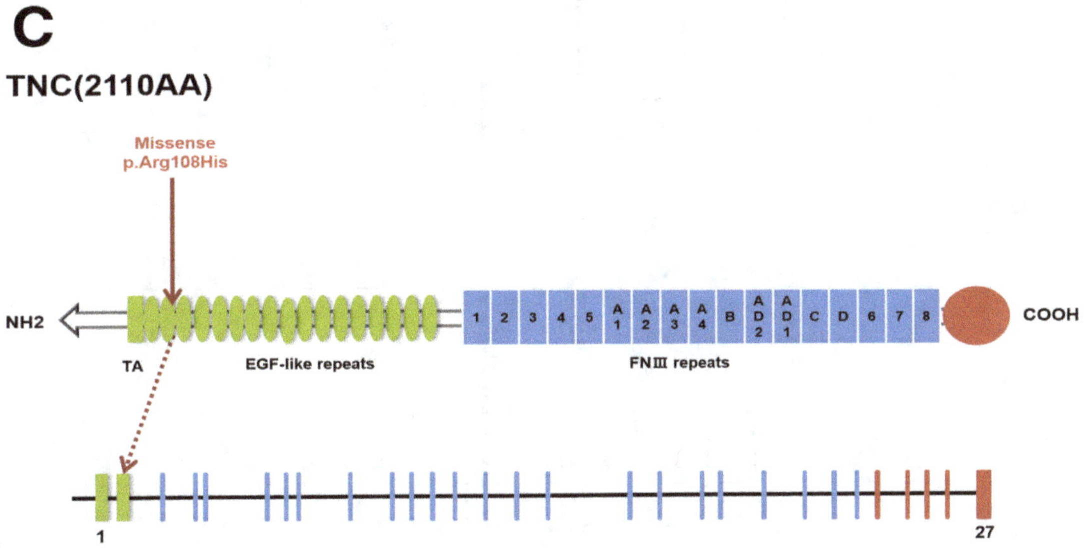

Figure 2. Schematic of *de novo* variants of *CREBBP*, *IGFALS*, and *TNC* in RSTS. (**A**) Genomic alterations and schematic drawing of proteins showing the predicted effects of selected missense mutations identified in *CREBBP*. The p.Thy1174Cys and p.Thr910Ala substitutions predicted by missense mutations do not affect known functional domains and are associated with a mild phenotype compared with the classic phenotype expected for mutations at other sites. The frameshift mutation p.Gln733Hisfs*5 is predicted to interrupt all of the following functional domains: BAD, CH2, HAT, CH3, and CTAD; (**B**) The *IGFALS* mutation site affects the LRR domain and (**C**) the *TNC* mutation one of the EGF-like repeats. The *de novo* variants are shown in red. CREBBP: CREB (cAMP response element-binding protein) binding protein; IGFALS: Insulin-like growth factor)-binding protein, acid labile subunit; TNC: Tenascin C; Protein domain names: (**A**) NHRD: Nuclear receptor-binding and receptor-interacting domain; NTAD: Amino-terminal transactivation domain; CH1: Cys/His-rich region; CREB/KIX: CREB-binding domain; BROMO/BRD: Bromo domain; HAT: Histone acetyltransferase domain; CH2: Cys/His-rich region 2; CH3: Cys/His-rich region 3; CTAD: C-terminal transactivation domain; (**B**) NH2: *N*-terminal; CH1: Cys-rich region 1; LRR: Leucine rich repeats; CH2: Cys-rich region 2; COOH: *C*-terminal; (**C**) TA: *N*-terminal tenascin assembly domain; EGF-like repeats: Epidermal growth factor-like repeats; FNIII repeats: Fibronectin type III-like repeats; FN Globe: *C*-terminal fibrinogen globe

Table 1. The three *de novo* variants validated by Sanger Sequencing.

Gene	*TNC*	*IGFALS*	*CREBBP*
Chromosome	chr9	chr16	chr16
Position	117852975	1841118	3823901
Reference Allele	C	G	C
Alternative Allele	T	A	–
Mutation Type	Missense	Missense	Frameshift
Sequence Variant	c.323G>A	c.1415C>T	c.2199delG
Protein Variant	p.Arg108His	p.Ala472Val	p.Gln733Hisfs*5
phyloP Score	2.369	0.598	1.492
GERP Score	1200.8	2536.4	476.2
SIFT Score	0	0.30	–
Mutation Assessor	1.87	0.995	–
Classification [1]	Likely pathogenic [2]	Variants of unknown significance	Pathogenic

[1] Variant Classification is based on the recommendations of Ambry Genetics, but pathogenicity of *de novo* variants in *TNC* and *IGFALS* are not certain; [2] *TNC* c.323G>A is reported in dbSNP as rs151119387, but MAF/MinorAlleleCount = 0.0002/1. Overall MAF in 1000 genomes, ESP6500, ExAc database is less than 0.0003. *TNC*: Tenascin C; *IGFALS*: Insulin-like growth factor-binding protein, acid labile subunit; *CREBBP*: CREB (cAMP response element-binding protein) binding protein; phyloP: Phylogenetic *p*-values; GERP: Genomic evolutionary rate profiling; SIFT: Sorting intolerant from tolerant.

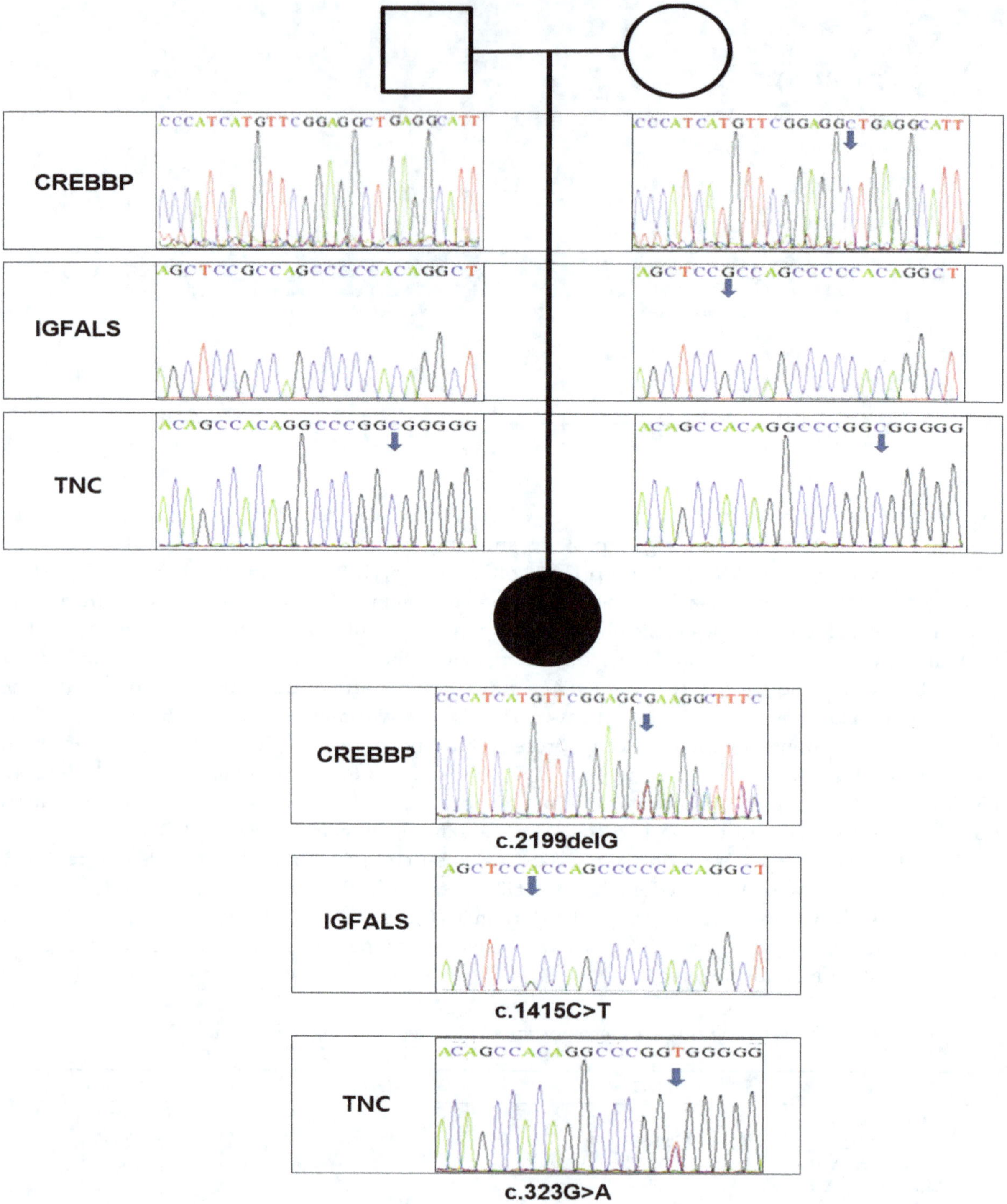

Figure 3. Sequences of *CREBBP*, *IGFALS*, and *TNC* for the family trio. A downward arrow indicates the mutated residue and nucleotides are shown in colored, single-letter codes. The black circle indicates the proband.

None of the observed sequence changes were observed in normal Korean subjects. The validation results from the normal population are shown in Figure 4.

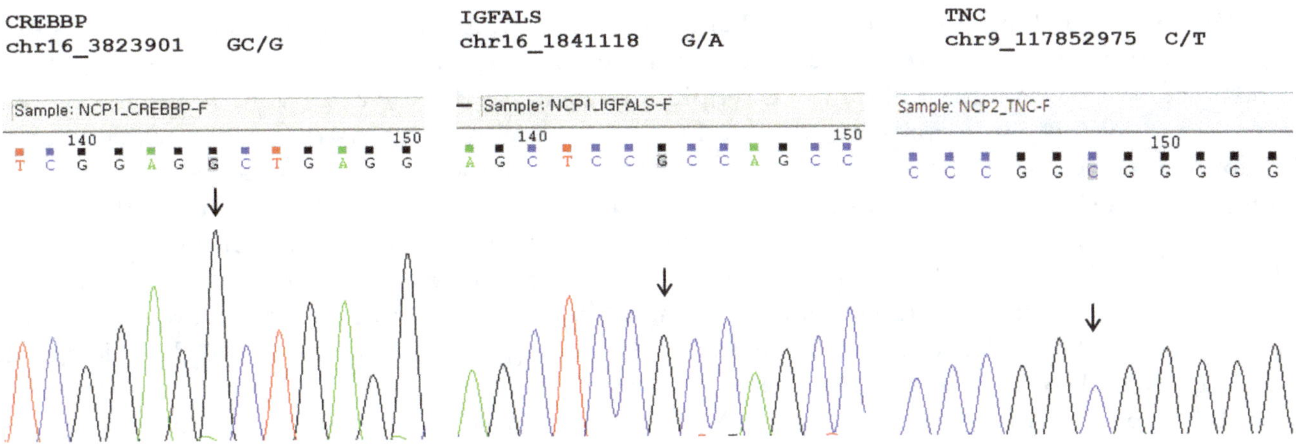

Figure 4. Validation results for *de novo* variants in *CREBBP*, *IGFALS*, and *TNC* in 80 normal Korean subjects. The downward arrow indicates the residue of *de novo* variants.

3. Discussion

We have shown that *de novo* variants in the *CREBBP*, *TNC*, and *IGFALS* genes are potential causes for RSTS by analyzing the whole genome of a female patient with RSTS. In WES analyses, we observed *de novo* variants in the *CREBBP*, *TNC*, and *IGFALS* genes. The girl showed typical morphological findings of RSTS, including abnormal features of the face, fingers, and toes, as well as growth retardation. Major characteristics of this patient were severe developmental/behavioral problems together with ASD with typical features that fulfilled the diagnostic criteria in multiple domains including communication, social interaction, specialized interests, and repetitive behavior.

Developmental/behavioral problems are common in patients with RSTS, with the most typical symptoms being moderate to severe mental retardation and language impairment [8,18]. There are no definitive reports regarding the specific frequency of psychiatric disorders in RSTS due to its low prevalence. In terms of autistic behavior, only a few reports have described this specific psychopathology associated with RSTS. In one relatively large-scale study exploring the socio-behavioral characteristics of RSTS, this syndrome was associated with behavioral problems such as a short attention span, motor stereotypies, and poor coordination [19]. These can also be part of the behavioral phenotype of ASD. The studies that have reported Autism-like phenotypes in patients with RSTS describe milder and atypical forms of ASD (*i.e.*, pervasive developmental disorder not otherwise specified; PDD NOS) in only a small proportion (8%) of the subjects [20–23].

Mutations in the *CREBBP* gene are one of the most commonly reported genetic etiologies of RSTS (Table S2). *CREBBP* mutations are found in 50%–60% of RSTS cases, whereas *EP300* (OMIM 602700) mutations are found in 5% of the cases [7,8]. RSTS is assumed to be a genetically heterogeneous disorder which is caused by mutations in the *CREBBP* gene as well as in other genes in up to 50% of cases [2]. The *CREBBP* mutations are heterogeneous, as 160 different mutations have been identified (Leiden Open Variation Database v.2.0 Build 35) [24]. The *CREBBP* gene is ubiquitously expressed and is involved in the transcriptional co-activation of many transcription factors [25]. *CREBBP* is also involved in multiple signaling pathways and in other cellular functions such as DNA repair, cell growth, differentiation, apoptosis, and tumor suppression [26]. The CREBBP protein plays an important role in regulating cell growth and division and is essential for normal fetal development. If one copy of *CREBBP* is deleted or mutated, cells make only half the normal amount of CREBBP protein. This reduction in the amount of this protein is thought to disrupt normal development before and after birth. The *CREBBP* mutation is known to be associated with more severe symptomatology than the *EP300* mutations [24]. Based on previous studies, the severe cognitive symptomatology of the subject of this study, including the ASD phenotype, could be attributed to the *CREBBP* mutation.

We can infer that the *de novo* sequence changes of the *TNC* and *IGFALS* genes, featuring as missense mutations observed in our study could potentially explain any additional phenotypes in patients with RSTS, but experimental validation is required to establish disease causation. Tenascin C (TNC), encoded by *TNC*, is a glycoprotein expressed in the extracellular matrix of various tissues during development, disease, or injury, as well as in restricted areas of the central nervous system involved in neurogenesis [27]. TNC expression changes during development until adulthood. In the developing central nervous system, it is involved in regulating the proliferation of both oligodendrocyte precursor cells and astrocytes [28]. TNC expression by radial glia precedes the onset of gliogenesis, and is thought to drive astrocyte differentiation. In the adult brain, TNC expression is downregulated in all areas except the hypothalamus and areas that maintain neurogenesis into adulthood [28]. Male-specific association signals have been found in the intronic region of the *TNC* gene [29]. A missense mutation c.5317G>A (p.V1773M) in exon 19 of the *TNC* gene was recently reported as a causative gene for nonsyndromic hearing loss in family-based exome sequencing and linkage analyses [30]. Based on the fact that pronounced-to-profound bilateral hearing loss or deafness is diagnosed more commonly in ASD than in the general population, the causality of deafness and ASD might have a partial overlap [31]. This study suggests that mutations in the *TNC* gene could contribute to sensory impairment in ASD, including hearing loss. The patient with RSTS in this study showed slight hearing problems (data now provided), but it is still not clear which specific aspect of the patient's phenotype can be attributed to the missense mutations in *TNC*.

To date, the presence of a genetic mutation in *CREBBP* has been linked with the behavioral phenotype in RSTS. For example, poor coordination is more prevalent in patients with RSTS and in subjects with genetic abnormalities in *CREBBP* than in those who have no abnormalities in this gene [19]. Severe cognitive impairments and autistic features have been reported in patients with large deletions in *CREBBP* [32]. This can be explained by the involvement of CREB-dependent gene transcription in long-term memory formation through signaling pathways that include multiple important kinases (protein kinase A, mitogen-activated protein kinase, and calcium/calmodulin-dependent kinase IV (CaMKIV)) in the nervous systems of many species [2]. The mental retardation and cognitive phenotype in patients with RSTS may be derived from impairments to the function of CREB-binding protein [2,13]. The role of the *CREBBP* mutation in long-term memory formation is supported by experiments showing that memory impairments in a $CREBBP^{+/-}$ mutant mouse model were ameliorated by phosphodiesterase 4 inhibitors [33]. Our observations suggest that *de novo* variants can have an additive effect and produce more severe and defined neurological/cognitive aberrations in subjects with RSTS.

The acid-labile subunit of insulin-like growth factor-binding protein (IGFALS) encoded by the *IGFALS* gene, is a serum protein that binds to IGFs. The IGFALS protein interacts with growth hormones to increase their half-life as well as their vascular localization [34]. *IGFALS*-dependent growth changes related to sex-specific body characteristics and bone size have been reported previously [35,36]. Defects in this gene cause acid-labile subunit deficiency which manifests as delayed and slow development during puberty [37]. The growth retardation in our patient, which has been present from birth until her current age, might be enhanced by the variants in the *IGFALS* gene.

One limitation of our study is that the analysis was restricted to only a single case. Validation of our results was also performed using relatively small samples from the general population. The precise function of the mutations and variants needs to be validated in future studies.

In conclusion, using WES, we observed *de novo* variants in the *CREBBP*, *TNC*, and *IGFALS* genes in a female patient with RSTS. To our knowledge, this is the first report suggesting that variants in the *TNC* and *IGFALS* genes can produce additional phenotypic effects. We assume that *de novo* variants in the *TNC* gene are related to the neurological phenotype and those in the *IGFALS* gene are related to growth retardation.

4. Methods

4.1. Ethics Statement

This study was approved by the Institutional Review Board (IRB) of the Seoul National University Bundang Hospital (Seongnam, Gyeonggi, Korea). Written informed consent was obtained from both parents of the patient.

4.2. Subject

The patient, a girl aged 6 years and 8 months, was examined in the child psychiatry clinic of the Seoul National University Bundang Hospital. She was thoroughly evaluated to assess problems related to delayed development and dysmorphology. A genetic assessment to diagnose RSTS, a possibility indicated during a previous diagnosis process, was also performed. The patient was the only child of a healthy non-consanguineous couple. Both biological parents were healthy with no clinically significant medical, developmental, or neuropsychological illnesses.

4.3. Clinical Evaluation

Thorough physical and laboratory evaluations were performed to confirm the diagnosis of RSTS and obtain detailed clinical and behavioral features. Physical, dental, ophthalmologic, and dermatologic examinations were performed. Chest and limb/digit X-ray radiography, urine and blood tests, a videofluoroscopic swallowing study, kidney ultrasonography, echocardiography, and electrocardiography were all performed as part of the laboratory analyses. Intelligence and adaptive functioning were assessed using the Korean version of the Wechsler preschool and primary scale of intelligence (K-WPPSI), the Leiter international performance scale [6,38], and the Vineland Adaptive Behavior scale (VABS) [39,40]. Two board-certified child psychiatrists evaluated the autistic symptoms. The Autism diagnostic observation schedule (ADOS), Module I [41,42], and the Autism diagnostic interview-revised (ADI-R) [43,44] were used, as well as the social communication questionnaire (SCQ) and social responsiveness scale (SRS) [45,46]. We measured the patients sleep quality using the Pittsburgh sleep quality index (PSQI) [47] and the "STOP" questionnaire (snoring, tiredness during daytime, observed apnea, high blood pressure) [48]. Brain magnetic resonance imaging (MRI) and electroencephalography (EEG) were performed to elucidate potential structural and functional abnormalities in the brain.

4.4. Genetic Analyses Using Bioinformatics Tools

Blood samples were drawn from the patient and both biological parents. Genomic DNA was extracted using the DNeasy Blood & Tissue kit (QIAGEN, Valencia, CA, USA). Raw reads in FASTQ format from exome sequencing were aligned to the hg19 reference genome from the UCSC genome browser using the Burrows–Wheeler Aligner (BWA) [49] with default parameters. Aligned reads were processed and polymerase chain reaction (PCR) duplicates were removed with SAMtools [50]. Single-nucleotide variants (SNVs) and insertions/deletions (indels) were identified using the Genome Analysis Toolkit (GATK) [51]. Regions near short indels were realigned using the IndelRealigner function in GATK according to default parameters. SNVs and indels affecting coding sequences or splicing sites were annotated by an in-house custom-made annotation system. All genomic changes were filtered against the Single Nucleotide Polymorphism Database (dbSNP; build 141) and the in-house control database comprising 54 Korean individuals.

We classified the *de novo* variants using the recommendations of Ambry Genetics (Scheme for AD and XD Mendelian disorders) into five categories: Benign, VLB (Variant, Likely benign), VUS (Variant, Unknown significance), VLP (Variant, Likely pathogenic), and Pathogenic mutation. Variants classified as VUS, VLP, and Pathogenic mutation were also confirmed using an IGV browser. To evaluate the mutations in the general population, we also applied Sanger sequencing for these mutations to 80 normal subjects belonging to the Korean ethnic group.

5. Conclusions

RSTS is a rare disorder characterized by facial, dental, and limb dysmorphology, growth retardation, and developmental disorders including intellectual disability and Autism spectrum disorder. Although many *de novo* mutations have been proposed as the genetic cause of RSTS, genetic analyses to identify mutations have often yielded inconsistent results due to inadequacies in the analysis methods, and many mutations are yet to be confirmed. The objective of this study was to investigate the genetic background of a young girl with RSTS presenting with an Autism phenotype, using whole exome sequencing (WES). We observed *de novo* variants in the *CREBBP*, *TNC*, and *IGFALS* genes. As far as the authors know, this is the first report to suggest that the *TNC* and *IGFALS* genes might contribute to clinical signs that are uncommon in RSTS patients.

Acknowledgments: A summary of this article was previously presented at the Annual Meeting of the American Society of Human Genetics, 2013, in Boston, MA, USA.

This work was supported by the Korea Healthcare Technology R&D project, Ministry of Health & Welfare, Republic of Korea [Grant Number A120029], Korean NRF grants (2011-0030049), and a grant from KRIBB Research Initiative Program.

Author Contributions: Hee Jeong Yoo and Seong-Hwan Rho recruited subjects. Hee Jeong Yoo and In Hyang Kim performed psychiatric and behavioral assessment of the subject. Namshin Kim, Hee Jeong Yoo and Ki Young Lee conceived and designed the experiments. Soon Ae Kim and Byung Yoon Choi performed the experiments. Kyung Kim and Namshin Kim analyzed the data. Kyung Kim, Hee Jeong Yoo, In Hyang Kim, Jong-Eun Park, and Namshin Kim wrote the paper.

References

1. Hennekam, R.C.; Stevens, C.A.; van de Kamp, J.J. Etiology and recurrence risk in Rubinstein-Taybi syndrome. *Am. J. Med. Genet. Suppl.* **1990**, *6*, 56–64. [PubMed]
2. Hallam, T.M.; Bourtchouladze, R. Rubinstein-Taybi syndrome: Molecular findings and therapeutic approaches to improve cognitive dysfunction. *Cell. Mol. Life Sci.* **2006**, *63*, 1725–1735. [CrossRef] [PubMed]
3. Rubinstein, J.H.; Taybi, H. Broad thumbs and toes and facial abnormalities. A possible mental retardation syndrome. *Am. J. Dis. Child.* **1963**, *105*, 588–608. [CrossRef] [PubMed]
4. Wiley, S.; Swayne, S.; Rubinstein, J.H.; Lanphear, N.E.; Stevens, C.A. Rubinstein-Taybi syndrome medical guidelines. *Am. J. Med. Genet. Part A* **2003**, *119A*, 101–110. [CrossRef]
5. Miller, R.W.; Rubinstein, J.H. Tumors in Rubinstein-Taybi syndrome. *Am. J. Med. Genet.* **1995**, *56*, 112–115. [CrossRef] [PubMed]
6. Hennekam, R.C.; Baselier, A.C.; Beyaert, E.; Bos, A.; Blok, J.B.; Jansma, H.B.; Thorbecke-Nilsen, V.V.; Veerman, H. Psychological and speech studies in Rubinstein-Taybi syndrome. *Am. J. Mental Retard.* **1992**, *96*, 645–660.
7. Hennekam, R.C. Rubinstein-Taybi syndrome. *Eur. J. Hum. Genet.* **2006**, *14*, 981–985. [CrossRef] [PubMed]
8. Roelfsema, J.H.; White, S.J.; Ariyurek, Y.; Bartholdi, D.; Niedrist, D.; Papadia, F.; Bacino, C.A.; den Dunnen, J.T.; van Ommen, G.J.; Breuning, M.H.; *et al.* Genetic heterogeneity in Rubinstein-Taybi syndrome: Mutations in both the *CBP* and *EP300* genes cause disease. *Am. J. Hum. Genet.* **2005**, *76*, 572–580. [CrossRef] [PubMed]
9. Bartsch, O.; Schmidt, S.; Richter, M.; Morlot, S.; Seemanova, E.; Wiebe, G.; Rasi, S. DNA sequencing of CREBBP demonstrates mutations in 56% of patients with Rubinstein-Taybi syndrome (RSTS) and in another patient with incomplete RSTS. *Hum. Genet.* **2005**, *117*, 485–493. [CrossRef] [PubMed]
10. Bentivegna, A.; Milani, D.; Gervasini, C.; Castronovo, P.; Mottadelli, F.; Manzini, S.; Colapietro, P.; Giordano, L.; Atzeri, F.; Divizia, M.T. Rubinstein-Taybi syndrome: Spectrum of *CREBBP* mutations in Italian patients. *BMC Med. Genet.* **2006**, *7*, 77. [CrossRef] [PubMed]
11. Negri, G.; Milani, D.; Colapietro, P.; Forzano, F.; Monica, M.D.; Rusconi, D.; Consonni, L.; Caffi, L.G.; Finelli, P.; Scarano, G.; *et al.* Clinical and molecular characterization of Rubinstein-Taybi syndrome patients carrying distinct novel mutations of the *EP300* gene. *Clin. Genet.* **2015**, *87*, 148–154. [CrossRef]
12. Spena, S.; Milani, D.; Rusconi, D.; Negri, G.; Colapietro, P.; Elcioglu, N.; Bedeschi, F.; Pilotta, A.; Spaccini, L.; Ficcadenti, A. Insights into genotype–phenotype correlations from *CREBBP* point mutation screening in a cohort of 46 Rubinstein-Taybi syndrome patients. *Clin. Genet.* **2014**. [CrossRef]

13. Petrij, F.; Giles, R.H.; Dauwerse, H.G.; Saris, J.J.; Hennekam, R.C.; Masuno, M.; Tommerup, N.; van Ommen, G.J.; Goodman, R.H.; Peters, D.J.; *et al.* Rubinstein-Taybi syndrome caused by mutations in the transcriptional co-activator CBP. *Nature* **1995**, *376*, 348–351. [CrossRef] [PubMed]
14. Tsai, A.C.-H.; Dossett, C.J.; Walton, C.S.; Cramer, A.E.; Eng, P.A.; Nowakowska, B.A.; Pursley, A.N.; Stankiewicz, P.; Wiszniewska, J.; Cheung, S.W. Exon deletions of the *EP300* and *CREBBP* genes in two children with Rubinstein-Taybi syndrome detected by aCGH. *Eur. J. Hum. Genet.* **2011**, *19*, 43–49. [CrossRef] [PubMed]
15. Kim, S.R.; Kim, H.J.; Kim, Y.J.; Kwon, J.Y.; Kim, J.W.; Kim, S.H. Cryptic microdeletion of the *CREBBP* gene from t(1;16) (p36.2;p13.3) as a novel genetic defect causing Rubinstein-Taybi syndrome. *Ann. Clin. Lab. Sci.* **2013**, *43*, 450–456. [PubMed]
16. Blough, R.I.; Petrij, F.; Dauwerse, J.G.; Milatovich-Cherry, A.; Weiss, L.; Saal, H.M.; Rubinstein, J.H. Variation in microdeletions of the cyclic AMP-responsive element-binding protein gene at chromosome band 16p13. 3 in the Rubinstein-Taybi syndrome. *Am. J. Med. Genet.* **2000**, *90*, 29–34. [CrossRef] [PubMed]
17. Gervasini, C.; Castronovo, P.; Bentivegna, A.; Mottadelli, F.; Faravelli, F.; Giovannucci-Uzielli, M.L.; Pessagno, A.; Lucci-Cordisco, E.; Pinto, A.M.; Salviati, L. High frequency of mosaic *CREBBP* deletions in Rubinstein–Taybi syndrome patients and mapping of somatic and germ-line breakpoints. *Genomics* **2007**, *90*, 567–573. [CrossRef] [PubMed]
18. Stevens, C.A.; Hennekam, R.C.; Blackburn, B.L. Growth in the Rubinstein-Taybi syndrome. *Am. J. Med. Genet. Suppl.* **1990**, *6*, 51–55. [PubMed]
19. Galera, C.; Taupiac, E.; Fraisse, S.; Naudion, S.; Toussaint, E.; Rooryck-Thambo, C.; Delrue, M.A.; Arveiler, B.; Lacombe, D.; Bouvard, M.P. Socio-behavioral characteristics of children with Rubinstein-Taybi syndrome. *J. Autism Dev. Disord.* **2009**, *39*, 1252–1260. [CrossRef] [PubMed]
20. Calì, F.; Failla, P.; Chiavetta, V.; Ragalmuto, A.; Ruggeri, G.; Schinocca, P.; Schepis, C.; Romano, V.; Romano, C. Multiplex ligation-dependent probe amplification detection of an unknown large deletion of the *CREB-binding protein* gene in a patient with Rubinstein-Taybi syndrome. *CEP* **2013**, *14025*, 220.
21. Hellings, J.A.; Hossain, S.; Martin, J.K.; Baratang, R.R. Psychopathology, GABA, and the Rubinstein-Taybi syndrome: A review and case study. *Am. J. Med. Genet.* **2002**, *114*, 190–195. [CrossRef] [PubMed]
22. Levitas, A.S.; Reid, C.S. Rubinstein-Taybi syndrome and psychiatric disorders. *J. Intellect. Disabil. Res.* **1998**, *42*, 284–292. [CrossRef] [PubMed]
23. Waite, J.; Moss, J.; Beck, S.R.; Richards, C.; Nelson, L.; Arron, K.; Burbidge, C.; Berg, K.; Oliver, C. Repetitive behavior in Rubinstein-Taybi syndrome: Parallels with Autism spectrum phenomenology. *J. Autism Dev. Disord.* **2014**. [CrossRef]
24. Lopez-Atalaya, J.P.; Valor, L.M.; Barco, A. Epigenetic factors in intellectual disability: The Rubinstein-Taybi syndrome as a paradigm of neurodevelopmental disorder with epigenetic origin. *Prog. Mol. Biol. Transl. Sci.* **2014**, *128*, 139. [PubMed]
25. Goodman, R.H.; Smolik, S. CBP/p300 in cell growth, transformation, and development. *Genes Dev.* **2000**, *14*, 1553–1577. [PubMed]
26. Marzuillo, P.; Grandone, A.; Coppola, R.; Cozzolino, D.; Festa, A.; Messa, F.; Luongo, C.; del Giudice, E.M.; Perrone, L. Novel cAMP binding protein-BP (*CREBBP*) mutation in a girl with Rubinstein-Taybi syndrome, GH deficiency, Arnold Chiari malformation and pituitary hypoplasia. *BMC Med. Genet.* **2013**, *14*, 28. [CrossRef] [PubMed]
27. Nies, D.E.; Hemesath, T.J.; Kim, J.-H.; Gulcher, J.R.; Stefansson, K. The complete cDNA sequence of human hexabrachion (Tenascin). A multidomain protein containing unique epidermal growth factor repeats. *J. Biol. Chem.* **1991**, *266*, 2818–2823. [PubMed]
28. Wiese, S.; Karus, M.; Faissner, A. Astrocytes as a source for extracellular matrix molecules and cytokines. *Front. Pharmacol.* **2012**, *3*, 120. [CrossRef] [PubMed]
29. Chang, S.C.; Pauls, D.L.; Lange, C.; Sasanfar, R.; Santangelo, S.L. Sex-specific association of a common variant of the *XG* gene with Autism spectrum disorders. *Am. J. Med. Genet. Part B* **2013**, *162*, 742–750. [CrossRef]
30. Zhao, Y.; Zhao, F.; Zong, L.; Zhang, P.; Guan, L.; Zhang, J.; Wang, D.; Wang, J.; Chai, W.; Lan, L.; *et al.* Exome sequencing and linkage analysis identified tenascin-C (*TNC*) as a novel causative gene in nonsyndromic hearing loss. *PLoS One* **2013**, *8*, e69549. [CrossRef] [PubMed]

31. Rosenhall, U.; Nordin, V.; Sandstrom, M.; Ahlsen, G.; Gillberg, C. Autism and hearing loss. *J. Autism Dev. Disord.* **1999**, *29*, 349–357. [CrossRef] [PubMed]
32. Schorry, E.; Keddache, M.; Lanphear, N.; Rubinstein, J.; Srodulski, S.; Fletcher, D.; Blough-Pfau, R.; Grabowski, G. Genotype–phenotype correlations in Rubinstein-Taybi syndrome. *Am. J. Med. Genet. Part A* **2008**, *146*, 2512–2519. [CrossRef]
33. Bourtchouladze, R.; Lidge, R.; Catapano, R.; Stanley, J.; Gossweiler, S.; Romashko, D.; Scott, R.; Tully, T. A mouse model of Rubinstein-Taybi syndrome: Defective long-term memory is ameliorated by inhibitors of phosphodiesterase 4. *Proc. Natl. Acad. Sci. USA* **2003**, *100*, 10518–10522. [CrossRef] [PubMed]
34. Leong, S.R.; Baxter, R.C.; Camerato, T.; Dai, J.; Wood, W.I. Structure and functional expression of the acid-labile subunit of the insulin-like growth factor-binding protein complex. *Mol. Endocrinol.* **1992**, *6*, 870–876. [PubMed]
35. Courtland, H.W.; DeMambro, V.; Maynard, J.; Sun, H.; Elis, S.; Rosen, C.; Yakar, S. Sex-specific regulation of body size and bone slenderness by the acid labile subunit. *J. Bone Miner. Res.* **2010**, *25*, 2059–2068. [CrossRef] [PubMed]
36. Domene, H.; Bengolea, S.; Jasper, H.; Boisclair, Y. Acid-labile subunit deficiency: Phenotypic similarities and differences between human and mouse. *J. Endocrinol. Investig.* **2004**, *28*, 43–46.
37. Domené, H.M.; Scaglia, P.A.; Lteif, A.; Mahmud, F.H.; Kirmani, S.; Frystyk, J.; Bedecarrás, P.; Gutiérrez, M.; Jasper, H.G. Phenotypic effects of null and haploinsufficiency of acid-labile subunit in a family with two novel *IGFALS* gene mutations. *J. Clin. Endocrinol. Metab.* **2007**, *92*, 4444–4450. [CrossRef] [PubMed]
38. Park, H.W.; Kwak, K.J.; Park, G.B. *Korean Wechsler Preschool and Primary Scale of Intelligence*; Special Education Publishing: Seoul, Korean, 2002.
39. Sparrow, S.; Balla, D.; Cichetti, D. *Vineland Adaptive Behavior Scales*; American Guidance Services: Circle Pines, MN, USA, 1984.
40. Aylward, G. *Practitioner's Guide to Developmental and Psychological Testing*; Springer: New York, NY, USA, 1994.
41. Lord, C.; Rutter, M.; DiLavore, P.D.; Risi, S. *Autism Diagnostic Observation Schedule*; Western Psychological Services: Los Angeles, CA, USA, 2001.
42. Lord, C.; Rutter, M.; Goode, S.; Heemsbergen, J.; Jordan, H.; Mawhood, L.; Schopler, E. Autism diagnostic observation schedule: A standardized observation of communicative and social behavior. *J. Autism Dev. Disord.* **1989**, *19*, 185–212. [CrossRef] [PubMed]
43. Le Couteur, A.; Lord, C.; Rutter, M. *The Autism Diagnostic Interview-Revised (ADI-R)*; Western Psychological Services: Los Angeles, CA, USA, 2003.
44. Lord, C.; Rutter, M.; Le Couteur, A. Autism diagnostic interview-revised: A revised version of a diagnostic interview for caregivers of individuals with possible pervasive developmental disorders. *J. Autism Dev. Disord.* **1994**, *24*, 659–685. [CrossRef] [PubMed]
45. Constantino, J.; Gruber, C.P. *Social Responsiveness Scale (SRS)*; Western Psychological Services: Los Angeles, CA, USA, 2005.
46. Rutter, M.; Bailey, A.; Lord, C. *Social Communication Questionnaire (SCQ)*; Western Psychological Services: Los Angeles, CA, USA, 2003.
47. Buysse, D.J.; Reynolds, C.F., III; Monk, T.H.; Berman, S.R.; Kupfer, D.J. The Pittsburgh sleep quality index: A new instrument for psychiatric practice and research. *Psychiatry Res.* **1989**, *28*, 193–213. [CrossRef] [PubMed]
48. Chung, F.; Yegneswaran, B.; Liao, P.; Chung, S.A.; Vairavanathan, S.; Islam, S.; Khajehdehi, A.; Shapiro, C.M. Stop questionnaire: A tool to screen patients for obstructive sleep apnea. *Anesthesiology* **2008**, *108*, 812–821. [CrossRef] [PubMed]
49. Li, H.; Durbin, R. Fast and accurate short read alignment with Burrows-Wheeler transform. *Bioinformatics* **2009**, *25*, 1754–1760. [CrossRef] [PubMed]
50. Li, H.; Handsaker, B.; Wysoker, A.; Fennell, T.; Ruan, J.; Homer, N.; Marth, G.; Abecasis, G.; Durbin, R.; Genome Project Data Processing Subgroup. The sequence alignment/map format and SAMtools. *Bioinformatics* **2009**, *25*, 2078–2079. [CrossRef] [PubMed]
51. McKenna, A.; Hanna, M.; Banks, E.; Sivachenko, A.; Cibulskis, K.; Kernytsky, A.; Garimella, K.; Altshuler, D.; Gabriel, S.; Daly, M.; *et al.* The genome analysis toolkit: A MapReduce framework for analyzing next-generation DNA sequencing data. *Genome Res.* **2010**, *20*, 1297–1303. [CrossRef] [PubMed]

52. Murata, T.; Kurokawa, R.; Krones, A.; Tatsumi, K.; Ishii, M.; Taki, T.; Masuno, M.; Ohashi, H.; Yanagisawa, M.; Rosenfeld, M,G.; *et al.* Defect of histone acetyltransferase activity of the nuclear transcriptional coactivator CBP in Rubinstein-Taybi syndrome. *Hum. Mol. Genet.* **2001**, *10*, 1071–1076. [CrossRef]
53. Bartsch, O.; Locher, K.; Meinecke, P.; Kress, W.; Seemanova, E.; Wagner, A.; Ostermann, K.; Rodel, G. Molecular studies in 10 cases of Rubinstein-Taybi syndrome, including a mild variant showing a missense mutation in codon 1175 of CREBBP. *J. Med. Genet.* **2002**, *39*, 496–501. [CrossRef] [PubMed]
54. Kalkhoven, E.; Roelfsema, J.H.; Teunissen, H.; den Boer, A.; Ariyurek, Y.; Zantema, A.; Breuning, M.H.; Hennekam, R.C.; Peters, D.J. Loss of CBP acetyltransferase activity by PHD finger mutations in Rubinstein-Taybi syndrome. *Hum. Mol. Genet.* **2003**, *12*, 441–450. [CrossRef] [PubMed]
55. Coupry, I.; Roudaut, C.; Stef, M.; Delrue, M.A.; Marche, M.; Burgelin, I.; Taine, L.; Cruaud, C.; Lacombe, D.; Arveiler, B. Molecular analysis of the *CBP* gene in 60 patients with Rubinstein-Taybi syndrome. *J. Med. Genet.* **2002**, *39*, 415–421. [CrossRef] [PubMed]
56. Kalkhoven, E. CBP and p300: HATs for different occasions. *Biochem. Pharmacol.* **2004**, *68*, 1145–1155. [CrossRef] [PubMed]
57. Udaka, T.; Samejima, H.; Kosaki, R.; Kurosawa, K.; Okamoto, N.; Mizuno, S.; Makita, Y.; Numabe, H.; Toral, J.F.; Takahashi, T.; *et al.* Comprehensive screening of CREB-binding protein gene mutations among patients with Rubinstein-Taybi syndrome using denaturing high-performance liquid chromatography. *Congenit. Anom. (Kyoto)* **2005**, *45*, 125–131. [CrossRef]

7

Participatory Art Activities Increase Salivary Oxytocin Secretion of ASD Children

Sanae Tanaka [1,†], Aiko Komagome [2,†], Aya Iguchi-Sherry [3,†], Akiko Nagasaka [4], Teruko Yuhi [5], Haruhiro Higashida [5], Maki Rooksby [6,7], Mitsuru Kikuchi [8], Oko Arai [2], Kana Minami [5,9], Takahiro Tsuji [5,10] and Chiharu Tsuji [5,*]

1 Division of Integrated Art and Sciences and Local Community Support, Research Center for Child Mental Development, Kanazawa University, Kanazawa 920-8640, Japan; tanakast@staff.kanazawa-u.ac.jp
2 The COI Site, Tokyo University of the Arts Tokyo 110-8714, Japan; komagome.aiko@ms.geidai.ac.jp (A.K.); tanaka.oko@ms.geidai.ac.jp (O.A.)
3 Artlink Central, Scotland FK8 1EA, UK; ayaiguchi@icloud.com
4 Department of Childhood Care and Education, Faculty of Social Work, Kinjo University, Hakusan 924-8511, Japan; ngsk-a4@kinjo.ac.jp
5 Department of Basic Research on Social Recognition, Research Center for Child Mental Development, Kanazawa University, Kanazawa 920-8640, Japan; y-teruko@med.kanazawa-u.ac.jp (T.Y.); haruhiro@med.kanazawa-u.ac.jp (H.H.); minami-k@staff.kanazawa-u.ac.jp (K.M.); tsuji-t@u-fukui.ac.jp (T.T.)
6 Adverse Childhood Experiences (ACE) Lab, Institute of Health and Wellbeing, University of Glasgow, Glasgow G12 8RZ, UK; Maki.Rooksby@glasgow.ac.uk
7 Social Brain in Action Lab, Institute of Neuroscience and Psychology, University of Glasgow, Glasgow G12 8QB, UK
8 Department of Psychiatry and Neurobiology, Graduate School of Medical Science, Kanazawa University, Kanazawa 920-8640, Japan; mitsuruk@med.kanazawa-u.ac.jp
9 Department of Health Development Nursing, Institute of Medical, Pharmaceutical and Health Sciences, Kanazawa University, Kanazawa 920-0942, Japan
10 Department of Ophthalmology, Faculty of Medical Sciences, University of Fukui, Fukui 910-1193, Japan
* Correspondence: ctsuji@med.kanazawa-u.ac.jp or higashida.c@gmail.com
† These authors contributed equally to this work.

Abstract: Autism spectrum disorder (ASD) occurs in 1 in 160 children worldwide. Individuals with ASD tend to be unique in the way that they comprehend themselves and others, as well as in the way that they interact and socialize, which can lead to challenges with social adaptation. There is currently no medication to improve the social deficit of children with ASD, and consequently, behavioral and complementary/alternative intervention plays an important role. In the present pilot study, we focused on the neuroendocrinological response to participatory art activities, which are known to have a positive effect on emotion, self-expression, sociability, and physical wellbeing. We collected saliva from 12 children with ASD and eight typically developed (TD) children before and after a visual art-based participatory art workshop to measure the levels of oxytocin, a neuropeptide involved in a wide range of social behaviors. We demonstrated that the rate of increase in salivary oxytocin following art activities in ASD children was significantly higher than that in TD children. In contrast, the change rate of salivary cortisol after participatory art activities was similar between the two groups. These results suggest that the beneficial effects of participatory art activities may be partially mediated by oxytocin release, and may have therapeutic potential for disorders involving social dysfunction.

Keywords: autism spectrum disorder; oxytocin; cortisol; group activity; stress; art

1. Introduction

Autism spectrum disorder (ASD) is estimated to occur in 1 in 160 children worldwide [1]; ASD tends to begin in childhood and tends to persist for life. Deficits in social skills are the defining symptoms of ASD [2], which greatly impede the ability of individuals to function in community settings throughout their lives. Effective social interaction is essential for building friendships and avoiding unnecessary aversive interactions with peers during the early years, while communication with coworkers and customers is necessary for successful work performance in adults. Thus, social deficits are likely to lead ASD individuals to socially withdraw or isolate. Despite these serious consequences of social deficits in ASD, there is currently no medication to attenuate the impairment of social behaviors.

Moreover, in many cases, depression and anxiety accompany social deficits and other core symptoms of ASD such as repetitive behaviors and a narrow range of interests [2,3]. Therefore, numerous studies have focused on the hypothalamic–pituitary–adrenal (HPA) axis with regard to level of cortisol (CORT), which is frequently used as a stress biomarker [4]. The HPA axis is a highly regulated system that enables stress adaptation and diurnal rhythm, and CORT is secreted when the HPA axis is activated [5,6]. Previous studies have shown that in children with ASD, diurnal rhythm of CORT differs from that in typically developed (TD) children; in addition, children with ASD exhibit hyperresponsive CORT secretions in the social evaluative context or social situations [7]. Dysfunction of the HPA axis has been shown to negatively affect mental health in TD children and children with ASD [3,8]. Thus, management of stress in children with ASD may help decrease the risk of a concurrent mental disorder.

Recently, the therapeutic use of oxytocin (OT), which has a diverse role in mammalian social behaviors, has gained increasing attention. OT is a nonapeptide produced by the hypothalamic neurons in the brain. It is released to the bloodstream to reach peripheral organs or within the hypothalamic and other limbic regions of the brain [9]. The involvement of OT in social recognition, selective social bonding, attachment, anxiety, and stress coping has been demonstrated in a considerable amount of animal studies [9,10]. Indeed, mice that have a deficiency in OT release, such as OT null mice or CD38 knockout mice, are unable to recognize previously encountered conspecifics [11,12]. Furthermore, OT has been shown to be important for mate-bonding in monogamous prairie voles [13], as well as in parent-infant bonding in prairie voles, sheep, and primates [14,15]. The OT system is activated in stressful, challenging, and threatening conditions, and functions to facilitate stress coping [9]. OT has also been implicated in human emotions and social behaviors [14]; for instance, physical interaction between parents and infants increase endogenous OT in both the mother and father, and the increase in OT correlates with the level of affectionate behavior of the mother [15].

Exogenously administrated OT has been shown to modulate social behaviors, stress, and anxiety both in healthy individuals and in patients with neuropsychiatric disorders [16]. Moreover, intranasal administration of OT affects social perception, in that it improves discrimination of facial expressions [17,18] and increases the gaze to the eye region [19]. In addition, OT application has been previously shown to enhance feelings of trust [20] and generosity [21]. Thus, the peripheral application of OT has been considered a potentially effective therapeutic treatment for autism and schizophrenia; however, recent clinical trials have shown conflicting results [22]. Although this is in part due to the underpowered design of the trials, the use of exogenous OT as a therapeutic agent is questionable given it has low blood brain barrier permeability and metabolic stability in plasma [23]. Therefore, nonpharmacological interventions that increase endogenous OT are needed to ameliorate the social deficit of patients with ASD, especially those that can effectively stimulate the release of OT in the brain.

The World Health Organization (WHO) recently summarized how art-based interventions can help improve health and well-being, as well as contribute to the prevention of, and recovery from mental and physical illness [24]. Participatory art, in which participants engage in creative activities during social interaction, is known for its beneficial effects on physical health and emotional well-being [25,26]. In fact, the experience of participating in the creative process itself improves mental health conditions, thereby building resilience, boosting social and communicative skills, and improving self-confidence [26–28]. More broadly, such activities are included in social prescribing, an emerging intervention modality that has garnered interest and attention in the academic and clinical communities [29]. With participatory art, as well as social prescribing, the approach to treating various health ailments is holistic and practical, whereby activities such as art, exercising, and gardening are supervised by trained specialists, many of whom are nonclinicians [30]. Because ASD is a neurodevelopmental disorder for which no specific intervention has been established, such activities may provide valuable coping mechanisms across the life span for those affected and their families.

In the present study, we conducted the preliminary study to investigate whether the salivary OT level changes following participation in visual art-based activities in ASD and typically developed (TD) children. Because ASD individuals often struggle to adapt to changes or a new environment, we also measured the salivary CORT level, which is often used as a psychological stress biomarker. To the best of our knowledge, this is the first study to assess the neuroendocrinological changes in individuals who have taken part in participatory art activities.

2. Materials and Methods

2.1. Participants

For this study, 10 TD children (aged 8–9 years) and 13 children (8–13 years) with ASD were recruited. All the children were volunteers; however, all children did not participate in all five sessions of visual art-based participatory workshops, and the data from children who participated less than twice were not used for analysis. Four boys and 4 girls, aged 8–9 years, who were TD and 11 boys and 1 girl, aged 8–13 years, who had ASD were analyzed (Table 1). ASD was diagnosed by children's psychiatrists or pediatricians, who used criteria from the American Psychiatric Association's Diagnostic and Statistical Manual of Mental Disorders, Fourth Edition, Text Revision (DSM-IV-TR) or Fifth Edition (DSM-V) or from the International Statistical Classification of Diseases and Related Health Problems, 10th edition (ICD-10). The evaluations included IQ testing, behavioral observation, and questionnaires; depending on the child, the Childhood Autism Rating Scale (CARS), Autism Diagnostic Observation Schedule (ADOS), Diagnostic Interview for Social and Communication Disorders (DISCO), or Pervasive Developmental Disorders Autism Society Japan Rating Scale (PARS) was used.

Table 1. Age, mean scores of Early Symptomatic Syndromes Eliciting Neurodevelopmental Clinical Examinations-Questionnaire (ESSENCE-Q) and education for each group of children.

	TD	ASD
Numbers	8 (male: 4, female: 4)	12 (male: 11, female: 1)
Age	96–119 months mean: 107, SD: 6.9	113–162 months mean: 135, SD: 16.7
ESSENCE-Q	Yes: 0.4, Maybe/A Little: 0.1/0.3	Yes: 2.83, Maybe/A Little: 1.58/2.83
Education	regular class	regular or special needs classes or special education support classes

The participants' parents were asked to respond to the Early Symptomatic Syndromes Eliciting Neurodevelopmental Clinical Examinations-Questionnaire (ESSENCE-Q) in order to screen the current status of TD children and children with ASD. The ESSENCE-Q is a brief screening questionnaire established specifically for the purpose of shortening the identification process of a wide variety of neurodevelopmental problems [31].

Among the children with ASD, 10 were enrolled in either regular or special needs classes at local schools in Japan. The other 2 children in this group were students at special support education schools.

2.2. Ethics Statement

The study was approved as a noninvasive medical study by Kanazawa University Graduate School of Medicine in 2018 (approval number #2790-2). The study was performed according to the Declaration of Helsinki and the Ethical Guidelines for Clinical Studies of the Ministry of Health, Labor and Welfare of Japan. After the children and their parents had been given a complete explanation of the study, they provided written informed consent. The participants were informed that they could choose not to supply their saliva on each occasion, even after agreeing to participate in the study.

2.3. Visual Art-Based Participatory Art Workshop

During the visual art-based participatory art workshops, participants created their own original stories and made characters and props with different kind of materials. Then participants used the Smoovie application on an iPad (Apple, Inc., Cupertino, CA, USA) to make their own movies with short stop-motion animation. The subjects of their stories varied from their everyday life to the objects that surrounded them; the theme of the project was fully participant led. The aim of this workshop was to let the participants express themselves as freely as possible and not to make them feel as if they were working on a school task or a job. We provided arts and crafts materials that stimulated different senses—paper (colored, textured, plain; different weights of paper), fabric (patterned, textured), tape (washi tape, colored tape), soft clay (colored, neutral), soft construction material (bubble wrap, wrapping material, cardboard), glue (hot glue gun, glue stick), paint, colored pens, and decorative material (sequins, gems, buttons).

The facilitators and supporters of the art workshop set up a comfortable venue, prepared the tools, explained how to use them, and provided a variety of materials. The art workshops conducted in this study were facilitated by a visual artist and supported by the art faculty, students from the University of the Arts, and a staff member who is licensed in special education. During the activity, the organizers interacted with the participants as and when appropriate and encouraged them throughout the creative processes of generating ideas and producing animations.

2.4. Assessment

The visual art-based participatory art workshops were held five times between 22 July–10 August in 2018 and 2019. The workshops in 2018 were held from 14:30–16:30, while those in 2019 were held from 14:00–15:30. Sessions for TD children and ASD children were organized separately. The saliva samples were collected within 10 min of arrival, and just after the participatory art was finished. The percentage of salivary OT or CORT for each session was determined as (concentration after session/concentration before session) × 100. The total number of sessions analyzed before and after the art workshop and the percentage after the workshops for TD and ASD group were 33 and 42, respectively. The personal average percentage after the workshops was calculated as a mean percentage of all the sessions that each child participated (8 subjects for TD group and 12 subjects for ASD group).

2.5. Saliva Collection and Analysis

The saliva samples (0.3–1.0 mL) were collected in a sterile 50 mL polypropylene tube (Greiner Bio-one Co. Ltd., Tokyo, Japan), and were immediately placed in ice for storage at −20 °C. Three to 5 days later, the samples were thawed and centrifuged twice at 4 °C at 1500× *g* for 10 min. The samples were divided into 1.5-mL microtubes, each containing 100 μL, and kept again at −80 °C until required for the assay. The salivary OT level was measured using a 96-plate commercial OT-ELISA kit (Enzo Life

Sciences, Farmingdale, NY, USA), as described previously [32–34]. The measurements were performed in duplicate. Samples (100 μL) without fractionation were treated according to the manufacturer's instructions. The optical density of the samples and standards was measured at wavelengths of 405 nm by a microplate reader (Bio-Rad, Richmond, CA, USA). The salivary CORT level was measured using a cortisol enzyme immunoassay kit (Salimetrics, State College, PA, USA) as previously described [35]. Samples (25 μL) were treated according to the manufacturer's instructions. The optical density of the samples and standards were measured at wavelengths of 450 nm by a microplate reader (Bio-Rad, Richmond, CA, USA). Measurements were performed in duplicate. Sample concentrations were calculated according to the relevant standard curve. The intraassay and interassay coefficients were <12.4% and <12.1%, respectively.

2.6. Statistical Analysis

Statistical analysis was performed using Prism 8 software (GraphPad Software Inc., San Diego, CA, USA). Wilcoxon rank-sum tests were used to compare the levels of salivary OT or CORT of TD children with children with ASD before and after each visual art-based workshop session. The Mann–Whitney *U* test was used to compare the average percentage of OT or CORT of TD children with children with ASD after each session. Two-tailed student's *t* test was used to assess the personal average percentage of salivary OT or CORT after each session in which a child participated. All data were calculated as means ± standard errors of the means. In all analyses, $p < 0.05$ was considered statistically significant.

3. Results

The salivary OT level after each session of visual art-based participatory art workshop showed a significant decrease in the TD group (before, 161.5 ± 19.4 pg/mL, after 136.6 ± 16.0 pg/mL; $p = 0.015$) (Figure 1a), whereas there was no significant difference in the ASD group (before 167.9 ± 17.9 pg/mL, after 175.5 ± 16.4 pg/mL; $p = 0.880$) (Figure 1a). However, the average percentage of salivary OT after each session of the ASD group was significantly higher than that of the TD group (TD, 90.8% ± 6.9%; ASD, 127.9% ± 11.8%; $p = 0.024$) (Figure 1b). Also, the personal average percentage of salivary OT after each participated session of the ASD group was significantly higher than that of the TD group (TD, 88.4% ± 4.8%; ASD, 134.5% ± 15.6%; $p = 0.03$) (Figure 1c).

The concentrations of salivary cortisol were not significantly different before and after the participatory art workshop in either the TD or ASD group (Figure 2a). No significant difference was observed between the TD and ASD groups with regards to the average percentage after each session, and/or in the average percentage of personal salivary CORT after each session (Figure 2b,c).

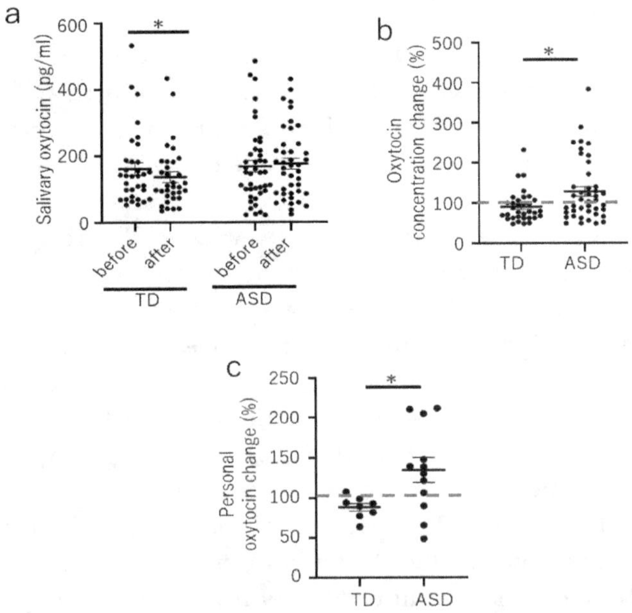

Figure 1. The salivary oxytocin levels before and after participatory art workshops. (**a**). Salivary oxytocin level before and after each session in the typically developed (TD) children and those with autism spectrum disorder (ASD). Note that not all children attended all five sessions of the art workshop (total number of sessions analyzed: 33 for the TD children and 42 for the children with ASD). (**b**). Percentage of salivary oxytocin in the TD children and those with ASD after each session. Note that not all children attended all five sessions of the art workshop (total number of sessions analyzed—33 for the TD children and 42 for the children with ASD). (**c**). Personal average percentage of salivary oxytocin level after each session in the TD and ASD groups (number of children assessed: TD, $n = 8$; ASD, $n = 12$). Data are mean ± sem. * $p < 0.05$.

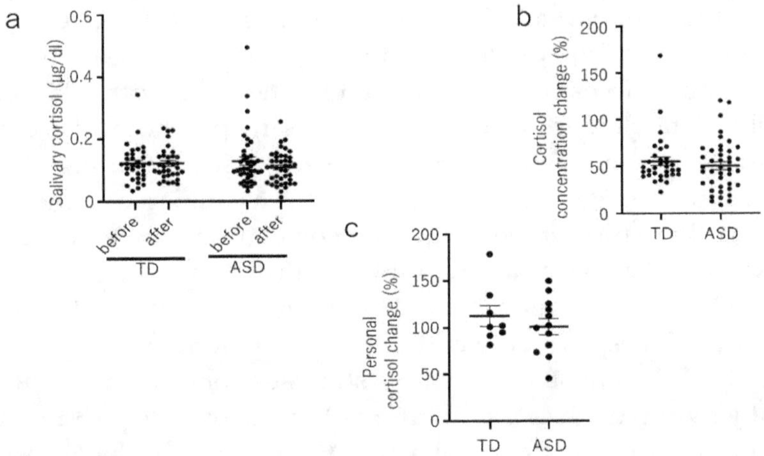

Figure 2. The salivary cortisol level before and after participatory art workshop. (**a**). Salivary cortisol level before and after each session in the TD and ASD groups. Note that not all children attended all five sessions of the art workshop (total number of sessions analyzed—33 for the TD children and 42 for the children with ASD). (**b**). Percentage of salivary cortisol after each session in the TD and ASD groups. Note that not all children attended all five sessions of the art workshop (total number of sessions analyzed—33 for the TD children and 42 for the children with ASD). (**c**). Personal average percentage of salivary cortisol level after each session in the TD and ASD groups (number of children assessed: TD, $n = 8$; ASD, $n = 12$). Data are mean ± sem.

4. Discussion

The current trial was a pioneering study to assess salivary OT and CORT concentrations in ASD and TD children in response to a positive social activity, participatory arts. Although we could not detect a statistical difference in OT levels after each session in the ASD group, the average percentage of salivary OT after each session, and the personal average percentage of salivary OT after each session were increased in ASD children. However, no significant difference in the cortisol level was detected before and after participatory art activities in either the ASD or TD group. Since the cortisol level did not change significantly during the participatory art activities, we suggest that OT is released as a result of positive social activities, rather than a response to stress.

Because all the children participated voluntarily in the visual art-based participatory art workshop, the TD children were expected not to feel anxious or stressed about their participation, and we initially assumed that their OT levels would increase after participatory art activities. However, the OT level decreased instead. As the CORT level in TD children did not change significantly, the decrease in the OT level may not be a result of the stress response. Because both groups of children enjoyed the art activities, the results suggest that the TD children may have felt driven to complete their artwork, which corresponded with a decrease in the OT level afterwards. A decrease in OT levels has been suggested to reflect a reduction in social qualities of attention or, more broadly, in social interaction [36]. In our case, the decrease in the TD group may correspond to a shift in attention upon completion of their work. The children with ASD, on the other hand, required the experience to form a part of their routine over the course of the workshop attendance and may have gained more pleasure out of the process of creativity. It has been reported that attention systems are disrupted and atypical in children with ASD [37]. It is possible that our participants with ASD required more sessions than the TD children in order to understand the structure of the workshops and to focus on their creative activities. Alternatively, there might have been an increase in the OT level in TD children during the activities, but the time course may have differed from that observed in the children with ASD. Larger sample sizes and further follow up will allow a better understanding of the process.

Our preliminary study had several limitations. First, the study was designed to examine the immediate OT response of participatory art activity. Although the percentage change of OT level was increased in ASD children, we failed to show a statistical difference in the salivary OT level before and after each of the workshop due to the modest sample size and the large variance in the OT concentration. Therefore, it is necessary to conduct a further trial with a larger sample size of ASD children to obtain reliable data. Second, we did not include any psychological, emotional, or behavioral measurement that may be relevant to the OT response. As shown in Figure 1c, there is a diverse variability in the personal percentage change in ASD children compared to the TD children; as a result, we need to conduct a further study to elucidate the correlation between the traits of children and the OT responsiveness to participatory art activities. Third, it is worth pointing out that our study did not include a control condition in order to disentangle the potential effect of participatory art from other more generic activities involving crafting or animation making. Such a control could have simply involved being in the premise for the workshop sessions, as in a wait-list group. However, each workshop typically required the entire duration of the children's visit in terms of staff cover and their families who need to fit in taking and collecting their children. Staffs and participants were all volunteers and we faced several practical difficulties which prevented from adding this important aspect to our design this time. We will be mindful for exploring options for adding the control in our future work.

The WHO recently summarized how art interventions can help improve health and well-being, and can help to prevent both mental and physical illness [24]. They also stated that while art is conceptually difficult to define, it is important to verify the effectiveness of art. Indeed, although a wide variety of studies use diverse methodologies, these are often based on psychological tests or subjective feedback. Our study aimed to capture the fluctuations in the neuroendocrine response to participatory art activities. In the future study, we will investigate the association of the neuroendocrine response and the traits of children in order to elucidate for whom and in what aspect participatory art activities can be effective. We will also evaluate the effectiveness of participatory arts activities in the long term. Further, experience in multi-sensory processing has been showing some promising results in children with autism spectrum disorders [38]. Given that crafting and creative activities are familiar and popular in typical as well as atypical development, it would be an important agenda to study the therapeutic role of multi-sensory experiences involved in activities such as participatory art. Ultimately, we would like to utilize our research findings related to the use of neuroendocrine responses in combination with psychological, emotional, or behavioral measurement to establish a method to verify the effectiveness of participatory art activities.

In the current study, ELISA was used to measure the saliva OT concentrations; however, with this technique, there remains the issue of antibody specificity. The antibody may not only detect the free form of the target analyte, but different forms, such as precursors and metabolites, or a form within other protein complexes. These phenomena may partially explain the differences in values observed between different ELISA kits, as well as between ELISA and HPLC-MS or radio immunoassay. Indeed, our detected OT concentration range is one digit higher than that reported by other studies [15,39,40]. However, since we have detected the relative change in salivary OT in the context of physical interaction and/or in social interaction [32,34,41], although the values may not be reflecting the absolute physiological value of free OT, the relative change in monitored values are likely to be comparable.

In conclusion, the current experiment was designed to assess salivary OT and CORT concentrations in ASD and TD children in response to participation in visual art-based activities, since art is known to improve mental and physical health and overall quality of life. We demonstrated increased OT release after participatory art activities that was unrelated to the stress response. Thus, our case study is the first to show the biological link between the social experience of participatory art and its positive psychosocial effects.

Author Contributions: S.T., A.K., A.I.-S. have contributed equally to this work. S.T. and C.T. recruited the participants; S.T., A.K., A.I.-S., M.R. and C.T. conceived and designed the experiments; S.T., A.K., A.I.-S., M.R., A.N., K.M., M.K., and O.A. performed and organized art workshop; T.Y. performed saliva assay; T.T., C.T., H.H. analyzed the data and data interpretation; H.H. contributed to provide analytical tools; C.T. prepared the initial draft and M.R. and C.T. revised the manuscript. All authors have read and agreed to the published version of the manuscript.

References

1. Elsabbagh, M.; Divan, G.; Koh, Y.J.; Kim, Y.S.; Kauchali, S.; Marcin, C.; Montiel-Nava, C.; Patel, V.; Paula, C.S.; Wang, C.; et al. Global prevalence of autism and other pervasive developmental disorders. *Autism Res.* **2012**, *5*, 160–179. [CrossRef]
2. Geschwind, D.H. Advances in autism. *Annu. Rev. Med.* **2009**, *60*, 367–380. [CrossRef]
3. Simonoff, E.; Pickles, A.; Charman, T.; Chandler, S.; Loucas, T.; Baird, G. Psychiatric disorders in children with autism spectrum disorders: Prevalence, comorbidity, and associated factors in a population-derived sample. *J. Am. Acad. Child. Adolesc. Psychiatry* **2008**, *47*, 921–929. [CrossRef]
4. Hellhammer, D.H.; Wust, S.; Kudielka, B.M. Salivary cortisol as a biomarker in stress research. *Psychoneuroendocrinology* **2009**, *34*, 163–171. [CrossRef]
5. Chrousos, G.P. Stress and disorders of the stress system. *Nat. Rev. Endocrinol.* **2009**, *5*, 374–381. [CrossRef]
6. de Kloet, E.R.; Joels, M.; Holsboer, F. Stress and the brain: From adaptation to disease. *Nat. Rev. Neurosci.* **2005**, *6*, 463–475. [CrossRef]
7. Taylor, J.L.; Corbett, B.A. A review of rhythm and responsiveness of cortisol in individuals with autism spectrum disorders. *Psychoneuroendocrinology* **2014**, *49*, 207–228. [CrossRef]
8. Shirtcliff, E.A.; Essex, M.J. Concurrent and Longitudinal Associations of Basal and Diurnal Cortisol with Mental Health Symptoms in Early Adolescence. *Dev. Psychobiol.* **2008**, *50*, 690–703. [CrossRef]
9. Jurek, B.; Neumann, I.D. The Oxytocin Receptor: From Intracellular Signaling to Behavior. *Physiol. Rev.* **2018**, *98*, 1805–1908. [CrossRef]
10. Modi, M.E.; Young, L.J. The oxytocin system in drug discovery for autism: Animal models and novel therapeutic strategies. *Horm. Behav.* **2012**, *61*, 340–350. [CrossRef]

11. Ferguson, J.N.; Young, L.J.; Hearn, E.F.; Matzuk, M.M.; Insel, T.R.; Winslow, J.T. Social amnesia in mice lacking the oxytocin gene. *Nat. Genet.* **2000**, *25*, 284–288. [CrossRef]
12. Jin, D.; Liu, H.X.; Hirai, H.; Torashima, T.; Nagai, T.; Lopatina, O.; Shnayder, N.A.; Yamada, K.; Noda, M.; Seike, T.; et al. CD38 is critical for social behaviour by regulating oxytocin secretion. *Nature* **2007**, *446*, 41–45. [CrossRef]
13. Tabbaa, M.; Paedae, B.; Liu, Y.; Wang, Z. Neuropeptide Regulation of Social Attachment: The Prairie Vole Model. *Compr. Physiol.* **2016**, *7*, 81–104. [CrossRef]
14. Feldman, R. Oxytocin and social affiliation in humans. *Horm. Behav.* **2012**, *61*, 380–391. [CrossRef]
15. Feldman, R.; Gordon, I.; Schneiderman, I.; Weisman, O.; Zagoory-Sharon, O. Natural variations in maternal and paternal care are associated with systematic changes in oxytocin following parent-infant contact. *Psychoneuroendocrinology* **2010**, *35*, 1133–1141. [CrossRef]
16. Andari, E.; Hurlemann, R.; Young, L.J. A Precision Medicine Approach to Oxytocin Trials. *Curr. Top. Behav. Neurosci.* **2018**, *35*, 559–590. [CrossRef]
17. Domes, G.; Heinrichs, M.; Michel, A.; Berger, C.; Herpertz, S.C. Oxytocin improves "mind-reading" in humans. *Biol. Psychiatry* **2007**, *61*, 731–733. [CrossRef]
18. Savaskan, E.; Ehrhardt, R.; Schulz, A.; Walter, M.; Schachinger, H. Post-learning intranasal oxytocin modulates human memory for facial identity. *Psychoneuroendocrinology* **2008**, *33*, 368–374. [CrossRef]
19. Yamasue, H.; Domes, G. Oxytocin and Autism Spectrum Disorders. *Curr. Top. Behav. Neurosci.* **2018**, *35*, 449–465. [CrossRef]
20. Kosfeld, M.; Heinrichs, M.; Zak, P.J.; Fischbacher, U.; Fehr, E. Oxytocin increases trust in humans. *Nature* **2005**, *435*, 673–676. [CrossRef]
21. Zak, P.J.; Stanton, A.A.; Ahmadi, S. Oxytocin increases generosity in humans. *PLoS ONE* **2007**, *2*, e1128. [CrossRef]
22. Young, L.J.; Barrett, C.E. Neuroscience. Can oxytocin treat autism? *Science* **2015**, *347*, 825–826. [CrossRef]
23. Gulliver, D.; Werry, E.; Reekie, T.A.; Katte, T.A.; Jorgensen, W.; Kassiou, M. Targeting the Oxytocin System: New Pharmacotherapeutic Approaches. *Trends Pharmacol. Sci.* **2019**, *40*, 22–37. [CrossRef]
24. Fancourt, D.; Finn, S. *What is the Evidence on the Role of the Arts in Improving Health and Well-Being? A Scoping Review*; (Health Evidence Network (HEN) Synthesis Report 67); WHO Regional Office for Europe: Copenhagen, Denmark, 2019.
25. Hacking, S.; Secker, J.; Kent, L.; Shenton, J.; Spandler, H. Mental health and arts participation: The state of the art in England. *J. R Soc. Promot. Health* **2006**, *126*, 121–127. [CrossRef]
26. Bone, T.A. Art and Mental Health Recovery: Evaluating the Impact of a Community-Based Participatory Arts Program through Artist Voices. *Community Ment Health J.* **2018**, *54*, 1180–1188. [CrossRef]
27. Hacking, S.; Secker, J.; Spandler, H.; Kent, L.; Shenton, J. Evaluating the impact of participatory art projects for people with mental health needs. *Health Soc. Care Community* **2008**, *16*, 638–648. [CrossRef]
28. Stickley, T.; Wright, N.; Slade, M. The art of recovery: Outcomes from participatory arts activities for people using mental health services. *J. Ment. Health* **2018**, *27*, 367–373. [CrossRef]
29. Bickerdike, L.; Booth, A.; Wilson, P.M.; Farley, K.; Wright, K. Social prescribing: Less rhetoric and more reality. A systematic review of the evidence. *BMJ Open* **2017**, *7*, e013384. [CrossRef]
30. Toma, M.; Morris, J.; Kelly, C.; Jinal-Snape, D. *The Impact of Art Attendance and Participation on Health and Wellbeing: Systematic Literature Review (Work Package 1)*; Glasgow Centre for Population Health: Glasgow, UK, 2014.
31. Hatakenaka, Y.; Fernell, E.; Sakaguchi, M.; Ninomiya, H.; Fukunaga, I.; Gillberg, C. ESSENCE-Q-a first clinical validation study of a new screening questionnaire for young children with suspected neurodevelopmental problems in south Japan. *Neuropsychiatr. Dis. Treat.* **2016**, *12*, 1739–1746. [CrossRef]
32. Tsuji, S.; Yuhi, T.; Furuhara, K.; Ohta, S.; Shimizu, Y.; Higashida, H. Salivary oxytocin concentrations in seven boys with autism spectrum disorder received massage from their mothers: A pilot study. *Front. Psychiatry* **2015**, *6*, 58. [CrossRef]
33. MacLean, E.L.; Gesquiere, L.R.; Gee, N.; Levy, K.; Martin, W.L.; Carter, C.S. Validation of salivary oxytocin and vasopressin as biomarkers in domestic dogs. *J. Neurosci. Methods* **2018**, *293*, 67–76. [CrossRef]
34. Yuhi, T.; Ise, K.; Iwashina, K.; Terao, N.; Yoshioka, S.; Shomura, K.; Maehara, T.; Yazaki, A.; Koichi, K.; Furuhara, K.; et al. Sex Differences in Salivary Oxytocin and Cortisol Concentration Changes during Cooking in a Small Group. *Behav. Sci.* **2018**, *8*, 101. [CrossRef]

35. Kumazaki, H.; Warren, Z.; Corbett, B.A.; Yoshikawa, Y.; Matsumoto, Y.; Higashida, H.; Yuhi, T.; Ikeda, T.; Ishiguro, H.; Kikuchi, M. Android Robot-Mediated Mock Job Interview Sessions for Young Adults with Autism Spectrum Disorder: A Pilot Study. *Front. Psychiatry* **2017**, *8*. [CrossRef]
36. Nishizato, M.; Fujisawa, T.X.; Kosaka, H.; Tomoda, A. Developmental changes in social attention and oxytocin levels in infants and children. *Sci. Rep. UK* **2017**, *7*. [CrossRef]
37. Guillon, Q.; Hadjikhani, N.; Baduel, S.; Roge, B. Visual social attention in autism spectrum disorder: Insights from eye tracking studies. *Neurosci. Biobehav. Rev.* **2014**, *42*, 279–297. [CrossRef]
38. Case-Smith, J.; Weaver, L.L.; Fristad, M.A. A systematic review of sensory processing interventions for children with autism spectrum disorders. *Autism* **2015**, *19*, 133–148. [CrossRef]
39. Schladt, T.M.; Nordmann, G.C.; Emilius, R.; Kudielka, B.M.; de Jong, T.R.; Neumann, I.D. Choir versus Solo Singing: Effects on Mood, and Salivary Oxytocin and Cortisol Concentrations. *Front. Hum. Neurosci.* **2017**, *11*, 430. [CrossRef]
40. Jong, T.R.; Menon, R.; Bludau, A.; Grund, T.; Biermeier, V.; Klampfl, S.M.; Jurek, B.; Bosch, O.J.; Hellhammer, J.; Neumann, I.D. Salivary oxytocin concentrations in response to running, sexual self-stimulation, breastfeeding and the TSST: The Regensburg Oxytocin Challenge (ROC) study. *Psychoneuroendocrinology* **2015**, *62*, 381–388. [CrossRef]
41. Yuhi, T.; Kyuta, H.; Mori, H.A.; Murakami, C.; Furuhara, K.; Okuno, M.; Takahashi, M.; Fuji, D.; Higashida, H. Salivary Oxytocin Concentration Changes during a Group Drumming Intervention for Maltreated School Children. *Brain Sci.* **2017**, *7*, 152. [CrossRef]

8

Parents' Attitudes toward Clinical Genetic Testing for Autism Spectrum Disorder—Data from a Norwegian Sample

Jarle Johannessen [1,5,*,†], Terje Nærland [1,4,†], Sigrun Hope [1,6], Tonje Torske [10], Anne Lise Høyland [7,8], Jana Strohmaier [9], Arvid Heiberg [3], Marcella Rietschel [9], Srdjan Djurovic [1,3,11] and Ole A. Andreassen [1,2]

1 NORMENT, KG Jebsen Centre for Psychosis Research, University of Oslo, Oslo 0424, Norway; ternae@ous-hf.no (T.N.); sighop@ous-hf.no (S.H.); srdjan.djurovic@medisin.uio.no (S.D.); ole.andreassen@medisin.uio.no (O.A.A.)
2 Division of Mental Health and Addiction, Oslo University Hospital, Oslo 0315, Norway
3 Department of Medical Genetics, Oslo University Hospital, Oslo 0424, Norway; arvhei@ous-hf.no
4 NevSom, Department of Rare Disorders and Disabilities, Oslo University Hospital, Oslo 0424, Norway
5 Autism Society Norway, Oslo 0609, Norway
6 Department of Neurohabilitation, Oslo University Hospital, Oslo 0424, Norway
7 Regional Centre for Child and Youth Mental Health and Child Welfare, Department of Mental Health, Faculty of Medicine and Health Sciences, Norwegian University of Science and Technology, Trondheim 7491, Norway; anne.lise.hoyland@ntnu.no
8 Department of Pediatrics, St. Olavs Hospital, Trondheim University Hospital, Trondheim 7006, Norway
9 Department of Genetic Epidemiology in Psychiatry, Central Institute of Mental Health, Medical Faculty Mannheim, University of Heidelberg, Mannheim 68159, Germany; Jana.Strohmaier@zi-mannheim.de (J.S.); Marcella.Rietschel@zi-mannheim.de (M.R.)
10 Division of Mental Health and Addiction, Vestre Viken Hospital Trust, Drammen 3004, Norway; tonje.torske@vestreviken.no
11 Department of Clinical Science, University of Bergen, Bergen 5021, Norway
* Correspondence: jarle@autismeforeningen.no
† The authors contributed equally to this work.

Academic Editor: Merlin G. Butler

Abstract: Clinical genetic testing (CGT) of children with autism spectrum disorder (ASD) may have positive and negative effects. Knowledge about parents' attitudes is needed to ensure good involvement of caregivers, which is crucial for accurate diagnosis and effective clinical management. This study aimed to assess parents' attitudes toward CGT for ASD. Parent members of the Norwegian Autism Society were given a previously untested questionnaire and 1455 answered. Linear regression analyses were conducted to evaluate contribution of parent and child characteristics to attitude statements. Provided it could contribute to a casual explanation of their child's ASD, 76% would undergo CGT. If it would improve the possibilities for early interventions, 74% were positive to CGT. Between 49–67% agreed that CGT could have a negative impact on health insurance, increase their concern for the child's future and cause family conflicts. Parents against CGT (9%) were less optimistic regarding positive effects, but not more concerned with negative impacts. The severity of the children's ASD diagnosis had a weak positive association with parent's positive attitudes to CGT (p-values range from <0.001 to 0.975). Parents prefer that CGT is offered to those having a child with ASD (65%), when the child's development deviates from normal (48%), or before pregnancy (36%). A majority of the parents of children with ASD are positive to CGT due to possibilities for an etiological explanation.

Keywords: ASD; autism; Asperger syndrome; clinical genetic testing; parents; attitudes; ethics; genetic counselling

1. Introduction

Autism spectrum disorder (ASD) is a set of heterogeneous conditions, characterized by early-onset difficulties in social communication and unusually restricted, repetitive behavior and interests [1]. The worldwide prevalence is about 1%, with a high global disease burden [2]. In Norway, the cumulative incidence for 11-year-olds has recently been estimated to be 0.8% [3].

ASD is among the most heritable neurodevelopmental conditions [4]. The recurrence risk for a sibling of an affected child is about 10–20%, which increases to 30–50% if the child has more than one sibling with ASD [5]. The etiology is still largely unknown, although it is clear that environmental factors are involved in addition to genetic susceptibility [1]. The etiology of ASD is very heterogeneous [6], and the search for genes that can explain the pathology is ongoing.

Recent advances in genetic technology have increased the diagnostic yield to 30–40% in clinical testing [7], and genetic testing is increasingly being used in the clinics, although not as a diagnostic tool [8]. In Norway, clinical genetic testing (CGT) is performed upon request by specialists in medical genetics, neurology or pediatrics and requires good phenotypic description. In cases of developmental delay and intellectual disability, as well as at least some features of ASD, chromosome 16p11.2 deletion syndrome is specifically tested for. Other copy number variants (CNVs) of diagnostic yield are emerging. A recent study on the use of ultra-high resolution chromosomal microarray analysis (CMA) found 15q11.2 BP1–BP2 microdeletion as the most common cytogenetic finding in those with ASD presenting for genetic services [9].

Meaningful interventions exist for ASD, but approved medications that target the core symptoms are absent. Finding effective treatments is regarded as the most important goal of ASD research [10], and the identification of a genetic etiology is a first step in the development of an individualized medical approach for these patients [5].

Towards the achievements of a new era of precision medicine [11], essential non-technological issues must be clarified. These issues include respecting the patients' autonomy and privacy and their need for protection from discriminations [12]. Good involvement of caregivers is needed to improve the accuracy of diagnosis, and to enable effective clinical management, tailored education [13,14], and genetic counseling, which involves complicated issues [15–17] that require a high degree of ethical reflection [15] informed by up-to-date knowledge about technological advancements [18,19] as well as of the views of those involved.

According to a recent report, professionals believe that genetic testing could improve the possibility for early intervention, enable the prevention of specific comorbid diseases, or relieve guilt [20]. Clarifying the role of specific genetic factors may contribute to parents' understanding of why their child has ASD [5]. Clinical relevance of genetic factors may include impact on the diagnostic process [15,21,22], on pharmacological and behavioral treatment [23], on adequate planning of actions [15] and on preparing parents for a life with an ASD child [22].

However, knowledge of specific genetic factors may also be potentially harmful, depending on the characteristics and roles of the genes involved, the family situation and clinical relevance of the genetic factors. A test showing that a child inherited a disease-causing gene may induce feelings of guilt and worry while a de novo mutation may relieve the parents from feelings of responsibility [21,24]. Genetic testing may also cause family conflicts [25]. Feelings of guilt and family conflicts are common in monogenic disorders [26,27]. The likelihood of recurrence of ASD in the family involved, i.e., the risk of getting another child with ASD [28–30], is also relevant for whether knowledge of specific genetic factors may be beneficial or harmful.

Current knowledge of parents´ attitudes toward CGT for ASD is limited. One study [31] found that more than 90% of the parents agreed that genetic testing is useful in health care, and that 86% of the parents are interested in finding out if genetic factors are causal in their child's ASD. Another study [32] shows that 80% of parents were interested in a genetic risk assessment test for ASD in an undiagnosed younger sibling. Both studies found that parents held a belief that the genetic test result could allow for closer monitoring and earlier access to evaluation and intervention. However, these studies included a small number of parents. Early identification is important for access to specialized evidence-based interventions [33], and prolonged diagnostic process is associated with stress in parents [34]. Parental stress or psychological well-being is not significantly different in parents of children across the ASD sub-diagnoses of infantile autism and Asperger syndrome [35]. However, we previously found very small significant differences in attitudes toward genetic research between parents of children with autism and parents of children with Asperger syndrome [36].

Perceived recurrence risk is found to influence reproductive decisions [37]. A survey of parents of children with fragile X syndrome (FXS) found that 59% indicated that the diagnosis affected their decision to have another child greatly while the rest was less affected. Those who indicated they were unaffected had already decided not to have more children [38,39]. A review found that concerns about increased risk of having a child with a given genetic condition influences decisions to undergo prenatal testing [40]. To the extent that these findings are applicable to ASD, they suggest that the reproductive decisions of parents of ASD individuals may be influenced by their perceived risk [39].

Genetic test results are also believed to reinforce stigmatization and discrimination, both by society in general and by insurance companies [25]. The stigma attached to mental illness is claimed to always lead to stress through discrimination in academic settings, in work, and in public, although often unintended [41]. Advocates for ASD fear the possible outcomes of genetic prenatal testing or treatment and argue that aggressively seeking interventions devalues autistic traits and tendencies [42]. Adults with ASD fear that people with ASD traits eventually will be eliminated through prenatal testing and selective abortion [42]. Despite genetic non-discrimination acts in most western countries [21,25], people with a disease mutation may be offered less favorable health insurance [25,43]. In some countries, it is explicitly allowed to use genetic risk information when the insurance payment exceeds a certain level [44,45].

To the best of our knowledge, most findings with respect to attitudes in the field are generated from small samples or samples that may be skewed due to selection bias or self-reference. Thus, there is a need for larger empirical investigations on parents' attitudes and outlooks of CGT in ASD. The objective of the current study was to describe and explore parents' attitudes to CGT for ASD. Our first hypothesis was that (1) parents would be positive toward CGT for ASD, due to learning more about their child's genetic risk and etiology of confirmed ASD. We also hypothesized that (2) small differences in attitudes to CGT exist between parents of children with autism and parents of children with Asperger syndrome. Health or life insurance discrimination is a potential negative effect of CGT for ASD risk. Thus, the third hypothesis was that (3) discrimination from insurance companies would be a reason to be opposed to CGT. Early diagnosis is important for early access to specialized evidence-based interventions and our fourth hypothesis was that (4) parents of children with ASD would prefer CGT for ASD risk to be offered as early as possible, i.e., during pregnancy. As a corollary, we also hypothesized that (5) parents of children with ASD would prefer CGT for ASD risk to be offered to all those interested, i.e., those doubting they are able to care for a child with ASD.

2. Results

2.1. Participants: Sociodemographic

As seen in Table 1, mean age of the parents was 46.7 years, and the mean age of their children with ASD was 16.5 years. Of the children with ASD, 81% were male and 19% were female, 49% had

Asperger syndrome and 51% had infantile autism or atypical autism (infantile autism 38%, atypical autism 13%).

Table 1. Demographics: Responding parents and their children with ASD.

Responding Parents n = 1444 [a]	Mean Age, (SD), Age Range, [count], %
Age: mean (SD) {range}	46.7 (8.6) {22–87}
Children with ASD of the responding parents: [count]	[1432] [b]
Age of the children with ASD: mean (SD) {range}	16.5 (7.6) {3–58}
Male gender of the children with ASD [c]	80.5%
ASD sub-diagnoses of the children with ASD of the responding parents [d]	
Asperger syndrome	49.3%
Infantile autism	37.6%
Other ASD	13.1%

Missing information: [a] n = 11; [b] n = 23; [c] n = 29; [d] n = 39; ASD: Autism spectrum disorder, SD: Standard deviation.

2.2. Possible Positive Effects of Clinical Genetic Testing

Proportions of participants agreeing to statements about expected positive and negative effects of CGT for ASD are presented in Table 2. Regression model summaries are listed in Table S1a,b.

Table 2. Parents' opinions on possible effects of CGT for ASD (n = 1455).

Positive Effects	Agree
Causal Explanation [a] I would only take a genetic test if it could help explain the cause of ASD in me or in my child.	76.4%
Intervention Planning [b] Early diagnosis based on a genetic test will improve the possibilities of planning for good interventions and facilitations.	74.8%
Treatment Relevance [c] I would only take a genetic test if it has a direct relevance for treatment or intervention.	53.1%
Recurrence Prevention [d] I would take a genetic test if it gave me the possibility to prevent having more children with ASD.	40.0%
Family Planning [e] Genetic testing is important for family planning.	24.1%
Negative Effects	**Agree**
Insurance Discrimination [f] A genetic test showing ASD risk will cause discrimination from insurance companies.	66.8%
Parental Concern [g] Early diagnosis based on a genetic test will increase the parents' concern for the future health and development of the child.	56.1%
Family Conflicts [h] Genetic testing may cause family conflicts.	48.9%

Missing information: [a] n = 33; [b] n = 74; [c] n = 42; [d] n = 36; [e] n = 38; [f] n = 68; [g] n = 71; [h] n = 76; CGT: Clinical genetic testing; ASD: Autism spectrum disorder.

Three quarters of the participants would only do CGT if it could contribute to explaining the etiology of ASD in their child (76%) and if the CGT could improve the possibilities of planning for good interventions and treatments (75%). Half of the respondents would do CGT only if it has a direct relevance for treatment or intervention (53%). A total of 40% would do CGT if it enabled them to prevent having further children with ASD, and 24% agreed that CGT is important for family planning.

Some parent and child characteristics had a small but significant influence on opinions regarding positive effects of clinical genetic testing. Parents of children with autism differed from parents of children with Asperger syndrome on how CGT is important for etiological explanation, for recurrence prevention and for family planning. Parents of children with autism parents agreed significantly more to the statements than parents of children with Asperger syndrome in all three models ($p < 0.001$). In a family planning model, age of parent contributed significantly ($p = 0.007$). Agreement to the family planning statement increases by age of the parent. The variances explained in the significant models are, however, small (p-values range from <0.001 to 0.009; R^2 range from 0.018 to 0.081). Regression model summaries are presented in Table S1a.

2.3. Possible Negative Effects of Clinical Genetic Testing

Two thirds (67%) of the parents agreed that a genetic test result showing risk for ASD will cause insurance company discrimination, and over half (56%) had increased concern for the child's future as a consequence of CGT. Half (49%) of the parents agreed that genetic testing may cause family conflicts. We found no significant association between age, gender or ASD sub-diagnosis and opinions of insurance discrimination, parental concern or family conflicts (p-values range from 0.055 to 0.404) (Table S1b).

2.4. Management of Clinical Genetic Testing: Who and When?

The proportions of participants' opinions concerning who should be offered CGT for ASD and when to offer CGT are listed in Table 3. Regression model summaries are listed in Table S2a,b.

Table 3. Parents' opinions on management of CGT (n = 1330).

Who Should Be Offered Testing	Agree
Parents of children with ASD Those already having a child with ASD	64.9%
Doubting able to care Those doubting ability to care for a child with ASD	15.6%
Worried about the fetus Those anxious/worried that there is something wrong with the fetus	14.7%
No pregnant women	11.3%
All pregnant women	9.5%
When Should Testing Be Offered	**Agree**
Development deviates When a child shows behavioral or developmental difficulties	47.7%
Before pregnancy	35.6%
During pregnancy	8.6%
Immediately after birth	8.1%

CGT: Clinical genetic testing; ASD: Autism spectrum disorder.

On opinions about who should be offered CGT for ASD risk, 65% of the respondents agreed to those who already have an ASD child, 16% agreed to those doubting they are able to care for a child with ASD and 15% agreed to those worried about the fetus. A total of 11% of the respondents agreed that CGT should be offered to no pregnant women, and 10% agreed to all pregnant women.

Regression analyses of the parent and child characteristics (see Table S2a) show small but significant contributions from ASD sub-diagnoses in the parents of children with an ASD model and in those worried about the fetus model. Parents of children with autism agree more than parents of children with Asperger syndrome that parents of children with ASD and those worried about the fetus should be offered CGT for ASD risk ($p < 0.001$).

On items about time of testing, 48% agreed to do CGT when development deviates, 36% before pregnancy, 9% during pregnancy and 8% immediately after birth. Regression analyses of the parent and child characteristics (see Table S2b) show small but significant contributions from ASD sub-diagnosis in the before pregnancy model ($p < 0.001$) and the during pregnancy model ($p = 0.015$). Parents of children with autism parents agreed more than parents of children with Asperger syndrome in both models. The variances explained in the significant models are, however, small ($p = 0.002$; $R^2 = 0.017$ and 0.018).

2.5. Participants Opposing Clinical Genetic Testing

One option on the question "When is the best time to offer genetic testing for ASD risk?" was "I am against genetic testing for ASD", to which 9% of the participants agreed. Of those opposing CGT, 31% agreed that they would do testing only if it could help explain the cause of ASD, 42% if it has directly treatment-relevant consequences, and 35% if that early diagnosis based on CGT will improve the possibilities of planning for good interventions and facilitations (Table 4).

Parents opposing CGT differ significantly from parents not explicitly opposing all statements (p-values range from <0.001 to <0.01). We found the largest differences in scores on the statements of positive effects and the smallest differences on negative effects. See Table 4 for details.

Table 4. Parents in favor versus parents opposed CGT.

Possible Positive Effects	Agree N	In Favor of CGT	Opposed CGT	MD	Sig.
Causal Explanation I would take a genetic test only if it could help explain the cause of ASD in me or in my child.	1422	80.7%	30.9%	1.9	**
Recurrence Prevention I would take a genetic test if it gave me the possibility to prevent getting more children with ASD.	1419	43.3%	4.9%	1.8	**
Intervention Planning Early diagnosis based on a genetic test will improve the possibilities of planning for good interventions and facilitations.	1381	78.6%	35.0%	1.4	**
Family Planning Genetic testing is important for family planning.	1417	26.3%	0.8%	1.4	**
Treatment Relevance I would take a genetic test only if it has directly treatment-relevant consequences for me or my child.	1413	54.1%	41.8%	0.7	**
Possible negative effects					
Family Conflicts Genetic testing may cause family conflicts.	1379	47.3%	66.7%	-0.9	**
Parental Concern Early diagnosis based on a genetic test will increase the parents' concern for the future health and development of the child.	1384	54.9%	68.9%	-0.7	**
Insurance Discrimination A genetic test showing ASD risk will cause discrimination from insurance companies.	1387	66.0%	74.4%	-0.4	*

CGT: Clinical genetic testing; ASD: Autism spectrum disorder; MD: Difference in means; Sig.: Significance probability; ** $p < 0.001$, * $p < 0.01$.

3. Discussion

The main result of this study is that parents of ASD individuals have a clearly positive view on CGT for ASD. Etiological explanation is the most frequent effect of CGT that our respondents agreed to in our survey. This seems to confirm our hypothesis #1. The second positive effect was improvement in the possibilities of planning for good interventions and facilitations. These results are in line with findings from a study of professionals who also believe that genetic testing implies benefits for the affected families, e.g., a better possibility for early intervention, prevention of specific comorbid diseases, or relief of guilt [20]. The current findings seem to provide mixed support for routine CGT for ASD, and could help in designing such programs.

Nine percent of our respondents seem to be clearly against CGT. However, this seems mostly due to doubts about the positive effects and less due to fears of negative effects. The large agreement to positive effects of CGT among the responders (Table 4) may indicate that they will become in favor of CGT when clinical utility and treatment implications improve. Taken together, these findings seem to indicate rather robust positive attitudes toward CGT for ASD among parents of children with ASD. Furthermore, the findings also suggest that there are very small differences between parents of children with autism and parents of children with Asperger syndrome, supporting our hypothesis #2.

Skepticism against beneficial effects of CGT rather than fear of negative consequences seems to be a general finding of the current analysis. The parents' attitudes could be interpreted as being cautious and focused on preventing negative consequences of introducing technological innovations into clinical practice prematurely, e.g., by giving inaccurate etiological diagnoses [46]. Their opinions seems to be in line with the recent guidelines of EuroGentest and the European Society of Human Genetics (ESHG) for diagnostic next-generation sequencing, which states that insufficiently validated tests present a threat to patients, and their use in a clinical diagnostic setting is unacceptable [47].

Discrimination from insurance companies is the negative effect of CGT most frequently stated in our sample. The difference between those in favor and those against CGT is small (see Table 4), supporting our hypothesis #3. Fear of discrimination from insurance companies may come as a surprise in the Norwegian context of our study. In Norway, genetic testing is covered by the compulsory state health insurance, and discrimination on the basis of genetic constitution is prohibited by law [48], as it is in most other western countries [21,25]. The UN Universal Declaration of the Human Genome and Human Rights also prohibit all forms of discrimination based on genetic characteristics [49]. However, the use of voluntary private health insurance (VPHI) has recently increased also among Norwegians, but VPHI typically do not cover treatments for psychiatric conditions [50]. Knowledge of risk is integral to the concept of insurance premiums [44] and some European countries explicitly allow the use of genetic risk information when the insurance payment exceeds a certain level, which usually applies for life insurance, illness/health insurance or insurance to protect income in the case of being disabled and unable to work [44,45]. Having a child with ASD is associated with long term sick leave, not being in the labor force and low income [51], and it seems prudent to be aware of issues of possible discriminations from health and life insurance companies both in relation to parents and to people with ASD.

While only 8% agree that it is best to offer CGT during pregnancy (i.e., prenatal diagnosis), half (48%) of the parents in our sample prefer CGT to be offered when a child shows behavioral or developmental challenges and more than a third (36%) before pregnancy. Hypothesis #4, saying that parents would prefer CGT as early as possible, i.e., during pregnancy, is thus refuted. In the event of a prenatal test for ASD, this result may indicate that the Norwegian practice of direct access to prenatal testing for Trisomies (21, 18, 13) for women 38 years or older, or in later pregnancies when one has a child with a severe disability, may be less relevant for parents of individuals with ASD. This may have consequences for genetic counselling practices of parents of children with ASD. Effective counselling may depend on professional exposure to individuals with ASD. In a Down syndrome (DS) context, it is claimed that what genetic counselors believe to be the most salient information to discuss with parents differs based on whether they practice in the prenatal or postnatal setting [52], which may be a point to consider in ASD as well.

We found that more than half (65%) of the parents of children with ASD prefer CGT to be offered to those already having a child with ASD. This contradicts our hypothesis #5 that parents would prefer all those interested, i.e., those doubting that they are able to care for a child with ASD, to be offered CGT. Fifteen percent of the respondents support our hypothesis #5, and 36% prefer CGT before pregnancy. Although not specified, testing before pregnancy is plausibly interpreted as carrier testing in parents, which is not likely in a complex disorder such as ASD. This may reflect a lack of knowledge in parents, but may as well be due to the questionnaire that asked to imagine the existence of a test saying "something about the risk of ASD". However, parents' recurrence risk perceptions have shown to be inaccurately high and to influence reproductive decisions [39], and our finding may be interpreted in line with this.

We found that 40% in our sample would do a CGT if it gave them the possibility to prevent having more children with ASD. This may be interpreted as our sample preferring CGT when a child shows behavioral or developmental challenges with the purpose of augmenting development, or for preventive purposes for those parents that already have children with ASD. In comparison, a study of parents of children with fragile X (FX) found that 59% agreed that the FX-test influenced their decision to have another child [38]. It is surprising that only 24% agree that CGT is important for family planning (Table 2) when 40% would do a CGT if it enabled them to prevent having further children with ASD (Table 2). According to the World Health Organization (WHO), "family planning allows people to attain their desired number of children and determine the spacing of pregnancies. It is achieved through use of contraceptive methods and the treatment of infertility" [53]. This is also the official standard use of the term in Norway. However, the term may have been interpreted as very different from preventive measures, perhaps because this was addressed explicitly in another questionnaire statement. Family planning may have been interpreted as a question of organizing the family life and about interventions in the parents' home as almost every child and teenager with ASD in Norway lives with their parents. Regarding genetic counselling and reproductive issues, this may warrant a focus on experienced and knowledgeable parents and collaboration between them and professionals, in addition to the current predominance of a "teaching model" that may not be optimal in supporting patients to make decisions relevant to their health care [54]. These results also seem to underscore the need for recurrence risk counselling.

Ethical concerns regarding genetic testing in a reproductive setting may vary with cultural, religious and societal value bases both in parents and professionals [55]. A collaborative climate that respects the autonomy of individuals and the values of the communities and groups to which they belong seems necessary [56]. It is also important to cover these ethical issues further than the scope of the present study, which may be limited by empirical foundations for such inquiries. Relevant issues for ethical inquiries include how society values people with ASD and their parents. Advocates for ASD fear the possible outcomes of prenatal genetic testing or treatment. They argue that aggressively seeking interventions devalues ASD traits and tendencies [42], and adults with ASD fear that people with these traits will eventually be eliminated through prenatal genetic testing and selective abortion [42].

Three quarters of our sample agreed that CGT is relevant for intervention planning. This seems in line with results from a study of the impact of CMA on clinical management [57]. Treatment plans targeting associated medical conditions and planned additional assessments were directly impacted for more than 40% of individuals with neurodevelopmental disorders, including ASD [58,59]. Furthermore, the current parents' views seem in line with recent findings that genetic testing may shorten the 'diagnostic odyssey' and provide a causal explanation, indicate a recurrence risk and enable access to appropriate early interventions and tailoring the care of affected individuals [8,32,59,60]. Interestingly, a recent study summarizing the results of over four years of real-world clinical ultra-high resolution CMA testing optimized for neurodevelopmental disorders found direct correlation between a higher rate of detected abnormalities and age in the ASD cohort, which suggests that earlier use of CMA and perhaps other genetic testing methods may be important for early intervention [9].

Overall, characteristics of the parents or their children seem to have only small influences on the informants' attitudes toward CGT of ASD. This underscores the general positive attitude toward the use of molecular genetic technology in this group of patients. Some differences were, however, present in parents of children with ASD. Whether the child had autism or Asperger syndrome influences the attitudes. Parents of children with autism are more optimistic about the clinical opportunities of genetic testing for ASD than parents of children with Asperger syndrome by rating the positive effects higher and the negative effects lower. The difference between Asperger syndrome and autism may be regarded as difference in disease severity. In contrast, no association between various FX severities and opinions about screening in caregivers have been found [61].

The stigma attached to mental illness is claimed to always lead to stress through discrimination in academic settings, in work, and in public, although often unintended [41]. For instance, in a future case of neonatal genetic screening for ASD, a child with a susceptibility genotype whose behavioral presentation is considered "odd" may be stigmatized as "autistic" despite not meeting the diagnostic criteria. Conversely, a child with a susceptibility genotype may be excused for "inappropriate" behavior [21]. In either case, less fortunate interventions or treatments may be initiated. Parents are also in danger of being blamed for their children's condition when the condition is inherited. It is important to avoid terminology that may be misused and cause unjust stigmatizing and blaming, as happened with Kanner's early characterization of parents [42]. If the ethical implications of genetic identities become uncertain as research gains more knowledge about how genes and environments interrelate [42], it is clear that empirical studies of attitudes, hopes and fears of all stakeholders, at pace with the technological advancements, are necessary.

Limitations

There is limited knowledge about the attitudes toward CGT among parents of children with ASD. Although the current study provides important new information about the attitudes toward CGT for ASD and collected information from a large numbers of parents, it has limitations. One limitation is a lack of comprehensive demographic information of the participants, and little information about disease severity or genetic origin of the ASD in their children. Our findings are also limited to opinions about the specific items of positive and negative effects stated in our questionnaire. The lack of explicit questions about attitudes toward prenatal diagnosis and the related issues of stigma and offence of such practice is also a limitation. The low number of parents that think CGT should be offered during pregnancy may indicate that this is an issue that should have been addressed in more detail.

Another potential limitation is that the previously untested questionnaire was inspired from a questionnaire about malignant melanoma, which is a disease quite different from ASD. Malignant melanoma is a deadly skin cancer disease while ASD is a disability. There are important differences between what is perceived as disease and what is perceived as disability. Disabilities, and particularly those involving mental capacities, raise existential issues of identity in a sense that issues of diseases do not. To determine identities through genetic testing is more controversial than to determine diseases. This difference may have made the questions generated from malignant melanoma studies less suitable for capturing attitudes toward CGT for ASD. A further limitation is that the questionnaire did not specify whether the questions concerned testing parents or testing the child, where it could mean either, which makes the accuracy of some of our findings uncertain.

It is also possible that our sample is biased by being recruited from an interest organization. Our large sample may not be representative of attitudes of parents of children with ASD in general. Despite it being the only ASD organization in Norway, with a high number of members, a significant proportion of parents of children with ASD are not members of the interest organization.

4. Materials and Methods

4.1. Participants

In collaboration with the Norwegian patient organization for ASD "Autism Society Norway", a questionnaire was sent by email or post to all of the parent members of the organization. The organization has no formal requirement for membership of parents, but 3539 members were registered as parents to one or more children with ASD. In order to reach as many as possible, two approaches were used. Members registered with email addresses were contacted by email, which contained a link to a web-based Response Form Questionnaire from the University of Oslo. Members without email addresses received paper mail with the questionnaire and a prepaid return envelope. Email reminders were sent to those not responding, while no paper mail reminders were sent. Answers were anonymous. A total of 3539 invitations were sent, n = 1990 by email and n = 1549 by paper letters. A total of n = 1455 responded (41%), n = 917 (46%) through email, and n = 538 (35%) by paper mail. The survey was closed after two reminders. No financial incentive or other rewards were provided.

4.2. Questionnaire

The questionnaire investigated attitudes toward clinical use of a potential genetic test for ASD. It was emphasized that, currently, a predictive genetic test for ASD is not available. The participants were asked to imagine the existence of a clinical test that could say "something" about the risk of ASD.

Some of the questions concerning attitudes were based on a survey of attitudes toward genetic research in families with a risk of malignant melanoma [62], others were composed and tested by our multi-professional team and selected representatives of the target group. One of the questions was also in line with a qualitative study of awareness and attitudes among parents of children with ASD [25]. The questionnaire as a whole has not been previously tested and the overall psychometric properties are unknown. Although difficult to establish, the validity seems high at face value. Our explorations of how responder characteristics influence the ratings provide some indications of the validity of the questionnaire. The answers were given on a 5-point Likert scale with alternatives "strongly disagree", "disagree", "neither disagree or agree", "agree" and "strongly agree", in addition to "Don´t know" or "Have no meaning" options [63].

The questions concerning attitudes were part of a questionnaire with 45 items in four sections. It took 10–15 min to complete the questionnaire. The first section of the questionnaire asked about age and gender of the parents. The second section asked about the parents' firstborn child with ASD diagnosis, the child´s ASD diagnosis (infantile autism or Asperger syndrome), the child´s age when first diagnosed with ASD, and the child´s comorbid somatic and psychiatric diagnoses. It was not asked how many children with ASD the participants have. International Statistical Classification of Diseases and Related Health Problems (ICD) criteria are used in Norway. The third section of the questionnaire asked about experiences with the specialist health services. The fourth section asked about attitudes toward genetic research and CGT. The questions about attitudes toward genetic research have been previously reported [36].

With a total of n = 1455 members responding, we estimate the response rate to be approximately 50%. Because the information to be collected was anonymized, the Regional Committee for Medical and Health Research Ethics (REC) concluded that the study did not require REC approval.

4.3. Data Handling and Analyses

SPSS version 23 (IBM, Armonk, NY, USA) was used for statistical analyses. The paper responses were scanned and read using ABBYY FlexiCapture 10 (ABBYY Europe, Munich, Germany) and subsequently imported into a SPSS file, while the online responses were imported directly.

First, descriptive statistics were performed. Percentages of agreement and disagreement to the attitude statements were obtained by dichotomizing the Likert-scale variables in the following way: Scores 1 ("Totally disagree") and 2 ("Somewhat disagree") were combined to a "disagree"—score, scores 4 ("Somewhat agree") and 5 ("Totally agree") were combined to an "agree"—score. Score 3 ("neither/nor") was merged with the "have no meaning"—and the "don't know"—scores in order to form an "NA"—score labelling the "no distinct negative or positive attitude available".

Forced entry linear regression analyses were conducted both on the original 5-point attitude variables and on the binary attitude variables [64] concerning management of CGT to analyze the effect of respondent age and gender, child age, child gender, and child ASD diagnose on the attitude items. Due to multiple comparisons, we used Bonferroni corrected significance thresholds, setting the significance limits to $p = 0.01$ per test (0.05/5 tests). Cases with missing values were excluded listwise in the regression analyses and deleted on an analysis-by-analysis basis in the independent sample *t*-tests.

5. Conclusions

Parents of children with ASD seem to be clearly positive toward CGT. Only one of ten is opposed to CGT and the reason is mainly skepticism about the possible benefits, not because they fear possible harm. This suggests that parents of children with ASD seem well informed, have a practical attitude to CGT, and have similar attitudes as health care personnel and ASD experts.

Few parents seem interested in prenatal diagnosis and family planning. They seem rather to prefer CGT when a child shows behavioral or developmental challenges with the purpose of augmenting development, or for preventive purposes for those that already have children with ASD. Further research is necessary in order to draw direct clinical implications of these results. However, the current results may form the basis for such testing procedures in the future when they will be more informative. It is important to avoid initiating premature CGT procedures.

Acknowledgments: We are thankful to the participants in the study and the Autism Society Norway. We are also thankful to Berge Solberg for valuable comments and suggestions. The project was supported by the Research Council of Norway (Grant Nos. 213694 and 223273) and the KG Jebsen Stiftelsen, and has received funding from the European Community's Seventh Framework Programme (FP7/2007–2013) under Grant No. 602450. This paper reflects only the author's views and the European Union is not liable for any use that may be made of the information contained therein. This study is part of the BUPgen Study group and the research network NeuroDevelop.

Author Contributions: Terje Nærland and Ole A. Andreassen designed the study, Jarle Johannessen and Terje Nærland collected and analysed data and wrote the first draft together with Ole A. Andreassen, Sigrun Hope, Marcella Rietschel, Tonje Torske, Anne Lise Høyland, Jana Strohmaier, Arvid Heiberg and Srdjan Djurovic participated in interpreting data. All authors contributed to the final version of the paper.

Abbreviations

ASD	Autism spectrum disorder
CGT	Clinical genetic testing
CMA	Chromosomal microarray
CNV	Copy number variant
DS	Down syndrome
ESHG	European Society of Human Genetics
FX	Fragile X
FXS	Fragile X syndrome
ICD	International Statistical Classification of Diseases and Related Health Problems
REC	Regional Committee for Medical and Health Research Ethics
VPHI	Voluntary private health insurance
WHO	World Health Organization

References

1. Lai, M.C.; Lombardo, M.V.; Baron-Cohen, S. Autism. *Lancet* **2014**, *383*, 896–910. [CrossRef]
2. Baxter, A.J.; Brugha, T.S.; Erskine, H.E.; Scheurer, R.W.; Vos, T.; Scott, J.G. The epidemiology and global burden of autism spectrum disorders. *Psychol. Med.* **2015**, *45*, 601–613. [CrossRef] [PubMed]
3. Surén, P.; Bakken, I.J.; Aase, H.; Chin, R.; Gunnes, N.; Lie, K.K.; Magnus, P.; Reichborn-Kjennerud, T.; Schjølberg, S.; Øyen, A.-S.; et al. Autism spectrum disorder, ADHD, epilepsy, and cerebral palsy in norwegian children. *Pediatrics* **2012**, *130*, e152–e158. [CrossRef] [PubMed]
4. Xu, L.; Carpenter-Aeby, T.; Aeby, V.G.; Lu, W. An integrated model of emotions, attitudes, and intentions associated with undergoing autism genetic testing. *Psychol. Cogn. Sci. Open J.* **2015**, *1*, 29–38. [CrossRef]

5. Schaefer, G. Clinical genetic aspects of ASD spectrum disorders. *Int. J. Mol. Sci.* **2016**, *17*, 180. [CrossRef] [PubMed]
6. Yuen, R.K.C.; Thiruvahindrapuram, B.; Merico, D.; Walker, S.; Tammimies, K.; Hoang, N.; Chrysler, C.; Nalpathamkalam, T.; Pellecchia, G.; Liu, Y.; et al. Whole-genome sequencing of quartet families with autism spectrum disorder. *Nat. Med.* **2015**, *21*, 185–191. [CrossRef] [PubMed]
7. Schaefer, G.B.; Mendelsohn, N.J. Clinical genetics evaluation in identifying the etiology of autism spectrum disorders: 2013 guideline revisions. *Genet. Med.* **2013**, *15*, 399–407. [CrossRef] [PubMed]
8. Heil, K.M.; Schaaf, C.P. The genetics of autism spectrum disorders—A guide for clinicians. *Curr. Psychiatry Rep.* **2013**, *15*, 334–342. [CrossRef] [PubMed]
9. Ho, K.; Wassman, E.; Baxter, A.; Hensel, C.; Martin, M.; Prasad, A.; Twede, H.; Vanzo, R.; Butler, M. Chromosomal microarray analysis of consecutive individuals with autism spectrum disorders using an ultra-high resolution chromosomal microarray optimized for neurodevelopmental disorders. *Int. J. Mol. Sci.* **2016**, *17*, 2070. [CrossRef] [PubMed]
10. Fischbach, R.L.; Harris, M.J.; Ballan, M.S.; Fischbach, G.D.; Link, B.G.; Charman, T.; Leake, A.R.; Sivberg, B. Is there concordance in attitudes and beliefs between parents and scientists about autism spectrum disorder? *Autism* **2015**, *6*, 207–214. [CrossRef] [PubMed]
11. Collins, F.S.; Varmus, H. A new initiative on precision medicine. *N. Engl. J. Med.* **2015**, *372*, 793–795. [CrossRef] [PubMed]
12. Julia, S.; Soulier, A.; Leonard, S.; Sanlaville, D.; Vigouroux, A.; Keren, B.; Heron, D.; Till, M.; Chassaing, N.; Bouneau, L. Ethical issues raised by the clinical implementation of new diagnostic tools for genetic diseases in children: Array comparative genomic hybridization (ACGH) as a case study. *J. Clin. Med. Res.* **2015**, *6*, 2.
13. Polyak, A.; Girirajan, S. A need for precision medicine to enable tailored special education. *Am. J. Med. Genet.* **2016**, *171*, 300. [CrossRef] [PubMed]
14. Polyak, A.; Kubina, R.M.; Girirajan, S. Comorbidity of intellectual disability confounds ascertainment of autism: Implications for genetic diagnosis. *Am. J. Med. Genet.* **2015**, *168*, 600–608. [CrossRef] [PubMed]
15. Hens, K.; Peeters, H.; Dierickx, K. The ethics of complexity. Genetics and autism, a literature review. *Am. J. Med. Genet.* **2016**, *171B*, 305–316. [CrossRef] [PubMed]
16. Burke, W.; Laberge, A.M.; Press, N. Debating clinical utility. *Public Health Genom.* **2010**, *13*, 215–223. [CrossRef] [PubMed]
17. Freitag, C.M. The genetics of autistic disorders and its clinical relevance: A review of the literature. *Mol. Psychiatry* **2007**, *12*, 2–22. [CrossRef] [PubMed]
18. McMahon, W.M.; Baty, B.J.; Botkin, J. Genetic counseling and ethical issues for autism. *Am. J. Med. Genet.* **2006**, *142C*, 52–57. [CrossRef] [PubMed]
19. Finucane, B.; Myers, S.M. Genetic counseling for autism spectrum disorder in an evolving theoretical landscape. *Curr. Genet. Med. Rep.* **2016**, *4*, 147–153. [CrossRef] [PubMed]
20. Hens, K.; Peeters, H.; Dierickx, K. Genetic testing and counseling in the case of an autism diagnosis: A caregivers perspective. *Eur. J. Hum. Genet.* **2016**, *59*, 452–458. [CrossRef] [PubMed]
21. Marchant, G.E.; Robert, J.S. Genetic testing for autism predisposition: Ethical, legal and social challenges. *Houst J. Health Law Policy* **2009**, *9*, 203–235.
22. Walsh, P.; Elsabbagh, M.; Bolton, P.; Singh, I. In search of biomarkers for autism: Scientific, social and ethical challenges. *Nat. Rev. Neurosc.* **2011**, *12*, 603–612. [CrossRef] [PubMed]
23. Lintas, C.; Persico, A.M. Autistic phenotypes and genetic testing: State-of-the-art for the clinical geneticist. *J. Med. Genet.* **2009**, *46*, 1–8. [CrossRef] [PubMed]
24. Scherer, S.W.; Dawson, G. Risk factors for autism: Translating genomic discoveries into diagnostics. *Hum. Genet.* **2011**, *130*, 123–148. [CrossRef] [PubMed]
25. Chen, L.S.; Xu, L.; Huang, T.Y.; Dhar, S.U. Autism genetic testing: A qualitative study of awareness, attitudes, and experiences among parents of children with autism spectrum disorders. *Genet. Med.* **2013**, *15*, 274–281. [CrossRef] [PubMed]
26. Rew, L.; Kaur, M.; McMillan, A.; Mackert, M.; Bonevac, D. Systematic review of psychosocial benefits and harms of genetic testing. *Issues Ment. Health Nurs.* **2010**, *31*, 631–645. [CrossRef] [PubMed]
27. Rew, L.; Mackert, M.; Bonevac, D. A systematic review of literature about the genetic testing of adolescents. *J. Spec. Pediatr. Nurs.* **2009**, *14*, 284–294. [CrossRef] [PubMed]

28. Gronborg, T.K.; Hansen, S.N.; Nielsen, S.V.; Skythhe, A.; Parner, E.T. Stoppage in autism spectrum disorders. *J. Autism. Dev. Disord.* **2015**, *45*, 3509–3519. [CrossRef] [PubMed]
29. Lauritsen, M.B.; Pedersen, C.B.; Mortensen, P.B. Effects of familial risk factors and place of birth on the risk of autism: A nationwide register-based study. *J. Child Psychol. Psychiatry* **2005**, *46*, 963–971. [CrossRef] [PubMed]
30. Ozonoff, S.; Young, G.S.; Carter, A.; Messinger, D.; Yirmiya, N.; Zwaigenbaum, L.; Bryson, S.; Carver, L.J.; Constantino, J.N.; Hutman, T.; et al. Recurrence risk for autism spectrum disorders: A baby siblings research consortium study. *Pediatrics* **2011**, *128*, e488–e495. [CrossRef] [PubMed]
31. Cuccaro, M.L.; Czape, K.; Alessandri, M.; Lee, J.; Deppen, A.R.; Bendik, E.; Dueker, N.; Nations, L.; Pericak-Vance, M.; Hahn, S. Genetic testing and corresponding services among individuals with autism spectrum disorder (ASD). *Am. J. Med. Genet.* **2014**, *164A*, 2592–2600. [CrossRef] [PubMed]
32. Narcisa, V.; Discenza, M.; Vaccari, E.; Rosen-Sheidley, B.; Hardan, A.Y.; Couchon, E. Parental interest in a genetic risk assessment test for autism spectrum disorders. *Clin. Pediatr.* **2013**, *52*, 139–146. [CrossRef] [PubMed]
33. Zwaigenbaum, L.; Bauman, M.L.; Stone, W.L.; Yirmiya, N.; Estes, A.; Hansen, R.L.; McPartland, J.C.; Natowicz, M.R.; Choueiri, R.; Fein, D.; et al. Early identification of autism spectrum disorder: Recommendations for practice and research. *Pediatrics* **2015**, *136*, S10–S40. [CrossRef] [PubMed]
34. Golfenshtein, N.; Srulovici, E.; Medoff-Cooper, B. Investigating parenting stress across pediatric health conditions: A systematic review. *Compr. Child. Adolesc. Nurs.* **2016**, *39*, 41–79. [CrossRef] [PubMed]
35. Lai, W.W.; Goh, T.J.; Oei, T.P.; Sung, M. Coping and well-being in parents of children with autism spectrum disorders (ASD). *J. Autism. Dev. Disord.* **2015**, *45*, 2582–2593. [CrossRef] [PubMed]
36. Johannessen, J.; Nærland, T.; Bloss, C.; Rietschel, M.; Strohmaier, J.; Gjevik, E.; Heiberg, A.; Djurovic, S.; Andreassen, O.A. Parents' attitudes toward genetic research in autism spectrum disorder. *Psychiatr. Genet.* **2016**, *26*, 74–80. [CrossRef] [PubMed]
37. Jones, M.B.; Szatmari, P. Stoppage rules and genetic studies of autism. *J. Autism. Dev. Disord.* **1988**, *18*, 31–40. [CrossRef] [PubMed]
38. Bailey, D.B.; Skinner, D.; Sparkman, K.L. Discovering fragile X syndrome: Family experiences and perceptions. *Pediatrics* **2003**, *111*, 407–416. [CrossRef] [PubMed]
39. Selkirk, C.G.; McCarthy Veach, P.; Lian, F.; Schimmenti, L.; Leroy, B.S. Parents' perceptions of autism spectrum disorder etiology and recurrence risk and effects of their perceptions on family planning: Recommendations for genetic counselors. *J. Genet. Couns.* **2009**, *18*, 507–519. [CrossRef] [PubMed]
40. Sivell, S.; Elwyn, G.; Gaff, C.L.; Clarke, A.J.; Iredale, R.; Shaw, C.; Dundon, J.; Thornton, H.; Edwards, A. How risk is perceived, constructed and interpreted by clients in clinical genetics, and the effects on decision making: Systematic review. *J. Genet. Couns.* **2008**, *17*, 30–63. [CrossRef] [PubMed]
41. Adler, B.A.; Minshawi, N.F.; Erickson, C.A. Evolution of autism: From Kanner to the DSM-V. In *Handbook of Early Intervention for Autism Spectrum Disorders: Research, Policy, and Practice*; Tarbox, J., Dixon, D.R., Sturmey, P., Matson, J.L., Eds.; Springer: New York, NY, USA, 2014; pp. 3–19.
42. Silverman, C. *Understanding Autism: Parents, Doctors, and the History of a Disorder*; Princeton University Press: Princeton, NJ, USA, 2012.
43. Campbell, E.; Ross, L.F. Parental attitudes and beliefs regarding the genetic testing of children. *Community Genet.* **2005**, *8*, 94–102. [CrossRef] [PubMed]
44. Soini, S. Genetic testing legislation in Western Europe—A fluctuating regulatory target. *J. Community Genet.* **2012**, *3*, 143–153. [CrossRef] [PubMed]
45. Kvale, H.; Gudmundsdóttir, L.H.; Stoll, J.; Faber, B.A. *Legislation on Biotechnology in the Nordic Countries—An Overview 2016*; NordForsk: Oslo, Norway, 2016.
46. Ashley, E.A. Towards precision medicine. *Nat. Rev. Genet.* **2016**, *17*, 507–522. [CrossRef] [PubMed]
47. Matthijs, G.; Souche, E.; Alders, M.; Corveleyn, A.; Eck, S.; Feenstra, I.; Race, V.; Sistermans, E.; Sturm, M.; Weiss, M.; et al. Guidelines for diagnostic next-generation sequencing. *Eur. J. Hum. Genet.* **2016**, *24*, 2–5. [CrossRef] [PubMed]
48. Bioteknologiloven. Lov om Humanmedisinsk Bruk av Bioteknologi m.m. (Bioteknologiloven). [Act of 5 December 2003 No. 100 Relating to the Application of Biotechnology in Human Medicine, etc]. Available online: http://app.uio.no/ub/ujur/oversatte-lover/data/lov-20031205-100-eng.pdf (accessed on 16 April 2017).

49. UN General Assembly. Universal declaration on the human genome and human rights. In *Resolution 53/152 of 9 December 1998*; United Nations Human Rights Office of the High Commissioner: Geneva, Switzerland, 1998.
50. Alexandersen, N.; Anell, A.; Kaarboe, O.; Lehto, J.S.; Tynkkynen, L.-K.; Vrangbaek, K. The development of voluntary private health insurance in the nordic countries. *Nordic J. Health Econ.* **2016**, *4*, 68–83. [CrossRef]
51. McEvilly, M.; Wicks, S.; Dalman, C. Sick leave and work participation among parents of children with autism spectrum disorder in the stockholm youth cohort: A register linkage study in Stockholm, Sweden. *J. Autism. Dev. Disord.* **2015**, *45*, 2157–2167. [CrossRef] [PubMed]
52. Acharya, K. Prenatal testing for intellectual disability: Misperceptions and reality with lessons from down syndrome. *Dev. Disabil. Res. Rev.* **2011**, *17*, 27–31. [CrossRef] [PubMed]
53. World Health Organization. Family Planning/Contraception. Available online: http://who.int/mediacentre/factsheets/fs351/en/ (accessed on 2 February 2017).
54. Skirton, H.; Cordier, C.; Ingvoldstad, C.; Taris, N.; Benjamin, C. The role of the genetic counsellor: A systematic review of research evidence. *Eur. J. Hum. Genet.* **2015**, *23*, 452–458. [CrossRef] [PubMed]
55. MacKenzie, M.J.; Baumeister, R.F. Meaning in life: Nature, needs, and myths. In *Meaning in Positive and Existential Psychology*; Batthyany, A., Russo-Netzer, P., Eds.; Springer: New York, NY, USA, 2014; pp. 25–37.
56. Blasimme, A.; Vayena, E. Becoming partners, retaining autonomy: Ethical considerations on the development of precision medicine. *BMC Med. Ethics* **2016**, *17*, 67–75. [CrossRef] [PubMed]
57. Tammimies, K.; Marshall, C.R.; Walker, S.; Kaur, G.; Thiruvahindrapuram, B.; Lionel, A.C.; Yuen, R.K.C.; Uddin, M.; Roberts, W.; Weksberg, R.; et al. Molecular diagnostic yield of chromosomal microarray analysis and whole-exome sequencing in children with autism spectrum disorder. *JAMA* **2016**, *314*, 895–903. [CrossRef] [PubMed]
58. Henderson, L.B.; Applegate, C.D.; Wohler, E.; Sheridan, M.B.; Hoover-Fong, J.; Batista, D.A.S. The impact of chromosomal microarray on clinical management: A retrospective analysis. *Genet. Med.* **2014**, *16*, 1–8. [CrossRef] [PubMed]
59. Tammimies, K.; Falck-Ytter, T.; Bölte, S. Quo vadis clinical genomics of ASD? *Autism* **2016**, *20*, 259–261. [CrossRef] [PubMed]
60. Reiff, M.; Giarelli, E.; Bernhardt, B.A.; Easley, E.; Spinner, N.B.; Sankar, P.L.; Mulchandani, S. Parents' perceptions of the usefulness of chromosomal microarray analysis for children with autism spectrum disorders. *J. Autism. Dev. Disord.* **2015**, *45*, 3262–3275. [CrossRef] [PubMed]
61. Bailey, D.B.; Bishop, E.; Raspa, M.; Skinner, D. Caregiver opinions about fragile X population screening. *Genet. Med.* **2012**, *14*, 115–121. [CrossRef] [PubMed]
62. Branstrom, R.; Kasparian, N.A.; Affleck, P.; Tibben, A.; Chang, Y.-m.M.; Azizi, E.; Baron-Epel, O.; Bergman, W.; Chan, M.; Davies, J.; et al. Perceptions of genetic research and testing among members of families with an increased risk of malignant melanoma. *Eur. J. Cancer* **2012**, *48*, 3052–3062. [CrossRef] [PubMed]
63. Bishop, P.A.; Herron, R.L. Use and misuse of the likert item responses and other ordinal measures. *Int. J. Exerc. Sci.* **2015**, *8*, 297–302. [PubMed]
64. Hellevik, O. Linear versus logistic regression when the dependent variable is a dichotomy. *Qual. Quant.* **2009**, *43*, 59–74. [CrossRef]

9

Sensory Profiles of Children with Autism Spectrum Disorder with and without Feeding Problems: A Comparative Study in Sicilian Subjects

Simonetta Panerai [1,*], Raffaele Ferri [1], Valentina Catania [1], Marinella Zingale [1], Daniela Ruccella [2], Donatella Gelardi [1], Daniela Fasciana [3] and Maurizio Elia [1]

1 Oasi Research Institute-IRCCS, 94018 Troina, Italy; rferri@oasi.en.it (R.F.); vacatania@oasi.en.it (V.C.); mzingale@oasi.en.it (M.Z.); dgelardi@oasi.en.it (D.G.); melia@oasi.en.it (M.E.)

2 Psychoeducational Service for Children with Autism and Intellectual Disability, Società Cooperativa Sociale "I Corrieri dell'Oasi" (CdO), 94100 Enna, Italy; danielaruccella82@gmail.com

3 Center for Diagnosis and Early Intensive Treatment of Autism Spectrum Disorder, 93100 ASP Caltanissetta, Italy; danifasciana@gmail.com

* Correspondence: spanerai@oasi.en.it

Abstract: The aim of this study is to better understand the relationship between sensory and feeding problems in Autism Spectrum Disorder (ASD) by comparing sensory responsiveness of ASD children with (ASD-W) and without (ASD-WO) feeding problems. The feeding and sensory characteristics of 111 children with ASD (37 ASD-W and 74 ASD-WO) were assessed by using two questionnaires tapping on feeding problems and two on sensory problems. A comparative study was carried out with between-group as well as intra-group comparisons design; a correlation analysis was also added. A statistically significant correlation was found between sensory and feeding problems. ASD-W children showed more severe and extensively impaired sensory responses than ASD-WO, with lower sensory adaptation and more generalized and severe deficits in all subdomains. Taste/Smell sensitivity was strongly impaired only in ASD-W, whereas in ASD-WO it was found to be a point of strength. Both groups showed a Hyporesponsive profile, though it was more marked in ASD-W. Both groups showed strengths in Visual/Auditory sensitivity, Low-Energy/Weak, and Movement sensitivity, again more marked in ASD-WO. These results might prove to be particularly useful for sensory training and psychoeducational treatment.

Keywords: autism spectrum disorder (ASD); sensory profile; sensory responsiveness; feeding problems; short sensory profile (SSP); sensory experience questionnaire (SEQ)

---

1. Introduction

Sensory impairments are frequent in children with Autism Spectrum Disorder (ASD) [1–7], with over 90% of cases presenting severe sensory symptoms in multiple sensory domains, as reported in some studies [2,4]. They form a group of disorders that involve challenges in modulation, integration, organization, and discrimination of sensory inputs, leading to either inappropriately responding to those inputs or experiencing disruptions in daily activities and emotional-behavioral patterns. In particular, sensory modulation disorders are classified into three subtypes: (1) over-responsivity (or hyperresponsiveness), characterized by exaggerated, rapid onset and/or prolonged reactions to sensory stimulation; (2) under-responsivity (or hyporesponsiveness), with unawareness or slow response to sensory input; and (3) seeking for, involving craving of, and interest in sensory experiences that are prolonged or intense [8]. Some patterns, such as hypo- and hyperresponsiveness, are also known to co-occur in children with ASD [9–12], especially in children showing a generalized sensory impairment [13]. Results of a meta-analysis by Ben Sasson et al. [14] showed a significantly high difference between ASD and Typically Developing (TD) groups in sensory modulation, with the greatest difference in under-responsivity, followed by over-responsivity and sensation seeking. Although the three sensory modulation disorder subtypes are hypothetical, some physiological research supports these distinctions. A review by Suarez [4] reported some results of these physiological studies: in over-responsivity a low threshold for one or multiple sensation channels has been hypothesized, resulting, for example, in exaggerated reactions to textures or noises. On the contrary, in under-responsivity, a high threshold has been hypothesized, so that only intense and sustained stimuli can obtain attention by children, resulting in diminished or no response, for example, to name or pain. Studies using physiological tools, such as electrodermal sensors or cardiac vagal tone index, found a decreased or increased activation of the electrodermal responses (in under-responsive and in over-responsive children respectively) and an impaired less effective parasympathetic system.

The most affected sensory modalities in children with ASD seem to be auditory filtering and tactile sensitivity [3,15–18]. Sensory dysfunctions also seem to be related to the severity of ASD [5,14,19] and to stereotyped interests and behaviors [16,20]. Limited and stereotyped behaviors, interests and activities can be observed also in the feeding domain [21,22] and a strong sensitivity to sensory information has been associated with feeding problems, especially food fussiness, in both children with typical and atypical development [23]. However, in children with atypical development, feeding concerns still persist beyond childhood. With age, children with typical development change their appetite, food preferences, and eating habits, but the social and emotional dimensions of food remain stable and expand over time. Furthermore, in children with ASD, feeding involves both the nutritional and the emotional-relational dimensions. The term "eating problems" typically refers to oral consumption of nutrients that deviates from the norm, enough to lead to negative emotional, social or health consequences. The prevalence of feeding problems in children with ASD is estimated to be approximately 90%, with 70% of children showing food selectivity [24–26]. It has been suggested that feeding problems might be related to sensory modulation disorders as well [4,27–30]. The study by Zobel-Lachiusa et al. [28] investigated differences in feeding behaviors and sensory characteristics of children with ASD compared to TD children. Statistically significant differences between the two groups were found in all the measures administered, as well as a moderate to strong positive correlation between feeding problems and sensory impairments in children with ASD. Nadon et al. [29] found a definite and probable difference in sensory processing (as measured by using the Short Sensory Profile—SSP) [31] in 65% of children ($N = 95$) with ASD, aged 3 to 10 years; these results were also related to increased feeding problems in the sample. Chistol et al. [30] found higher levels of food refusal in ASD children with atypical oral sensitivity compared to those showing a typical oral sensitivity. McCormick et al. [7] showed no significant differences between ASD and Developmentally Delayed children, except for the Taste/Smell and Visual/Auditory sensitivity (SSP subsections).

Children with ASD present with higher sensory problems than TD, with a prevalence ranging from 65.3% to 84.8% [3,28,32]; moreover, sensory and feeding problems seem to be correlated. Objective of our study was to investigate whether ASD children with feeding problems (ASD-W) show the same sensorimotor features as the ASD without feeding problems (ASD-WO): which sensory modalities are impaired and to what extent? Our study is not directed to feeding per se, as a purely physiological process, but to the behavioral components accompanying the feeding act.

Our hypothesis is that sensory profiles might present different characteristics in specific subgroups of children with autism (with and without feeding problems), and that ASD-W children might show higher sensory impairments than ASD-WO, with Taste/Smell sensitivity mostly affected. In order to carry out this assessment, we used four measures: two questionnaires for the detection of feeding problems, and two for the detection of sensorimotor features. We are not aware of previous studies in the literature on such a topic. A better understanding of the association between feeding problems and sensory factors in children with autism, might bring benefits for the physical health of ASD children, since it might provide some ideas and guide for treatment: for example, feeding training might include behavioral techniques to gradually decrease the negative sensory experiences related to food consumption, and encourage familiarity and acceptance of foods.

2. Materials and Methods

2.1. Study Design

A comparative study was carried out. The four questionnaires were administered by clinical psychologists, working in the diagnostic services of three Sicilian specialized centers, throughout interviews to parents, as part of the psychological and psychoeducational assessment. Recruitment and organization of the sample are described in the following paragraph.

2.2. Participants

A total of 111 children with ASD, aged 2 to 12 years (86 males and 25 females; median chronological age 62 months, interquartile range 44–75 months), were consecutively recruited from specialized services of diagnosis and treatment of autism during the year 2019, in three specialized centers of Eastern Sicily provinces (Enna, Caltanissetta and Catania). All participants were diagnosed by a multidisciplinary team, following the DSM-5 criteria [21]. The severity of their disorders was classified into three levels (1 to 3) accordingly. Approximately 65% (N = 72) of children showed a severity level of 3, about 27% (N = 30) a severity level of 2, and about 8% (N = 9) a severity level of 1; moreover, the majority of them (91%, N = 101) presented with comorbid Intellectual Disability (ID). Diagnoses were further confirmed using at least one of the most common diagnostic scales (the Autism Diagnostic Interview-Revised, the Autism Diagnostic Observation Schedules or the Childhood Autism Rating Scale-Second edition). Based on the results obtained at the Brief Autism Mealtime Behaviors Inventory (BAMBI-18) [33], the sample was divided into two subgroups, which included ASD-W (N = 37, 33%; scores at BAMBI ≥ 34) and ASD-WO (N = 74, 67%; scores at BAMBI < 34) children. The characteristics of the two subgroups are shown in Table 1 (N of males and females, level of severity, chronological ages, total and sub-domain scores obtained at mealtime behavior measures).

Table 1. Characteristics of the sample and scores obtained at BAMBI 18 and CEBQ, expressed as medians and interquartile ranges.

TitleSample Features	ASD-W	ASD-WO	z =	$p \leq$	Effect Size [3] r
N =	37	74			
Males/Females	30/7	56/18		NS [1]	
Severity level 3/2/1	27/8/2	45/22/7		NS [1]	
Chronological age, months	60 (44–76)	63.5 (45.2–74.0)		NS [2]	
BAMBI 18 total scores	41 (38–46)	26.5 (22.25–29.75)	−8.44	0.00001 [2]	0.8
BAMBI 18 subdomains					
Food Selectivity	14 (12–16)	9 (7–11)	−7.1	0.00001 [2]	0.67
Disruptive Behaviors	13 (10–16)	7.5 (6–9)	−6.48	0.00001 [2]	0.61
Food Refusal	7 (5–9)	4 (3–4.75)	−7.02	0.00001 [2]	0.67
Mealtime Rigidity	8 (6–11)	4 (3–7)	−5.69	0.00001 [2]	0.54
CEBQ	93 (84–105)	10 (7–16)	−8.54	0.00001 [2]	0.81
CEBQ subdomains					
Food Responsiveness	12 (7–16)	10 (7–16)	−0.424	NS [2]	
Emotional Over-eating	5 (4–8)	6 (4–7)	0.237	NS [2]	
Enjoyment of food	13 (10–16)	16 (13–17)	2.939	0.038 [2]	0.28
Desire to Drink	7 (5–9)	6 (5–8)	−0.88	NS [2]	
Satiety responsiveness	12 (10–15)	11 (8–13)	−2.36	0.018 [2]	0.22
Slowness in Eating	12 (10–15)	9 (8–12)	−2.13	0.033 [2]	0.2
Emotional Under-eating	10 (6–12)	8 (6–12)	−1.84	NS [2]	
Food Fussiness	21 (18–26)	16 (12–19)	−4.58	0.00001 [2]	0.435

ASD = Autism Spectrum Disorder; ASD-W = ASD With feeding problems; ASD-WO = ASD WithOut feeding problems; Severity level: 3 = requiring very substantial support, 2 = requiring substantial support, 1 = requiring support; BAMBI = Brief Autism Mealtime Behaviour Inventory; CEBQ = Child Eating Behaviour Questionnaire; NS = Not Significant; [1] Chi-square test; [2] Mann-Whitney's U Test; [3] Effect size calculated by using $r = z/\sqrt{N}$ formula.

2.3. Measures

BAMBI 18 [33,34] is an 18-item interview for assessing mealtime behavior problems. A 5-point Likert scale is used, ranging from 1 = never/rarely to 5 = always, including a neutral midpoint; a total frequency score is derived from the sum of the items; higher scores indicate more problematic mealtime behaviors. Undesirable behaviors can be analyzed also on the basis of four main factors, and namely: limited variety/food selectivity, disruptive mealtime behaviors, food refusal and mealtime rigidity [34]. Original test-retest reliability was reported at 0.87 (TD children $N = 40$ and ASD children $N = 68$, aged 3 to 11 years), and interrater reliability at 0.78 [31]. The scale internal consistency was 0.88 (Cronbach's alpha). A cut-off total score of 34 was found by DeMand et al. [34].

CEBQ [35] is a tool for assessing children's eating styles. It is an interview including 35 items; a 5-point Likert scale is used, ranging from 1 = never to 5 = always. It includes eight scales: Food responsiveness, Emotional over-eating, Enjoyment of food, Desire to drink, Satiety responsiveness, Slowness in eating, Emotional under-eating, and Food fussiness. Internal reliability, derived from two samples ($N = 177$ and $N = 222$, respectively) for the eight factors, ranged from 0.72 to 0.91 (Cronbach's alpha). Test-retest reliability ($N = 160$) ranged from 0.52 to 0.87.

SSP [31] is a 38-item caregiver questionnaire, scored on a 5-point Likert scale (ranging from 1 = always to 5 = never). The lower the score, the more atypical sensory responses. The SSP consists of a total score and 7 subsection scores: Tactile sensitivity (7 items, mostly focusing on tactile avoiding and expression of distress: for example, fights or cries during hair cutting, fingernail cutting or face washing; emotional or aggressive reactions to touch; difficulty in standing in line or close to other people; avoids going barefoot, especially over sand or grass); Taste/Smell sensitivity (4 items, focusing on food avoiding and selectivity: for example, avoiding certain tastes or food smells that are typically part of children's diet; eating only certain foods or limiting to particular food textures/temperatures; picky eating); Movement sensitivity (3 items, focusing on anxiety due to specific postures: for example, becoming anxious or distressed when feet leave the ground, disliking activities where head is upside down); Under-responsive/Seeks sensation (7 items, focusing on actions adding more intense sensations and inattention during social interactions: for example, seeking to make noises, or enjoying strange noises; fidgeting, and not seating still; seeking all kinds of movement, touching people and objects, jumping from one activity to another, not noticing messy face or hands); Auditory Filtering (6 items, focusing on distraction and inattention caused by auditory stimuli in the environment: for example, being distracted by noises, and impossibility to work with background noises; not hearing what he/she is told, not responding to his/her name, ignoring persons interacting with him/her); Low Energy/Weak (6 items, focusing on weakness and easy fatigue: for example, getting easily tired, especially when standing or holding particular body positions; weak grasping; not lifting heavy objects in comparison to children with the same age); Visual/Auditory sensitivity (5 items, focusing on negative responses to unexpected or loud stimuli: for example, negative responses to unexpected or loud noises, protecting ears from sound or eyes from light, being bothered by bright light). The SSP total score and the subsection scores can be used to classify children's sensory impairments into three categories: Typical Performance, Probable Difference, and Definite Difference. Cut-off points to define these categories are available for the total and the subsection scores. A discriminant validity > 95% in differentiating children with and without sensory impairments was found [36]. The internal reliability was reported as ranging between 0.70 to 0.90. Internal validity correlations for the subsections ranged from 0.25 to 0.76 and were all significant at $p < 0.01$ [31].

The Sensory Experience Questionnaire (SEQ Version 1) [10,37] is a brief caregiver interview designed to assess sensory problems in young children with ASD and related Developmental Disorders. A 5-point Likert scale is used, ranging from 1 = almost never to 5 = almost always. Higher scores indicate higher sensory problems. The SEQ measures the Hyper- and Hyporesponsive patterns across social and nonsocial contexts. Hypo- is considered as a lack of or delayed response to sensory stimuli [14,38]). Hyper- is defined as an exaggerated or avoidant response to sensory stimuli [39,40]. SEQ yields both a total score as well as four-dimensional subscale scores. The psychometric properties of SEQ were evaluated by Little et al. [35] by means of 358 caregiver questionnaires; internal consistency and test–retest reliability were 0.80 (Cronbach's coefficient alpha); intraclass correlation coefficients was 0.92.

2.4. Statistical Analysis

Non-parametric statistics were used because most of the variables did not show a normal distribution, based on asymmetry and kurtosis. The between-group comparisons were carried out by means of the Mann-Whitney's U test; the significance level was set at $p < 0.05$. Effect sizes were calculated by means of the $r = z/\sqrt{N}$ formula, where N is the total number of the sample participants. The r value of 0.1, 0.3 and 0.5 indicated a small, a medium, and a large effect size respectively; the absolute value of r has been reported. The Chi-square test was used for frequency data, including the intra-group comparisons; effect size was calculated by means of the Cramer's V test, where scores ≤0.2 indicate a small effect size, while scores between 0.2 and ≤ 0.6 a moderate effect size, and >0.6 a strong effect size. For intra-group comparisons, the Friedman and the Wilcoxon matched pair tests were used. Effect sizes were calculated by means of $r = z/\sqrt{N}$ formula. A correlation analysis between sensory and feeding problems was carried out for the whole sample, by using the Spearman's test.

2.5. Ethics Committee Approval

Approval was obtained from the Local Ethics Committee "Comitato Etico IRCCS Sicilia–Oasi Maria SS.", approval date 7 July 2018, approval code: 2018/07/18/CE-IRCCS-OASI/14. All parents provided written informed consent prior to the administration of the questionnaires.

3. Results

No significant differences were found between ASD-W and ASD-WO subgroups, neither in the chronological ages, nor in the number of male and female participants, or in the levels of disorder severity (Table 1); therefore, the two subgroups were comparable.

Table 1 shows statistically significant differences at BAMBI and CEBQ questionnaires, both investigating feeding problems. In all the BAMBI subdomains (selectivity, disruptive behaviors, refusal, and mealtime rigidity), statistically significant differences were obtained with medium to large effect sizes. In the CEBQ, the statistically significant differences were found only in some subdomains, namely enjoyment of food, satiety responsiveness, slowness in eating, and, above all, food fussiness, including food selectivity items. Therefore, the two subgroups turned out to be clearly distinguished from each another as for feeding behaviors.

3.1. Comparisons Between ASD-W and ASD-WO Subgroups

Statistically significant differences were found in the comparisons between ASD-W and ASD-WO subgroups (Mann Whitney's U test; Table 2).

Table 2. Scores obtained from ASD-W and ASD-WO subgroups at the SSP and SEQ, expressed as medians and interquartile ranges.

MeasuresTitle	ASD-W break//$N = 37$	ASD-WO $N = 74$	$z =$	$p \leq$ [1]	Effect Size $r =$ [2]
SEQ Total scores	51 (41–62)	46.5 (39–57)	−1.94	0.026	0.18
SEQ subsections					
HY	21 (18–28)	19 (16–23)	−2.49	0.006	0.24
HY-S	11 (8–15)	10 (7–12)	−1.75	0.04	0.17
HY-NS	11 (10–13)	10 (7.25–12)	−2.52	0.006	0.24
HO	29 (23–34)	29 (22–34)	−1.03	NS	
HO-S	8 (5–9)	7 (5–9)	−1.13	NS	
HO-NS	22 (18–24)	20 (17–25.75)	−0.89	NS	

Table 2. *Cont.*

MeasuresTitle	ASD-W break//$N = 37$	ASD-WO $N = 74$	$z =$	$p \leq$ [1]	Effect Size $r =$ [2]
SSP Total scores	132 (113–149)	156 (140.25–165.5)	4.5	0.00001	0.43
SSP subsections					
Tactile sensitivity	27 (23–31)	30.5 (28–33)	2.99	0.0014	0.28
Taste/Smell sensitivity	9 (7–13)	18 (14–20)	5.42	0.00001	0.515
Movement sensitivity	13 (10–15)	15 (11.25–15)	1.87	0.03	0.18
Under-responsive/Seeks sensation	21 (17–22)	24.5 (19.25–27.75)	3.43	0.0003	0.33
Auditory filtering	16 (14–22)	22 (20–24)	3.79	0.00008	0.36
Low energy/Weak	26 (20–28)	28 (25.25–30)	2.77	0.028	0.26
Visual/Auditory sensitivity	20 (17–22)	21 (18–23)	1.004	NS	

ASD = Autism Spectrum Disorder; ASD-W = ASD With feeding problems; ASD-WO = ASD WithOut feeding problems; SEQ = Sensory Experience Questionnaire; HY = Hyperresponsiveness; HY-S = HY social items; HY-NS = HY non-social items; HO = Hyporesponsiveness; HO-S = HO social items; HO-NS = HO non-social items; SSP = Short Sensory Profile; NS = Not significant; [1] Mann Whitney's U Test; [2] Effect size calculated by using the formula: $r = z/\sqrt{N}$.

As far as the SSP results are concerned, differences were found in the total score, with a medium effect size, and in almost all the subsections, with a large effect size in Taste/Smell sensitivity, a medium effect size in Auditory Filtering and Under-responsive/Seeks sensation, and a small effect size in Tactile sensitivity, Low Energy/Weak, and Movement sensitivity. Higher sensory impairments turned out to characterize the ASD-W subgroup. No differences were found in the Visual/Auditory sensitivity.

Statistically significant differences emerged from SEQ, both in the total score, with a small effect size, and in the Hyperresponsiveness subsection (in total score and responsiveness toward social and non-social stimuli), with most impairments in the ASD-W subgroup. No statistically significant differences were found in Hyporesponsiveness subsection, impaired in both subgroups (see median scores). Table 3 shows the SSP performance categories (Definite Difference, Probable Difference, and Typical Performance in both total and subsection scores), expressed in percentages of children, and the results from the comparisons between the two subgroups (Chi Square test).

Table 3. SSP performances from the whole ASD sample and from each of the ASD-W and ASD-WO subgroups (expressed as percentages of children); statistically significant differences between ASD-W and ASD-WO subgroups; percentages of children as reported in other studies.

SSP Performance CategoriesTitle	All ASD (N = 111)	ASD-W (N = 37)	ASD-WO (N = 74)	ASD-W vs. ASD-WO $p \leq$ [1]	Cramer's V Effect Size	Tomchek and Dunn, 2007 [3]	Nadon et al., 2011 [29]	AL-Heizan et al., 2015 [32]
SSP Total scores								
Definite Difference	43.2	73	28.4			83.6	65.3 [2]	84.8
Probable Difference	15.3	10.8	17.6	0.00001 [3]	0.46	11.4	21.1	8.7
Typical Performance	41.4	16,2	54			5	13.7	6.5
SSP subsections: Tactile sensitivity								
Definite Difference	28.8	48.6	19			60.9	36.8	60.9
Probable Difference	22.5	21.6	23	0.000015 [4]	0.33	18.5	24.2	21.7
Typical Performance	48.7	29.7	58			20.6	37.9	17.4
Taste/Smell sensitivity								
Definite Difference	28.8	62.2	12.2			54.1	48.4	52.2
Probable Difference	18.9	16.2	20.2	0.00001 [5]	0.54	13.9	15.8	19.6
Typical Performance	52.3	21.6	67.6			32	34.7	28.26
Movement sensitivity								
Definite Difference	14.4	24.3	9.5			23.1	28.4	50
Probable Difference	17.1	8.1	21.6	0.0013 [6]	0.26	21	20	15.2
Typical Derformance	68.5	67.6	68.9			55.9	51.6	34.8
Under-responsive/Seeks sensation								
Definite Difference	54.1	78.4	41.9			86.1	67.4	89.1
Probable Difference	22.5	13.5	27	0.00001 [7]	0.38	7.5	16.8	2.2
Typical Derformance	23.4	8	31.1			6.4	15.8	8.7
Auditory Filtering								
Definite Difference	39.6	70.3	24.3			77.6	55.8	73.9
Probable Difference	23.5	8.1	31.1	0.00001 [8]	0.47	14.6	24.2	8.7
Typical Derformance	36.9	21.6	44.6			7.8	20	17.4
Low Energy/Weak								
Definite difference	26.1	37.8	20.2			23.1	43.2	58.7
Probable difference	7.2	10.8	5.4	0.0035 [9]	0.24	18.9	12.6	10.9
Typical performance	66.7	51.3	74.3			58	44.2	30.4
Visual/Auditory sensitivity								
Definite difference	10.8	13.5	9.5			43.8	22.1	34.8
Probable difference	23.4	27	21.6	NS		25.3	31.6	19.6
Typical performance	65.8	59.4	68.9			31	46.3	45.7

ASD = Autism Spectrum Disorder; ASD-W = ASD With feeding problems; ASD-WO = ASD WithOut feeding problems; SSP = Short Sensory Profile; NS = Not significant; [1] Chi-square test; [2] In this group a mean of 15.5 ± 6 presented with feeding problems; Definite difference vs. Typical performance: [3] $p < 0.00001$, Cramer's V = 0.49; [4] $p < 0.00001$, Cramer's V = 0.38; [5] $p < 0.00001$, Cramer's V = 0.59; [6] $p < 0.00001$, Cramer's V = 0.18; [7] $p < 0.00001$, Cramer's V = 0.38; [8] $p < 0.0018$, Cramer's V = 0.415; [9] $p < 0.0017$, Cramer's V = 0.23.

The percentage of Definite Difference in ASD-W subgroup was higher than ASD-WO in both the SSP total score and the subsections; on the contrary, higher percentages of ASD-WO children fell into the Typical Performance of SSP total and subsection scores. Statistically significant differences were found in the comparisons between the two subgroups, with moderate effect sizes in the total score and in all the subsections, except for Visual/Auditory sensitivity performance, in which no statistically significant difference was found. When comparing Definite Differences vs. Typical performance, statistically significant differences and moderate effect sizes were found.

3.2. *ASD-WO Intra-Group Analysis*

In the ASD-WO subgroup, a statistically significant difference ($p < 0.00001$; Friedman's test) was found between the SSP subsection scores, expressed as medians of the ratios between the scores obtained and the maximum possible scores; the medians of the ratios ranged from 0.8 to 1, (the highest SSP score, the lowest impairment) in the following subdomains: Tactile, Taste/Smell, Movement, Visual/Auditory sensitivity and Low Energy/Weak; and from 0.7 to 0.75 in Under-responsive/Seeks sensation and Auditory Filtering (Figure 1A).

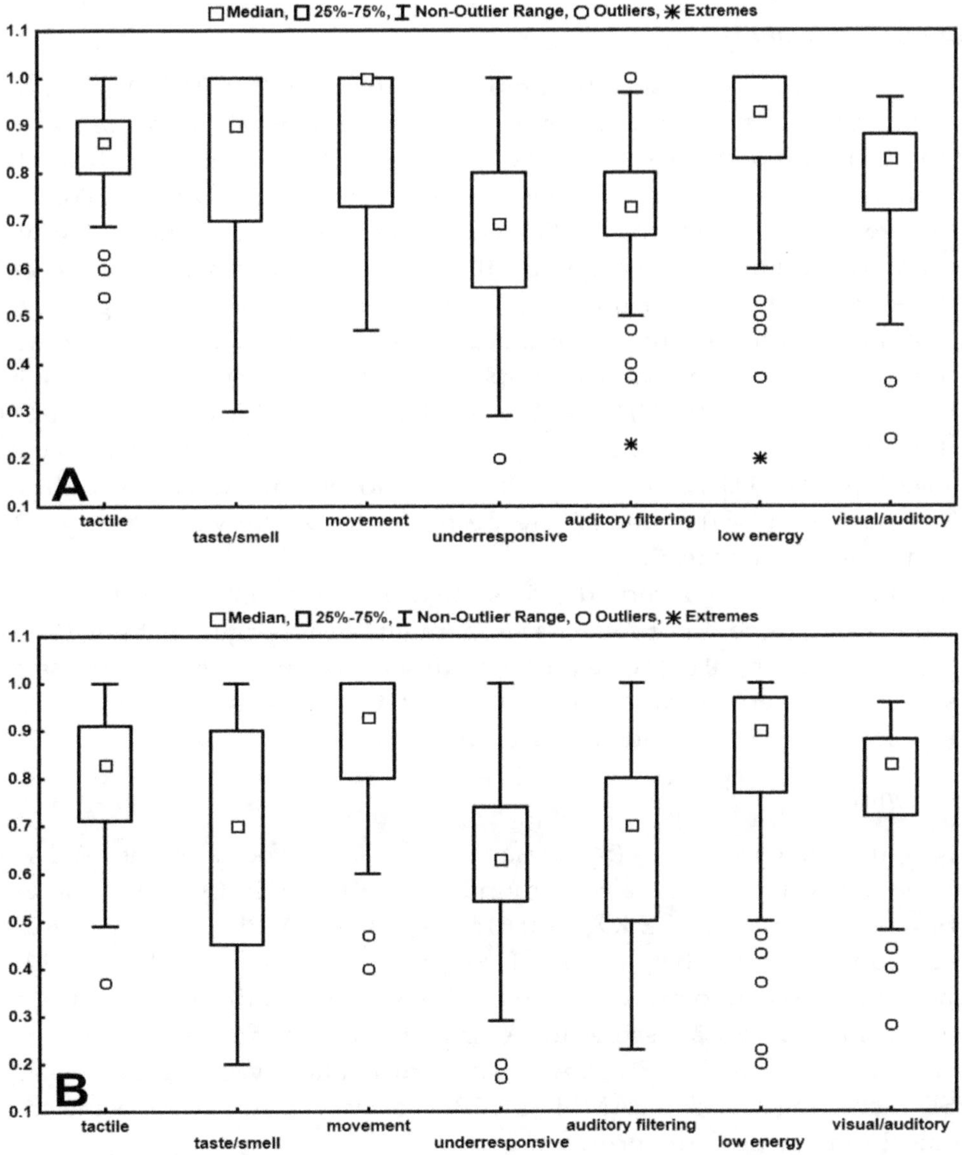

Figure 1. Scores obtained from ASD-WO (**A**) and ASD-W (**B**) in the SSP subdomains (expressed as medians of the ratios between obtained scores and maximum possible scores).

Both Under-responsive/Seeks sensation (US) and Auditory Filtering (AF) showed statistically significant differences (Wilcoxon matched pairs test) when compared to the other SSP subdomains, and namely: US vs. Tactile, Movement, and Low Energy $p < 0.000001$, with large effect sizes ($z = 6.78$, 6.45, 5.98 respectively; $r = 0.79$, 0.75, 0.69 respectively); US vs. Visual/Auditory $p < 0.000002$, with large effect size ($z = 4.73$; $r = 0.55$); US vs. Taste/Smell $p = 0.000014$, with large effect size ($z = 4.35$; $r = 0.506$); US vs. AF $p = 0.012$, with small effect size ($z = 2.51$; $r = 0.29$); AF vs. Tactile, Movement, Low Energy $p < 0.000001$, with large effect sizes ($z = 5.76$, 5.53, 5.98 respectively; $r = 0.67$, 0.64, 0.69 respectively); AF vs. Taste/Smell $p = 0.001$, with medium effect size ($z = 3.27$; $r = 0.38$), AF vs. Visual/Auditory $p = 0.002$, with medium effect size ($z = 3.1$; $r = 0.36$).

As far as the SEQ is concerned, a statistically significant difference with large effect size between the Hyperresponsiveness and Hyporesponsiveness subdomains (Wilcoxon matched pairs test, $p < 0.00001$, $z = -5.22$, $r = 0.07$) was found, with higher scores in Hyporesponsiveness. Within the Hyporesponsiveness subdomain, a statistically significant difference with medium effect size was found between responses to social and non-social stimuli (Wilcoxon matched pairs test, $p = 0.006$, $z = 2.73$, $r = 0.036$), with response to non-social stimuli being more impaired. Within the Hyperresponsiveness subdomain, no significant difference was found between responses to social and non-social stimuli.

3.3. ASD-W Intra-Group Analysis

In the ASD-W subgroup, a statistically significant difference ($p < 0.00001$, Friedman's test) was found between the SSP subsection scores, expressed as medians of the ratios between the scores obtained and the maximum possible scores. The medians of the ratios ranged from 0.75 to 0.9 in the following subdomains: Tactile, Movement, Visual/Auditory and Low Energy/Weak; from 0.53 and 0.45 in Auditory Filtering, Under-responsive/Seeks sensation, and Taste/Smell sensitivity (Figure 1 B). No statistically significant differences were found either between Taste/Smell and both Under-responsive and Auditory Filtering, or between Under-responsive and Auditory filtering (Wilcoxon matched pairs test). Taste/Smell, Under-responsive and Auditory Filtering subsections showed statistically significant differences and large effect sizes in comparison with the others SSP subdomains, and namely: Taste/Smell (TS) vs. Tactile $p = 0.000004$, $z = 4.62$, $r = 0.76$; TS vs. Movement $p = 0.000003$, $z = 4.71$, $r = 0.77$; TS vs. Low Energy $p = 0.000016$, $z = 4.32$, $r = 0.71$; TS vs. Visual/Auditory $p = 0.000017$, $z = 4.31$, $r = 0.71$; US vs. Tactile $p = 0.000002$, $z = 4.8$, $r = 0.79$; US vs. Movement and Visual/Auditory $p = 0.000001$, $z = 5.1$ and 4.82 respectively; $r = 0.84$ and 0.79 respectively; US vs. Low Energy $p = 0.000007$, $z = 4.51$, $r = 0.74$ (Wilcoxon matched pairs test).

As far as the SEQ is concerned, a statistically significant difference between the Hyperresponsiveness and Hyporesponsiveness subdomains and a large effect size (Wilcoxon matched pairs test $p < 0.015$, $z = -3.39$, $r = 0.09$) were found, with sensory Hyporesponsiveness being prevalent; no statistically significant differences were found either in Hyperresponsiveness or Hyporesponsiveness subdomains (responses to social and non-social stimuli).

3.4. Correlation Analysis

Statistically significant correlations (Spearman's test; $p < 0.05$) between the total scores of sensory and mealtime behaviors questionnaires were found (BAMBI vs. CEBQ = 0.61; SSP vs. SEQ = −0.59; SSP vs. BAMBI = −0.46; SSP vs. CEBQ = −0.61; SEQ vs. BAMBI = 0.3; SEQ vs. CEBQ = 0.33). A positive correlation was found between the two questionnaires on feeding problems (increased scores in one questionnaire corresponded to increased scores in the other), and between SEQ and each of the mealtime measures (increasing scores in feeding problems corresponded to increasing scores in sensory impairments, investigated by SEQ). A negative correlation was found between each mealtime measure and SSP: increasing scores in BAMBI or CEBQ corresponded to decreasing scores in SSP, that is, decreased typical sensory performances.

4. Discussion

Children with ASD seem to show more sensory problems than children with TD, and a relationship between sensory and feeding problems was hypothesized by some authors [4,26–29]. To the best of our knowledge, no studies on ASD sensory processing have so far reported any comparisons between sensory characteristics of ASD children with and without feeding problems. The aim of our study was to shed light on this aspect, starting from the hypothesis that ASD-W children presented with higher sensory impairments than ASD-WO, with Taste/Smell sensitivity particularly affected.

In our ASD sample, the percentage of feeding problems turned out to be lower than those reported in other studies [24,25,41,42], probably due to the specific cut-off used in our study for classifying children with feeding problems. This result should be further investigated in future studies with larger samples.

The Spearman's test showed a statistically significant correlation between feeding behaviors and responses to sensory stimuli, especially between SSP and the two mealtime behaviors measures, thus confirming the findings of the studies above mentioned [4,27–30].

Results obtained from the between-group comparisons seem to confirm our hypothesis. Statistically significant differences in the total scores of both SSP and SEQ were found, with higher impairments in the ASD-W subgroup. As stated by O'Donnell et al. [43], the SSP total score is considered as the most sensitive indicator of sensory dysfunction. As for the SSP subsections, differences turned out to be particularly marked in the Taste/Smell sensitivity, and this is certainly consistent with our expectations, since the Taste/Smell sensitivity is a factor that strongly influences feeding behaviors. The presence of olfactory and gustatory dysfunctions in children with ASD have already been reported in the literature [44,45], even if they remain still understudied. The olfactory system is mainly implicated in detection, identification, memory and recognition of odors. The principal function of taste is to analyze chemosensory, somesthetic and hedonic features of gustatory stimuli. Results from the few studies in which physiological measures were used, found significant differences in odor and taste identification in children with ASD compared with TD, but not in detection thresholds, thus suggesting cortical rather than brainstem dysfunction [45]. A recent study by Koehler et al. [46] on odor threshold and odor identification in children with ASD, using structural magnetic resonance imaging, found decreased threshold and identification functions, and a decreased activation of the pyriform cortex, suggesting that olfactory impairments in people with ASD has its correspondence in the primary olfactory cortex. A study by Avery et al. [47] on taste reactivity in ASD found an aberrant function of the primary gustatory cortex (anterior insula and frontal operculum) and other brain regions associated with social functioning. Taste and smell cerebral pathways present some similarities, since they both involve regions such as the orbitofrontal cortex, the insula, the limbic system and the hypothalamus. However, studies have so far found no clear link between impaired responses to sensory stimuli and the underlying brain sensory processing; therefore, the unusual sensory responses in children with autism still need a reliable explanation. We know that these cortex areas are connected not only to the olfactory and gustatory systems, but also to emotions and social behaviors; therefore, it is possible to hypothesize that the altered perception of taste/smell stimuli in children with autism can contribute to their social and emotional deficits.

As far as the other results of our study are concerned, statistically significant differences were found in all the other SSP subsections, especially in Auditory Filtering and Under-responsive/Seeks sensation (Tables 2 and 3), and also in Tactile sensitivity, Movement sensitivity and Low Energy/Weak (Table 3). These results indicate that feeding behaviors of children with autism seem to be affected not only by Taste/Smell sensitivity, but also by multiple sensory experiences, and that a generalized impairment of all sensory modalities occurs more in children with ASD-W than in children with ASD-WO. This generalized sensory impairment, especially in children with ASD-W, might find an explanation in the theory of imbalance in excitatory and inhibitory processes in the brain, resulting in increased excitation (greater glutamatergic signaling) and reduced inhibition (reduced GABA inhibitory neurotransmitters) [48,49]. Increased activation was found in children with ASD in primary sensory cortices, amygdala, hippocampus and orbitofrontal cortex, also related to cognitive, emotional, and social processing; reduced GABA levels were found in auditory, motor and frontal cortex. However, a link between changes in neurotransmitters and the anomalous behavioral responses to sensory stimuli has not been established yet.

The presence and severity of sensory dysfunctions in our sample seemed to be related to feeding problems, rather than to the autism severity (as stated by some authors) [7,15,18]; in fact, the two subgroups did not differ from each other as for the severity of autistic symptoms (see Table 1). Visual/Auditory sensitivity did not seem to affect feeding behaviors: a high percentage of children (about 60% of ASD-W and 70% of ASD-WO) showed a Typical Performance in this sensory modality, therefore it was not widely impaired in our whole sample.

In a study by Lane et al. [50], using the SSP, four distinct sensory subtypes were identified: sensory adaptive, consisting in typical functioning in five of the seven SSP subsections; taste smell sensitive, consisting in extreme Taste/Smell sensitivity and clinically significant concerns in Auditory Filtering and Under-responsive/Seeks sensation; postural inattentive, consisting in extreme score in Low Energy/Weak and clinically significant concerns in Auditory Filtering and Under-responsive/Seeks sensation; and generalized sensory difference, in which all sensory domains were affected. We applied these subtypes to both ASD-W and ASD-WO children, thus confirming our results as described above: ASD-W children fell into the Taste/Smell sensitive subtype, and showed a more generalized sensory difference than the ASD-WO subgroup; on the contrary, ASD-WO children were sensory adaptive in about half of the cases.

The SSP performance classifications in our study appeared to be different from those obtained in previous studies [3,29,32] (Table 3), either in the whole ASD sample, or in the ASD-WO subgroup. In fact, the percentages of Definite Differences were lower, while those of Typical Performance higher; our percentages were close to those of the studies mentioned above only in the case of the ASD-W subgroup. This might be due to the fact that these studies included ASD children with and without feeding problems, but their percentages were not specified. Nadon et al. [29], however, suggested that the presence of feeding problems might have affected the results of their study.

As far as the SEQ is concerned, Hyporesponsiveness turned out to be impaired in both ASD-W and ASD-WO children. This is consistent with previous studies [14] and confirms data obtained in the SSP Under-responsive/Seeks sensation subsection. Statistically significant differences were found by comparing the two subgroups, both in the SEQ total score and Hyperresponsive subsection, and ASD-W appeared to be more affected than ASD-WO children; however, the effect sizes were small, therefore these results need to be confirmed by further studies. In the ASD-W subgroup the dysfunctioning seemed to be more generalized, because no differences were found in the responses to social and non-social stimuli in Hyporesponsiveness.

Results from the intra-group SSP analysis (Figure 1) are also consistent with those described above: in the ASD-WO children, the Under-responsive/Seeks sensations and Auditory Filtering subsections appeared to be the most impaired, unlike Tactile, Taste/Smell, Movement, Low Energy/Weak, and Visual-Auditory subsections, which turned out to be points of strength. The strengths of the ASD-W subgroup seem to be Movement, Low Energy/Weak, and Visual/Auditory sensitivity, unlike Under-responsive/Seeks sensation, Auditory Filtering, and Taste/Smell subsections, which turned out to be strongly impaired.

Results from our study might offer some suggestions about the opportunity to include individualized sensory training within the psychoeducational treatments. Whereas these trainings seem to be useful for ASD-WO children with no typical performance, they become essential for children with ASD-W, because of their generalized sensory dysfunctioning that requires a multisensory stimulation treatment. The multisensory stimulation treatment should be individually designed to decrease the functional limitations due to the impaired sensory modulation and should involve active participation of children to produce adaptive responses. A play context might encourage children participation. Individualized sensory trainings might provide multiple benefits: (1) normalizing the deficient responses to tactile, olfactory and tasting stimuli, so as to provide the opportunity for learning adequate mealtime behaviors and other functional self-care skills; (2) providing the appropriate required level of sensory stimulation—through Applied Behavior Analysis procedures—that would replace sensations typically experienced from repetitive behaviors or stereotypies; (3) capturing and maintaining attention on the provided stimuli (especially auditory stimuli); (4) using visual/auditory and kinesthetic stimulation (in which the ASD-W children appear to be more adapted) as a bridge to more easily accept sensory stimuli generally avoided.

Our study has some limitations: first of all, the absence of a TD control group. The comparison with TD peers would highlight any statistically significant differences with ASD sensory profiles, especially for the ASD-WO subjects, who showed more adaptive sensory responsiveness. Second, the absence of other clinical control groups, for example peers with ID, with and without feeding problems, that might allow us to better understand whether different clinical populations would show different sensory profiles. To this regard, for example, McCormick et al. [7] did not find any differences between ASD and Developmentally Delayed children in the SSP total scores, except for Taste/Smell and Visual/Auditory sensitivities. Third, the relatively small sample size, especially the ASD-W subgroup: a future study with larger samples might confirm the similarities and differences found here between ASD-W and ASD-WO sensory profiles; moreover, larger samples might be useful to establish whether changes in the sensory processing occur across different age ranges. Finally, our sample mainly included children with moderate to severe disorder (predominantly showing severity levels 2 and 3), therefore our results might be not generalizable to ASD children with a severity level 1. Fourth, to investigate children's response to sensory stimuli we used only questionnaires to parents, that present a certain degree of subjectivity. More psychophysical investigations are needed in order to decrease the subjectivity of data, although the biological mechanisms underlying sensory processing are not easy to determine due to the heterogeneity of the disorder and the difficulty in applying physiological measures to low functioning and little collaborating subjects.

5. Conclusions

We were able to confirm our original hypothesis of the existence of a significant correlation between sensory and feeding problems in ASD. We may suggest that ASD-W children show a more severe and more extensive impaired sensory processing than ASD-WO children, and that feeding behaviors of children with autism are affected not only by Taste/Smell, but also by multiple sensory experiences. ASD-W and ASD-WO subgroups showed a Hyporesponsive profile. Both subgroups showed impairments in Under-responsive/Seeks sensation and Auditory Filtering, more marked in ASD-W than in ASD-WO children. Taste/Smell sensitivity was strongly impaired only in ASD-W, whereas in ASD-WO subgroup it turned out to be a strength. ASD-W showed a more severe impairment also in Tactile sensitivity. Both subgroups showed strengths in Visual/Auditory sensitivity, Low-Energy/Weak, and Movement sensitivity, though more marked in ASD-WO. Based on our results, some useful suggestions on sensory trainings and psychoeducational treatments might be provided. However, a deeper knowledge of sensory dysfunctions in larger samples of ASD-W and ASD-WO children would be desirable for better orienting psychoeducational treatments by providing pointily suggestions about specific and individualized sensory trainings.

Author Contributions: Conceptualization, S.P. and M.E.; Data curation, V.C., M.Z., D.R., D.G. and D.F.; Formal analysis, S.P. and R.F.; Methodology, S.P.; Supervision, R.F.; Writing—original draft, S.P.; Writing—review & editing, S.P., R.F. and M.E. All authors have read and agreed to the published version of the manuscript.

Acknowledgments: We acknowledge the valuable contribution of all families who joined the study. We are grateful to Rosa Di Giorgio for her contribution to the final version of this paper. We are also grateful to the "I Corrieri dell'Oasi" Professional Team–Enna and Adrano (Psychologists, Pedagogues, Professional Educators, Speech-therapists, Psychomotor Therapists, Rehabilitation Therapists, Occupational Therapists, Art Teachers, and Health Care Assistants), to Danila Polizzi (Pedagogue), and Michele Lipani (Coordinator of the Center for Diagnosis and EIT for children with ASD-Caltanissetta).

References

1. Watling, R.; Deitz, J.; White, O. Comparison of sensory profile scores of young children with and without autism spectrum disorders. *Am. J. Occup. Ther.* **2001**, *55*, 416–423. [CrossRef] [PubMed]
2. Leekam, S.R.; Nieto, C.; Libby, S.J.; Wing, L.; Gould, J. Describing the sensory abnormalities of children and adults with autism. *J. Autism Dev. Disord.* **2007**, *37*, 894–910. [CrossRef] [PubMed]
3. Tomchek, S.D.; Dunn, W. Sensory processing in children with and without autism: A comparative study using the short sensory profile. *Am. J. Occup. Ther.* **2007**, *61*, 190–200. [CrossRef] [PubMed]
4. Suarez, M.A. Sensory processing in children with autism spectrum disorders and impact on functioning. *Pediatr. Clin. N. Am.* **2012**, *59*, 203–214. [CrossRef]
5. Brockevelt, B.L.; Nissen, R.; Schweinle, W.E.; Kurtz, E.; Larson, K.J. A comparison of the Sensory Profile scores of children with autism and an age- and gender-matched sample. *S. D. J. Med.* **2013**, *66*, 463–465.
6. Green, D.; Chandler, S.; Charman, T.; Simonoff, E.; Baird, G. Brief Report: DSM-5 Sensory behaviours in children with and without an Autism Spectrum Disorder. *J. Autism Dev. Disord.* **2016**, *46*, 3597–3606. [CrossRef]
7. McCormick, C.; Hepburn, S.; Young, G.S.; Rogers, S.J. Sensory symptoms in children with autism spectrum disorder, other developmental disorders and typical development: A longitudinal study. *Autism* **2016**, *20*, 572–579. [CrossRef]
8. Miller, L.J.; Anzalone, M.E.; Lane, S.; Cermak, S.A.; Osten, E. Concept evolution in sensory integration: A proposed nosology for diagnosis. *Am. J. Occup. Ther.* **2007**, *61*, 135–140. [CrossRef]
9. Ausderau, K.; Sideris, J.; Furlong, M.; Little, L.; Bulluck, J.C.; Baranek, G.T. National survey of sensory features in children with ASD: Factor structure of the sensory experience questionnaire (3.0). *J. Autism Dev. Disord.* **2014**, *44*, 915–925. [CrossRef]
10. Baranek, G.T.; David, F.J.; Poe, M.D.; Stone, W.L.; Watson, L.R. Sensory Experiences Questionnaire: Discriminating sensory features in young children with autism, developmental delays, and typical development. *J. Child Psychol. Psychiatry* **2006**, *47*, 591–601. [CrossRef]
11. Lane, A.E.; Young, R.L.; Baker, A.E.; Angley, M.T. Sensory processing subtypes in autism: Association with adaptive behavior. *J. Autism Dev. Disord.* **2010**, *40*, 112–122. [CrossRef] [PubMed]
12. Liss, M.; Saulnier, C.; Fein, D.; Kinsbourne, M. Sensory and attention abnormalities in autistic spectrum disorders. *Autism* **2006**, *10*, 155–172. [CrossRef] [PubMed]
13. Ausderau, K.K.; Furlong, M.; Sideris, J.; Bulluk, J.; Little, L.M.; Watson, L.R.; Boyd, B.A.; Belger, A.; Dickie, V.A.; Baranek, G.T. Sensory subtypes in children with autism spectrum disorder: Latent profile transition analysis using a national survey of sensory features. *J. Child Psychol. Psychiatry* **2014**, *55*, 935–944. [CrossRef] [PubMed]
14. Ben-Sasson, A.; Hen, L.; Fluss, R.; Cermak, S.A.; Engel-Yeger, B.; Gal, E. A meta-analysis of sensory modulation symptoms in individuals with autism spectrum disorders. *J. Autism Dev. Disord.* **2009**, *39*, 1–11. [CrossRef]
15. Ashburner, J.; Ziviani, J.; Rodger, S. Sensory processing and classroom emotional, behavioral, and educational outcomes in children with autism spectrum disorder. *Am. J. Occup. Ther.* **2008**, *62*, 564–573. [CrossRef]
16. Wiggins, L.D.; Robins, D.L.; Bakeman, R.; Adamson, L.B. Brief report: Sensory abnormalities as distinguishing symptoms of autism spectrum disorders in young children. *J. Autism Dev. Disord.* **2009**, *39*, 1087–1091. [CrossRef]
17. Fernández-Andrés, M.I.; Pastor-Cerezuela, G.; Sanz-Cervera, P.; Tárraga-Mínguez, R. A comparative study of sensory processing in children with and without autism spectrum disorder in the home and classroom environments. *Res. Dev. Disabil.* **2015**, *38*, 202–212. [CrossRef]
18. Sanz-Cervera, P.; Pastor-Cerezuela, G.; González-Sala, F.; Tárraga-Mínguez, R.; Fernández-Andrés, M.I. Sensory processing in children with autism spectrum disorder and/or attention deficit/hyperactivity disorder in the home and classroom context. *Front. Psychol.* **2017**, *8*, 1772. [CrossRef]
19. Sanz-Cervera, P.; Pastor-Cerezuela, G.; Fernández-Andrés, M.I.; Tárraga-Mínguez, R. Sensory processing in children with autism spectrum disorder: Relationship with non-verbal IQ, autism severity and attention deficit/hyperactivity disorder symptomatology. *Res. Dev. Disabil.* **2015**, *45*, 188–201. [CrossRef]

20. Kargas, N.; López, B.; Reddy, V.; Morris, P. The relationship between auditory processing and restricted, repetitive behaviors in adults with autism spectrum disorders. *J. Autism Dev. Disord.* **2015**, *45*, 658–668. [CrossRef]
21. American Psychiatric Association. *Diagnostic and Statistical Manual of Mental Disorders*, 5th ed.; American Psychiatric Publishing: Arlington, VA, USA, 2013.
22. Balikçi, Ö.S.; Çiyiltepe, M. Feeding problems of children with autism. *Int. J. Soc. Sci.* **2017**, *3*, 870–880. [CrossRef]
23. Smith, B.; Rogers, S.L.; Blisset, J.; Ludlow, A.K. The relationship between sensory sensitivity, food fussiness and food preferences in children with neurodevelopmental disorders. *Appetite* **2020**, *150*, 104643. [CrossRef] [PubMed]
24. Kodak, T.; Piazza, C.C. Assessment and behavioral treatment of feeding and sleeping disorders in children with autism spectrum disorders. *Child Adolesc. Psychiatr. Clin. N. Am.* **2008**, *17*, 887–905. [CrossRef] [PubMed]
25. Twachtman-Reilly, J.; Amaral, S.C.; Zebrowsk, P.P. Addressing feeding disorders in children on the autism spectrum in school- based settings: Physiological and behavioral issues. *Lang. Speech Hear. Serv.* **2008**, *39*, 261–272. [CrossRef]
26. Panerai, S.; Suraniti, G.S.; Catania, V.; Carmeci, R.; Elia, M.; Ferri, R. Improvements in mealtime behaviors of children with special needs following a day-center-based behavioral intervention for feeding problems. *Riv. Psichiatr.* **2018**, *53*, 299–308. [CrossRef]
27. Cermak, S.A.; Curtin, C.; Bandini, L.G. Food selectivity and sensory sensitivity in children with autism spectrum disorders. *J. Am. Diet. Assoc.* **2010**, *110*, 238–246. [CrossRef]
28. Zobel-Lachiusa, J.; Andrianopoulos, M.V.; Mailloux, Z.; Cermak, S.A. Sensory differences and mealtime behavior in children with Autism. *Am. J. Occup. Ther.* **2015**, *69*, 6905185050p1–6905185050p8. [CrossRef]
29. Nadon, G.; Feldman, D.E.; Dunn, W.; Gisel, E. Association of sensory processing and eating problems in children with autism spectrum disorders. *Autism Res. Treat.* **2011**, *2011*, 541926. [CrossRef]
30. Chistol, L.T.; Bandini, L.G.; Must, A.; Phillips, S.; Cermak, S.A.; Curtin, C. Sensory sensitivity and food selectivity in children with autism spectrum disorder. *J. Autism Dev. Disord.* **2018**, *48*, 583–591. [CrossRef]
31. Dunn, W. *The Sensory Profile: User's Manual*; Psychological Corporation: San Antonio, TX, USA, 1999.
32. Al-Heizan, M.O.; AlAbdulwahab, S.S.; Kachanathu, S.J.; Natho, M. Sensory processing dysfunction among Saudi children with and without autism. *J. Phys. Ther. Sci.* **2015**, *27*, 1313–1316. [CrossRef]
33. Lukens, C.T.; Linscheid, T.R. Development and validation of an inventory to assess mealtime behavior problems in children with autism. *J. Autism Dev. Disord.* **2008**, *38*, 342–352. [CrossRef] [PubMed]
34. DeMand, A.; Johnson, C.; Foldes, E. Psychometric Properties of the Brief Autism Mealtime Behaviors Inventory. *J. Autism Dev. Disord.* **2015**, *45*, 2667–2673. [CrossRef] [PubMed]
35. Wardle, J.; Guthrie, C.A.; Sanderson, S.; Rapoport, L. Development of the children's eating behaviour questionnaire. *J. Child Psychol. Psychiatry* **2001**, *42*, 963–970. [CrossRef] [PubMed]
36. McIntosh, D.N.; Miller, L.J.; Shyu, V. Development and validation of the short sensory profile (SSP). In *The Sensory Profile: Examiner's Manual*; Dunn, W., Ed.; The Psychological Corporation: San Antonio, TX, USA, 1999; pp. 59–73.
37. Little, L.M.; Freuler, A.C.; Houser, M.B.; Guckian, L.; Carbine, K.; David, F.J.; Baranek, G.T. Psychometric validation of the sensory experiences questionnaire. *Am. J. Occup. Ther.* **2011**, *65*, 207–210. [CrossRef] [PubMed]
38. Baranek, G.T.; Watson, L.R.; Boyd, B.A.; Poe, M.D.; David, F.J.; McGuire, L. Hyporesponsiveness to social and nonsocial sensory stimuli in children with autism, children with developmental delays, and typically developing children. *Dev. Psychopathol.* **2013**, *25*, 307–320. [CrossRef]
39. Baranek, G.T.; Boyd, B.A.; Poe, M.D.; David, F.J.; Watson, L.R. Hyperresponsive sensory patterns in young children with autism, developmental delay, and typical development. *Am. J. Ment. Retard.* **2007**, *112*, 233–245. [CrossRef]
40. Schoen, S.A.; Miller, L.J.; Green, K.E. Pilot study of the sensory over-responsivity scales: Assessment and inventory. *Am. J. Occup. Ther.* **2008**, *62*, 393–406. [CrossRef]
41. Ledford, J.R.; Gast, D.L. Feeding problems in children with autism spectrum disorders: A review. *Focus Autism Dev. Disabil.* **2006**, *21*, 153–166. [CrossRef]

42. Sharp, W.G.; Berry, R.C.; McCracken, C.; Nuhu, N.; Marvel, E.; Saulnier, C.A.; Klin, A.; Jones, W.; Jaquess, D.L. Feeding problems and nutrient intake in children with autism spectrum disorders: A meta-analysis and comprehensive review of the literature. *J. Autism Dev. Disord.* **2013**, *43*, 2159–2173. [CrossRef]
43. O'Donnell, S.; Deitz, J.; Kartin, D.; Nalty, T.; Dawson, G. Sensory processing, problem behavior, adaptive behavior, and cognition in preschool children with autism spectrum disorders. *Am. J. Occup. Ther.* **2012**, *66*, 586–594. [CrossRef]
44. Boudjarane, M.A.; Grandgeorge, M.; Marianowski, R.; Misery, L.; Lemonnier, E. Perception of odors and tastes in autism spectrum disorders: A systematic review of assessments. *Autism Res.* **2017**, *10*, 1045–1057. [CrossRef] [PubMed]
45. Bennetto, L.; Kuschner, E.S.; Hyman, S.L. Olfaction and taste processing in autism. *Biol. Psychiatry* **2007**, *62*, 1015–1021. [CrossRef] [PubMed]
46. Baum, S.H.; Stevenson, R.A.; Wallace, M.T. Behavioral, perceptual, and neural alterations in sensory and multisensory function in autism spectrum disorder. *Prog. Neurobiol.* **2015**, *134*, 140–160. [CrossRef] [PubMed]
47. Avery, J.A.; Ingeholm, J.E.; Wohltjen, S.; Collins, M.; Riddell, C.D.; Gotts, S.J.; Kenworthy, L.; Wallace, G.L.; Simmons, W.K.; Martin, A. Neural correlates of taste reactivity in autism spectrum disorder. *NeuroImage Clin.* **2018**, *19*, 38–46. [CrossRef] [PubMed]
48. Mikkelsen, M.; Wodka, E.L.; Mostofsky, S.H.; Puts, N.A.J. Autism spectrum disorder in the scope of tactile processing. *Dev. Cogn. Neurosci.* **2018**, *29*, 140–150. [CrossRef] [PubMed]
49. Koehler, L.; Fournel, A.; Albertowski, K.; Roessner, V.; Gerber, J.; Hummel, C.; Hummel, T.; Bensafi, M. Impaired odor perception in autism spectrum disorder is associated with decreased activity in olfactory cortex. *Chem. Senses* **2018**, *43*, 627–634. [CrossRef]
50. Lane, A.E.; Molloy, C.A.; Bishop, S.L. Classification of children with autism spectrum disorder by sensory subtype: A case for sensory-based phenotypes. *Autism Res.* **2014**, *7*, 322–333. [CrossRef]

10

Modulation of the Genome and Epigenome of Individuals Susceptible to Autism by Environmental Risk Factors

Costas Koufaris and Carolina Sismani *

Department of Cytogenetics and Genomics, the Cyprus Institute of Neurology and Genetics, P.O. Box 3462, Nicosia 1683, Cyprus; costask@cing.ac.cy

* Author to whom correspondence should be addressed; csismani@cing.ac.cy

Academic Editor: Merlin G. Butler

Abstract: Diverse environmental factors have been implicated with the development of autism spectrum disorders (ASD). Genetic factors also underlie the differential vulnerability to environmental risk factors of susceptible individuals. Currently the way in which environmental risk factors interact with genetic factors to increase the incidence of ASD is not well understood. A greater understanding of the metabolic, cellular, and biochemical events involved in gene x environment interactions in ASD would have important implications for the prevention and possible treatment of the disorder. In this review we discuss various established and more alternative processes through which environmental factors implicated in ASD can modulate the genome and epigenome of genetically-susceptible individuals.

Keywords: xenobiotic; immune; endocrine; epigenome; gut microbes; oxidative stress; transposable elements; endocrine disruptors; transgenerational; gene environment interactions; seizures; genotype

---

1. Introduction

Autism spectrum disorders (ASD) are a collection of neurodevelopmental disorders typically diagnosed in the first three years of life, characterized by deficits in verbal and nonverbal communication, repetitive behaviors, and impairments in social interactions [1]. ASD is caused by the genetic or epigenetic disruption of genes that are essential for normal neurodevelopment, with hundreds of candidate susceptibility genes identified so far. Genetic variations associated with ASD include large chromosomal abnormalities, copy number variants (CNV), indels/deletions, and single nucleotide variants (SNV). The genetic variants implicated in ASD are either inherited from parents to affected individuals or form *de novo* in the patients. Inherited genetic factors (both common and rare variants) have been estimated to explain ~40% of ASD risk [2], while *de novo* mutations are thought to contribute to 15%–20% of cases [3]. Recurrent mutations found in ASD patients implicate disruption of certain biological pathways as particularly important in ASD, such as post-synaptic density [4], phosphoinositide 3-kinase (PI3K)-mammalian target of rapamycin (mTOR) [5], and ubiquitin processing [6].

Strong evidence now also implicates epigenetic dysregulation with ASD development. For example, the epigenetic regulator methyl CpG binding protein 2 (*MECP2*) is well established as being implicated in ASD [7], while altered DNA and histone epigenetic markers have been identified in brain tissue and immune-cell derived cells from autistic patients [8–11]. The biological significance of the observed epigenetic alterations in ASD is supported by the observation that they affect the expression of genes implicated in ASD such as *MECP2*, retinoic acid related orphan receptor A (*RORA*), and engrailed-2 (*EN-2*) [8–11].

Of particular interest to both researchers and the general public is the substantial evidence linking exposure to environmental agents with the incidence of ASD. Epidemiological studies have associated diverse prenatal and perinatal environmental exposures to an increased risk of ASD [12–14], while discordance between monozygotic twins in the incidence of the disorder also supports the importance of environmental influences [15]. Additionally, the largest genetic study reported so far also indicated a large influence of environmental factors on the development of ASD [2]. A sensible hypothesis, based on the importance of both genetic and environmental factors on ASD, is that the interactions between these two components influence the incidence of the disorder. Indeed, a number of recent reviews have discussed the evidence from genetic, epidemiological, and animal studies that support the influence of gene x environment interactions on ASD [16–19]. However, our understanding of the biological mechanisms underlying genotype-environment interactions in ASD is currently inadequate.

2. Disruption of the Genome and Epigenome of Genetically Susceptible Individuals by ASD Environmental Risk Factors

Environmental ASD risk factors are those non-genetic factors that can influence the development of the disorder in genetically-susceptible individuals. These have been suggested to include dietary factors, maternal diabetes, pre-and-perinatal stress, parental age, medications, zinc deficiencies, supplements, pesticides, and infections. Ultimately the environmental risk factors act by disrupting the genome/epigenome of developing neurons. This review will not aim to provide an overview of the numerous proposed environmental ASD risk factors. Rather here we will focus on how environmental factors can modulate the genome and epigenome of individuals susceptible to develop ASD. An increased understanding of this gene-environment interaction would have great implications for the prevention and treatment of the disorder. For example, identifying genetically vulnerable individuals would allow targeted strategies for reducing their exposure to ASD risk factors. Taking into account genotype-environment interactions could also improve the consistency and interpretation of association and epidemiological studies, which often fail to replicate. Finally, elucidating the mechanisms of genotype-environment interactions could also inform the identification of novel therapeutic targets in ASD patients.

2.1. Defective Xenobiotic Metabolism of ASD Environmental Risk Factors

The initial interaction between environmental toxins and biological organisms involves xenobiotic metabolic enzymes, specialized systems responsible for detoxifying and removing harmful chemicals from the body. Although the liver is considered the primary organ where xenobiotic metabolism takes place, detoxification in the brain is also known to occur [20]. Xenobiotic metabolic enzymes are also involved with the biochemical processing of neurotoxicants and environmental ASD risk factors. For example, 2,2',4,4'-tetrabromodiphenyl ether (BDE-47), a main component of the flame retardant polybrominated diphenyl ethers (PBDE) linked to ASD [21], is metabolised to its more harmful metabolites by action of CYP2B6 [22]. It is also the case that several environmental risk factors associated with ASD risk are established mutagens, possibly acting by increasing the incidence of mutations in key neurodevelopmental genes [23]. The majority of mutagenic compounds have to be metabolically converted from non-mutagenic to mutagenic forms by the action of cytochrome p450 (CYP450) enzymes, thus are also strongly affected by the functioning of xenobiotic metabolic activity.

Xenobiotic enzymes display extensive variation in copy number between individuals and ethnic groups. Additionally, SNVs are also known to affect the activity of xenobiotic enzymes. Polymorphisms in xenobiotic enzymes are an important source of individual variability in the response to environmental agents. Indeed, such a mode of action is widely accepted to influence individual susceptibility to environmental carcinogens [24]. A reasonable hypothesis then is that genetic variability that affects the metabolism of environmental ASD risk factors can render subsets of the population particularly vulnerable to environmental chemicals that modulate the genome or epigenome. However, so far few studies have examined the association between polymorphisms affecting xenobiotics metabolic enzymes and ASD incidence. One interesting case involves paraoxonase (*PON1*), a gene involved in the removal from the body of organophosphate pesticides. D'Amelio *et al.* [25] reported that variants of the *PON1* gene were associated with increased incidence of ASD in USA populations, but not in Italian populations. The authors interpreted these observations as relating to the higher levels of organophosphate to which the USA population is exposed. A second study reported an association between *PON1* polymorphisms and neurodevelopment in children exposed in utero to organophosphate pesticides [26]. Five studies have examined the association between *PON1* polymorphisms and ASD. These studies have had mixed results, with only three out of the five studies finding an association between the genetic variants and the disorder [27].

A study by Serajee *et al.* [28] examined the association between polymorphisms affecting six xenobiotic metabolism genes and ASD in 196 families and reported a significant association for a polymorphism affecting the metal-regulatory transcription factor 1 (*MTF1*). Buyske *et al.* [29] examined the association between deletions of the glutathione *S*-transferase M1 (*GSTM1*) allele and autism. This enzyme is involved in the detoxification of electrophilic compounds. In this study a significant association was found for homozygous deletion of *GSTM1* and ASD risk. In conclusion, genetic variability affecting the functioning of xenobiotic enzymes can render individuals more sensitive to environmental ASD risk factors. Taking into account exposures to environmental factors and variants affecting xenobiotic enzymes might potentially improve the design and interpretation of epidemiological studies, as demonstrated by D'Amelio *et al.* [25].

2.2. Increased Sensitivity to Endocrine-Disrupting Chemicals

Increasing evidence indicates that defects in the physiological sex hormone-dependent processes can influence ASD development [30,31]. Diagnosis of ASD is four times more frequent in males compared to females, which might be partly attributed to hormonal involvement in the development of the disease. Fetal testosterone affects brain organization [32] and investigation of amniotic fluid found elevated levels of sex steroid hormones in boys diagnosed with autism [33]. Importantly for our purposes, diverse environmental agents (including plasticizers, flame retardants, drugs, and pesticides) are acknowledged to be able to block or mimic normal hormone signaling by affecting the synthesis of hormones or by interacting with their receptors. Such environmental agents, termed endocrine-disruptor chemicals (EDC), have been implicated with the development of diverse human diseases, including ASD [34]. In support of the influence of EDC on ASD, epidemiological studies have linked gestational exposure to EDC with behavioral problems relating to ASD development [35,36].

Vulnerability to EDC exposures is known to be highly dependent on individual genotype. For example, disruption of male reproductive development in juvenile mice following EDC exposure varied more than 16-fold between mouse strains [37]. Individual variability in sensitivity to EDC can arise by various means, for example different basal levels of sex hormones or binding affinity of hormone receptors. Genetic variants affecting the sex hormones signaling axis in the developing brain could render individuals more susceptible to low EDC doses that induce abnormal brain development and ASD. One study has reported an association between polymorphisms of the androgen receptor and ASD [38]. A second recent study examined the association between 29 single nucleotide polymorphisms (SNP) in genes relating to sex steroids and ASD-like traits belonging to a subset (n = 1771) from The Child and Adolescent Twin Study in Sweden (CATSS) [39]. The authors reported two SNPs to be associated with autism-like traits, one located in the 3'UTR of the estrogen receptor and the other a non-synonymous variant affecting the 3-oxo-5-α-steroid 4-dehydrogenase 2 (SRD5A2) enzyme that is involved in testosterone metabolism. Another interesting observation is the reduced expression of RORA, a gene involved in the transcriptional regulation of genes that convert male to female hormones, in the brain and lymphocytes of ASD patients [9]. Nevertheless there is inadequate understanding at present of how abnormal sex hormone signaling can disrupt normal neurodevelopment and neurobiology in order to contribute to ASD.

2.3. Increased Susceptibility to Agents that Induce Oxidative Stress

Oxidative stress refers to an imbalance between the generation and removal of reactive oxygen species (ROS) in biological systems. Accumulating evidence supports that oxidative stress is also implicated with the development of ASD [40–42]. ROS can directly attack and damage DNA, thus increasing the incidence of mutations that can potentially contribute to ASD. A second possible consequence of oxidative stress is destabilization of the epigenome. In conditions of oxidative stress the enhanced requirement for the antioxidant glutathione can impair synthesis of *S*-adenosyl methionine (SAM), the major methyl donor used for DNA methylation, thus diminishing the available pool of methyl donors used for methylating DNA. The subsequent loss of normal methylation patterns results in the loss of normal regulation and aberrant gene expression. In addition, DNA hypomethylation can also lead to genomic instability [43]. A third detrimental consequence of ROS is the induction of mitochondrial dysfunction, which can initiate vicious cycles of increased ROS generation from the damaged mitochondria. Mitochondrial dysfunction can affect biological functions of the organelle that are important in normal neuronal functioning, such as regulation of neurotransmission [44]. The brain is considered to be particularly vulnerable to ROS due to the fact that it contains non-replicating cells that can become permanently dysfunctional or undergo necrotic or apoptotic cell death.

Increased oxidative stress has been reported in autistic patients [45] and a more oxidized microenvironment is associated with a more favourable development [40]. Additionally, mitochondrial disease and markers of mitochondrial dysfunction are much higher in ASD population compared to control populations [41]. A recent study has also found decreased tryptophan metabolism in lymphoblastoid cells from ASD patients [42]. Aberrant tryptophan metabolism is important because this amino acid is the precursor of molecules that are important for mitochondrial energy generation and anti-oxidant defenses [46]. Tryptophan metabolism is involved in the generation of NAD^+ involved in mitochondrial energy generation through oxidative phosphorylation. Tryptophan is also ultimately involved in the generation of melatonin, which acts as a scavenger of free radicals [46].

Importantly, diverse types of environmental factors can act to either augment or protect against oxidative stress. Subsets of individuals with inherently higher rates of ROS formation or reduced anti-oxidative capabilities would therefore be more vulnerable to environmental conditions that favor a pro-oxidant microenvironment that can contribute to ASD development. Recently published studies have reported that oxidative stress induces more prominent mitochondrial dysfunction in lymphoblastoid cells derived from subsets of ASD patients [47,48]. Damage in the mitochondria can also lead to even greater oxidative stress as ROS are released from the damaged mitochondria. In an interesting recent study it has been reported that exposure of lymphoblasts to bisphenol A results in greater levels of oxidative stress and mitochondrial dysfunction in ASD individuals compared to unaffected siblings [49].

At present the greatest effort to identify the underlying genetic basis for an increased vulnerability of ASD patients to environmental agents has been carried out in relation to ROS and mitochondrial dysfunction [40–42,42,45,45,47,47–49]. Work in animal models also supports that genes implicated with ASD affect ROS and mitochondria. Examples are conditional phosphatase and tensin homolog (*Pten*) haplo-insufficient mice which display aberrant social behavior coupled with mitochondrial dysfunction [50] and neuroligin knockout *Caenorhabditis elegans* that show both abnormal behavior and increased sensitivity to oxidative stress [51]. However, since these two proteins have multiple biological functions it is not possible to exclude that loss of these genes contributes to ASD development through alternative mechanisms. Association studies have revealed an increased frequency of genetic variants affecting Methylenetetrahydrofolate reductase (*MTHFR*) [52] and superoxide dismutase 1 (*SOD1*) [53], enzymes that affect cellular anti-oxidative machinery, in ASD patients. MTHFR is a crucial enzyme of the folate pathway and is involved in the generation of the anti-oxidant glutathione and in generating methyl units that are used for repairing genetic and epigenetic damage caused by ROS. Intriguingly, a SNP that results in reduced activity of the MTHFR was associated with greater incidence of autism, but only in countries with low levels of folate fortification during pregnancy [51]. SOD1 is a member of the superoxide dismutase family that are important participants in antioxidant defense mechanisms. Researchers have recently reported the presence of rare variants within the non-coding potentially regulatory regions of the *SOD1* gene. Although not verified experimentally, the authors consider a plausible hypothesis to be that these variants will affect the regulation of this gene and subsequently the ability of individuals to respond to oxidative stress [53].

A number of recent studies have also identified increased frequencies of genetic variants that affect mitochondrial functions in ASD patients. Smith *et al.* [54] found an increased presence of CNV affecting genes involved in mitochondrial oxidative phosphorylation. Nava *et al.* [55] identified mutations affecting trimethyllysine dioxygenase (*TMLHE*), an enzyme catalyzing the first step of carnitine biosynthesis, in ASD patients. Carnitine is a molecule that is essential for mitochondrial fatty acid metabolism, as well as having anti-oxidant functions. Dysfunction in the mitochondrial aspartate/glutamate carrier (*AGC1*) involved in calcium homeostasis has also been reported in autism [56]. Another alternative mechanism that could render individuals more sensitive to environmental inducers of oxidative stress is the presence of persistent inflammation and immune dysregulation. In these individuals the immune system would result in the continuous generation of excess ROS that will act to drain the available anti-oxidative defenses of cells, rendering them more vulnerable to environmental agents [57].

2.4. *Susceptibility to Epigenomic Dysregulation*

Epigenetic markers such as DNA methylation and histone modifications regulate gene expression in eukaryotic cells. The proper epigenetic marking of DNA is crucial for the normal development of human tissues and organs. Studies of ASD patients have found aberrant patterns of epigenetic regulation, both in the brain and in lymphoblastoid cells [8–11,58]. Aberrant epigenetic mechanisms can contribute to ASD development by causing abnormal gene expression patterns or due to increased genomic damage occurring subsequent to DNA hypomethylation. By their very nature epigenetic mechanisms are at the interface between the genome and environmental factors. A variety of environmental factors can affect the epigenome, such as exposure to heavy metals and levels of dietary folate. Genetic factors that influence the interaction between environmental factors and the epigenome could therefore be important in determining the risk of ASD developing in exposed individuals. In one interesting study it was shown that mice with a truncated version of *Mecp2*, a regulator of the epigenome in neuronal cells, demonstrated social behavioral defects when exposed prenatally to the organic pollutant PBDE. Decreased sociability was associated with reduced global DNA methylation in the female but not in the male mice [21]. As mentioned previously, SNPs that reduce activity of MTHFR have been associated with increased risk of ASD in countries with low fortification [52]. One of the effects of reduced MTHFR activity is lower generation of methyl groups by the folate cycle that can be used for methylating DNA. An increased propensity towards a dysregulated epigenome could also arise due to an inherently higher baseline level of ROS, which use one-carbon units for the generation of glutathione, in ASD patients (discussed in Section 2.3).

An alternative mechanism that would render individuals more susceptible to environmental modulators of the epigenome has been proposed by La Salle [16]. According to this hypothesis large-scale genomic differences between individuals in the size of their repetitive regions can affect their vulnerability to environmental factors that influence the epigenome. It is being increasingly recognized that large-scale genomic differences exist between individuals. Polymorphic regions in the human region include duplications, deletions, inversions, microsatellite repeats, ribosomal DNA repeats, and interstitial telomeric repeats. Since the repetitive regions of the genome act as major drains of methyl donors, it is suggested that individuals with greater genomic size of repetitive elements will be more vulnerable to environmental factors that interact with the DNA methylome [16].

2.5. *Hyperactive Transposable Elements*

Transposable elements are DNA sequences that can mobilize themselves to new regions of the genome, thus acting as mutagens. Long interspersed element-1 (L1) is the most abundant autonomous transposable element in the human genome. Importantly, the L1 retrotransposition is active in neural progenitor cells [59]. Additionally, L1 retrotransposition is enhanced by a large variety of chemical treatments [60]. Intriguingly, reduced activity of Mecp2, a gene implicated in Rett syndrome and ASD, is associated with a higher occurrence of L1 retrotransposition [61]. Therefore, a propensity to a hyperactive mobility of L1 elements in neurons in response to environmental exposures is a plausible mechanism that can drive the incidence of the pathogenic mutations that in turn drive the development of the disease. The precise mechanisms by which environmental agents activate L1 retrotransposition are diverse and probably differ between environmental agents. For example, heterocyclic amines activate L1 mobility through activation of ligand-bound transcription factors [62] and alcohol affecting methylation [63]. As of yet, clear experimental evidence for an increased susceptibility to L1 retrotransposition hyperactivity caused by environmental agents in ASD remains to be reported.

2.6. Increased Genomic Instability

Genomic rearrangements lead to the formation of CNV through deletions, duplications, inversions, and complex rearrangements. Importantly, genes involved in neurodevelopmental disorders including ASD are often flanked by segmental duplications or repetitive elements which drive genomic rearrangements and disruption of gene function [64]. An interesting observation is that ASD patients possess significantly elevated CNV load, even when removing rare and pathogenic events [65]. This finding suggests that beyond the sampling bias this population is also characterized by an increased rate of genomic rearrangements [65]. Environmental agents such as ionizing radiation and genotoxic chemicals are known to be able to initiate genomic rearrangements which subsequently lead to CNV formation. An increased genomic instability in individuals following exposure to such environmental agents could contribute to ASD by enhancing the rate of genomic rearrangements that involve genes implicated in the disorder. Increased genomic instability could be the result of defects in the machinery involved in DNA repair and recombination [65]. So far one study has suggested a link between defective DNA repair and ASD development. Fanconi-associated nuclease 1 (*FAN1*) is a relatively recently identified nuclease involved in the repair of DNA inter-strand cross-links. In a recent study rare variants affecting the FAN1 have been suggested to be candidate drivers of ASD [66]. A decreased ability to repair DNA damage caused by environmental agents could also arise due to the presence in the genome of susceptible individuals of regions with significant sequence homology that flank genes important for normal neurodevelopment. Such genomic regions can act as substrates to allow improper chromosomal recombination (non-allelic homologous recombination or microhomology-mediated break-induced replication) to occur, resulting in loss or gain of the intervening genes.

2.7. Abnormal Immune Activation

Several studies have reported abnormalities in the peripheral immune system of ASD individuals and a number of genes that are frequently mutated in ASD relate to immune function [67]. Additionally recent epidemiological reports link infections in early pregnancy to an increased incidence of autism [12]. Increased neuronal inflammation is also observed in the central nervous system of ASD patients [67]. Consequently, it is firmly established that the immune system is dysregulated in autism and it has been suggested that this could be a contributing factor to the development of the disorder [67,68]. Cytokines receptors are expressed in the brain and cytokines released by immune cells are able to affect both the development and function of the neuronal system. Imbalanced cytokine release can therefore disrupt physiological neurodevelopment [69]. Prenatal maternal inflammation can also disrupt global and gene-specific methylation patterns in the brain [70]. Chronic inflammation can also be a source of ROS contributing to oxidative stress [40,41] which has been implicated in ASD (see Section 2.3).

Environmental exposures that trigger immune responses include infections, toxins that impact the immune system, and allergens. An increased propensity to immune dysregulation predisposing to ASD could be due to inappropriate activation of immune responses, prolonged and persistent immune responses, and autoimmunity [67,68]. Abnormal immune activation can also occur due to defective clearance of environmental toxicants by xenobiotic metabolic enzymes. In one interesting study Ashwood *et al.* [71] showed that peripheral blood mononuclear cells from control and autistic individuals resulted in qualitatively different profiles of secreted cytokines following bacterial lipopolysaccharide (LPS) exposure when pre-treated with environmental toxins PBDEs. This experiment suggested an inherently different immune response of ASD individuals to PBDE exposure compared to controls. Evidence in support of genotype-environment interactions for the immune system is also available from animal studies. Mouse research has shown a link between maternal immune activation and ASD behavior [67]. In a recent interesting study comparing two mice strains, C57BL/6J and Black and Tan BRachyury *T* + *tf*/J (BTBR), it was shown that the immune responses and their propensity for the development of ASD-like phenotypes in the offspring differed following exposure to viral mimics, with the BTBR strain displaying a greater susceptibility [72]. Consequently, this study supports the importance of gene x environment interactions in the development of immune system dysregulation and ASD. The genetic factors associated with the greater susceptibility of the BTBR strain were not clarified in this study, although Disrupted in Schizophrenia 1 (*Disc1*), a gene that this strain lacks and is involved in immunological responses, has been suggested as a potential candidate. In another recent study researchers showed that haploinsufficiency of tuberous sclerosis complex (*TSC*), a gene for which mutations are associated with a greatly increased risk of ASD development, interacted with infection to disrupt social behavior in adult mice [73]. In this case specific gene x environment interactions and their effects on normal behavior, at least in adult mice, were demonstrated.

2.8. Gut Microbiota

Gut microbiota are the collection of thousands of microbial species that are found within the intestine. The gut microbiota affects multiple biological systems such as gut permeability, immune system, and metabolism. Gut microbiota can also affect neuronal development, functioning, and signaling by interacting with the immune system, neural, and hormonal pathways [74]. As discussed in Section 2.7 abnormal immune system activation has been associated with ASD development. The gut microbiota also induce the generation of ROS in epithelial cells which can contribute to immune dysfunction and to oxidative stress [75]. Studies have reported differences in the gut microbiota between ASD patients and control cohorts [76,77]. In an intriguing recent study it was reported that in a mouse model of ASD altering the gut microbiota ameliorates behavioral abnormalities [78]. Importantly the gut microbiome is highly flexible and is affected by a person's age, geographic region, environment, health, and genotype [79]. Studies in mice support that the genotype of animals is a strong determinant of the type of microbial species present in the animals guts [80,81]. Differences in the composition of the gut microbiota in humans could therefore potentially render them more susceptible to ASD environmental factors through distinct mechanisms e.g., increased sensitivity to environmental agents that disrupt the immune system. Currently we are not aware of any published studies that have investigated whether an individual's gut microbiota can render them more or less susceptible to environmental risk factors for autism.

2.9. Transgenerational Environmental Effects

The transmission of the effects of environmental exposures across generations has been suggested to be involved in various human diseases, including autism and other behavioral disorders [82,83]. There is considerable debate about the mechanisms by which transgenerational information can be transmitted, although miRNA, DNA methylation, and histone modification are considered as primary candidates. Although highly speculative at present, it is possible that defects in epigenetic machinery could render individuals more susceptible to transgenerational epigenetic defects caused by environmental exposures. In one study gestational exposure to bisphenol A was linked to transgenerational behavioral abnormalities in mice [82]. A second study found that exposure to valproic acid *in utero* was associated with abnormal gut microbiome across multiple generation, as well as with immune and neurological abnormalities [83,84]. By causing transgenerational epigenetic effects, environmental factors could interact with genetic factors to promote ASD in individuals that were not exposed to the environmental agents directly.

2.10. Exacerbation of Environmental Effects by Seizures

Seizures are the result of abnormal electrical activity in the brain and can result in loss of consciousness and involuntary muscle contractions. Importantly, there is evidence for a link between seizures and ASD. There is a much higher prevalence of epilepsy in ASD children compared to controls [85]. Seizures are also associated with the exacerbation of ASD clinical features [86,87]. The interaction between seizures and autism could be important for two different reasons. First, seizures can modulate the incidence and clinical features of ASD associated with a given genotype. Second, seizures could render individuals more susceptible to environmental agents that disrupt normal neurodevelopment to promote ASD development. One proposed mechanism by which seizures can affect ASD is the downregulation of the Fragile X mental retardation protein (*FMRP*). It has long been known that Fragile X syndrome (FXS) is associated with increased incidence of ASD [88]. In recent years post-mortem examination of brain tissue from idiopathic ASD patients has also found deregulated FMRP [89,90]. Interesting research has found that seizures disrupt the normal functioning of the FMRP. In a rat model of seizures it has been found that this results in abnormal FMRP phosphorylation, localization, and function of the protein [91].

3. Conclusions

So far substantially more research effort has been invested into cataloging the presence of genetic and epigenetic aberrations in ASD individuals compared to how and why these emerge in the first place. We have presented here a number of processes through which environmental ASD risk factors can modulate the genome and epigenome of genetically-susceptible individuals (Table 1). Some of these mechanisms have currently more supportive evidence (for example oxidative stress and immune dysregulation) while others are more speculative (for example transgenerational inheritance). Crucially, these different mechanisms do not act in isolation but can interact to enhance their detrimental effects. In Figure 1 we present examples of how different genetic and environmental factors and biological processes can interact to produce the genetic and epigenetic aberrations that promote ASD development. For example we have previously discussed the potential contribution of oxidative stress to ASD (Section 2.3). Defective one-carbon metabolism or dysfunctional mitochondria can increase the susceptibility of individuals to pro-oxidant diet or toxin exposures. Aberrant immune responses can also contribute to oxidative stress through the generation of ROS as a consequence of inflammation. Altered gut microbiota which disrupt the immune system could also possibly contribute to the generation of a state of oxidative stress. An integrative analysis of the multiple mechanisms of gene x environment interactions will be required to understand the development of ASD.

The susceptibility of individuals to environmental ASD risk factors is restricted to the early stages of life, especially during embryonic and fetal life, when the developing brain is uniquely sensitive to environmental agents [92,93]. The biological mechanisms described here should therefore only be relevant to ASD if they affect normal neurodevelopment *in utero* or possibly during very early post-natal stages. This observation raises the possibility that the genetically-susceptible individuals on which environmental risk factors act may not be the ASD patients themselves but their parents. For example an increased mutation rate as a consequence of environmental exposures (due to an inherently greater genomic instability or oxidative stress) could act to increase the presence of pathogenic mutations in the gametes and offspring. In this case mutations occurring in somatic tissues post-natally will not be relevant to ASD development. For many of the proposed mechanisms it is not clear at present whether environmental factors act on the ASD patients themselves or on their parents, a question of potential clinical significance.

It is important to remember when interpreting studies examining the association between exposure to environmental agents and ASD development that correlation does not necessarily imply causation. This is especially the case when the mechanisms through which environmental factors increase ASD risk are of a more speculative nature. Moreover, it is possible that environmental agents associated with ASD act to increase the incidence of the disorder through different mechanisms than the ones considered to be the primary candidates. Finally, in cases where environmental agents may act through multiple distinct mechanisms it can be difficult to determine which are the most relevant. For example, in conditions of low dietary folate MTHFR variants that affect the activity of the enzyme could increase the incidence of ASD by affecting oxidative stress, the epigenome or mutation rates (or all three). Uncovering the implicated mechanism could be of great therapeutic importance since epigenetic aberrations, unlike genetic aberrations, are in principle reversible.

Table 1. Mechanisms modulating the genome and epigenome of susceptible individuals.

Mechanisms	Effects on Genome and Epigenome	Environmental Factors	Genetic Factors
Oxidative stress	DNA damage; Mitochondria dysfunction; Disruption of the epigenome; Deregulated gene expression	Pro-oxidant toxicants; Diet low in one-carbon donors; Immunogens	Defective one-carbon metabolism; Defective anti-oxidant defenses; Abnormal immune activation; mitochondrial dysfunction
Abnormal immune activation	Autoantibody generation; CNS inflammation; Cytokine secretion; Gut permeability	Infections; Allergens; Immunogens	Defective xenobiotic metabolism; Autoimmune diseases; Hypersensitivity to immunogens
Genomic instability	Increased incidence of mutations predisposing to autism	DNA damaging agents; Diet low in one-carbon donors	Defective DNA repair; Defective xenobiotic metabolism; Genomic architecture
Epigenome dysregulation	Loss of normal gene regulation; Genomic instability	Heavy metals and toxins; CNS inflammation; Diet low in one-carbon donors	Defective one-carbon metabolism; Genomic architecture
Altered gut microbiome	Gut permeability; Neurotransmitter release; Immune dysfunction	Infections; Diet composition	Interaction of immune system with microbiota
Hyperactive transposable elements	Mutations affecting genes implicated in ASD	Chemicals activating retrotransposition	Reduced Mecp2 activity
Transgenerational inheritance	Abnormal gene expression patterns during neurodevelopment in unexposed generations	Perinatal stress; Endocrine disruptors; Effects on gut microbiome	Mechanisms are currently controversial

Elucidating the relevance of the candidate mechanisms by which environmental agents affect the genome and epigenome will require the usage of diverse research strategies. Family and population association studies that specifically examine genotype-environment interactions can provide strong evidence for the importance of such mechanisms in the disorder and identify genetic factors that increase individual susceptibility. We have previously discussed how variants affecting *MTHFR* have been associated with ASD risk according to folate fortification [52]. Another recent study reported that variants in the *MET* gene interact with air pollution exposure to increase ASD risk [94]. However, association studies examining genotype-environment interactions have low statistical power, necessitating very large study populations. Consequently, such studies are difficult to set up. A second limitation is that even when statistically significant gene x environmental factor interactions are detected by association studies, it can still be difficult to pinpoint the biological mechanisms by which these occur.

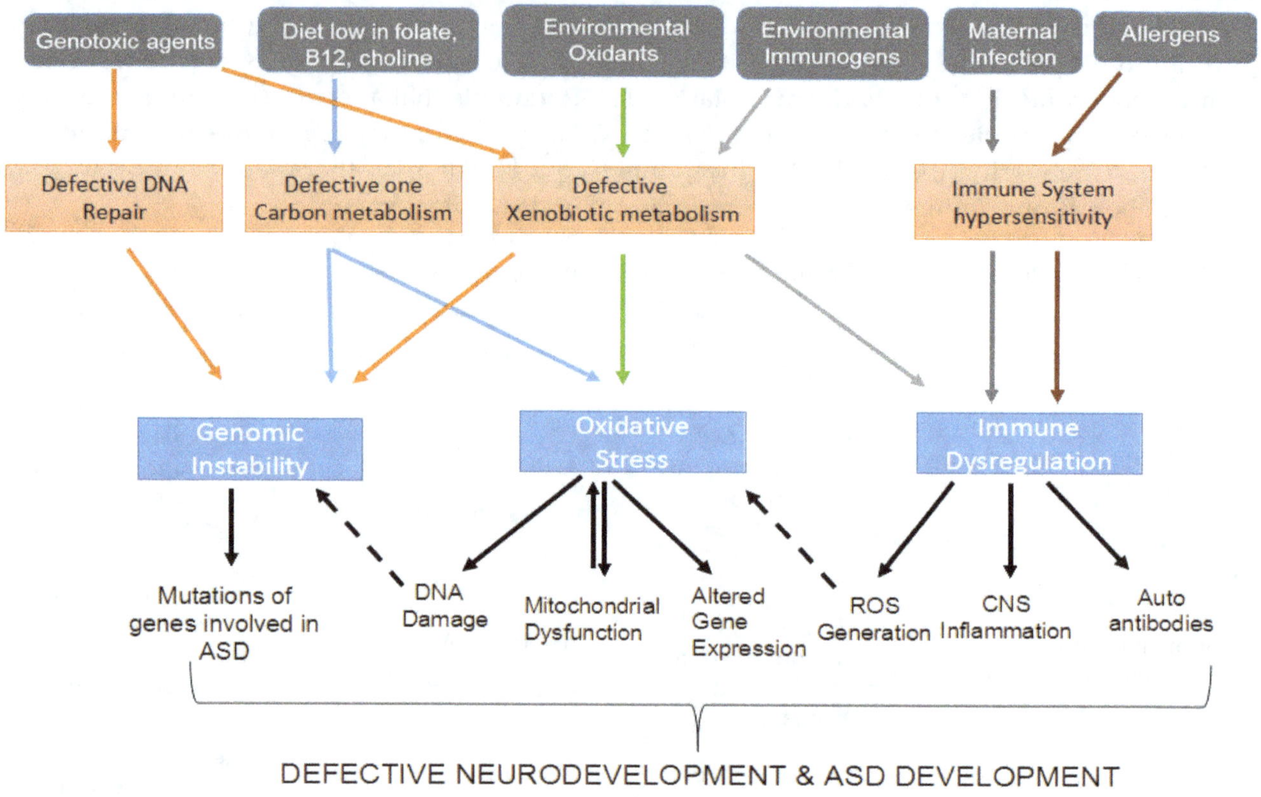

Figure 1. The figure illustrates the complex interactions between environmental and genetic factors that modulate the genome and epigenome of susceptible individuals. Environmental factors are shown in grey boxes, genetic factors in orange boxes, and the biological mechanism in blue boxes. The biological mechanisms shown in this figure are abnormal immune activation, oxidative stress, and genomic instability. The solid, colored arrows indicate interactions between environmental and genetic factors that eventually contribute to genomic instability, oxidative stress or immune activation. Orange colored lines indicate the effects of genotoxic agents, blue lines the effects of diets that are low in sources of one-carbon units, green lines indicate environmental agents, light gray lines indicate environmental immunogens, dark gray maternal infection, and red lines indicate allergens. Solid black lines link genomic instability, oxidative stress, and immune dysregulation to processes which contribute to ASD development. Dashed lines indicate interactions between biological processes involved in ASD e.g., DNA damage caused by oxidative stress also contributes to genomic instability and ROS generated by the immune system contribute to oxidative stress. As can be seen not only are multiple genotype-environmental interactions implicated in modulating the genome and epigenome of susceptible individuals, but interactions also occur between the different biological mechanisms.

Highly useful for studies investigating the mechanisms of genotype-environment interactions in ASD are the repositories of biomaterials and phenotypic and genotypic data for ASD patients and unaffected relatives, such as the AGRE and SFARI depositories. Patient-derived lymphoblastoid cells can be highly informative as gene expression profiles of immune cells reflect to a surprising extent those of human tissues, including the brain [95]. Additionally, the utilization of induced pluripotent stem cells (iPSC) is becoming an increasingly more powerful methodology for simulating neurodevelopmental disorders in patients. The lymphoblastoid and iPSC from ASD patients and controls can be used to investigate differences in the vulnerabilities of ASD patients to environmental factors. Cell line based investigations can be performed much cheaper and quicker than association studies that require the recruitment of large numbers of patients. An additional advantage is that cell lines can be easily genetically manipulated, something that can be used for examining the biological mechanisms by which environmental agents interact with genetic factors. An example of a recent study using this approach to investigate a potential inherent susceptibility of autistic individuals was conducted by Main *et al.*, 2013 [96]. In this study the researchers compared the effects of treatment with hydrogen peroxide and *S*-nitroprusside on lymphoblastoid cell lines from six ASD-normal sibling pairs. They reported finding that the autistic individuals were more sensitive to necrotic death but not to DNA damage induced by this treatments. Although innovative this study was limited in its use of a very small sample size and in not examining the epigenetic susceptibilities of the cell lines derived from ASD individuals (for example by determining disruption of global and gene specific patterns of DNA and histone methylation).

A big limitation of *in vitro* methods is that they are not applicable to the study of neurodevelopmental or behavioural processes. Consequently a variety of animal models have been developed for use in ASD research, with different advantages and disadvantages. Lower order species such as *C. elegans* and zebrafish can be genetically manipulated relatively quickly and at a lower cost, while using mammalian models is trickier and more expensive, but can better replicate human neurobiology and complex social behavior. Animal models also provide powerful tools for investigating genotype X environment interactions in ASD. For example, studies have demonstrated that neuroligin-deficient *C. elegans* are more vulnerable to oxidative stress [51] and hippocampal-slices from Mecp2 mice are more sensitive to hypoxia [97]. A large number of animal models for ASD have already been developed, which can be used in the future for studies investigating gene X environment interactions.

An increased understanding of genotype-environment interactions in ASD is important for identifying key genetic variants and environmental risk factors, reducing the exposure of vulnerable individuals to environmental risk factors, increasing the power and efficacy of epidemiological and clinical traits, and could facilitate the development of personalized treatments. A priority of autism research in the coming years should therefore be to increase the investment of time and resources into elucidating the nature, extent, and importance of genotype-environment interactions in autism. This will require the systematic application of research approaches that will facilitate progress in the field of genotype-environment interactions in ASD.

Acknowledgments: The authors of this manuscript have been supported by the Cyprus Institute of Neurology and Genetics.

Author Contributions: Costas Koufaris drafted the manuscript and Carolina Sismani revised the manuscript.

References

1. Geschwind, D.H. Advances in autism. *Annu. Rev. Med.* **2009**, *60*, 367–380. [CrossRef] [PubMed]
2. Hallmayer, J.; Cleveland, S.; Torres, A.; Phillips, J.; Cohen, B.; Torigoe, T.; Miller, J.; Fedele, A.; Collins, J.; Smith, K.; *et al.* Genetic heritability and shared environmental factors among twin pairs with autism. *Arch. Gen. Psychiatry* **2011**, *68*, 1095–1102. [CrossRef] [PubMed]
3. Devlin, B.; Scherer, S.W. Genetic architecture in autism spectrum disorder. *Curr. Opin. Genet. Dev.* **2012**, *22*, 229–237. [CrossRef] [PubMed]
4. Leblond, C.S.; Nava, C.; Polge, A.; Gauthier, J.; Huguet, G.; Lumbroso, S.; Giuliano, F.; Stordeur, C.; Depienne, C.; Mouzat, K.; *et al.* Meta-analysis of SHANK mutations in autism spectrum disorders: A gradient of severity in cognitive impairments. *PLoS Genet.* **2014**, *10*, e1004580. [CrossRef] [PubMed]
5. Clipperton-Allen, A.E.; Page, D.T. Pten haploinsufficient mice show broad brain overgrowth but selective impairments in autism-relevant behavioral tests. *Hum. Mol. Genet.* **2014**, *23*, 3490–3505. [CrossRef] [PubMed]
6. Tsai, N.P.; Wilkerson, J.R.; Guo, W.; Maksimova, M.A.; DeMartino, G.N.; Cowan, C.W.; Huber, K.M. Multiple autism-linked genes mediate synapse elimination via proteasomal degradation of a synaptic scaffold PSD-95. *Cell* **2012**, *151*, 1581–1594. [CrossRef] [PubMed]

7. Shepherd, G.M.; Katz, D.M. Synaptic microcircuit dysfunction in genetic models of neurodevelopmental disorders: Focus on *Mecp2* and *Met*. *Curr. Opin. Neurobiol.* **2011**, *21*, 827–833. [CrossRef] [PubMed]
8. James, S.J.; Shpyleva, S.; Melnyk, S.; Pavliv, O.; Pogribny, I.P. Elevated 5-hydroxymethylcytosine in the Engrailed-2 (EN-2) promoter is associated with increased gene expression and decreased MeCP2 binding in autism cerebellum. *Transl. Psychiatry* **2014**, *4*, e460. [CrossRef] [PubMed]
9. Nguyen, A.; Rauch, T.A.; Pfeifer, G.P.; Hu, V.W. Global methylation profiling of lymphoblastoid cell lines reveals epigenetic contributions to autism spectrum disorders and a novel autism candidate gene, *RORA*, whose protein product is reduced in autistic brain. *FASEB J.* **2010**, *24*, 3036–3051. [CrossRef] [PubMed]
10. Ladd-Acosta, C.; Hansen, K.D.; Briem, E.; Fallin, M.D.; Kaufmann, W.E.; Feinberg, A.P. Common DNA methylation alterations in multiple brain regions in autism. *Mol. Psychiatry* **2014**, *19*, 862–871. [CrossRef] [PubMed]
11. James, S.J.; Shpyleva, S.; Melnyk, S.; Pavliv, O.; Pogribny, I.P. Complex epigenetic regulation of the Engrailed-2 (EN-2) homeobox gene in the autism cerebellum. *Transl. Psychiatry* **2013**, *3*, e232. [CrossRef] [PubMed]
12. Atladóttir, H.O.; Thorsen, P.; Østergaard, L.; Schendel, D.E.; Lemcke, S.; Abdallah, M.; Parner, E.T. Maternal infection requiring hospitalization during pregnancy and autism spectrum disorders. *J. Autism Dev. Disord.* **2010**, *40*, 1423–1430. [CrossRef] [PubMed]
13. Roberts, A.L.; Lyall, K.; Hart, J.E.; Laden, F.; Just, A.C.; Bobb, J.F.; Koenen, K.C.; Ascherio, A.; Weisskopf, M.G. Perinatal air pollutant exposures and autism spectrum disorder in the children of Nurses' Health Study II participants. *Environ. Health Perspect.* **2013**, *121*, 978–984. [PubMed]
14. Surén, P.; Roth, C.; Bresnahan, M.; Haugen, M.; Hornig, M.; Hirtz, D.; Lie, K.K.; Lipkin, W.I.; Magnus, P.; Reichborn-Kjennerud, T.; *et al.* Association between maternal use of folic acid supplements and autism risk in children. *JAMA* **2013**, *309*, 570–577. [CrossRef] [PubMed]
15. Herbert, M.R. Contributions of the environment and environmentally vulnerable physiology to autism spectrum disorders. *Curr. Opin. Neurol.* **2010**, *23*, 103–110. [CrossRef] [PubMed]
16. LaSalle, J.M. A genomic-point-of-view on environmental factors influencing the human brain methylome. *Epigenetics* **2011**, *6*, 862–869. [CrossRef] [PubMed]
17. Chaste, P.; Leboyer, M. Autism risk factors: Genes, environment, and gene-environment interactions. *Dialogues Clin. Neurosci.* **2012**, *14*, 281–292. [PubMed]
18. LaSalle, J.M. Epigenomic strategies at the interface of genetic and environmental risk factors for autism. *J. Hum. Genet.* **2013**, *58*, 396–401. [CrossRef] [PubMed]
19. Stamou, M.; Streifel, K.M.; Goines, P.E.; Lein, P.J. Neuronal connectivity as a convergent target of gene × environment interactions that confer risk for Autism Spectrum Disorders. *Neurotoxicol. Teratol.* **2013**, *36*, 3–16. [CrossRef] [PubMed]
20. Miksys, S.; Tyndale, R.F. Cytochrome P450-mediated drug metabolism in the brain. *J. Psychiatry Neurosci.* **2013**, *38*, 152–163. [CrossRef] [PubMed]
21. Woods, R.; Vallero, R.O.; Golub, M.S.; Suarez, J.K.; Ta, T.A.; Yasui, D.H.; Chi, L.-H.; Kostyniak, P.J.; Pessah, I.N.; Berman, R.F.; *et al.* Long lived epigenetic interactions between perinatal PBDE exposure and Mecp22308 mutation. *Hum. Mol. Genet.* **2012**, *21*, 2399–2411. [CrossRef] [PubMed]
22. Feo, M.L.; Gross, M.S.; McGarrigle, B.P.; Eljarrat, E.; Barceló, D.; Aga, D.S.; Olson, J.R. Biotransformation of BDE-47 to potentially toxic metabolites is predominantly mediated by human CYP2B6. *Environ. Health Perspect.* **2013**, *121*, 440–446. [CrossRef] [PubMed]
23. Kinney, D.K.; Barch, D.H.; Chayka, B.; Napoleon, S.; Munir, K.M. Environmental risk factors for autism: Do they help cause de novo genetic mutations? *Med. Hypotheses* **2010**, *74*, 102–106. [CrossRef] [PubMed]
24. Turesky, R.J. The role of genetic polymorphisms in the metabolism of carcinogenic heterocyclic amines. *Curr. Drug Metab.* **2004**, *5*, 169–180. [CrossRef] [PubMed]
25. D'Amelio, M.; Ricci, I.; Sacco, R.; Liu, X.; D'Agruma, L.; Muscarella, L.A.; Guarnieri, V.; Militerni, R.; Bravaccio, C.; Elia, M.; *et al.* Paraoxonase gene variants are associated with autism in North America, but not in Italy: Possible regional specificity in gene-environment interactions. *Mol. Psychiatry* **2005**, *10*, 1006–1016. [CrossRef] [PubMed]
26. Eskenazi, B.; Huen, K.; Marks, A.; Harley, K.G.; Bradman, A.; Barr, D.B.; Holland, N. PON1 and neurodevelopment in children from the CHAMACOS study exposed to organophosphate pesticides in utero. *Environ. Health Perspect.* **2010**, *118*, 1775–1781. [CrossRef] [PubMed]

27. Rossignol, D.A.; Genuis, S.J.; Frye, R.E. Environmental toxicants and autism spectrum disorders: A systematic review. *Transl. Psychiatry* **2014**, *4*, e360. [CrossRef] [PubMed]
28. Serajee, F.J.; Nabi, R.; Zhong, H.; Huq, M. Polymorphisms in xenobiotic metabolism genes and autism. *J. Child Neurol.* **2004**, *19*, 413–417. [PubMed]
29. Buyske, S.; Williams, T.A.; Mars, A.E.; Stenroos, E.S.; Ming, S.X.; Wang, R.; Sreenath, M.; Factura, M.F.; Reddy, C.; Lambert, G.H.; *et al.* Analysis of case-parent trios at a locus with a deletion allele: Association of GSTM1 with autism. *BMC Genet.* **2006**, *7*, 8. [CrossRef] [PubMed]
30. Baron-Cohen, S.; Knickmeyer, R.C.; Belmonte, M.K. Sex differences in the brain: Implications for explaining autism. *Science* **2005**, *310*, 819–823. [CrossRef] [PubMed]
31. Werling, D.M.; Geschwind, D.H. Sex differences in autism spectrum disorders. *Curr. Opin. Neurol.* **2013**, *26*, 146–153. [CrossRef] [PubMed]
32. Lombardo, M.V.; Ashwin, E.; Auyeung, B.; Chakrabarti, B.; Taylor, K.; Hackett, G.; Bullmore, E.T.; Baron-Cohen, S. Fetal testosterone influences sexually dimorphic grey matter in the brain. *J. Neurosci.* **2012**, *32*, 674–680. [CrossRef] [PubMed]
33. Baron-Cohen, S.; Auyeung, B.; Nørgaard-Pedersen, B.; Hougaard, D.M.; Abdallah, M.W.; Melgaard, L.; Cohen, A.S.; Chakrabarti, B.; Ruta, L.; Lombardo, M.V. Elevated fetal steroidogenic activity in autism. *Mol. Psychiatry* **2015**, *20*, 369–376. [CrossRef] [PubMed]
34. Kajta, M.; Wójtowicz, A.K. Impact of endocrine-disrupting chemicals on neural development and the onset of neurological disorders. *Pharmacol. Rep.* **2013**, *65*, 1632–1639. [CrossRef] [PubMed]
35. Miodovnik, A.; Engel, S.M.; Zhu, C.; Ye, X.; Soorya, L.V.; Silva, M.J.; Calafat, A.M.; Wolff, M.S. Endocrine disruptors and childhood social impairments. *Neurotoxicology* **2011**, *32*, 261–267. [CrossRef] [PubMed]
36. Braun, J.M.; Kalkbrenner, A.E.; Just, A.C.; Yolton, K.; Calafat, A.M.; Sjödin, A.; Hauser, R.; Webster, G.M.; Chen, A.; Lanphear, B.P. Gestational exposure to endocrine-disrupting chemicals and reciprocal social, repetitive, and stereotypic behaviors in 4- and 5-year-old children: The HOME study. *Environ. Health Perspect.* **2014**, *122*, 513–520. [PubMed]
37. Spearow, J.L.; Doemeny, P.; Sera, R.; Leffler, R.; Barkley, M. Genetic variability in susceptibility to endocrine disruptors in mice. *Science* **1999**, *285*, 1259–1261. [CrossRef] [PubMed]
38. Henningsson, S.; Jonsson, L.; Ljunggren, E.; Westberg, L.; Gillberg, C.; Råstam, M.; Anckarsäter, H.; Nygren, G.; Landén, M.; Thuresson, K.; *et al.* Possible association between the androgen receptor gene and autism spectrum disorder. *Psychoneuroendocrinology* **2009**, *34*, 752–761. [CrossRef] [PubMed]
39. Zettergren, A.; Jonsson, L.; Johansson, D.; Melke, J.; Lundström, S.; Anckarsäter, H.; Lichtenstein, P.; Westberg, L. Associations between polymorphisms in sex steroid related genes and autistic-like traits. *Psychoneuroendocrinology* **2013**, *38*, 2575–2584. [CrossRef] [PubMed]
40. Frye, R.E.; Delatorre, R.; Taylor, H.; Slattery, J.; Melnyk, S.; Chowdhury, N.; James, S.J. Redox metabolic abnormalities in autistic children associated with mitochondrial disease. *Transl. Psychiatry* **2013**, *3*, e273. [CrossRef] [PubMed]
41. Rossignol, D.A.; Frye, R.E. Mitochondrial dysfunction in autism spectrum disorders: A systematic review and meta-analysis. *Mol. Psychiatry* **2012**, *17*, 290–314. [CrossRef] [PubMed]
42. Boccuto, L.; Chen, C.-F.; Pittman, A.R.; Skinner, C.D.; McCartney, H.J.; Jones, K.; Bochner, B.R.; Stevenson, R.E.; Schwartz, C.E. Decreased tryptophan metabolism in patients with autism spectrum disorders. *Mol. Autism* **2013**, *4*, 16. [CrossRef] [PubMed]
43. Li, J.; Harris, R.A.; Cheung, S.W.; Coarfa, C.; Jeong, M.; Goodell, M.A.; White, L.D.; Patel, A.; Kang, S.-H.; Shaw, C.; *et al.* Genomic hypomethylation in the human germline assosiates with selective structural mutability in the human genome. *PLoS Genet.* **2012**, *8*, e1002692. [CrossRef] [PubMed]
44. Li, Z.; Okamoto, K.-I.; Hayashi, Y.; Sheng, M. The importance of dendritic mitochondria in the morphogenesis and plasticity of spines and synapses. *Cell* **2004**, *119*, 873–887. [CrossRef] [PubMed]
45. James, S.J.; Melnyk, S.; Jernigan, S.; Cleves, M.A.; Halsted, C.H.; Wong, D.H.; Cutler, P.; Bock, K.; Boris, M.; Bradstreet, J.J.; *et al.* Metabolic endophenotype and related genotypes are associated with oxidative stress in children with autism. *Am. J. Med. Genet. Part B* **2006**, *141B*, 947–956. [CrossRef]
46. Schwartz, C.E. Aberrant tryptophan metabolism: The unifying biochemical basis for autism spectrum disorders? *Biomark. Med.* **2014**, *8*, 313–315. [CrossRef] [PubMed]

47. Rose, S.; Frye, R.E.; Slattery, J.; Wynne, R.; Tippett, M.; Pavliv, O.; Melnyk, S.; James, S.J. Oxidative stress induces mitochondrial dysfunction in a subset of autism lymphoblastoid cell lines in a well-matched case control cohort. *PLoS ONE* **2014**, *9*, e85436. [CrossRef] [PubMed]
48. Rose, S.; Frye, R.E.; Slattery, J.; Wynne, R.; Tippett, M.; Melnyk, S.; James, S.J. Oxidative stress induces mitochondrial dysfunction in a subset of autistic lymphoblastoid cell lines. *Transl. Psychiatry* **2014**, *4*, e377. [CrossRef] [PubMed]
49. Kaur, K.; Chauhan, V.; Gu, F.; Chauhan, A. Bisphenol A induces oxidative stress and mitochondrial dysfunction in lymphoblasts from children with autism and unaffected siblings. *Free Radic. Biol. Med.* **2014**, *76C*, 25–33. [CrossRef] [PubMed]
50. Napoli, E.; Ross-Inta, C.; Wong, S.; Hung, C.; Fujisawa, Y.; Sakaguchi, D.; Angelastro, J.; Omanska-Klusek, A.; Schoenfeld, R.; Giulivi, C. Mitochondrial dysfunction in Pten haplo-insufficient mice with social deficits and repetitive behavior: Interplay between Pten and p53. *PLoS ONE* **2012**, *7*, e42504. [CrossRef] [PubMed]
51. Hunter, J.W.; Mullen, G.P.; McManus, J.R.; Heatherly, J.M.; Duke, A.; Rand, J.B. Neuroligin-deficient mutants of C. elegans have sensory processing deficits and are hypersensitive to oxidative stress and mercury toxicity. *Dis. Model. Mech.* **2010**, *3*, 366–376. [CrossRef] [PubMed]
52. Pu, D.; Shen, Y.; Wu, J. Association between *MTHFR* gene polymorphisms and the risk of autism spectrum disorders: A meta-analysis. *Autism Res.* **2013**, *6*, 384–392. [CrossRef] [PubMed]
53. Kovač, J.; Macedoni Lukšič, M.; Trebušak Podkrajšek, K.; Klančar, G.; Battelino, T. Rare single nucleotide polymorphisms in the regulatory regions of the superoxide dismutase genes in autism spectrum disorder. *Autism Res.* **2014**, *7*, 138–144. [CrossRef] [PubMed]
54. Smith, M.; Flodman, P.L.; Gargus, J.J.; Simon, M.T.; Verrell, K.; Haas, R.; Reiner, G.E.; Naviaux, R.; Osann, K.; Spence, M.A.; *et al.* Mitochondrial and Ion Channel gene alterations in autism. *Biochim. Biophys. Acta* **2012**, *1817*, 1796–1802. [CrossRef] [PubMed]
55. Nava, C.; Lamari, F.; Héron, D.; Mignot, C.; Rastetter, A.; Keren, B.; Cohen, D.; Faudet, A.; Bouteiller, D.; Gilleron, M.; *et al.* Analysis of the chromosome X exome in patients with autism spectrum disorders identified novel candidate genes, including TMLHE. *Transl. Psychiatry* **2012**, *2*, e179. [CrossRef] [PubMed]
56. Napolioni, V.; Persico, A.M.; Porcelli, V.; Palmieri, L. The mitochondrial aspartate/glutamate carrier AGC1 and calcium homeostasis: Physiological links and abnormalities in autism. *Mol. Neurobiol.* **2011**, *44*, 83–92. [CrossRef] [PubMed]
57. Rossignol, D.A.; Frye, R.E. A review of research trends in physiological abnormalities in autism spectrum disorders: Immune dysregulation, inflammation, oxidative stress, mitochondrial dysfunction and environmental toxicant exposures. *Mol. Psychiatry* **2012**, *17*, 389–401. [CrossRef] [PubMed]
58. Zhu, L.; Wang, X.; Li, X.-L.; Towers, A.; Cao, X.; Wang, P.; Bowman, R.; Yang, H.; Goldstein, J.; Li, Y.-J.; *et al.* Epigenetic dysregulation of SHANK3 in brain tissues from individuals with autism spectrum disorders. *Hum. Mol. Genet.* **2014**, *23*, 1563–1578. [CrossRef] [PubMed]
59. Muotri, A.R.; Chu, V.T.; Marchetto, M.C.N.; Deng, W.; Moran, J.V.; Gage, F.H. Somatic mosaicism in neuronal precursor cells mediated by L1 retrotransposition. *Nature* **2005**, *435*, 903–910. [CrossRef] [PubMed]
60. Terasaki, N.; Goodier, J.L.; Cheung, L.E.; Wang, Y.J.; Kajikawa, M.; Kazazian, H.H.; Okada, N. *In vitro* screening for compounds that enhance human L1 mobilization. *PLoS ONE* **2013**, *8*, e74629. [CrossRef] [PubMed]
61. Muotri, A.R.; Marchetto, M.C.N.; Coufal, N.G.; Oefner, R.; Yeo, G.; Nakashima, K.; Gage, F.H. L1 retrotransposition in neurons is modulated by MeCP2. *Nature* **2010**, *468*, 443–446. [CrossRef] [PubMed]
62. Okudaira, N.; Okamura, T.; Tamura, M.; Iijma, K.; Goto, M.; Matsunaga, A.; Ochiai, M.; Nakagama, H.; Kano, S.; Fujii-Kuriyama, Y.; *et al.* Long interspersed element-1 is differentially regulated by food-borne carcinogens via the aryl hydrocarbon receptor. *Oncogene* **2013**, *32*, 4903–4912. [CrossRef] [PubMed]
63. Wilhelm-Benartzi, C.S.; Houseman, E.A.; Maccani, M.A.; Poage, G.M.; Koestler, D.C.; Langevin, S.M.; Gagne, L.A.; Banister, C.E.; Padbury, J.F.; Marsit, C.J. In utero exposures, infant growth, and DNA methylation of repetitive elements and developmentally related genes in human placenta. *Environ. Health Perspect.* **2012**, *120*, 296–302. [CrossRef] [PubMed]
64. Mefford, H.C.; Eichler, E.E. Duplication hotspots, rare genomic disorders, and common disease. *Curr. Opin. Genet. Dev.* **2009**, *19*, 196–204. [CrossRef] [PubMed]

65. Girirajan, S.; Johnson, R.L.; Tassone, F.; Balciuniene, J.; Katiyar, N.; Fox, K.; Baker, C.; Srikanth, A.; Yeoh, K.H.; Khoo, S.J.; *et al.* Global increases in both common and rare copy number load associated with autism. *Hum. Mol. Genet.* **2013**, *22*, 2870–2880. [CrossRef] [PubMed]
66. Ionita-Laza, I.; Xu, B.; Makarov, V.; Buxbaum, J.D.; Roos, J.L.; Gogos, J.A.; Karayiorgou, M. Scan statistic-based analysis of exome sequencing data identifies FAN1 at 15q13.3 as a susceptibility gene for schizophrenia and autism. *Proc. Natl. Acad. Sci. USA* **2014**, *111*, 343–348. [CrossRef] [PubMed]
67. Goines, P.; van de Water, J. The immune system's role in the biology of autism. *Curr. Opin. Neurol.* **2010**, *23*, 111–117. [CrossRef] [PubMed]
68. Onore, C.; Careaga, M.; Ashwood, P. The role of immune dysfunction in the pathophysiology of autism. *Brain. Behav. Immun.* **2012**, *26*, 383–392. [CrossRef] [PubMed]
69. Deverman, B.E.; Patterson, P.H. Cytokines and CNS development. *Neuron* **2009**, *64*, 61–78. [CrossRef] [PubMed]
70. Basil, P.; Li, Q.; Dempster, E.L.; Mill, J.; Sham, P.C.; Wong, C.C.; McAlonan, G.M. Prenatal maternal immune activation causes epigenetic differences in adolescent mouse brain. *Transl. Psychiatry* **2014**, *2*, e434. [CrossRef]
71. Ashwood, P.; Schauer, J.; Pessah, I.N.; van de Water, J. Preliminary evidence of the *in vitro* effects of BDE-47 on innate immune responses in children with autism spectrum disorders. *J. Neuroimmunol.* **2009**, *208*, 130–135. [CrossRef] [PubMed]
72. Schwartzer, J.J.; Careaga, M.; Onore, C.E.; Rushakoff, J.A.; Berman, R.F.; Ashwood, P. Maternal immune activation and strain specific interactions in the development of autism-like behaviors in mice. *Transl. Psychiatry* **2013**, *3*, e240. [CrossRef] [PubMed]
73. Ehninger, D.; Sano, Y.; de Vries, P.J.; Dies, K.; Franz, D.; Geschwind, D.H.; Kaur, M.; Lee, Y.-S.; Li, W.; Lowe, J.K.; *et al.* Gestational immune activation and Tsc2 haploinsufficiency cooperate to disrupt fetal survival and may perturb social behavior in adult mice. *Mol. Psychiatry* **2012**, *17*, 62–70. [CrossRef] [PubMed]
74. Cryan, J.F.; Dinan, T.G. Mind-altering microorganisms: The impact of the gut microbiota on brain and behaviour. *Nat. Rev. Neurosci.* **2012**, *13*, 701–712. [CrossRef] [PubMed]
75. Jones, R.M.; Mercante, J.W.; Neish, A.S. Reactive oxygen production induced by the gut microbiota: Pharmacotherapeutic implications. *Curr. Med. Chem.* **2012**, *19*, 1519–1529. [CrossRef] [PubMed]
76. Finegold, S.M.; Molitoris, D.; Song, Y.; Liu, C.; Vaisanen, M.-L.; Bolte, E.; McTeague, M.; Sandler, R.; Wexler, H.; Marlowe, E.M.; *et al.* Gastrointestinal microflora studies in late-onset autism. *Clin. Infect. Dis.* **2002**, *35*, S6–S16. [CrossRef] [PubMed]
77. Parracho, H.M.R.T.; Bingham, M.O.; Gibson, G.R.; McCartney, A.L. Differences between the gut microflora of children with autism spectrum disorders and that of healthy children. *J. Med. Microbiol.* **2005**, *54*, 987–991. [CrossRef] [PubMed]
78. Hsiao, E.Y.; McBride, S.W.; Hsien, S.; Sharon, G.; Hyde, E.R.; McCue, T.; Codelli, J.A.; Chow, J.; Reisman, S.E.; Petrosino, J.F.; *et al.* Microbiota modulate behavioral and physiological abnormalities associated with neurodevelopmental disorders. *Cell* **2013**, *155*, 1451–1463. [CrossRef] [PubMed]
79. Holmes, E.; Li, J.V.; Marchesi, J.R.; Nicholson, J.K. Gut microbiota composition and activity in relation to host metabolic phenotype and disease risk. *Cell Metab.* **2012**, *16*, 559–564. [CrossRef] [PubMed]
80. McKnite, A.M.; Perez-Munoz, M.E.; Lu, L.; Williams, E.G.; Brewer, S.; Andreux, P.A.; Bastiaansen, J.W.M.; Wang, X.; Kachman, S.D.; Auwerx, J.; *et al.* Murine gut microbiota is defined by host genetics and modulates variation of metabolic traits. *PLoS ONE* **2012**, *7*, e39191. [CrossRef] [PubMed]
81. Parks, B.W.; Nam, E.; Org, E.; Kostem, E.; Norheim, F.; Hui, S.T.; Pan, C.; Civelek, M.; Rau, C.D.; Bennett, B.J.; *et al.* Genetic control of obesity and gut microbiota composition in response to high-fat, high-sucrose diet in mice. *Cell Metab.* **2013**, *17*, 141–152. [CrossRef] [PubMed]
82. Wolstenholme, J.T.; Edwards, M.; Shetty, S.R.J.; Gatewood, J.D.; Taylor, J.A.; Rissman, E.F.; Connelly, J.J. Gestational exposure to bisphenol a produces transgenerational changes in behaviors and gene expression. *Endocrinology* **2012**, *153*, 3828–3838. [CrossRef] [PubMed]
83. Lim, J.P.; Brunet, A. Bridging the transgenerational gap with epigenetic memory. *Trends Genet.* **2013**, *29*, 176–186. [CrossRef] [PubMed]
84. De Theije, C.G.M.; Wopereis, H.; Ramadan, M.; van Eijndthoven, T.; Lambert, J.; Knol, J.; Garssen, J.; Kraneveld, A.D.; Oozeer, R. Altered gut microbiota and activity in a murine model of autism spectrum disorders. *Brain. Behav. Immun.* **2014**, *37*, 197–206. [CrossRef] [PubMed]

85. Viscidi, E.W.; Triche, E.W.; Pescosolido, M.F.; McLean, R.L.; Joseph, R.M.; Spence, S.J.; Morrow, E.M. Clinical characteristics of children with epilepsy and co-occuring autism. *PLoS ONE* **2013**, *8*, e67797. [CrossRef] [PubMed]
86. Van Eeghen, A.M.; Pulsifer, M.B.; Merker, V.L.; Neumeyer, A.M.; van Eeghen, E.E.; Thibert, R.L.; Cole, A.J.; Leigh, F.A.; Plotkin, S.R.; Thiele, E.A. Understanding relationships between autism, intelligence, and epilepsy: A cross-disorder approach. *Dev. Med. Child Neurol.* **2013**, *55*, 146–153. [CrossRef] [PubMed]
87. Hara, H. Autism and epilepsy: A retrospective follow-up study. *Brain Dev.* **2007**, *29*, 486–490. [CrossRef] [PubMed]
88. Hagerman, R.; Hoem, G.; Hagerman, P. Fragile X and autism: Intertwined at the molecular level leading to targeted treatments. *Mol. Autism* **2010**, *1*, 12. [CrossRef] [PubMed]
89. Fatemi, S.H.; Folsom, T.D. Dysregulation of fragile × mental retardation protein and metabotropic glutamate receptor 5 in superior frontal cortex of individuals with autism: A postmortem brain study. *Mol Autism.* **2011**, *2*, 1–11. [CrossRef] [PubMed]
90. Rustan, O.G.; Folsom, T.D.; Yousefi, M.K.; Fatemi, S.H. Phosphorylated fragile X mental retardation protein at serine 499, is reduced in cerebellar vermis and superior frontal cortex of subjects with autism: Implications for fragile X mental retardation protein-metabotropic glutamate receptor 5 signaling. *Mol. Autism.* **2013**, *4*, 41. [CrossRef] [PubMed]
91. Bernard, P.B.; Castano, A.M.; O'Leary, H.; Simpson, K.; Browning, M.D.; Benke, T.A. Phosphorylation of FMRP and alterations of FMRP complex underlie enhanced mLTD in adult rats triggered by early life seizures. *Neurobiol. Dis.* **2013**, *59*, 1–17. [CrossRef] [PubMed]
92. Grandjean, P.; Landrigan, P.J. Developmental neurotoxicity of industrial chemicals. *Lancet* **2006**, *368*, 2167–2178. [CrossRef] [PubMed]
93. Miodovnik, A. Environmental neurotoxicants and the developing brain. *Mt. Sinai J. Med.* **2011**, *78*, 58–77. [CrossRef] [PubMed]
94. Volk, H.E.; Kerin, T.; Lurmann, F.; Hertz-Picciotto, I.; McConnell, R.; Campbell, D.B. Autism spectrum disorder: Interaction of air pollution with the MET receptor tyrosine kinase gene. *Epidemiology* **2014**, *25*, 44–47. [CrossRef] [PubMed]
95. Kohane, I.S.; Valtchinov, V.I. Quantifying the white blood cell transcriptome as an accessible window to the multiorgan transcriptome. *Bioinform. Oxf. Engl.* **2012**, *28*, 538–545. [CrossRef]
96. Main, P.A.E.; Thomas, P.; Esterman, A.; Fenech, M.F. Necrosis is increased in lymphoblastoid cell lines from children with autism compared with their non-autistic siblings under conditions of oxidative and nitrosative stress. *Mutagenesis* **2013**, *28*, 475–484. [CrossRef] [PubMed]
97. Fischer, M.; Reuter, J.; Gerich, F.J.; Hildebrandt, B.; Hägele, S.; Katschinski, D.; Müller, M. Enhanced hypoxia susceptibility in hippocampal slices from a mouse model of rett syndrome. *J. Neurophysiol.* **2009**, *101*, 1016–1032. [CrossRef] [PubMed]

11

Increased Force Variability is Associated with Altered Modulation of the Motorneuron Pool Activity in Autism Spectrum Disorder (ASD)

Zheng Wang [1,2,3], MinHyuk Kwon [1,2,3], Suman Mohanty [4], Lauren M. Schmitt [1,2,3], Stormi P. White [4], Evangelos A. Christou [5] and Matthew W. Mosconi [1,2,3,*]

1 Schiefelbusch Institute for Life Span Studies, University of Kansas, 1000 Sunnyside Ave., Lawrence, KS 66045, USA; zhengwang@ku.edu (Z.W.); minhyuk.kwon@marquette.edu (M.K.); lmschmitt@ku.edu (L.M.S.)

2 Clinical Child Psychology Program, University of Kansas, 1000 Sunnyside Ave., Lawrence, KS 66045, USA

3 Kansas Center for Autism Research and Training (K-CART), University of Kansas Medical School, Overland Park, KS 66213, USA

4 Center for Autism and Developmental Disabilities, University of Texas Southwestern Medical Center, Dallas, TX 75390, USA; smohanty3@humana.com (S.M.); Stormi.White@UTsouthwestern.edu (S.P.W.)

5 Department of Applied Physiology and Kinesiology, University of Florida, Gainesville, FL 32611, USA; eachristou@hhp.ufl.edu

* Correspondence: mosconi@ku.edu

Academic Editor: Merlin G. Butler

Abstract: Force control deficits have been repeatedly documented in autism spectrum disorder (ASD). They are associated with worse social and daily living skill impairments in patients suggesting that developing a more mechanistic understanding of the central and peripheral processes that cause them may help guide the development of treatments that improve multiple outcomes in ASD. The neuromuscular mechanisms underlying force control deficits are not yet understood. Seventeen individuals with ASD and 14 matched healthy controls completed an isometric index finger abduction test at 60% of their maximum voluntary contraction (MVC) during recording of the first dorsal interosseous (FDI) muscle to determine the neuromuscular processes associated with sustained force variability. Central modulation of the motorneuron pool activation of the FDI muscle was evaluated at delta (0–4 Hz), alpha (4–10 Hz), beta (10–35 Hz) and gamma (35–60 Hz) frequency bands. ASD patients showed greater force variability than controls when attempting to maintain a constant force. Relative to controls, patients also showed increased central modulation of the motorneuron pool at beta and gamma bands. For controls, reduced force variability was associated with reduced delta frequency modulation of the motorneuron pool activity of the FDI muscle and increased modulation at beta and gamma bands. In contrast, delta, beta, and gamma frequency oscillations were not associated with force variability in ASD. These findings suggest that alterations of central mechanisms that control motorneuron pool firing may underlie the common and often impairing symptoms of ASD.

Keywords: autism spectrum disorder (ASD); index finger abduction; force variability; motorneuron pool; first dorsal interosseus (FDI) muscle; decomposition-based electromyography (dEMG)

1. Introduction

Sensorimotor impairments are common in autism spectrum disorder (ASD) [1,2]. Disrupted sensorimotor developments may be among the earliest emerging symptoms of ASD, and they are associated with increased severity of social-communication, cognitive, and daily living impairments [3–6]. Sensorimotor deficits also represent an important target for determining physiological processes disrupted in ASD. Specifically, sensorimotor processes are supported by central and peripheral nervous system mechanisms that are relatively well-understood. By determining patterns of sensorimotor deficits in ASD, and clarifying their underlying physiology, studies of sensorimotor control in patients may provide new insights into neurobiological processes associated with the disorder.

Multiple types of sensorimotor abnormalities have been identified in individuals with ASD, including reduced eye movement accuracy [7,8], postural instability [9,10], increased gait variability [11,12], and atypical handwriting [13]. Reduced ability to control force output also has been repeatedly documented in studies of ASD. Specifically, studies of grip force control in ASD have suggested reduced strength [6,14,15], increased sustained force variability, and reduced force accuracy [16,17]. Force control is essential for everyday tasks requiring manual dexterity (e.g., writing, feeding, and buttoning clothes), and thus determining the physiological processes associated with these deficits may identify new targets for treatments aimed at increasing daily living skills and functional independence.

Force control involves excitatory cortical commands relayed from primary motor cortex (M1) to spinal motor neurons which innervate skeletal muscle fibers [18]. Motor neurons and muscle fibers collectively form individual motor units which work together with other motor units within a motorneuron pool to generate force and maintain target force production. Force production during voluntary contractions involves increasing the number of motor units recruited and their rate of discharge action potentials [19–21]. During increases in force production, slow-twitch motor units are recruited early and followed by a gradual recruitment of fast-twitch motor units (the "size principle") [22]. During sustained force production, recruited motor units show an increase in their discharge rate over time to support a constant level of force output [19,23].

Motorneuron pool firing is coordinated by descending central commands generated at multiple frequencies to dynamically ensure precise force production [18]. Simultaneous recordings of brain and muscle during slow isometric force production have identified a low frequency 0–4 Hz delta oscillation "common drive" generated neocortically that modulates motorneuron pool activation [20,24]. The central origin of this drive is not yet determined, though delta oscillations are seen in premotor and supplementary motor areas during force production [25]. Alpha rhythms from 4 to 10 Hz also are observed during healthy individuals' slow phasic arm movements and isometric force production [26–28].

Beta band (10–35 Hz) frequency modulation of the motorneuron pool coincides with a default mode of cortical innervation from contralateral M1 during tasks involving low to moderate force contractions [29–33]. Increased beta modulation of the motorneuron pool is associated with greater force accuracy in healthy individuals suggesting that strengthened M1 cortical communication to skeletal muscles supports motor precision [34,35]. Gamma frequency (35–60 Hz) modulation of the motorneuron pool activity has been documented during individuals' maximal voluntary force production with its origins likely located in basal ganglia and frontal cortex [30]. Consistent with this hypothesis, studies have reported reduced gamma modulation in untreated individuals with Parkinson's disease along with a gradual recovery of gamma synchronization after patients received dopaminergic treatment [30,31,36]. Increased gamma power also is associated with reduced variability of sustained force production [31,37,38].

Defining alterations in the central modulation of the motorneuron pool activity associated with the increased force variability previously documented in ASD [16,17,39–41] may offer insights into both the musculophysiological processes that underpin motor deficits, and key central and peripheral processes that are disrupted. To address this critical issue, we applied Delsys decomposition-based quantitative electromyography (dEMG; Delsys, Inc., Boston, MA, USA) recording during participants' isometric index finger abduction test. The Delsys system collects four-channel surface EMG (sEMG) signal from participants' hand, from which specific skeletal muscle generates force. sEMG time series were then decomposed offline into distinct motor unit action potential trains using Delsys' decomposition algorithms (v42) [42,43] to allow us evaluating motorneuron pool activity of the muscle, thus further reveal mechanisms of the central modulation of skeletal muscles at the periphery.

Three study aims were pursued in the present study. First, whereas deficits in controlling grip force may reflect impairments in coordinating force production across multiple effectors, we tested whether individuals with ASD show deficits controlling sustained force produced by one finger in isolation. Second, we examined motorneuron pool firing properties and central modulation of the motorneuron pool at different frequency bands (delta: 0–4 Hz, alpha: 4–10 Hz, beta: 10–35 Hz, and gamma: 35–60 Hz) during isometric index finger abduction in order to characterize neuromuscular properties underlying increased force variability in ASD (Figure 1). Third, we compared the relationships between force production and motorneuron pool activity in both individuals with ASD and healthy controls to determine whether force output is controlled by separate neuromuscular processes in patients. We hypothesized that patients would show increased force variability when attempting to maintain a constant level of force by abducting their index finger. We also predicted that increased force variability in ASD would be associated with increased motorneuron pool discharge rate, increased motorneuron pool discharge rate variability, and atypical central modulation of the motorneuron pool at multiple frequency bands, especially delta, beta and gamma as these frequencies are highly associated with force production and variability in healthy individuals. Consistent with previous findings, we also expected that healthy controls would show a positive association between force variability and 0–4 Hz modulation of the motorneuron pool, and inverse relationships between force variability and modulation of the motorneuron pool at 10–35 and 35–60 Hz. For individuals with ASD, we predicted that these associations would be attenuated suggesting reduced central organization of motorneuron pool activation. Based on prior studies showing that force control impairments may be associated with core symptoms of ASD [15–17,39], we also hypothesized impaired force production and modulation of the motorneuron pool activity in individuals with ASD would be related to the severity of their ASD symptoms, including clinically rated social-communication abnormalities [4,5].

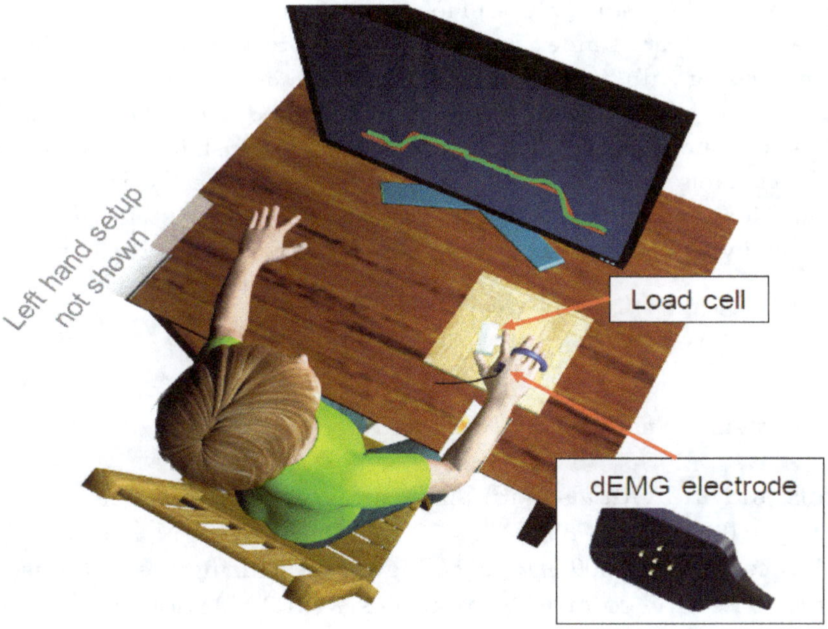

(A)

Figure 1. *Cont.*

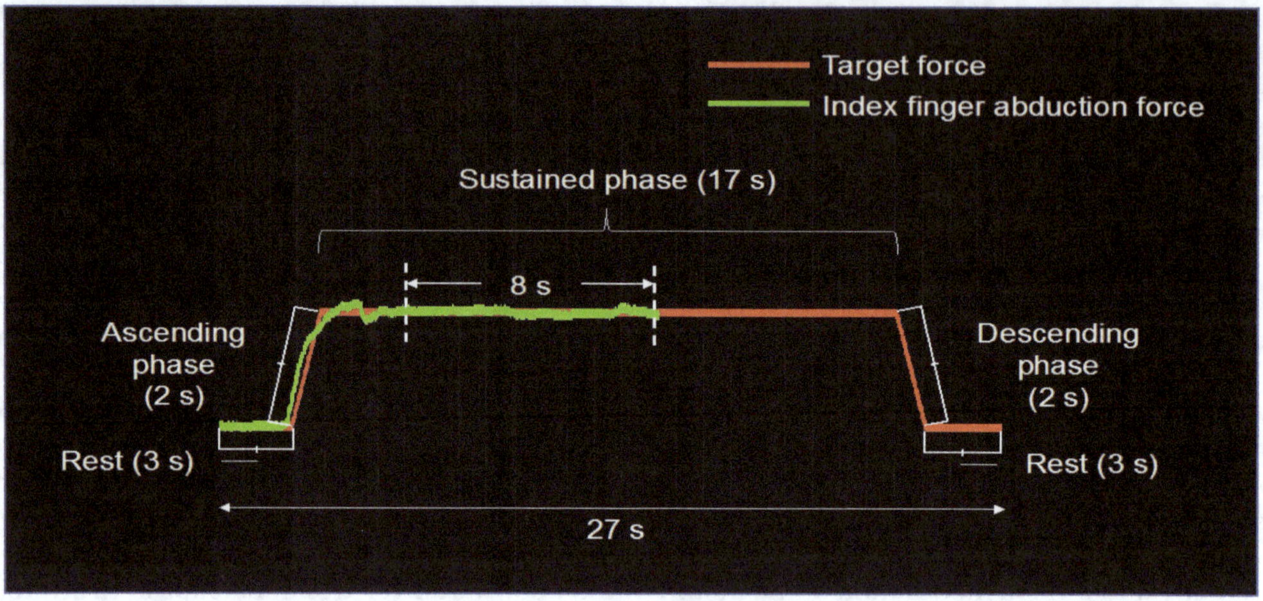

Figure 1. A participant pressed against a load cell with an abductive movement of his right index finger while viewing and tracing the red trapezoidal target template displayed on the monitor (**A**); the participant's middle, ring and little fingers were isolated and restricted to move on the hand plate. Delsys surface EMG (sEMG) electrode was attached to the back of the participant's hand in alignment with his first dorsal interosseus (FDI) muscle fibers to record muscle activity during each trial. The left index finger was used for left-handed individuals during the test (setup not shown). The duration of each trial was 27 s (**B**). The red trapezoidal target template includes a 2-s ascending phase, a 17-s sustained phase, and a 2-s descending phase of force production as well as two 3-s rest periods before and after each trial. Participant's index finger abduction force was displayed on the monitor as a light green line proceeding with time from left to right with its upward displacement representing force increase and downward movement representing force reduction. For each trial, time series of an 8-s force and its corresponding sEMG time series within the sustained phase of force production were randomly selected for evaluation of participants' behavioral performance (i.e., mean force and standard deviation of force) and motorneuron pool activity of the FDI muscle (i.e., mean discharge rate, discharge rate variability and normalized power of the motorneuron pool activity).

2. Results

2.1. Isometric Index Finger Abduction Force and Variability

Healthy controls and individuals with ASD showed similar levels of maximum voluntary contraction (MVC) ($F_{1,30} = 0.007$, $p = 0.935$; CNT = 22.500 N, SE = 2.198 N; ASD = 22.747 N, SE = 2.055 N) and mean sustained force ($F_{1,30} = 0.009$, $p = 0.924$; Figure 2A) during the test of isometric index finger abduction. Compared to healthy controls, individuals with ASD showed increased sustained force variability ($F_{1,30} = 6.641$, $p = 0.015$; Figure 2B).

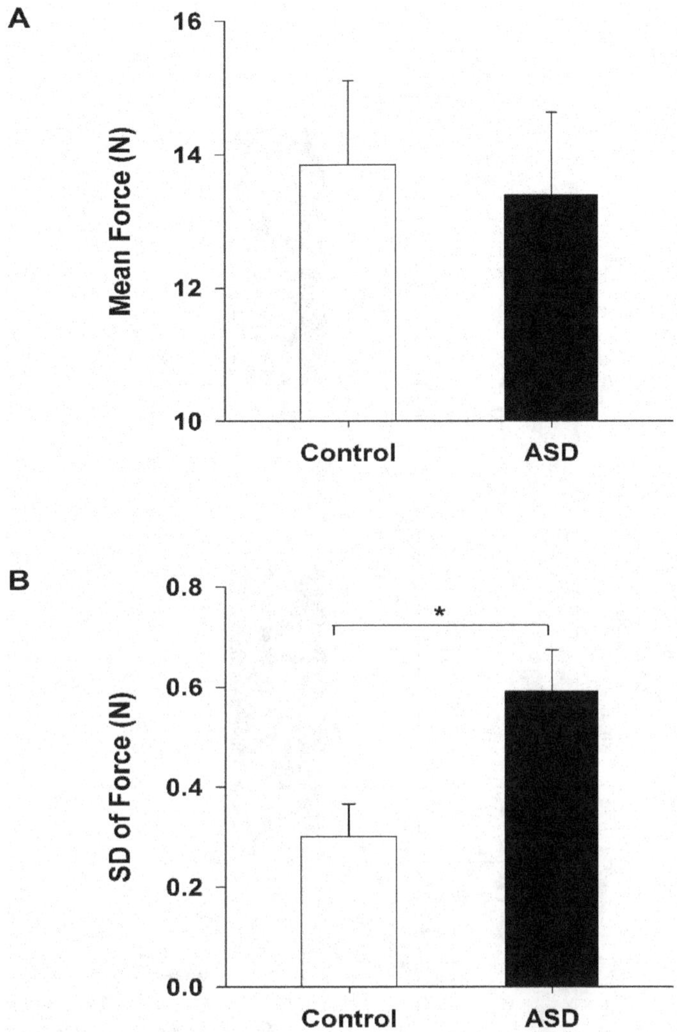

Figure 2. Isometric index finger abduction mean force (**A**); and standard deviation of force (**B**) in healthy controls and individuals with autism spectrum disorder (ASD). Both groups showed similar levels of mean force, although individuals with ASD showed a greater level of sustained force variability than healthy controls. * represents between group significance at the alpha level of 0.05. Error bars represent standard error.

2.2. decomposition-Based Electromyography (dEMG) Assessments of Motorneuron pool Activituy of the First Dorsal Interosseous (FDI) Muscle

Individuals with ASD and healthy controls showed similar FDI muscle motorneuron pool mean discharge rate ($F_{1,30} = 3.316$, $p = 0.079$; Figure 3A) and discharge rate variability ($F_{1,30} = 1.023$, $p = 0.320$; Figure 3B). For normalized power of the motorneuron pool, the main effect of frequency band ($F_{1.557,45.157} = 59.379$, $p = 0.000$) and the interactive effect of frequency band and group ($F_{1.557,45.157} = 5.173$, $p = 0.015$) were significant (Figure 3C). Normalized beta power (10–35 Hz) was significantly greater than power at other frequencies, whereas gamma power (35–60 Hz) was significantly lower than other frequency bands (delta (0–4 Hz): 26.976% ± 1.945%; alpha (4–10 Hz): 21.807% ± 1.091%; beta (10–35 Hz): 39.467% ± 1.097%; gamma (35–60 Hz): 11.750% ± 0.737%). Normalized power was significantly lower in individuals with ASD compared to controls at delta band (ASD-Control = −9.787% ± 3.889% , $p = 0.018$), while patients showed greater normalized power than controls at beta (10–35 Hz: ASD-Control = 5.546% ± 2.194%, $p = 0.017$) and gamma (35–60 Hz: ASD-Control = 3.445 ± 1.474%, $p = 0.027$) frequencies. No differences between groups were found for alpha band power.

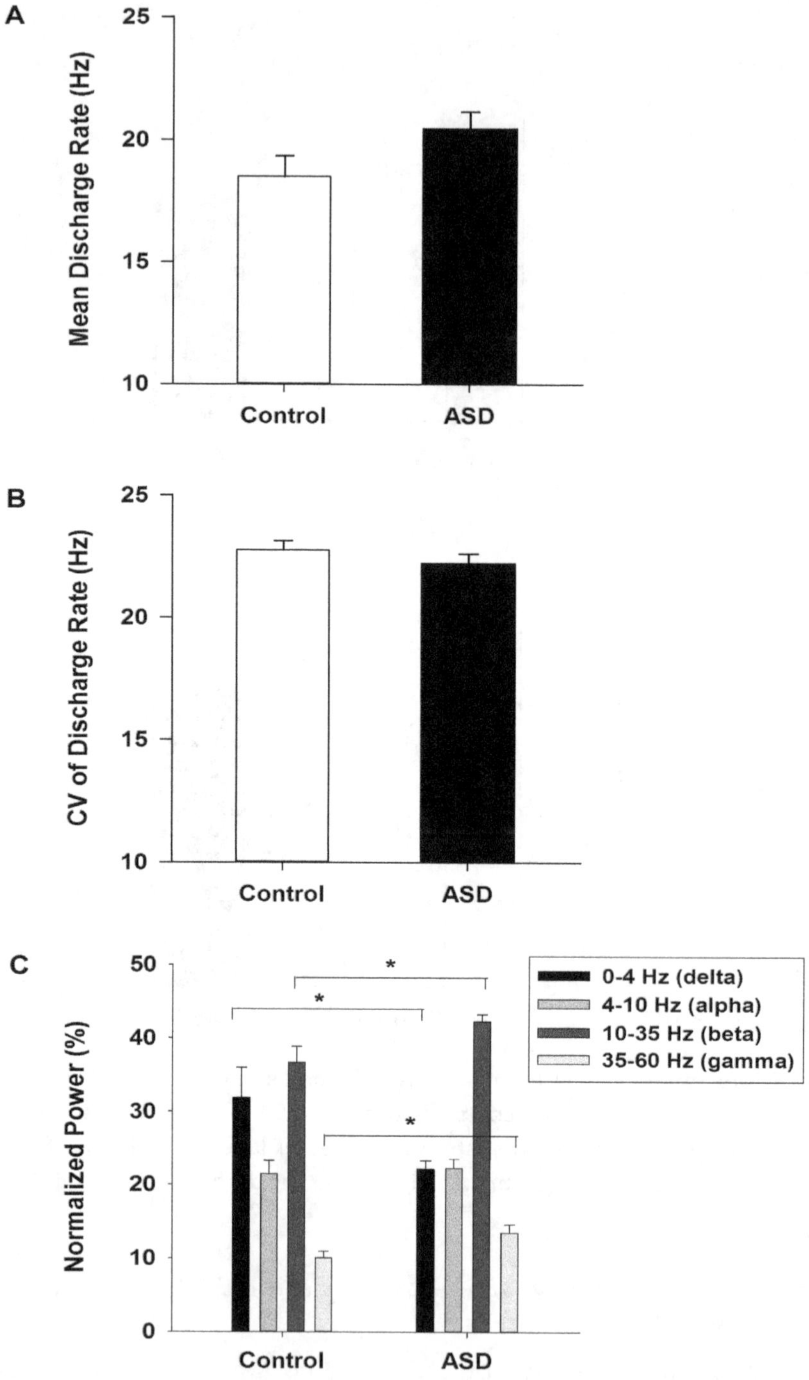

Figure 3. Mean discharge rate (**A**); coefficient of variation of mean discharge rate (**B**); and normalized power (**C**) of the first dorsal interosseous (FDI) muscle motorneuron pool for healthy controls and individuals with ASD. No between group differences were observed for mean discharge rate or discharge rate variability. Individuals with ASD showed greater normalized power at discharge rate of 10–35 (beta) and 35–60 (gamma) Hz, while they also showed lower normalized power at 0–4 (delta) Hz compared to healthy controls. * represents between group significance at the level of 0.05. Error bars represent standard error.

2.3. Relationship between Force Performance and Modulation of the FDI Muscle Motorneuron Pool Activity

For control participants, increased sustained force variability was associated with increased modulation of the motorneuron pool at delta band (0–4 Hz; Figure 4A) and reduced modulation at frequencies of beta (10–35 Hz; Figure 4C) and gamma (35–60 Hz; Figure 4D) bands. For individuals with ASD, the relationships between force variability and modulation of the motorneuron pool at different frequency bands were not significant. The relationships between sustained force variability and modulation of the motorneuron pool at alpha band (4–10 Hz) were not significant for healthy controls or individuals with ASD (Figure 4B).

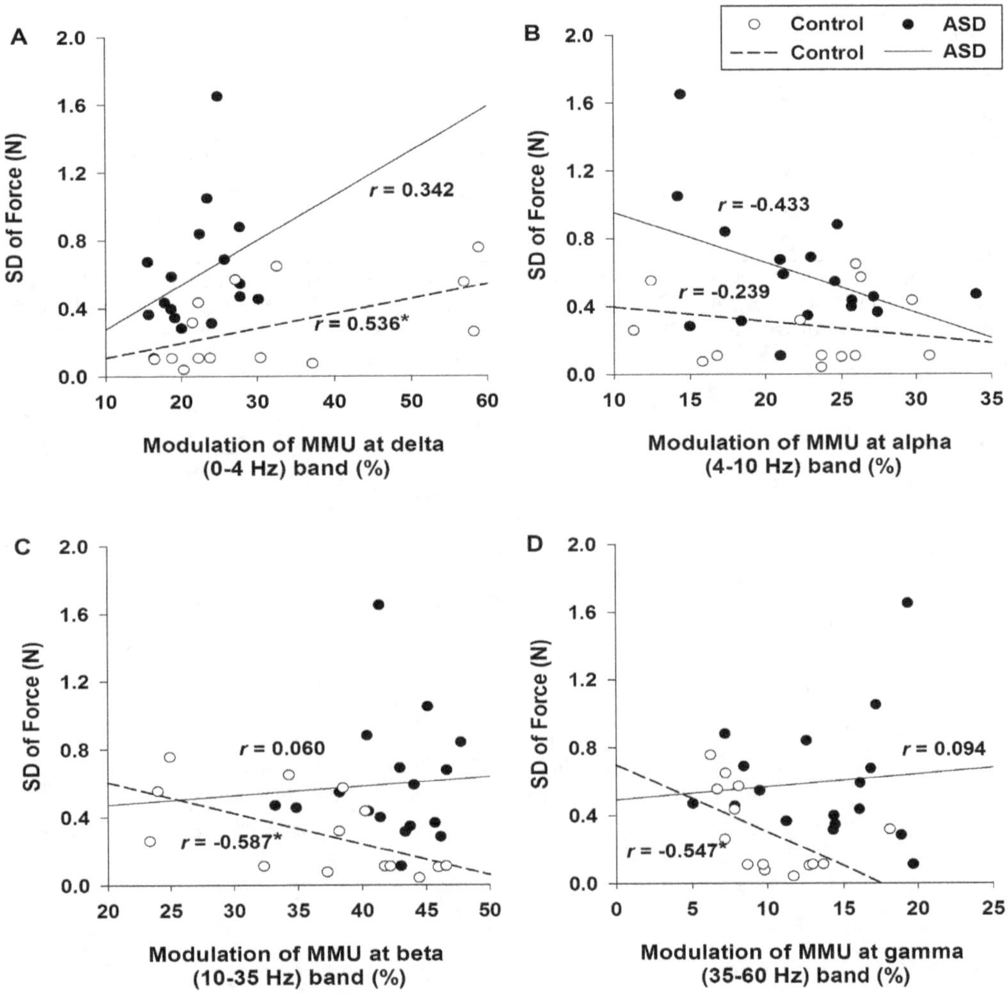

Figure 4. Relationships between the standard deviation of force and motorneuron pool activity of the FDI muscle at frequency bands of: delta, 0–4 Hz (**A**); alpha, 4–10 Hz (**B**); beta, 10–35 Hz (**C**); and gamma, 35–60 Hz (**D**). Behavioral–neuromuscular correlations were observed not significant for individuals with ASD at any frequency bands. Increased force variability was significantly associated with increased modulation of the motorneuron pool firing at 0–4 Hz in healthy controls. Force variability reduction was also significantly associated with increased modulation of motor units at beta (10–35 Hz) and gamma (35–60 Hz) frequency bands in healthy participants. * represents p value less than 0.05 and the absolute value of the correlation coefficient ($|r|$) greater than 0.5.

2.4. Demographic and Clinical Correlations

Neither force variability nor neuromuscular measurements were associated with intelligence quotient (IQ) scores for healthy controls or individuals with ASD (Table 1). For healthy controls, greater MVC was associated with higher full-scale and performance IQs (Figure 5A). Increased age was associated with reduced force variability for healthy controls (Figure 5B). For individuals with ASD, greater MVCs were associated with increased age but not IQ scores. Higher clinically rated social-communication deficits were associated with lower MVCs (Figure 5C) and greater motorneuron pool mean discharge rate for individuals with ASD (Figure 5D). No correlations were observed between clinically rated restricted, repetitive behaviors ratings and either force or neuromuscular measurements in individuals with ASD.

Table 1. Relationships between force and decomposition-based electromyography (dEMG) measurements with demographic, cognitive and clinical dimensions.

Control (n = 14)	Age	FSIQ	PIQ	VIQ		
MVC	0.399	0.590 *	0.640 *	0.477		
SD force	−0.576 *	0.172	0.033	0.270		
Mean discharge rate	0.462	−0.175	−0.067	−0.235		
ASD (n = 17)	**Age**	**FSIQ**	**PIQ**	**VIQ**	**ADOS.soc.com**	**ADOS.rrb**
MVC	0.787 **	0.296	0.310	0.230	−0.709 **	−0.058
SD force	0.143	−0.300	−0.108	−0.453	0.026	0.329
Mean discharge rate	−0.470	−0.388	−0.332	−0.397	0.674 **	0.1474

MVC: maximum voluntary contraction; SD Force: standard deviation of force; FSIQ: full scale IQ; PIQ: performance IQ; VIQ: verbal IQ; ADOS.sco.com: ADOS-2 social-communication algorithm total; ADOS.rrb: ADOS-2 restricted and repetitive behavior algorithm total; Statistical significance at * $\alpha = 0.05$; ** $\alpha = 0.01$ and $r > |0.5|$.

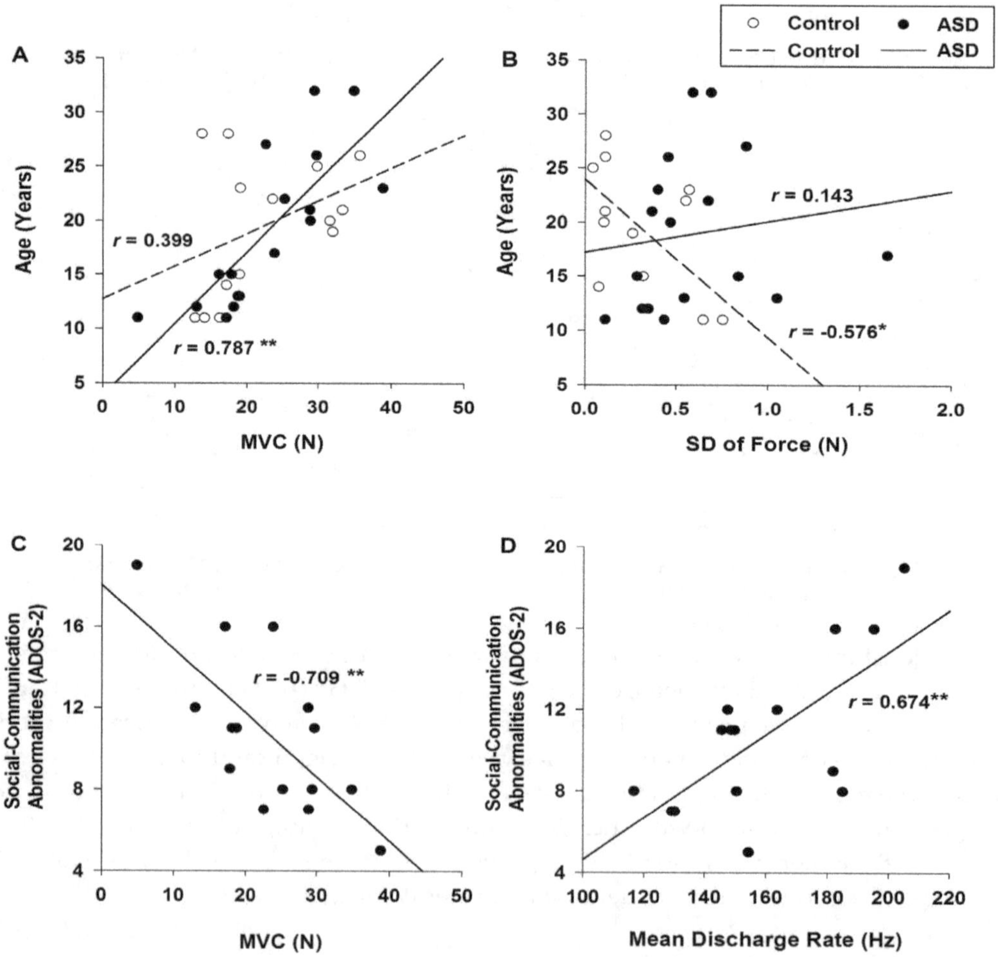

Figure 5. Relationships between age and isometric index finger abduction maximum voluntary contraction (MVC) (**A**) and standard deviation of force (**B**) for both groups. Relationships between clinical ratings of social-communication abnormalities on Autism diagnostic observation schedule-2 (ADOS-)2 and measures of MVC (**C**) and mean discharge rate of motorneuron pool activity (**D**) in individuals with ASD. * represents p value less than 0.05, ** represents p-value less than 0.01 and the absolute value of the correlation coefficient ($|r|$) greater than 0.5.

3. Discussion

The present study adds to the growing literature documenting deficits of voluntary hand movements and force production in ASD. Our findings also provide new evidence that motorneuron pool activity power during isometric index finger force production is abnormal in ASD at delta (0–4 Hz), beta (10–35 Hz), and gamma (35–60 Hz) frequency bands. Results further indicate that neuromuscular oscillations at these frequency bands are tightly linked to force control in healthy individuals, but that the central-peripheral communication processes that support the attenuation of force output variability in ASD are distinct and less organized. Taken together, alterations of central modulation of the motorneuron pool activity of the FDI muscle during constant force production may represent a key neurophysiological deficit related to both motor impairment and ASD symptoms.

3.1. Altered Force Production in Autism Spectrum Disorder (ASD)

Our findings were consistent with prior studies showing increased variability of manual motor output in ASD during precision gripping [16,17,39], writing [13], object lifting [40,41] and the use of simple finger gestures [44]. As the task of isometric index finger abduction only involves the FDI muscle, our study suggests that failure to precisely adjust force control and motor output in response to visual feedback is evidenced even when actions are restricted to a single muscle group as opposed to requiring coordination across different effectors or muscles. Given that manual motor deficits appear to be associated with increased severity of social-communication symptoms and daily living skills in ASD [3–6], our findings indicate that the compromised ability of patients to adjust motor output online in response to visual feedback may serve as a component of multiple key clinical issues and functional outcomes.

3.2. Altered Motorneuron Pool Activation during Force Control in ASD

Relative to controls, individuals with ASD showed similar levels of FDI muscle motorneuron pool discharge rate (Figure 3A) and discharge rate variability (Figure 3B). While these findings suggest intact central-to-peripheral modulation of skeletal muscles, it remains possible that impairments exist during recruitment of fast-twitch motor units and when increasing the firing rate of low-twitch motor units as has been seen in other developmental disorders [45]. Our findings of increased beta (10–35 Hz) and gamma (35–60 Hz) modulation of the motorneuron pool in individuals with ASD (Figure 3C) indicate atypical central modulation of the FDI muscle during isometric index finger abduction. Increased beta and gamma power may be attributable to increased central noise and/or compensatory modulation processes used to achieve specific motor goals. Increased inherent noise of central oscillators likely would involve elevation of signal power across different frequency bands. As our results showed a reduction of 0–4 Hz delta power in ASD and similar power in ASD and controls at higher frequencies from 4 to 10 Hz, it is likely that increased modulation of the motorneuron pool in ASD reflects compensatory modulation processes used to achieve specific force production.

Motorneuron pool oscillations within the delta band (0–4 Hz) represent a default mode of neural processing with the reductions seen as individuals engage in skilled actions, and associated with greater sustained motor precision [20,24]. At relatively higher force levels, such as the 60% MVC target studied here, output variability increases as delta power is increased due to greater muscle sensitivity to low frequency modulations [21,38,46,47]. In contrast, power of beta (10–35 Hz) and gamma (35–60 Hz) frequency oscillations are increased after visuomotor skill learning and during tasks involving greater attentional and cognitive demands [34,48,49]. Beta oscillations (10–35 Hz) represent co-activation of a large scale central network involving primary sensorimotor and inferior posterior parietal cortex, particularly during visuomotor tests requiring low and medium levels of force production [50,51]. Gamma (35–60 Hz) frequency oscillations, on the other hand, channel primary motor cortex as well as basal ganglia innervation during high level force production and slow phasic movements [26–28,30,31,36]. The relationship between reduced force variability and greater modulation of the motorneuron pool at beta and gamma bands thus reflects direct cortical communication to skeletal muscles of the hand that facilitates more precise motor output.

The nature of these compensatory processes remains unclear. Consistent with prior studies, we found that increased modulation of the motorneuron pool at beta (10–35 Hz) and gamma (35–60 Hz) as well as decreased modulation at delta (0–4 Hz) were highly associated with force variability reduction in healthy individuals [21,38,46,47]. These associations were not evident for individuals with ASD, suggesting the neurophysiological processes involved in central modulation of the motorneuron pool activity and control of force output are distinct from healthy individuals. These processes appear sufficient to allow patients to produce a similar level of MVC and mean force as healthy individuals, though they are not sufficient to stabilize motor output during continuous activity. Findings that individuals with ASD utilize unique neurophysiological processes during basic sensorimotor tasks are consistent with prior studies showing that prefrontal-striatal brain systems are more involved in basic movements in ASD than for controls, whereas cerebellar-cortical brain systems typically dedicated to controlling simple visuomotor actions are less involved in movement control in ASD [52,53]. Direct measurements of how modulation of the motorneuron pool varies across different force levels in individuals with ASD may be informative for determining central-to-peripheral mechanisms of force control and hand dexterity deficits in patients.

Unlike with controls, we did not find any relationship in ASD between modulation of motorneuron pool at beta and gamma bands and sustained force variability suggesting that excessive central oscillations were needed to support patients maintaining the target force level, but that these central processes had no effect on the precision of motor output. These findings suggest that central modulations may not be organized in ASD in the same manner as they are in health. For example, it is possible that, for individuals with ASD, fast-twitch and fatigable motor units are not recruited [45] or are recruited earlier than slow-twitch, fatigue resistant motor units. Alternatively, changes in the precise relation between firing rate and the mechanical twitch properties of motor units may also impair force production. In particular, when motor unit firing rates drop to the point where partial fusion of muscle twitches is reduced, muscle contractions become less efficient and more effort must be expended to achieve a force goal. Such increased effort may allow a target force to be reached, but it also likely leads to an increase in the variability of the force output [54].

3.3. *Neuromotor Deficits, Demographic Characteristics and Clinical Symptoms in ASD*

MVC production was more strongly associated with age in ASD compared to controls suggesting that increases in strength during development likely are delayed in ASD. This finding may help explain inconsistencies of prior studies showing both reductions in manual strength [6,14,15] and relatively intact manual strength [16,39]. It also is possible that we did not find MVC differences whereas grip strength has been shown to be impaired in ASD because gripping involves co-contraction of agonist and antagonist hand muscles, central modulation of which might be disrupted in individuals with ASD. It has been documented that motor units from different motorneuron pools respond to central modulation in a synergetic manner during co-contraction due to the fact that these motor units activate as a group according to the task goal and the advantage of this synergetic modulation is to reduce the computational load of central processing [25,55,56]. As our study showed atypical modulation of the motorneuron pool of a single muscle, it is possible that each individual's hand muscles are modulated in atypical and non-synergetic ways with the resultant effects being augmented during contraction of multiple muscles or co-contractions involving both agonist and antagonist muscles.

Increased age was associated with greater force variability reduction (Figure 5B) in healthy controls, but not in individuals with ASD (Figure 5A), suggesting persistent deficits in controlling force variability in patients. We also found that MVC reductions (Figure 5C) and greater mean discharge rates (Figure 5D) are associated with more severe clinically-rated social-communication abnormalities in ASD. Previous studies also have shown that social-communication symptom severity is related to different aspects of force control deficits in ASD, including reduced sustained force accuracy [39], lower complexity of force outputs [16], and greater target force overshooting during the ascending phase of force production [17]. Together, these findings suggest that social-communication and motor deficits in ASD may reflect common neurodevelopmental mechanisms [4,5], including central processes involved in modulating sensory-motor output. For example, increased motor variability in ASD has been shown to emerge early in development [44], and be linked to failures to understand the movements of others [57] and develop age-appropriate social and cognitive abilities [4–6]. Clarifying the timing and course of atypical modulation of motorneuron pool activity in ASD will be important for developing a more mechanistic understanding of motor, social-communication, and cognitive disturbances in patients and their dysmaturation.

3.4. Study Limitation

While the present study documents several novel findings useful for understanding neuromuscular processes underpinning force control deficits in ASD, our results should be considered in the context of multiple limitations. First, our sample spans a relatively broad age range. The small sample size may have contributed to insufficient power for characterizing the developmental trajectory of hand MVC and force variability increases in ASD. Further, the high functioning individuals may show less force variability as opposed to patients with lower IQ scores. Second, some of the participants with ASD in our sample may have shown comorbid conditions that are common in this disorder (e.g., Attention deficit hyperactivity disorder (ADHD) and depression). Systematic studies of contributions of these comorbid conditions to force variability increase as well as atypical central modulation of the motorneuron pool at different frequency bands in ASD are needed. Third, interpretations of our current findings, particularly the central origins of delta, alpha, beta and gamma frequency bands will need to be tested by integrating simultaneous measures of central oscillations using electroencephalogram (EEG) or magnetoencephalography (MEG). Such studies, in combination with EMG recording, will allow us to better understand altered central-to-peripheral mechanisms related to both motor and the defining symptoms of ASD. Lastly, antihypertensive and antidepressant medications have unclear effects on psychomotor functioning, with studies documenting both improvement and decline [58–61]. However, it is unlikely performance was impacted in participants taking either of these medications given that these medications appear to have minimal effect on basic motor functioning and peripheral processes [62].

4. Materials and Methods

4.1. Participants

Seventeen individuals with ASD and 14 healthy controls matched on age, gender, IQ and handedness (Table 2) performed an isometric index finger abduction test at 60% of their MVC. Tests of 20% and 40% MVC also were administered, though off-line observation of the surface-based EMG signals showed insufficient signal-to-noise ratio; thus, data analyses were conducted only for the 60% MVC condition. IQ was assessed using the Wechsler Abbreviated Scales of Intelligence [63], and handedness was determined using the Edinburgh questionnaire [64]. Individuals with ASD were recruited through community advertisements and local clinical programs. Diagnoses of ASD were confirmed using the ADOS-2 [65] and based on expert clinical opinion using DSM-5 criteria [66]. When possible, the Autism Diagnostic Inventory-Revised (ADI-R) [67] also was used to establish an ASD diagnosis. As parents of several adults with ASD in our study were not available, the ADI-R could only be conducted on 6/17 patients.

Table 2. Demographic characteristics (mean ± SD) of healthy controls and participants with autism spectrum disorder (ASD).

Demographic Characteristics	Control (n = 14)	ASD (n = 17)	t	p
Age (yr)	19.57 ± 6.24	18.95 ± 7.14	0.067	0.798
Range	11–28	11–32		
% Male *	85.7 (12/14)	94.14 (16/17)	0.576	0.425
% Right-handed *	92.9 (13/14)	88.23 (15/17)	0.653	0.422
Verbal IQ	112.62 ± 17.74	107.63 ± 17.14	0.589	0.449
Range	82–140	71–126		
Performance IQ	112.69 ± 13.68	106.81 ± 17.68	0.965	0.335
Range	85–133	79–129		
Full-scale IQ	114.77 ± 16.41	108.31 ± 18.34	0.975	0.449
Range	82–138	78–131		

* Chi-square (χ^2) statistics.

Participants with ASD were excluded if they had a known genetic or metabolic disorder associated with ASD (e.g., Fragile-X syndrome, Rett syndrome, and Tuberous sclerosis) or history of non-febrile seizures. Healthy controls were recruited from the community and were required to have a score of 8 or lower on the Social Communication Questionnaire (SCQ) [68]. Control participants were excluded for current or past history of psychiatric or neurological disorders, family history of ASD in first-, second- or third-degree relatives, or a history in first-degree relatives of a developmental or learning disorder, psychosis, or obsessive compulsive disorder.

No participants were taking medications known to affect sensorimotor control at the time of testing, including antipsychotics, stimulants, or anticonvulsants [62]. Seven individuals with ASD were taking antidepressant medication and two were taking antihypertensive medication at the time of testing. No participant had a history of head injury, birth injury, or seizure disorder. After a complete description of the study, written informed consent was obtained from adult participants, and informed parental consent and written assent were obtained for individuals aged less than 18 years. Study procedures were approved by the Institutional Review Board at Children's Medical Center Dallas (IRB # 062011-010) on 29 April 2012. Participants who are 18 years of age or older provided written consent and minors provided assent in addition to written consent from their legal guardian.

4.2. Apparatus and Procedures

Participants were seated in a darkened room facing a 27-inch Dell (Dell Inc., Dallas, TX, USA) LCD monitor (resolution: 1920 × 1080; refresh rate: 120 Hz) located 60 cm in front of them. They sat with their shoulder abducted at 45°, elbow flexed and forearm resting on a customized arm brace (Figure 1A). The arm brace was clamped to a table to keep participants' arm position stable throughout the test. Participants' dominant hand (i.e., the left hand was used for left handed individuals) was pronated and laid flat with digits comfortably extended on a hand plate with their middle, ring and little fingers isolated and restricted from moving. This setup only allows isometric index finger abduction at the metacarpophalangeal joint in the horizontal plane, which is a movement exclusively involving contractions of the FDI muscle [19,36]. Participants used the index finger of their dominant hand to press against a precision load cell (capacity: 100 lbf (≈445 N), Miniature Beam Load Cell, Interface Inc., Berwyn, PA, USA) that was securely attached to the hand plate and connected to a Bagnoli-16 surface EMG (sEMG) System (Delsys, Inc., Boston, MA, USA). Participants' index finger abduction force recorded from the load cell was sampled at a rate of 20 KHz using the Bagnoli-16 sEMG System (Delsys, Inc., Boston, MA, USA).

Prior to testing, each individual's index finger MVC was measured for their dominant hand. Participants completed three separate 5-s trials in which they were instructed to press against the load cell with as much force as possible by abducting their index finger. The amount of force they generated was displayed on the monitor as a red bar moving upwards with increased force. Participants rested for 1-min between consecutive trials to minimize the effect of muscle fatigue. The average maximum force across trials was calculated as the estimate of each participant's index finger MVC [16,17,39].

Prior to sEMG sensor attachment, individuals' skin over the FDI muscle was shaved and cleansed with rubbing alcohol to remove oil, debris and dead skin cells. A reference electrode was taped over the lateral epicondyle of participants' humerus. Subsequently, a specialized sEMG sensor (dEMG^{TM}, Delsys Inc.) was placed on the back of participants' hand in alignment with their FDI muscle. The sEMG electrode consists of five non-invasive probes (0.5 mm diameter of each) with four arranged in a square and the fifth probe located in the center of the square at a fixed distance of 3.6 mm from each of the surrounding four probes. Pairwise signal subtraction of these probes results in four differential sEMG channels from the FDI muscle. The sEMG time series was then amplified at 1 K, sampled at 20 KHz, and band-pass filtered at 20–450 Hz. Four-channel sEMG time series were decomposed offline into distinct motor unit action potential trains using Delsys decomposition algorithms (v42) [42,43] to evaluate the motorneuron pool activity of the FDI muscle.

During the test, participants viewed a red trapezoidal template displayed on the monitor with a target plateau set at 60% of their own MVC. Participants were instructed to accurately trace the template by adjusting the amount of force generated by abducting their index finger (Figure 1B). Participants' finger force was displayed as a light green line on the monitor that moved from left to right over time, upward with increased force, and downward with decreased force. Participants adjusted their finger force to keep the light green line as close as possible to the red trapezoidal template throughout the trial. Each trial was 27 s in duration. The red trapezoidal template consisted of three distinct phases, including: (1) a 2-s ascending phase during which participants gradually increased their force; (2) a 17-s sustained phase during which participants attempted to maintain a constant level of force; and (3) a 2-s descending phase during which participants slowly decreased their force. Two 3-s rest phases in addition to a 1 min break were administered before and after each trial to quantify baseline noise of the sEMG signal. During these rest phases, participants kept their index finger away from the load cell. Participants completed a block of three trials for each target force level, as well as practice trials at 30% MVC in order to confirm that they understood task instructions. The test consisted of 3 trials (×3 force levels) alternated with 1-min rest blocks. Total testing time including the electrode attachment, MVC testing, practice trials and task trials lasted 15–20 min.

4.3. *Data Processing and Analyses*

The trial on which the force trace best followed the trapezoidal template was selected for data analyses [38,69]. For each selected trial, the initial and final 5-s of force data was removed from analyses in order to limit variable effects related to initiating sustained force production and fatigue at the end of trials (Figure 1B). Thus, the middle 8-s of abduction force and its corresponding sEMG time series were analyzed off-line using custom-written Matlab programs and Delsys decomposition algorithms (v42) [42,43], respectively.

4.3.1. Force Data

Each raw force trace was digitally filtered using a 4th order low-pass Butterworth filter at a cutoff frequency of 20 Hz and detrended afterwards. Participants' behavioral performance was quantified using the mean and standard deviation of their 8-s index finger abduction force at 60% MVC.

4.3.2. sEMG Data and Decomposition Procedures for Motor Units' Activities

The sEMG time series of each trial was decomposed into distinct motor units. As shown in Figure 6, the action potentials of identified motor units were displayed in order from the smallest to the largest waveforms. To determine the accuracy of the decomposition procedure, a Decompose-Synthesize-Decompose-Compare (DSDC) test was conducted on the action potential train of each motor unit to reduce the incidence of false identification, which further increased the accuracy of validated wave forms [43,70]. Motor units were retained only when their firing was less than 10% of the false identification rate [38,70]. Among those retained motor units, we identified a range of 11–36 and 8–38 motor units for healthy participants and individuals with ASD, respectively.

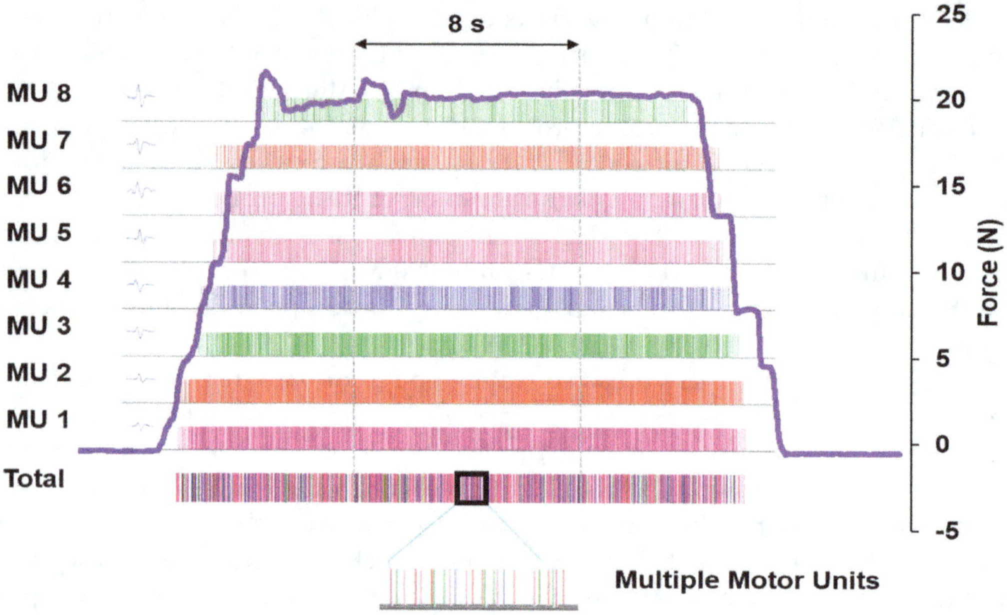

Figure 6. A representative index finger abduction force trace overlaid on eight identified and validated motor units' action potential firing trains of the FDI muscle. Eight motor units' action potential patterns were orderly displaced on the left from the smallest waveform located at the bottom to the largest at the top. The total action potential firing train representing motorneuron pool activituy of the FDI muscle was derived by summarizing action potential firing trains of all eight selected motor units. The summarized action potential train thus represents the motorneuron pool activity of the FDI muscle during a trial. The double-sided arrow shows an 8-s period during which force and eight motor unit action potential firing trains were selected for behavioral and FDI muscle activity assessments.

In order to compare the same number of motor units across groups, the smallest number of validated motor units across participants (n = 8) was selected from each trial to represent motorneuron pool activation of the FDI muscle and included in analyses of the mean discharge rate of the motorneuron pool. For those trials with a total number of retained motor units greater than eight, we selected eight motor units based on the following procedures: (1) the smallest and largest motor units were identified as the first (MU1) and the last (MU8) recruited motor units; (2) assigning motor units in the middle of the scale as the fourth (MU4) and fifth (MU5) recruited motor units; (3) assigning motor units in the middle of MU1 and MU4 as the second (MU2) and third (MU3) recruited motor units; and (4) assigning motor units in the middle of MU5 and MU8 as the sixth (MU6) and seventh (MU7) recruited motor units (for detailed procedures, see Appendix A). We then retained eight selected motor units for each trial with the wave forms of their action potentials evenly distributed across the motorneuron pool to ensure an unbiased comparison between individuals with ASD and healthy controls [38]. Motorneuron pool activity of the FDI muscle was derived by summarizing action potential trains of these eight selected motor units.

For each trial, mean discharge rate of the motorneuron pool was examined as the average of the inter-spike intervals. The discharge rate variability of the motorneuron pool was quantified as the coefficient of variation (CV) of the inter-spike intervals calculated using the formula below:

$$\text{CV of Discharge Rate} = \frac{\text{Standar deviation of interspike unterval}}{\text{Mean discharge rate}} \times 100\% \tag{1}$$

Modulation of the motorneuron pool activity was quantified using power spectrum analyses in the frequency domain. Inter-spike intervals of the motorneuron pool were initially transformed into a continuous time series by interpolating each trial [38]. Then, finite Fourier transformation was applied to quantify the power spectrum of the motorneuron pool [38,49,71] with frequencies separated into four bands: delta (0–4 Hz), alpha (4–10 Hz), beta (10–35 Hz) and gamma (35–60 Hz). For each frequency band, the normalized power spectrum of the motorneuron pool was calculated using the formula below:

$$\text{Normalized Power } (\%) = \frac{\left(\sum \text{power(specific frequency band)}/\text{Hz}\right)}{\sum \text{power}(0 - 60 \text{ Hz})} \times 100\% \quad (2)$$

Each specific frequency bin refers to each of the four frequency bands; thus, normalized power was derived for delta (0–4 Hz), alpha (4–10 Hz), beta (10–35 Hz) and gamma (35–60 Hz) frequency bands.

4.4. Clinical Measures

The ADOS-2 was used to confirm participants' diagnosis and rate ASD symptoms based on the observation of each participant's behavior [65]. The ADOS-2 is a semi-structured assessment of play, social abilities, communication skills, and imaginative use of materials performed with each individual with ASD by an examiner trained to research reliability. For the ADOS-2, higher scores reflect more severe abnormality in a given domain.

4.5. Statistical Analyses

A student *t*-test was used to compare index finger MVCs between individuals with ASD and healthy controls. A series of one-way ANOVAs were conducted to examine between-group (ASD vs. Control) differences on mean sustained force, standard deviation of force, mean discharge rate and discharge rate variability of the FDI muscle motorneuron pool. A 2 (group) × 4 (frequency band: delta (0–4 Hz), alpha (4–10 Hz), beta (10–35 Hz) and gamma (35–60 Hz)) fixed effect repeated measure ANOVA was applied to identify between-group differences in motorneuron pool activations of the FDI muscle across the power spectrum. For all analyses, results were interpreted as significant if $p < 0.05$. Where Mauchly's test indicated a violation of sphericity, the Greenhouse–Geisser estimate was used to provide a conservative test of ANOVA main and interaction effects.

To determine the relationships between FDI muscle motorneuron pool activity at each frequency band and force variability, Pearson correlations were conducted separately for individuals with ASD and healthy controls. Pearson correlation coefficients also were used to examine the relationships between individuals' muscle strength (i.e., index finger abduction MVC), force and dEMG measurements found to be different between groups and age, IQ and clinical ratings of ASD severity from the ADOS-2. Results were interpreted as significant if alpha was less than 0.05 and the absolute value of the correlation coefficient ($|r|$) was greater than 0.5.

5. Conclusions

Our results demonstrate that individuals with ASD show atypical central modulation of the motorneuron pool of a single hand muscle during isometric index finger abduction. Increased central modulations at beta (10–35 Hz) and gamma (35–60 Hz) frequency bands as well as delta (0–4 Hz) band reduction were all associated with lower force variability in healthy participants, although these relationships were all attenuated in patients. These findings suggest a lack of central communication to skeletal muscles in ASD as well as less organized motor unit recruitment at the periphery. An emerging literature has indicated that early motor developmental abnormalities are among the earliest signs of ASD [3,4,6], combined with our findings that neuromuscular impairments are associated with age and clinically rated social-communication abnormalities in ASD, these results suggest that studies of the development of force control and underlying neuromuscular properties in ASD may provide important insights into neurodevelopmental mechanisms that cause ASD and the emergence of sensorimotor and other core symptoms during childhood.

Acknowledgments: This study was supported by NIMH K23 Research Career Development Award (MH092696), the Kansas Center for Autism Research and Training (KCART) Research Investment Council Strategic Initiative Grant to Mosconi, and the NICHD U54 Kansas Intellectual and Developmental Disabilities Research Center Award (HD090216-01) to John Colombo.

Author Contributions: Matthew W. Mosconi and Suman Mohanty are responsible for the conception and design of the study; Lauren M. Schmitt and Stormi P. White performed ADI-R, ADOS-2 and IQ diagnostic tests for individuals with ASD and healthy controls and assisted in the interpretation of clinical data; Lauren M. Schmitt administered the testing protocol to participants; MinHyuk Kwon prepared the Matlab scoring program and scored the raw data; MinHyuk Kwon and Zheng Wang performed statistical analyses; Evangelos A. Christou, MinHyuk Kwon, Matthew W. Mosconi and Zheng Wang interpreted the experimental results; MinHyuk Kwon and Zheng Wang prepared figures and drafted the manuscript; each author edited the manuscript; and Evangelos A. Christou, Matthew W. Mosconi and Zheng Wang revised the manuscript. All authors have approved the final version of the manuscript.

Abbreviations

ASD	Autism spectrum disorder
ADOS-2	Autism diagnostic observation schedule-2
ADI-R	Autism diagnostic inventory-Revised
sEMG	Surface electromyography
dEMG	Decomposition-based quantitative electromyography
MVC	Maximum voluntary contraction
FDI muscle	First dorsal interosseus muscle
Motor unit	A single motorneuron and the muscle fiber that it innervates
Motorneuron pool	A motorneuron pool consists of all individual motorneurons that innervate a single muscle
Motor unit recruitment or Modulation of motor units	The CNS is responsible for the orderly recruitment of motorneurons through two distinct ways: spatial and temporal recruitment. Spatial recruitment activates more motor units to produce greater force. Temporal recruitment, or rate coding, deals with the frequency or activation rate of motor units firing
Size principle	Henneman's size principle [22] explains spatial recruitment of motor units, in which motor units are recruited from smallest to largest based on the amount of force production. For smaller force, slow twitch, low-force, fatigue-resistant muscle fibers are activated prior to the recruitment of the fast twitch, high-force, less fatigue-resistant muscle fibers
Motor unit discharge rate	Motor unit discharge rate describes temporal recruitment of motor units represented by spike firing frequency or rate of action potentials

Appendix A. Motor Unit Selection

MU1 and MU8 always represent the smallest and largest motor units in the motorneuron pool of FDI muscle, respectively. If the total number of recruited MUs is greater than 11, we used formulas below to identify MU2 through MU7 [38]:

$$\text{MU2} = round(\frac{1 \times (a-1)}{7})$$

$$\text{MU3} = round(\frac{2 \times (a-1)}{7})$$

$$\text{MU4} = round(\frac{3 \times (a-1)}{7})$$

$$\text{MU5} = round(\frac{4 \times (a-1)}{7})$$

$$\text{MU6} = round(\frac{5 \times (a-1)}{7})$$

$$\text{MU7} = round(\frac{6 \times (a-1)}{7})$$

where *a* stands for the total number of MUs identified using Delsys decomposition algorithms (v42) [67,68]; and *round* stands for rounding up the element within parentheses to its nearest integer. If the total number of identified MUs is 9, 10 and 11, the above listed formulas cannot be used due to overlapping assignments of specific MUs. For example, it is possible that the smallest MU will be assigned as both MU1 and MU2. If this happens, the following manual selection chart will apply:

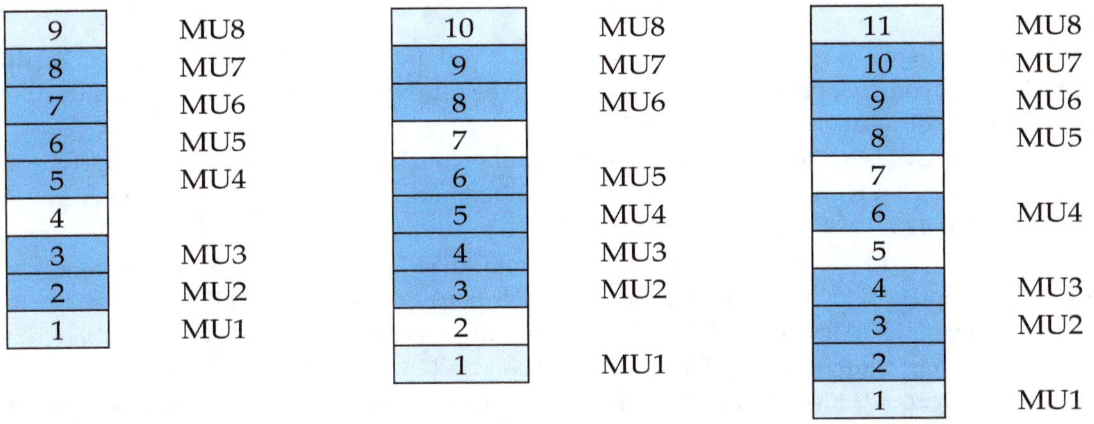

Light blue boxes represent MU1 and MU8, which are always the first and the last MU in the motorneuron pool, respectively; and dark blue boxes represent manually selected MUs with their order assigned on their right.

References

1. Fournier, K.A.; Hass, C.J.; Naik, S.K.; Lodha, N.; Cauraugh, J.H. Motor Coordination in Autism Spectrum Disorders: A Synthesis and Meta-Analysis. *J. Autism Dev. Disord.* **2010**, *40*, 1227–1240. [CrossRef] [PubMed]
2. Ming, X.; Brimacombe, M.; Wagner, G.C. Prevalence of motor impairment in autism spectrum disorders. *Brain Dev.* **2007**, *29*, 565–570. [CrossRef] [PubMed]
3. Loh, A.; Soman, T.; Brian, J.; Bryson, S.E.; Roberts, W.; Szatmari, P.; Smith, I.M.; Zwaigenbaum, L. Stereotyped motor behaviors associated with autism in high-risk infants: A pilot videotape analysis of a sibling sample. *J. Autism Dev. Disord.* **2007**, *37*, 25–36. [CrossRef] [PubMed]
4. Landa, R.J. Diagnosis of autism spectrum disorders in the first 3 years of life. *Nat. Clin. Pract. Neurol.* **2008**, *4*, 138–147. [CrossRef] [PubMed]
5. Hannant, P.; Tavassoli, T.; Cassidy, S. The Role of Sensorimotor Difficulties in Autism Spectrum Conditions. *Front. Neurol.* **2016**, *7*, 124. [CrossRef] [PubMed]
6. Travers, B.G.; Bigler, E.D.; Duffield, T.C.; Prigge, M.D.; Froehlich, A.L.; Lange, N.; Alexander, A.L.; Lainhart, J.E. Longitudinal development of manual motor ability in autism spectrum disorder from childhood to mid-adulthood relates to adaptive daily living skills. *Dev. Sci.* **2016**. [CrossRef] [PubMed]
7. Takarae, Y. Oculomotor abnormalities parallel cerebellar histopathology in autism. *J. Neurol. Neurosurg. Psychiatry* **2004**, *75*, 1359–1361. [CrossRef] [PubMed]
8. Schmitt, L.M.; Cook, E.H.; Sweeney, J.A.; Mosconi, M.W. Saccadic eye movement abnormalities in autism spectrum disorder indicate dysfunctions in both cerebellum and brainstem. *Mol. Autism* **2014**, *5*, 47. [CrossRef] [PubMed]
9. Minshew, N.J.; Sung, K.; Jones, B.L.; Furman, J.M. Underdevelopment of the postural control system in autism. *Neurology* **2007**, *63*, 2056–2061. [CrossRef]
10. Wang, Z.; Hallac, R.R.; Conroy, K.C.; White, S.P.; Kane, A.A.; Collinsworth, A.L.; Sweeney, J.A.; Mosconi, M.W. Postural orientation and equilibrium processes associated with increased postural sway in autism spectrum disorder (ASD). *J. Neurodev. Disord.* **2016**, *8*, 43. [CrossRef] [PubMed]
11. Hallett, M.; Lebiedowska, M.K.; Thomas, S.L.; Stanhope, S.J.; Benckla, M.B.; Rumsey, J. Locomotion of autistic adults. *Arch. Neurol.* **1993**, *50*, 1304–1308. [CrossRef] [PubMed]
12. Kindregan, D.; Gallagher, L.; Gormley, J. Gait deviations in children with autism spectrum disorders: A review. *Autism Res. Treat.* **2015**, *2015*, 741480. [CrossRef] [PubMed]
13. Fuentes, C.T.; Mostofsky, S.H.; Bastian, A.J. Children with autism show specific handwriting impairments. *Neurology* **2009**, *73*, 1532–1537. [CrossRef] [PubMed]

14. Hardan, A.Y.; Kilpatrick, M.; Keshavan, M.S.; Minshew, N.J. Motor Performance and Anatomic Magnetic Resonance Imaging (MRI) of the Basal Ganglia in Autism. *J. Child Neurol.* **2003**, *18*, 317–324. [CrossRef] [PubMed]
15. Kern, J.K.; Geier, D.A.; Adams, J.B.; Troutman, M.R.; Davis, G.; King, P.G.; Young, J.L.; Geier, M.R. Autism severity and muscle strength: A correlation analysis. *Res. Autism Spectr. Disord.* **2011**, *5*, 1011–1015. [CrossRef]
16. Mosconi, M.W.; Mohanty, S.; Greene, R.K.; Cook, E.H.; Vaillancourt, D.E.; Sweeney, J.A. Feedforward and feedback motor control abnormalities implicate cerebellar dysfunctions in autism spectrum disorder. *J. Neurosci.* **2015**, *35*, 2015–2025. [CrossRef] [PubMed]
17. Wang, Z.; Magnon, G.C.; White, S.P.; Greene, R.K.; Vaillancourt, D.E.; Mosconi, M.W. Individuals with autism spectrum disorder show abnormalities during initial and subsequent phases of precision gripping. *J. Neurophysiol.* **2015**, *113*, 1989–2001. [CrossRef] [PubMed]
18. Grosse, P.; Cassidy, M.J.; Brown, P. EEG-EMG, MEG-EMG and EMG-EMG frequency analysis: Physiological principles and clinical applications. *Clin. Neurophysiol.* **2002**, *113*, 1523–1531. [CrossRef]
19. De Luca, C.J.; LeFever, R.S.; McCue, M.P.; Xenakis, A.P. Behaviour of human motor units in different muscles during linearly varying contractions. *J. Physiol.* **1982**, *329*, 113–128. [CrossRef] [PubMed]
20. De Luca, C.J.; LeFever, R.S.; McCue, M.P.; Xenakis, A.P. Control scheme governing concurrently active human motor units during voluntary contractions. *J. Physiol.* **1982**, *329*, 129–142. [CrossRef] [PubMed]
21. Moritz, C.T.; Barry, B.K.; Pascoe, M.A.; Enoka, R.M. Discharge rate variability influences the variation in force fluctuations across the working range of a hand muscle. *J. Neurophysiol.* **2005**, *93*, 2449–2459. [CrossRef] [PubMed]
22. Henneman, E. Organization of the motorneuron pool: The size principle. In *Medical Physiology*, 14th ed.; Mountcastle, V.B., Ed.; Mosby: St. Louis, MO, USA, 1980; pp. 718–741.
23. Seki, K.; Marusawa, M. Firing rate modulation of human motor units in different muscles during isometric contraction with various forces. *Brain Res.* **1996**, *719*, 1–7. [CrossRef]
24. De Luca, C.J.; Erim, Z. Common drive of motor units in regulation of muscle force. *Trends Neurosci.* **1994**, *17*, 299–305. [CrossRef]
25. De Luca, C.J.; Erim, Z. Common drive in motor units of a synergistic muscle pair. *J. Neurophysiol.* **2002**, *87*, 2200–2204. [CrossRef] [PubMed]
26. Vallbo, A.B.; Wessberg, J. Organisation of motor output in slow finger movements in man. *J. Physiol.* **1993**, *469*, 673–691. [CrossRef] [PubMed]
27. Wessberg, J.; Vallbo, A.B. Coding of pulsatile motor output by human muscle afferents during slow finger movements. *J. Physiol.* **1995**, *485*, 271–282. [CrossRef] [PubMed]
28. Marsden, C.D. Origins of normal and pathological tremor. In *Movement Disorders: Tremor*; Findley, L.J., Capideo, R., Eds.; MacMillan Press: London, UK, 1984; pp. 37–84.
29. Conway, B.A.; Halliday, D.M.; Farmer, S.F.; Shahani, U.; Maas, P.; Weir, A.I.; Rosenberg, J.R. Synchronization between motor cortex and spinal motorneuronal pool during the performance of a maintained motor task in man. *J. Physiol.* **1995**, *489*, 917–924. [CrossRef] [PubMed]
30. Salenius, S.; Portin, K.; Kajola, M.; Salmelin, R.; Hari, R. Cortical control of human motorneuron firing during isometric contraction. *J. Neurophysiol.* **1997**, *77*, 3401–3405. [PubMed]
31. Chakarov, V.; Naranjo, J.R.; Schulte-Monting, J.; Omlor, W.; Huethe, F.; Kristeva, R. β-Range EEG-EMG Coherence With Isometric Compensation for Increasing Modulated Low-Level Forces. *J. Neurophysiol.* **2009**, *102*, 1115–1120. [CrossRef] [PubMed]
32. Brown, P. Cortical drives to human muscle: The Piper and related rhythms *Prog. Neurobiol.* **2000**, *60*, 97–108. [CrossRef]
33. Engel, A.K.; Fries, P. Beta-band oscillations-signalling the status quo? *Curr. Opin. Neurobiol.* **2010**, *20*, 156–165. [CrossRef] [PubMed]
34. Witte, M.; Patino, L.; Andrykiewicz, A.; Hepp-Reymond, M.C.; Kristeva, R. Modulation of human corticomuscular β-range coherence with low-level static forces. *Eur. J. Neurosci.* **2007**, *26*, 3564–3570. [CrossRef] [PubMed]
35. Kristeva, R.; Patino, L.; Omlor, W. β-Range cortical motor spectral power and corticomuscular coherence as a mechanism for effective corticospinal interaction during steady-state motor output. *Neuroimage* **2007**, *36*, 785–792. [CrossRef] [PubMed]

36. Brown, P. Muscle sounds in Parkinson's disease. *Lancet* **1997**, *349*, 533–535. [CrossRef]
37. Tracy, B.L.; Maluf, K.S.; Stephenson, J.L.; Hunter, S.K.; Enoka, R.M. Variability of motor unit discharge and force fluctuations across a range of muscle forces in older adults. *Muscle Nerve* **2005**, *32*, 533–540. [CrossRef] [PubMed]
38. Park, S.H.; Kwon, M.; Solis, D.; Lodha, N.; Christou, E.A. Motor control differs for increasing and releasing force. *J. Neurophysiol.* **2016**, *115*, 2924–2930. [CrossRef] [PubMed]
39. Neely, K.A.; Mohanty, S.; Schmitt, L.M.; Wang, Z.; Sweeney, J.A.; Mosconi, M.W. Motor Memory Deficits Contribute to Motor Impairments in Autism Spectrum Disorder. *J. Autism Dev. Disord.* **2016**. [CrossRef] [PubMed]
40. David, F.J.; Baranek, G.T.; Giuliani, C.A.; Mercer, V.S.; Poe, M.D.; Thorpe, D.E. A Pilot Study: Coordination of Precision Grip in Children and Adolescents with High Functioning Autism. *Pediatr. Phys. Ther.* **2009**, *21*, 205–211. [CrossRef] [PubMed]
41. David, F.J.; Baranek, G.T.; Wiesen, C.; Miao, A.F.; Thorpe, D.E. Coordination of precision grip in 2–6 years-old children with autism spectrum disorders compared to children developing typically and children with developmental disabilities. *Front. Integr. Neurosci.* **2012**, *6*, 122. [PubMed]
42. De Luca, C.J.; Adam, A.; Wotiz, R.; Gilmore, L.D.; Nawab, S.H. Decomposition of surface EMG signals. *J. Neurophysiol.* **2006**, *96*, 1646–1657. [CrossRef] [PubMed]
43. Nawab, S.H.; Chang, S.S.; De Luca, C.J. High-yield decomposition of surface EMG signals. *Clin. Neurophysiol.* **2010**, *121*, 1602–1615. [CrossRef] [PubMed]
44. Anzulewicz, A.; Sobota, K.; Delafield-Butt, J.T. Toward the Autism Motor Signature: Gesture patterns during smart tablet gameplay identify children with autism. *Sci. Rep.* **2016**, *6*, 31107. [CrossRef] [PubMed]
45. Rose, J.; McGill, K.C. Neuromuscular activation and motor-unit firing characteristics in cerebral palsy. *Dev. Med. Child Neurol.* **2005**, *47*, 329–336. [CrossRef] [PubMed]
46. Yoshitake, Y.; Shinohara, M. Low-frequency component of rectified EMG is temporally correlated with force and instantaneous rate of force fluctuations during steady contractions. *Muscle Nerve* **2013**, *47*, 577–584. [CrossRef] [PubMed]
47. Moon, H.; Kim, C.; Kwon, M.; Chen, Y.T.; Onushko, T.; Lodha, N.; Christou, E.A. Force control is related to low-frequency oscillations in force and surface EMG. *PLoS ONE* **2014**, *9*, e109202. [CrossRef] [PubMed]
48. Perez, M.A.; Lundbye-Jensen, J.; Nielsen, J.B. Changes in corticospinal drive to spinal motorneurones following visuo-motor skill learning in humans. *J. Physiol.* **2006**, *573*, 843–855. [CrossRef] [PubMed]
49. Onushko, T.; Baweja, H.S.; Christou, E.A. Practice improves motor control in older adults by increasing the motor unit modulation from 13 to 30 Hz. *J. Neurophysiol.* **2013**, *110*, 2393–2401. [CrossRef] [PubMed]
50. Classen, J.; Gerloff, C.; Honda, M.; Hallett, M. Integrative visuomotor behavior is associated with interregionally coherent oscillations in the human brain. *J. Neurophysiol.* **1998**, *79*, 1567–1573. [PubMed]
51. Brovelli, A.; Ding, M.; Ledberg, A.; Chen, Y.T.; Nakamura, R.; Bressler, S.L. Beta oscillations in a large-scale sensorimotor cortical network: Directional influences revealed by Granger causality. *Proc. Natl. Acad. Sci. USA* **2004**, *101*, 9849–9854. [CrossRef] [PubMed]
52. Takarae, Y.; Minshew, N.J.; Luna, B.; Sweeney, J.A. Atypical involvement of frontostriatal systems during sensorimotor control in autism. *Psychiatry Res.* **2007**, *156*, 117–127. [CrossRef] [PubMed]
53. Allen, G.; Muller, R.A.; Courchesne, E. Cerebellar function in autism: Functional magnetic resonance image activation during a simple motor task. *Biol. Psychiatry* **2004**, *56*, 269–278. [CrossRef] [PubMed]
54. Hu, X.; Suresh, A.K.; Li, X.; Rymer, W.Z.; Suresh, N.L. Impaired motor unit control in paretic muscle post stroke assessed using surface electromyography: A preliminary report. *Conf. Proc. IEEE Eng. Med. Biol. Soc.* **2012**, *2012*, 4116–4119. [PubMed]
55. De Luca, C.J.; Mambrito, B. Voluntary control of motor units in human antagonist muscles: Coactivation and reciprocal activation. *J. Neurophysiol.* **1987**, *58*, 525–542. [PubMed]
56. Negro, F.; Holobar, A.; Farina, D. Fluctuations in isometric muscle force can be described by one linear projection of low-frequency components of motor unit discharge rates. *J. Physiol.* **2009**, *587*, 5925–5938. [CrossRef] [PubMed]
57. Cook, J.L.; Blakemore, S.J.; Press, C. Atypical basic movement kinematics in autism spectrum conditions. *Brain* **2013**, *136*, 2816–2824. [CrossRef] [PubMed]
58. Kalra, L.; Swift, C.G.; Jackson, H.D. Psychomotor performance and antihypertensive treatment. *Br. J. Clin. Pharmacol.* **1994**, *37*, 165–172. [CrossRef] [PubMed]

59. Arora, E.; Khajuria, V.; Tandon, V.R.; Sharma, A.; Choudhary, N. Comparative evaluation of aliskiren, ramipril, and losartan on psychomotor performance in healthy volunteers: A preliminary report. *Perspect. Clin. Res.* **2014**, *5*, 190–194. [PubMed]
60. Dumont, G.J.; de Visser, S.J.; Cohen, A.F.; van Gerven, J.M.; Biomarker Working Group of the German Association for Applied Human, P. Biomarkers for the effects of selective serotonin reuptake inhibitors (SSRIs) in healthy subjects. *Br. J. Clin. Pharmacol.* **2005**, *59*, 495–510. [CrossRef] [PubMed]
61. Schrijvers, D.; Maas, Y.J.; Pier, M.P.; Madani, Y.; Hulstijn, W.; Sabbe, B.G. Psychomotor changes in major depressive disorder during sertraline treatment. *Neuropsychobiology* **2009**, *59*, 34–42. [CrossRef] [PubMed]
62. Reilly, J.L.; Lencer, R.; Bishop, J.R.; Keedy, S.; Sweeney, J.A. Pharmacological treatment effects on eye movement control. *Brain Cogn.* **2008**, *68*, 415–435. [CrossRef] [PubMed]
63. Wechsler, D. *Wechsler Abbreviated Scale of Intelligence*, 1st ed.; Psychological Corporation: New York, NY, USA, 1999.
64. Oldfield, R.C. The assessment and analysis of handedness: The Edinburgh inventory. *Neuropsychologia* **1971**, *9*, 97–113. [CrossRef]
65. Lord, C.; Rutter, M.; DiLavore, P.C.; Risi, S.; Gotham, K.; Bishop, S. *Autism Disgnostic Observation Schedule*, 2nd ed.; Western Psychological Services: Torrance, CA, USA, 2012.
66. Association, A.P. *Diagnostic and Statistical Manual of Mental Disorders*, 5th ed.; American Psychiatric Association: Washington, DC, USA, 2013.
67. Lord, C.; Rutter, M.; Le Couteur, A. Autism Diagnostic Interveiw-Revised: A revised version of a diagnostic interview for caregivers of individuals with possible pervasive developmental disorders. *J. Autism Dev. Disord.* **1994**, *24*, 659–685. [CrossRef] [PubMed]
68. Rutter, M.; Bailey, A.; Lord, C. *The Social Communication Questionnaire: Manual*, 1st ed.; Western Psychological Services: Torrance, CA, USA, 2003.
69. Taylor, A.M.; Christou, E.A.; Enoka, R.M. Multiple features of motor unit activity influence force fluctuations during isometric contractions. *J. Neurophysiol.* **2003**, *90*, 1350–1361. [CrossRef] [PubMed]
70. Kline, J.C.; De Luca, C.J. Error reduction in EMG signal decomposition. *J. Neurophysiol.* **2014**, *112*, 2718–2728. [CrossRef] [PubMed]
71. Mottram, C.J.; Christou, E.A.; Meyer, F.G.; Enoka, R.M. Frequency modulation of motor unit discharge has task-dependent effects on fluctuations in motor output. *J. Neurophysiol.* **2005**, *94*, 2878–2887. [CrossRef] [PubMed]

12

Cerebrospinal Fluid Findings of 36 Adult Patients with Autism Spectrum Disorder

Kimon Runge [1,2], Ludger Tebartz van Elst [1,2,*], Simon Maier [1,2], Kathrin Nickel [1,2], Dominik Denzel [1,2], Miriam Matysik [1,2], Hanna Kuzior [1,2], Tilman Robinson [3], Thomas Blank [4], Rick Dersch [3], Katharina Domschke [2,5] and Dominique Endres [1,2]

1 Section for Experimental Neuropsychiatry, Department of Psychiatry and Psychotherapy, Medical Center, Faculty of Medicine, University of Freiburg, Freiburg im Breisgau, Germany; kimon.runge@uniklinik-freiburg.de (K.R.); simon.maier@uniklinik-freiburg.de (S.M.); kathrin.nickel@uniklinik-freiburg.de (K.N.); dominik.denzel@uniklinik-freiburg.de (D.D.); miriam.matysik@uniklinik-freiburg.de (M.M.); hanna.kuzior@uniklinik-freiburg.de (H.K.); dominique.endres@uniklinik-freiburg.de (D.E.)

2 Department of Psychiatry and Psychotherapy, Medical Center, Faculty of Medicine, University of Freiburg, Freiburg im Breisgau, Germany; katharina.domschke@uniklinik-freiburg.de

3 Department of Neurology, Medical Center, Faculty of Medicine, University of Freiburg, Freiburg im Breisgau, Germany; tilman.robinson@uniklinik-freiburg.de (T.R.); rick.dersch@uniklinik-freiburg.de (R.D.)

4 Institute of Neuropathology, Medical Center, Faculty of Medicine, University of Freiburg, Freiburg im Breisgau, Germany; thomas.blank@uniklinik-freiburg.de

5 Center for Basics in Neuromodulation, Faculty of Medicine, University of Freiburg, Freiburg im Breisgau, Germany

* Correspondence: tebartzvanelst@uniklinik-freiburg.de

Abstract: Autism spectrum disorder (ASD) is a common neurodevelopmental disorder characterized by difficulties with social interaction, repetitive behavior, and additional features, such as special interests. Its precise etiology is unclear. Recently, immunological mechanisms, such as maternal autoantibodies/infections, have increasingly been the subject of discussion. Cerebrospinal fluid (CSF) investigations play a decisive role in the detection of immunological processes in the brain. This study therefore retrospectively analyzed the CSF findings of adult patients with ASD. CSF basic measures (white blood cell count, total protein, albumin quotient, immunoglobulin G (IgG) index, and oligoclonal bands) and various antineuronal antibody findings of 36 adult patients with ASD, who had received lumbar puncture, were compared with an earlier described mentally healthy control group of 39 patients with idiopathic intracranial hypertension. CSF protein concentrations and albumin quotients of patients with ASD were significantly higher as compared to controls (age corrected: $p = 0.003$ and $p = 0.004$, respectively); 17% of the patients with ASD showed increased albumin quotients. After correction for age and gender, the group effect for total protein remained significant ($p = 0.041$) and showed a tendency for albumin quotient ($p = 0.079$). In the CSF of two ASD patients, an intrathecal synthesis of anti-glutamate decarboxylase 65 (GAD65) antibodies was found. In total, more of the ASD patients (44%) presented abnormal findings in CSF basic diagnostics compared to controls (18%; $p = 0.013$). A subgroup of the patients with adult ASD showed indication of a blood–brain barrier dysfunction, and two patients displayed an intrathecal synthesis of anti-GAD65 antibodies; thus, the role of these antibodies in patients with ASD should be further investigated. The results of the study are limited by its retrospective and open design. The group differences in blood–brain barrier markers could be influenced by a different gender distribution between ASD patients and controls.

Keywords: Asperger syndrome; autism spectrum disorder; adults; cerebrospinal fluid; antibodies; blood–brain barrier; GAD65

---

1. Introduction

Autism spectrum disorder (ASD) is a common neurodevelopmental disorder characterized by deficits in social interaction and communication, unusually narrowed interests, and repetitive behavior in different situations [1]. Furthermore, the disorder involves specific alterations in social and sensory perception as well as in language [2]. The description of ASD in the Diagnostic and Statistical Manual of Mental Disorders, version 5 (DSM-5) demonstrates the clear tendency of the scientific community to subsume the various previous autism subtypes of the DSM-IV and of the International Statistical Classification of Diseases and Related Health Problems, version 10 (ICD-10) (childhood autism (ICD-10 F84.0, corresponding in the DSM-IV to autistic disorder 299.00), atypical autism (ICD-10 F84.1, not listed in the DSM-IV), and Asperger syndrome (ICD-10 F84.5, DSM-IV 299.80)) under a single diagnostic category [1,3,4]. ASD is a lifelong condition affecting predominantly males that is already present in early childhood, persists into adulthood, and is often accompanied by a variety of psychiatric comorbidities [1,2]. Despite the growing public and scientific interest in ASD over the past decades [5], which reflects increasing prevalence rates that are well above 1% and up to 2.7% depending on the populations studied [6,7], the disorder's precise etiology and pathophysiology remain elusive.

Genetic mechanisms certainly play an important role, and strong causal effects on ASD have long been known [8] for several rare genetic variants, such as tuberous sclerosis [9] and the fragile X syndrome [10]. Further genetic studies have shown the association of hundreds of distinct gene variants with autism, accounting, however, for only a fraction of ASD diagnoses [8,11]. Only recently, in the largest genome-wide association study (GWAS) for ASD to date, several single loci with genome-wide significance for association with ASD were reported for the first time [12]. Not only the phenotypic expression of ASD but also its etiology appear to be heterogeneous [13,14].

In recent studies, immunological mechanisms have increasingly been discussed as risk factors for altered neuronal development in ASD patients [15]. In particular, there is increasing evidence that maternal immune-dysfunction during gestation may lead to an ASD-like phenotype in susceptible offspring [11,16]. The first hints of the role of maternal prenatal infections were identified in the context of a significant increase in ASD after a rubella epidemic in the US in 1964 [17,18]. Furthermore, studies in large Danish registries found an elevated likelihood of ASD in children whose mothers were hospitalized during pregnancy due to a viral infection [19]. The possible importance of immune-dysfunction for an increased ASD risk is further supported by Scandinavian registry studies that reported a significant association between positive family history for autoimmune diseases and ASD [20,21]. Likewise, children of mothers with systemic lupus erythematosus have a doubled risk for ASD [22]. Potential mechanisms for an accentuated immune activation to affect neurological development are via cytokines, autoantibodies [11], or maternal anti-fetal brain antibodies [23,24]. In line with this, in post-mortem brains and the cerebrospinal fluid (CSF) of ASD patients, a proinflammatory cytokine profile has been found with activated microglia and astrocytes as signs of neuroinflammation [25].

In patients, CSF analysis is the most precise method for investigating subtle inflammation in the central nervous system (CNS) [26–28]. Furthermore, there is evidence that CSF circulation, which usually supplies growth hormones and signal molecules and cleanses the brain of harmful substances for proper brain development, is impaired in ASD [29]. Earlier CSF studies in ASD have analyzed children and infants as well as post-mortem material but not adult patients. This may be due to the fact that diagnostic procedures of potential brain disease are initiated at time of diagnosis (i.e., earlier in development and not in adulthood). Another reason might be that no CSF sampling is performed in adult ASD patients who are not characterized by mental retardation or further psychiatric/neurological symptoms. Therefore, this study's rationale is to retrospectively analyze the CSF findings of adult patients with ASD.

2. Participants and Methods

The study was part of a larger project of retrospective biomarker detection that was approved by the local ethics committee (Faculty of Medicine, Freiburg University, 396/18).

2.1. Study Sample

We included 36 patients with ASD who had received a lumbar puncture at our tertiary care hospital from 2010 to 2018. The patients were diagnosed by experienced senior physicians following German guidelines [30] as described in detail in earlier papers [31,32] and were classified following ICD-10. Patients with neurodegenerative disorders were excluded from the study; examples include mild cognitive impairment (ICD-10: F06.7) or dementia (ICD-10: F03), substance abuse (ICD-10: F1x.2), or severe neurological diseases other than epilepsy (because of its known association with ASD) [33,34]. The presence of other common comorbid conditions in patients with ASD was not defined as an exclusion criterion; examples include affective disorders (ICD-10: F30-F39), or neurodevelopmental disorders such as attention deficit hyperactivity disorder (ADHD; ICD-10: F90.x), or Tourette syndrome (ICD-10: F95.2).

The control group comprised 39 mentally healthy controls with idiopathic intracranial hypertension (IIH; ICD-10: G93.2), a non-inflammatory neurological disease characterized by increased intracranial pressure of unknown origin. All controls with clearly identifiable secondary forms of intracranial hypertension, those being treated with psychotropic drugs at the time of the lumbar puncture, and those with a history of psychiatric or neurological disorders (except headache) were excluded. This control group was collected in the context of a previous CSF study [35–37].

All the clinical and demographic data of the ASD patients were extracted from medical reports. Patients' psychometric data had been collected as part of routine clinical documentation, including the Clinical Global Impression (CGI) score [38], the Global Assessment of Functioning (GAF) score [4], and psychopathological scores based on the German Association for Methodology and Documentation in Psychiatry (AMDP) [39].

2.2. CSF and Instrument-Based Diagnostics

All of the included participants were informed about the lumbar puncture and gave their written informed consent. The CSF analyses were performed in the CSF laboratory at the Department of Neurology (https://www.uniklinik-freiburg.de/neurologie/klinik/diagnostische-einrichtungen/liquor-labor.html) as described in previous studies [40–42]. Routine CSF analysis included the determination of white blood cell (WBC) count, total protein concentration, albumin quotient (AQ), immunoglobulin G (IgG) index, and oligoclonal bands (OCBs). Antibodies against cell surface antigens (NMDA-receptor, LGI1, CASPR2, AMPA1/2-receptor, GABA-B-receptor) were identified in the CSF using fixed-cell assays (Euroimmun®). Antibodies in serum against paraneoplastic intracellular antigens (Yo, Hu, CV2/CRMP5, Ri, Ma1/2, SOX1, Tr, Zic4, glutamate decarboxylase 65 (GAD65), amphiphysin) were screened using immunoblots (Ravo line assay®). In individual cases, the anti-GAD65 antibody levels were measured in serum and CSF additionally using a radioimmunoassay (Medipan®, see [28] for comparison). All ASD patients received cerebral magnetic resonance imaging (MRI) assessed by experienced neuroradiologists as well as electroencephalograms (EEGs) assessed by the attending physicians.

2.3. Statistical Analyses

Data analysis was conducted with Statistical Package for the Social Sciences, version 25 (IBM Corp., Armonk, NY, USA). Group comparisons of categorical variables were conducted with Pearson's Chi-squared test. If the result in any of the cells of the contingency table was below 5, Fisher's exact test was used. One-way analyses of covariance (ANCOVAs) were conducted to determine whether there was a statistically significant difference between the patients and the controls in their CSF basis findings while controlling for the effect of age. Spearman's rank correlation coefficient was used for correlation analysis between CSF parameters (WBC count, protein concentration, AQ, and IgG index) of the ASD group and their psychometric scores, such as CGI, GAF, and AMDP as well as the number of inpatient stays, suicide attempts, and age. Further ANCOVAs were performed to detect significant influences of gender as well as the presence of abnormalities in EEGs or MRI on CSF parameters of ASD patients while controlling for the effect of age. To control the false discovery rate in multiple testing we calculated adjusted *p*-values with R (R Core Team, 2019) using the Benjamini–Hochberg procedure [43]. Thereby the *p*-values of the CSF basic diagnostics were adjusted together, then the *p*-values of the number of subjects with abnormal CSF diagnostics as a separate group and finally the *p*-values of each correlation of a CSF parameter with the psychometric data. A *p*-value of less than 0.05 was considered statistically significant.

3. Results

3.1. Clinical and Demographic Data

For clinical and demographic data of the patient and control samples see Table 1. The ASD and the control cohort differed significantly in gender ratio ($p < 0.001$) and age ($p = 0.03$). According to the ICD-10 subgroups of ASD, 34 patients were coded as diagnosed with Asperger syndrome (ICD-10: F84.5) and two with atypical autism (ICD-10: F84.1). All ASD patients had psychiatric comorbidities, of which depression was the most prevalent (75%).

Table 1. Clinical and demographic data of patients and controls.

	Patients with Autism ($n = 36$)	Controls ($n = 39$)	Statistics
Gender	13 F:23 M	33 F:6 M	$p < 0.001$
Average age at time of lumbar puncture (age range)	28.94 ± 9.9 (18–53 years)	34.6 ± 12.0 (18–61 years)	$p = 0.03$
Diagnosis			
F84.5	$n = 34$ (94.4%)	-	
F84.1	$n = 2$ (5.6%)	-	
G93.2	-	$n = 39$ (100%)	
Neuropsychiatric comorbidity			
Depression	$n = 27$ (86.1%)	-	
ADHD	$n = 6$ (16.7%)	-	
Schizophreniform disorders	$n = 5$ (13.9%)	-	
History of epilepsy	$n = 2$ (5.6%)	-	
Obsessive compulsive disorder	$n = 2$ (5.6%)	-	
Personality disorder	$n = 2$ (5.6%)	-	
Others	$n = 7$ * (19.4%)	-	
Civil status			
Single	$n = 31$ (86.1%)		
Married	$n = 3$ (8.3%)		
Unknown	$n = 2$ (5.6%)		
Educational level			
Low	$n = 5$ (13.9%)		
Intermediate	$n = 14$ (38.9%)		
High	$n = 14$ (38.9%)		
Unknown	$n = 3$ (8.3%)		
Employment			
Unemployed	$n = 7$ (19.4%)		
Working	$n = 11$ (30.6%)		
Education/training	$n = 11$ (30.6%)		
Occupational disability	$n = 4$ (11.1%)		
Others/unknown	$n = 3$ (8.3%)		
Living situation			
Alone	$n = 13$ (36.1%)		
With partner/family	$n = 2$ (5.6%)		
With parents/custodian	$n = 17$ (47.2%)		
Psychiatric transitional arrangement	$n = 1$ (2.8%)		
Others/unknown	$n = 3$ (8.3%)		

Table 1. *Cont.*

	Patients with Autism (n = 36)	Controls (n = 39)	Statistics
Family history for any psychiatric disease **			
Positive	n = 23 (63.9%)		
Negative	n = 9 (25.0%)		
Unknown	n = 4 (11.1%)		
Number of previous inpatient stays			
None	n = 12 (33.3%)		
1	n = 4 (11.1%)		
2	n = 7 (19.4%)		
3	n = 3 (8.3%)		
More than 3	n = 7 (19.4%)		
Unknown	n = 3 (8.3%)		
Burden of acute events			
None	n = 6 (16.7%)		
Mild	n = 17 (47.2%)		
Intermediate	n = 5 (13.9%)		
Severe	n = 4 (11.1%)		
Extreme	n = 1 (2.8%)		
Unknown	n = 3 (8.3%)		
Burden of long-term life circumstances			
None	n = 2 (5.6%)		
Mild	n = 10 (27.8%)		
Intermediate	n = 9 (25.0%)		
Severe	n = 9 (25.0%)		
Extreme	n = 2 (5.6%)		
Unknown	n = 4 (11.1%)		
Number of suicide attempts			
None	n = 28 (77.8%)		
1	n = 6 (16.7%)		
2	n = 1 (2.8%)		
Unknown	n = 1 (2.8%)		

* Bipolar disorder, anorexia nervosa, narcolepsy, Tourette syndrome, insomnia, substance induced psychotic disorder, dissociative disorder. ** In first-degree relatives. Abbreviations: F = female, M = male, ADHD = attention deficit hyperactivity disorder, n = number.

Most of the ASD patients were single (86.1%), lived with their parents/guardians (47.2%) and were either working (30.6%) or in training (30.6%). The majority had achieved intermediate (38.9%) to high (38.9%) education. Most patients had a positive family history for some psychiatric disease in first-degree relatives (63.9%).

3.2. CSF Diagnostics

At the time of lumbar puncture, most of the ASD patients (75%) were treated with psychotropic medications, of which the most prevalent were atypical neuroleptics (52.8%) and antidepressants (55.6%). An exact listing of psychotropic medications used at the time of lumbar puncture is provided in Table 2.

Of the 36 ASD patients, three (8.3%) showed a slightly elevated WBC count, 12 (33.3%) an increased total protein, and six (16.7%) an increased age-dependent AQ. CSF-specific OCBs were found in one patient with ASD (2.8%) and in none of the control patients, and no patient showed an increased IgG index. In summary, 16 of the 36 patients (44.4%) presented abnormal CSF basic diagnostic findings, which differed significantly ($p = 0.013$) from respective findings in controls with abnormal CSF measures (7 of 39; 18%). The ANCOVAs conducted with age correction showed a significant difference between ASD patients and controls in total protein ($F_{(1,73)} = 6.450$, $p = 0.003$) and AQ ($F_{(1,73)} = 5.878$, $p = 0.004$), but not regarding WBC counts or IgG index. For this analysis, data from 36 ASD patients and 39 controls were evaluated except for the WBC count, for which data from only 35 controls were available. All results of the CSF basic diagnostic are summarized in Tables 3 and 4.

In a secondary analysis, we additionally investigated the effect of gender and the interaction between age and gender in these ANCOVAs. Here, the group effect for total protein remained significant ($F_{(1,70)} = 4.327$, $p = 0.041$) and for AQ a tendency could still be observed ($F_{(1,70)} = 3.167$, $p = 0.079$). We found a significant interaction between age and gender in the ANCOVAs for total protein ($F_{(1,70)} = 6.510$, $p = 0.013$) as well as AQ ($F_{(1,70)} = 5.299$, $p = 0.024$), but gender alone had no significant effect on the models for total protein ($F_{(1,70)} = 2.073$, $p = 0.154$) and AQ ($F_{(1,70)} = 1.834$, $p = 0.180$). For WBC count and IgG index no significant group effects or interactions were detected.

Most ASD patients additionally received screenings for antineuronal antibodies against cell surface antigens ($n = 31$) or intracellular antigens ($n = 34$) (Table 5). Two of the patients tested were positive for anti-GAD65 antibodies in serum and CSF, and one patient had a nonspecific reaction for anti-Yo antibodies in serum.

Table 2. Psychotropic medication at time of lumbar puncture.

	Patients with ASD ($n = 36$)
Class of Medication	
Selective serotonin reuptake inhibitor	$n = 6$ (16.7%)
Selective serotonin/noradrenaline reuptake inhibitor	$n = 4$ (11.1%)
Tricyclic antidepressants	$n = 6$ (16.7%)
Bupropion	$n = 3$ (8.3%)
Mirtazapine	$n = 2$ (5.6%)
Typical neuroleptics	$n = 1$ (2.8%)
Atypical neuroleptics	$n = 19$ (52.8%)
Lithium	$n = 1$ (2.8%)
Anticonvulsants	$n = 7$ (19.4%)
Benzodiazepine	$n = 1$ (2.8%)
Methylphenidate	$n = 2$ (5.6%)
Melatonin	$n = 5$ (13.9%)
Others	$n = 4$ * (11.1%)
Number of Different Medication Classes per Patient	
Same class/only one drug	$n = 9$ (25.0%)
Two drugs	$n = 7$ (19.4%)
Three drugs	$n = 9$ (25.0%)
More than three	$n = 2$ (5.6%)
Unmedicated	$n = 9$ (25.0%)

The number refers to different drug classes. If several drugs of the same class were taken, only one was included. * One patient with comorbid ADHD received atypical off-label treatment with levodopa + carbidopa (this was changed to bupropion after lumbar puncture); another patient took biperiden and clonidine. Abbreviations: ASD = Autism spectrum disorder; ADHD = attention deficit hyperactivity disorder; n = number.

Table 3. CSF basis diagnostics.

	Reference [44]	**ASD Patients ($n = 36$)**	**Controls ($n = 39$)**	**Statistics (Unadjusted p-Value)**
WBC count (Mean ± SD)	<5/μL	1.94 ± 1.37	2.60 ± 7.59 *	$p = 0.698$ (0.698)
Total protein (Mean ± SD)	≤450 mg/L	478.14 ± 391.1	309.33 ± 142.5	**$p = 0.009$ (0.003)**
Albumin quotient (Mean ± SD)	<40 years: 6.5×10^{-3}; 40–60 years: 8×10^{-3}; >60 years: 9.3×10^{-3}	5.84 ± 5.66	3.93 ± 1.81	**$p = 0.009$ (0.004)**
IgG index (Mean ± SD)	≤0.7 mg/L	0.50 ± 0.39	0.50 ± 0.038	$p = 0.257$ (0.193)

The control group was created for an earlier project and the results were published earlier [35–37]. Abbreviations: CSF = cerebrospinal fluid; WBC = white blood cell, SD = standard deviation, IgG = immunoglobulin G, n = number. * Data of only 35 controls are available. One of them suffered from pleocytosis (46 cells/μL), which normalized independently, and was interpreted as reactive pleocytosis. p-Values adjusted by Benjamini–Hochberg procedure. Bold = significant at $p \leq 0.05$.

Table 4. Number of subjects with abnormal CSF diagnostics.

	ASD Patients ($n = 36$)	Controls ($n = 39$)	Statistics (Unadjusted p-Value)
Increased WBC count (≥5/μL)	$n = 3$ (8.3%) *	$n = 1$ (2.9%) **	$p = 0.115$ (0.086)
Increased total protein (>450 mg/L)	$n = 12$ (33.3%)	$n = 6$ (15.4%)	$p = 0.115$ (0.069)
Increased age-dependent albumin quotient (<40 years: 6.5×10^{-3}; 40–60 years: 8×10^{-3}; >60 years: 9.3×10^{-3})	$n = 6$ (16.7%)	$n = 2$ (5.1%)	$p = 0.191$ (0.143)
Increased IgG index (>0.7 mg/L)	$n = 0$	$n = 0$	-
CSF specific OCBs	$n = 1$ (2.8%) ***	$n = 0$ ****	$p = 0.324$ (0.324)
Patients with abnormal CSF basis diagnostics	16/36 (44.4%)	7/39 (18%)	$p = 0.013$

The control group was created for an earlier project and the results previously published (see [35–37]). The number of patients with abnormalities in CSF diagnostics, as a summary of previous tests, was not corrected for multiple testing. Abbreviations: WBC = white blood cell; SD = standard deviation; IgG = immunoglobulin G; OCBs = oligoclonal bands; n = number. * 5, 6 and 6 white blood cells without blood admixture. ** Only data of 35 controls are available. One of them suffered from reactive pleocytosis (46 cells/μL), which regressed independently to normal WBC counts and was interpreted as reactive pleocytosis. *** Two additional findings were not considered positive: one patient had an isolated OCB in the CSF, another patient had 1–2 very weak bands in the CSF. **** Only available from 38 (of 39) control patients. p-Values adjusted by Benjamini–Hochberg procedure. Bold = significant at $p \leq 0.05$.

Table 5. Antineuronal autoantibody findings.

Patients with ASD ($n = 36$)	Antibodies against Cell Surface Antigens in CSF	Antibodies against Paraneoplastic Intracellular Antigens in Serum
Not analyzed	$n = 5$ (13.9%)	$n = 2$ (5.6%)
Negative	$n = 31$ (86.1%)	$n = 32$ (88.2%)
Positive	$n = 0$	$n = 2$ * (5.6%)

* Two patients displayed anti-glutamate decarboxylase 65 (GAD65) antibodies, additionally one patient had a non-specific reaction for anti-Yo antibodies, which was not rated as a positive result. Abbreviations: ASD = Autism spectrum disorder, CSF = cerebrospinal fluid; n = number.

3.3. *Instrument-Based Diagnostics*

All patients received an EEG and an MRI scan of the brain. Sixteen ASD patients (44.4%) showed abnormalities in their MRI scans, the most frequent being white matter lesions/cerebral microangiopathy (25%). In the EEGs, generalized intermittent slow activity was found in five patients (13.9%) and focal slowing in three patients (8.3%). One patient (2.8%) had a history of epilepsy and showed corresponding epileptiform discharges with frontal spike wave complexes (Table 6).

Table 6. MRI and EEG pathologies in the ASD patient group.

MRI Abnormalities	Patients ($n = 36$)
White matter lesions/cerebral microangiopathy	$n = 12$ (33.3%)
Generalized cortical atrophy	$n = 2$ (5.6%)
Localized cortical atrophy	$n = 1$ (2.8%)
Pineal cyst	$n = 4$ (11.1%)
Other anatomical variants	$n = 4$ * (11.1%)
More than one abnormality	$n = 7$ (19.4%)
Normal findings	$n = 20$ (55.6%)
Total number of MRI abnormalities	16/36 patients (44.4%)
EEG pathologies	**Patients ($n = 36$)**
Continuous generalized/regional slow activity	-
Intermittent generalized slow activity	$n = 5$ (13.9%)
Intermittent focal slow activity	$n = 3$ (8.3%)
Epileptiform discharges	$n = 1$ (2.8%)
Absence of EEG pathologies	$n = 28$ (77.8%)
Total number of EEG pathologies	8/36 patients (22.2%)

* Arachnoidal cyst, asymmetric lateral ventricles, asymmetric vertebral artery, enlarged Virchow–Robin's space. Abbreviations: MRI = magnetic resonance imaging; EEG = electroencephalogram; n = number.

3.4. Clinical Characteristics of ASD Patients with Anti-GAD65 Antibodies

The two ASD patients who tested positive for anti-GAD65 antibodies in serum (patient (1): 14 U/mL; patient (2) 101 U/mL; reference <2.0 U/mL) displayed an increased antibody index (patient (1): 50.4, patient (2): 20.3; reference ≤1.5) indicating an intrathecal anti-GAD65 antibody synthesis. Both patients were relatively young, patient (1) was male and patient (2) was female. Both patients suffered from comorbid depression; patient (1) also suffered from tic disorder and patient (2) from anxious jitteriness and Hashimoto thyroiditis. Both patients had no diabetes mellitus (HbA1c levels were in the normal range) and no epilepsy. However, in patient (1), initially a slightly elevated WBC count in the CSF (6/μL; reference <5/μL; with normalization in the follow-up), increased streptolysin antibody levels, as well as anatomical alterations in the form of asymmetric lateral ventricles in the MRI and abnormal frontal slow waves in the EEG (which were partly generalized) were identified. A complementary [^{18}F] fluorodeoxyglucose positron emission tomography of the brain showed age-appropriate cerebral glucose utilization without patterns for an acute inflammatory CNS disease. In patient (2), the laboratory results, MRI, EEG, and CSF basis diagnostics were all essentially normal.

3.5. Correlation Analyses

For the ASD group we found significant negative correlations between WBC count and AMDP scores for formal thought disorders (r = −0.336, p = 0.045; n = 36) and delusion (r = −0.457, p = 0.005; n = 36) as well as number of suicide attempts (r = −0.405, p = 0.014; n = 36). This corresponds to moderate effect sizes of the correlation coefficients according to Cohen but were not significant after adjustments that control for the false discovery rate (p = 0.27/0.09/0.126). Furthermore, age correlated with total protein (r = 0.338, p = 0.043; n = 36) and AQ (r = 0.474, p = 0.004; n = 36). All other correlations between the CSF basic diagnostic parameters and the psychometric data were not significant. No significant influence of gender or the presence of EEG or MRI abnormalities on CSF parameters of ASD patients was detected.

4. Discussion

The main findings of this study are higher CSF levels of AQs in patients with ASD indicate potential blood–brain barrier (BBB) dysfunction and an intrathecal synthesis of anti-GAD65 antibodies in two patients with ASD. Overall, we found abnormal CSF basic findings in almost half of the ASD patients—significantly more than in the control group.

4.1. Significance of Increased CSF Protein Levels

Altogether the ASD group presented significantly higher CSF levels of total protein (478.1 vs. 309.3 mg/dL) and AQs (5.84 vs. 3.93) compared to the control group. Accordingly, 33.3% of ASD patients had an increased total protein and 16.7% an increased albumin ratio, which compares well to figures in similarly aged patients with schizophreniform psychosis (total protein increase in psychosis in 42.4%, increased AQs in 21.8%) [40] and to the previously reported proportion of neurological patients with a non-inflammatory disease of the CNS with isolated BBB dysfunction (17.5%) [45]. The serum/CSF AQ is clinically considered the "gold standard" for the assessment of BBB function [46]. Since albumin is only produced in the liver, it can reach the CSF only via the BBB. Nevertheless, it is still a matter of debate whether BBB dysfunction as measured with elevated AQs is the sequel of "leakage" at the site of small vessels and capillaries or a reduced CSF drainage in the context of disturbances of CSF flow [47,48]. For ASD, an altered CSF flow was suggested by Shen et al. [29]. In their study of the MRIs of infants who later developed autism, the authors observed an increased extra-axial CSF volume as a possible sign of reduced CSF circulation [49]. Interestingly, the protein concentration in the extra-axial CSF was also significantly elevated compared to healthy children [29]. Thus, it has been suggested that an impaired CSF circulation may lead to an altered distribution of growth factors and signal molecules in the brain as well as a disturbed cleansing of neurotoxins, which can cause neuroinflammation when they accumulate [29].

4.2. EEG and MRI Findings

The link between epilepsy and autism is well known, and thus an EEG is an important diagnostic procedure in patients with ASD. However, in addition to the detection of epileptiform discharges in a subgroup of patients, increased nonspecific EEG abnormalities in the form of, for example, slowing or asymmetries [50], as well as hints of long-range underconnectivity [51] in ASD patients have been described. The current study included one patient with comorbid epilepsy and epileptiform discharges, and 19% of the patients presented only focal or generalized slow activity. A previous study with a small sample size discerned a statistically significant difference between ASD patients and healthy controls in the rate of slow activity after hyperventilation [52]. One quarter of ASD patients in the current study showed nonspecific white matter alterations in their MRI. Other mental illnesses, such as depression, present similar rates [41]. It is assumed that these are caused by micro- or macroangiopathic diseases resulting from a dysfunction of the neurovascular unit, which can also lead to a BBB dysfunction [53]. Neuroinflammation can lead to defects in the neovascular unit and, reciprocally, defects in the neurovascular unit can also promote neuroinflammatory processes in the brain. However, the significance and clinical relevance of these white matter alterations remain unclear. Further studies in larger and more homogeneous subgroups of ASD patients are needed to develop a better understanding.

4.3. Antibody Findings

The presence of brain-reactive antibodies in patients with ASD has been reported in numerous studies [54]. Accordingly, Singer et al. [55] observed a greater prevalence of autoantibodies in the serum of autistic children than in their non-autistic siblings or healthy controls (in human brain slices of the caudate nucleus, putamen, prefrontal cortex, cerebellum, and cingulate gyrus). Moreover, the presence of brain-reactive antibodies in either the patient or the mother is associated with a more severe degree of autism [56] and has been reported to lead to markedly greater brain enlargement in preschool children who later develop ASD [57]. In the current study, the authors identified two patients (5.6%) who presented an intrathecal synthesis of anti-GAD65 antibodies. GAD65 is an enzyme that catalyzes the intracellular synthesis of the inhibitory neurotransmitter γ-amino butyric acid (GABA) through the decarboxylation of glutamate in brain cells and the pancreatic islet β-cells of the pancreas. Autoantibodies against GAD65 are common at the onset of type I diabetes but have also been reported in various neurological disorders, such as stiff person syndrome, cerebral ataxia, and, in some cases, in epilepsy and limbic encephalitis [58,59]. Interestingly, type I diabetes is a common co-morbidity not only of patients with ASD but also of their mothers and first-degree relatives [54,60,61]. In the healthy population, the prevalence of anti-GAD65 antibodies ranged from 0.5% to 1.1% [62,63]. Small studies in patients with ASD have described a higher incidence in ASD patients, ranging from 5% (three of 60 patients) [64] to 15% (three of 20 patients) [65]. There are, however, contradictory findings that may be related to diverse subgroups of ASD patients or to measurement techniques for anti-GAD65 antibodies [66]. It is important to note that most studies only tested antibodies in serum and did not comment on BBB integrity or the presence of antibodies in the CSF. Presumably, the antibodies are relevant for brain alteration only when they can reach the brain tissue from the serum through a "leaky" BBB due, for instance, to injury or inflammation or when they are synthesized intrathecally [67]. Although why are anti-GAD65 antibodies associated with diabetes mellitus in one patient, stiff person syndrome in another, and with autism in a third? The time at which antibodies reach specific organs as well as genetic predispositions (HLA haplotype) seem to play important roles [68], and environmental factors may be important. The pathophysiology of neuropsychiatric disease in association with anti-GAD65 antibodies is poorly understood to date. The gene expression of GAD65 appears to be reduced in ASD patients in certain brain regions, such as the cerebellar dentate nuclei [69,70], and also in the cortex of mice whose mothers during pregnancy received the anti-epileptic drug valproate, which is associated with a high risk of autism [71]. Moreover, hypermethylation of the *GAD1* promoter has been observed in the offspring of mice that received a nonspecific immune response by means of a poly (I:C) injection during pregnancy [72]. One possible pathomechanism is the direct intracellular binding of anti-GAD65 antibodies to the cytoplasmic GAD65 through unknown mechanisms leading to a change in GABAergic transmission. While a strong binding has been demonstrated in vitro [73], the application of anti-GAD65 antibodies in the CSF of mice in vivo did not lead to a change in hippocampal GABAergic transmission [74]. Thus, the pathophysiological functioning of anti-GAD65 antibodies seems to be more complex than, for example, in the case of the immunoglobulin G antibodies against the surface N-methyl D-aspartate receptor. In this context, we need to consider that GAD65 antibodies themselves may not be pathophysiologically active, but rather an immunological epiphenomenon of an unknown underlying pathomechanism [75]. Thus, the formation of anti-GAD65 antibodies could be secondary to the destruction of GABAergic neurons by, for instance, hitherto unidentified antibodies and the release of intracellular GAD into CSF [75,76]. This would also explain the clinical heterogeneity of diseases associated with anti-GAD65 antibodies and their different responsiveness to immunosuppressive therapies. In all cases, anti-GAD65 antibodies function at least as a disease marker of an unknown but most likely immune mediated process [76].

Case reports have described severe neurological diseases in association with anti-GAD65 antibodies, such as limbic encephalitis and epilepsy, that barely responded to classical immunotherapy, such as steroids or intravenous immunoglobulins (IVIGs), and required more aggressive treatment with monoclonal antibodies, such as basiliximab or rituximab [77,78]. Nevertheless, it has been reported at least in one patient with ASD with clinically relevant high anti-GAD65 antibodies and comorbid type I diabetes, that there was a relevant benefit from therapy with IVIGs [64].

4.4. Limitations

This study was performed openly and retrospectively. The decision to conduct lumbar punctures followed clinical criteria to exclude a secondary organic pathology and was not a routine procedure; therefore, the patient group is not representative of all patients with ASD. In addition, the control group's unclear IIH pathophysiology may have introduced a confounder to data in this group. In patients with IIH, larger amounts of CSF were removed due to therapy. Given that a clear reduction of the AQ between the first 4 mL and the last 4 mL of a total of 24 mL of CSF of a lumbar puncture has been described [79,80], false low values in the control group are possible. Moreover, the AQ may vary due to body weight, smoking, degenerative disc disease, hypothyroidism, or gender [80,81]. Particularly noteworthy is the gender difference between our patient and control groups. However, we did not find a gender effect in our secondary analysis of the CSF parameters but in the gender corrected ANOVA, however, only the group difference in the protein concentrations was still significant, whereas the AQ showed only a tendential increase in the ASD patients. Our findings could therefore be partly caused by a gender difference. Furthermore, the measured values for total protein and sometimes additionally AQ of one third of the ASD patients were also increased compared to established reference values. Differences on other CSF parameters like WBC and IgG due to gender have not been observed.

Psychotropic medication may also have had an influence on the total protein in the CSF and AQs. While three quarters of the ASD patients were medicated, the control group did not receive psychiatric medication. It has been indicated that, for example, antipsychotic drugs in bipolar patients may lead to an increased AQ [82]. However, other studies found no influence of antipsychotic [83–85] or antidepressant [86] medication on CSF properties. Finally, depression and other comorbidities may have confounded our results.

5. Conclusions

The present retrospective study on CSF measures provides no clear-cut positive evidence for relevant inflammatory alterations in adult ASD, however, it does suggest a trend toward a BBB dysfunction in some adult patients with ASD. The identification of anti-GAD65 antibodies in some patients with ASD may be relevant for future research in an effort to define etiological and clinical sub-phenotypes of ASD informing more personalized treatment approaches.

Author Contributions: K.R., L.T.v.E., and D.E. designed the study. K.R. and D.E. performed the data research and created the structure of the paper. H.K. and M.M. supported data search. K.R. wrote the first manuscript, and D.E. critically revised it. T.R. and R.D. helped in interpreting the CSF basic analyses. T.B. supported the neuroanatomical interpretation. S.M. supported statistical analyses. L.T.v.E., K.N., D.D., M.M., H.K., and K.D. critically revised the clinical interpretation of our findings. All authors were critically involved in the theoretical discussion and composition of the manuscript. All authors have read and approved the final version of the manuscript.

Acknowledgments: D.E. was supported by the Berta-Ottenstein-Programme for Advanced Clinician Scientists, Faculty of Medicine, University of Freiburg.

Abbreviations

ADHD	Attention deficit hyperactivity disorder
AMDP	Association for Methodology and Documentation in Psychiatry (in German: Arbeitsgemeinschaft für Methodik und Dokumentation in der Psychiatrie)
ANCOVA	One-way analysis of covariance
AQ	Albumin quotient
ASD	Autism spectrum disorder
BBB	Blood–brain barrier
CGI	Clinical Global Impression
CNS	Central nervous system
CSF	Cerebrospinal fluid
EEG	Electroencephalography
F	Female
GABA	γ-amino butyric acid
GAD65	Glutamate decarboxylase 65
GAF	Global Assessment of Functioning
GWAS	Genome-wide association study
IgG	Immunoglobulin G
IIH	Idiopathic intracranial hypertension
IVIG	Intravenous immunoglobulins
M	Male
MRI	Magnetic resonance imaging
n	Number
OCB	Oligoclonal band
SD	Standard deviation
WBC	White blood count
y	Years

References

1. World Health Organization. *ICD-10 International Statistical Classification of Diseases and Related Health Problems: 10th Revision ICD-10*, 5th ed.; World Health Organization: Geneva, Switzerland, 2016.
2. Van Elst, L.T.; Pick, M.; Biscaldi, M.; Fangmeier, T.; Riedel, A. High-functioning autism spectrum disorder as a basic disorder in adult psychiatry and psychotherapy: Psychopathological presentation, clinical relevance and therapeutic concepts. *Eur. Arch. Psychiatry Clin. Neurosci.* **2013**, *263*, 189–196. [CrossRef] [PubMed]

3. American Psychiatric Association. *Diagnostic and Statistical Manual of Mental Disorders: DSM-5*, 5th ed.; American Psychiatric Publishing: Washington, DC, USA, 2013.
4. American Psychiatric Association. *Diagnostic and Statistical Manual of Mental Disorders: DSM-IV-TR*, 4th ed.; American Psychiatric Association: Arlington, VA, USA, 2009.
5. Lai, M.-C.; Lombardo, M.V.; Baron-Cohen, S. Autism. *Lancet* **2014**, *383*, 896–910. [CrossRef]
6. Baio, J.; Wiggins, L.; Christensen, D.L.; Maenner, M.J.; Daniels, J.; Warren, Z.; Kurzius-Spencer, M.; Zahorodny, W.; Robinson, C.; Rosenberg, C.R.; et al. Prevalence of Autism Spectrum Disorder Among Children Aged 8 Years—Autism and Developmental Disabilities Monitoring Network, 11 Sites, United States, 2014. *MMWR. Surveill. Summ.* **2018**, *67*, 1–23. [CrossRef] [PubMed]
7. Kim, Y.S.; Leventhal, B.L.; Koh, Y.-J.; Fombonne, E.; Laska, E.; Lim, E.-C.; Cheon, K.-A.; Kim, S.-J.; Kim, Y.-K.; Lee, H.; et al. Prevalence of Autism Spectrum Disorders in a Total Population Sample. *Am. J. Psychiatry* **2011**, *168*, 904–912. [CrossRef]
8. Vorstman, J.A.S.; Parr, J.R.; Moreno-De-Luca, D.; Anney, R.J.L.; Nurnberger, J.I., Jr.; Hallmayer, J.F. Autism genetics: Opportunities and challenges for clinical translation. *Nat. Rev. Genet.* **2017**, *18*, 362–376. [CrossRef]
9. Crino, P.B.; Nathanson, K.L.; Henske, E.P. The Tuberous Sclerosis Complex. *N. Engl. J. Med.* **2006**, *355*, 1345–1356. [CrossRef]
10. Kidd, S.A.; Lachiewicz, A.; Barbouth, D.; Blitz, R.K.; Delahunty, C.; McBrien, D.M.; Visootsak, J.; Berry-Kravis, E. Fragile X Syndrome: A Review of Associated Medical Problems. *Pediatrics* **2014**, *134*, 995–1005. [CrossRef]
11. Meltzer, A.; Van De Water, J. The Role of the Immune System in Autism Spectrum Disorder. *Neuropsychopharmacology* **2016**, *42*, 284–298. [CrossRef]
12. Grove, J.; Ripke, S.; Als, T.D.; Mattheisen, M.; Walters, R.K.; Won, H.; Pallesen, J.; Agerbo, E.; Andreassen, O.A.; Autism Spectrum Disorder Working Group of the Psychiatric Genomics Consortium; et al. Identification of common genetic risk variants for autism spectrum disorder. *Nat. Genet.* **2019**, *51*, 431–444. [CrossRef]
13. Happé, F.; Ronald, A.; Plomin, R. Time to give up on a single explanation for autism. *Nat. Neurosci.* **2006**, *9*, 1218–1220. [CrossRef]
14. Levy, S.E.; Mandell, D.S.; Schultz, R.T. Autism. *Lancet* **2009**, *374*, 1627–1638. [CrossRef]
15. Edmiston, E.; Ashwood, P.; Van De Water, J. Autoimmunity, Autoantibodies, and Autism Spectrum Disorder. *Boil. Psychiatry* **2016**, *81*, 383–390. [CrossRef] [PubMed]
16. Onore, C.; Careaga, M.; Ashwood, P. The role of immune dysfunction in the pathophysiology of autism. *Brain Behav. Immun.* **2011**, *26*, 383–392. [CrossRef] [PubMed]
17. Chess, S.; Fernandez, P.; Korn, S. Behavioral consequences of congenital rubella. *J. Pediatr.* **1978**, *93*, 699–703. [CrossRef]
18. Chess, S. Autism in children with congenital rubella. *J. Autism Dev. Disord.* **1971**, *1*, 33–47. [CrossRef] [PubMed]
19. Atladóttir, H.Ó.; Thorsen, P.; Østergaard, L.; Schendel, D.E.; Lemcke, S.; Abdallah, M.; Parner, E. Maternal Infection Requiring Hospitalization During Pregnancy and Autism Spectrum Disorders. *J. Autism Dev. Disord.* **2010**, *40*, 1423–1430. [CrossRef]
20. Atladóttir, H.Ó.; Pedersen, M.G.; Thorsen, P.; Mortensen, P.B.; Deleuran, B.; Eaton, W.W.; Parner, E.; Sutton, R.M.; Niles, D.E.; Nysaether, J.; et al. Association of Family History of Autoimmune Diseases and Autism Spectrum Disorders. *Pediatrics* **2009**, *124*, 687–694. [CrossRef]
21. Keil, A.P.; Daniels, J.L.; Forssén, U.; Hultman, C.; Cnattingius, S.; Söderberg, K.C.; Feychting, M.; Sparén, P. Parental Autoimmune Diseases Associated With Autism Spectrum Disorders in Offspring. *Epidemiology* **2010**, *21*, 805–808. [CrossRef]
22. Vinet, E.; Pineau, C.A.; Clarke, A.; Scott, S.; Fombonne, E.; Joseph, L.; Platt, R.; Bernatsky, S. Increased Risk of Autism Spectrum Disorders in Children Born to Women With Systemic Lupus Erythematosus: Results From a Large Population-Based Cohort. *Arthritis Rheumatol.* **2015**, *67*, 3201–3208. [CrossRef]
23. Braunschweig, D.; Ashwood, P.; Krakowiak, P.; Hertz-Picciotto, I.; Hansen, R.; Croen, L.A.; Pessah, I.N.; Van De Water, J. Autism: Maternally derived antibodies specific for fetal brain proteins. *NeuroToxicology* **2007**, *29*, 226–231. [CrossRef]
24. Braunschweig, D.; Krakowiak, P.; Duncanson, P.; Boyce, R.; Hansen, R.L.; Ashwood, P.; Hertz-Picciotto, I.; Pessah, I.N.; Van De Water, J. Autism-specific maternal autoantibodies recognize critical proteins in developing brain. *Transl. Psychiatry* **2013**, *3*, e277. [CrossRef]

25. Vargas, D.L.; Nascimbene, C.; Krishnan, C.; Zimmerman, A.W.; Pardo, C.A. Neuroglial activation and neuroinflammation in the brain of patients with autism. *Ann. Neurol.* **2004**, *57*, 67–81. [CrossRef]
26. Bechter, K. CSF diagnostics in psychiatry—Present status—Future projects. *Neurol. Psychiatry Brain Res.* **2016**, *22*, 69–74. [CrossRef]
27. Endres, D.; Bechter, K.; Prüss, H.; Hasan, A.; Steiner, J.; Leypoldt, F.; Van Elst, L.T. Autoantikörper-assoziierte schizophreniforme Psychosen: Klinische Symptomatik. *Der Nervenarzt* **2019**, *90*, 547–563. [CrossRef]
28. Van Elst, L.T.; Bechter, K.; Prüss, H.; Hasan, A.; Steiner, J.; Leypoldt, F.; Endres, D. [Autoantibody-associated schizophreniform psychoses: Pathophysiology, diagnostics, and treatment]. *Der Nervenarzt* **2019**, *90*, 745–761. [CrossRef]
29. Shen, M.D. Cerebrospinal fluid and the early brain development of autism. *J. Neurodev. Disord.* **2018**, *10*, 39. [CrossRef]
30. Arbeitsgemeinschaft der Wissenschaftlichen Medizinischen Fachgesellschaften (AWMF). Autismus-Spektrum-Störungen im Kindes-, Jugend- und Erwachsenenalter. 2016. Available online: https://www.awmf.org/uploads/tx_szleitlinien/028-018l_S3_Autismus-Spektrum-Stoerungen_ASS-Diagnostik_2016-05.pdf (accessed on 15 December 2019).
31. Van Elst, L.T.; Maier, S.; Fangmeier, T.; Endres, D.; Mueller, G.T.; Nickel, K.; Ebert, D.; Lange, T.; Hennig, J.; Biscaldi, M.; et al. Disturbed cingulate glutamate metabolism in adults with high-functioning autism spectrum disorder: Evidence in support of the excitatory/inhibitory imbalance hypothesis. *Mol. Psychiatry* **2014**, *19*, 1314–1325. [CrossRef]
32. Endres, D.; Van Elst, L.T.; Meyer, S.A.; Feige, B.; Nickel, K.; Bubl, A.; Riedel, A.; Ebert, D.; Lange, T.; Glauche, V.; et al. Glutathione metabolism in the prefrontal brain of adults with high-functioning autism spectrum disorder: An MRS study. *Mol. Autism* **2017**, *8*, 10. [CrossRef]
33. Patterson, P.H. Maternal infection and immune involvement in autism. *Trends Mol. Med.* **2011**, *17*, 389–394. [CrossRef]
34. van Tebartz Elst, L.; Perlov, E. *Epilepsie und Psyche: Psychische Störungen bei Epilepsie—Epileptische Phänomene in der Psychiatrie*, 1st ed.; Kohlhammer: Stuttgart, Germany, 2013.
35. Kuzior, H.; Fiebich, B.; Yousif, N.M.; Saliba, S.W.; Ziegler, C.; Nickel, K.; Maier, S.; Süß, P.; Runge, K.; Matysik, M.; et al. Increased IL-8 Concentrations in the Cerebrospinal Fluid of Patients with Unipolar Depression. **2020**, under review.
36. Balla, A.; Endres, D.; Fiebich, B.; Stich, O.; Dersch, R.; van Tebartz Elst, L. The role of intrathecal-specific antibody synthesis against neurotropic infectious agents in patients with schizophreniform disorders. Poster-Session P-02. Poster 009. In Proceedings of the WPA XVII World Congress of Psychiatry Berlin 2017, Berlin, Germany, 8–12 October 2017.
37. Kuzior, H.; Fiebich, B.; Saliba, S.W.; Yousif, N.; Gargouri, B.; Blank, T.; Ziegler, C.; van Tebartz Elst, L.; Endres, D. Erhöhte Interleukin-8 Levels im Liquor von Patienten mit unipolaren Depressionen. In Proceedings of the Poster 012, DGPPN Congress Berlin 2018, Berlin, Germany, 28 November–1 December 2018.
38. Rush, A.J. *Handbook of Psychiatric Measures*, 1st ed.; American Psychiatric Association: Washington, DC, USA, 2000.
39. *Das AMDP-System: Manual zur Dokumentation Psychiatrischer Befunde*, 10th ed.; Hogrefe: Göttingen, Germany, 2018.
40. Endres, D.; Perlov, E.; Baumgartner, A.; Hottenrott, T.; Dersch, R.; Stich, O.; Van Elst, L.T. Immunological findings in psychotic syndromes: A tertiary care hospital's CSF sample of 180 patients. *Front. Hum. Neurosci.* **2015**, *9*, 897. [CrossRef]
41. Endres, D.; Perlov, E.; Dersch, R.; Baumgärtner, A.; Hottenrott, T.; Berger, B.; Stich, O.; Van Elst, L.T. Evidence of cerebrospinal fluid abnormalities in patients with depressive syndromes. *J. Affect. Disord.* **2016**, *198*, 178–184. [CrossRef]
42. Endres, D.; Dersch, R.; Hottenrott, T.; Perlov, E.; Maier, S.; Van Calker, D.; Hochstuhl, B.; Venhoff, N.; Stich, O.; Van Elst, L.T. Alterations in Cerebrospinal Fluid in Patients with Bipolar Syndromes. *Front. Psychol.* **2016**, *7*, 1689. [CrossRef]
43. Benjamini, Y.; Hochberg, Y. Controlling the False Discovery Rate: A Practical and Powerful Approach to Multiple Testing. *J. R. Stat. Soc. Ser. B* **1995**, *57*, 289–300. [CrossRef]

44. Hufschmidt, A.; Lücking, C.H.; Rauer, S.; Glocker, F.X. (Eds.) *Neurologie Compact: Für Klinik und Praxis*, 7th ed.; Georg Thieme Verlag: Stuttgart, Germany; New York, NY, USA, 2017.
45. Brettschneider, J.; Claus, A.; Kassubek, J.; Tumani, H. Isolated blood–cerebrospinal fluid barrier dysfunction: Prevalence and associated diseases. *J. Neurol.* **2005**, *252*, 1067–1073. [CrossRef]
46. Reiber, H.; Peter, J.B. Cerebrospinal fluid analysis: Disease-related data patterns and evaluation programs. *J. Neurol. Sci.* **2001**, *184*, 101–122. [CrossRef]
47. Asgari, M.; De Zélicourt, D.; Kurtcuoglu, V. Barrier dysfunction or drainage reduction: Differentiating causes of CSF protein increase. *Fluids Barriers CNS* **2017**, *14*, 14. [CrossRef]
48. Reiber, H. Flow rate of cerebrospinal fluid (CSF)—A concept common to normal blood-CSF barrier function and to dysfunction in neurological diseases. *J. Neurol. Sci.* **1994**, *122*, 189–203. [CrossRef]
49. Shen, M.D.; Kim, S.H.; McKinstry, R.C.; Gu, H.; Hazlett, H.C.; Nordahl, C.W.; Emerson, R.W.; Shaw, D.; Elison, J.T.; Swanson, M.R.; et al. Increased Extra-axial Cerebrospinal Fluid in High-Risk Infants Who Later Develop Autism. *Boil. Psychiatry* **2017**, *82*, 186–193. [CrossRef]
50. Keller, R.; Basta, R.; Salerno, L.; Elia, M. Autism, epilepsy, and synaptopathies: A not rare association. *Neurol. Sci.* **2017**, *38*, 1353–1361. [CrossRef]
51. O'Reilly, C.; Lewis, J.D.; Elsabbagh, M. Is functional brain connectivity atypical in autism? A systematic review of EEG and MEG studies. *PLoS ONE* **2017**, *12*, e0175870. [CrossRef]
52. Endres, D.; Maier, S.; Feige, B.; Posielski, N.A.; Nickel, K.; Ebert, D.; Riedel, A.; Philipsen, A.; Perlov, E.; Van Elst, L.T. Altered Intermittent Rhythmic Delta and Theta Activity in the Electroencephalographies of High Functioning Adult Patients with Autism Spectrum Disorder. *Front. Hum. Neurosci.* **2017**, *11*, 27. [CrossRef]
53. Najjar, S.; Pearlman, D.; Devinsky, O.; Najjar, A.; Zagzag, D. Neurovascular unit dysfunction with blood-brain barrier hyperpermeability contributes to major depressive disorder: A review of clinical and experimental evidence. *J. Neuroinflamm.* **2013**, *10*, 142. [CrossRef]
54. Hughes, H.K.; Ko, E.M.; Rose, D.; Ashwood, P. Immune Dysfunction and Autoimmunity as Pathological Mechanisms in Autism Spectrum Disorders. *Front. Cell. Neurosci.* **2018**, *12*, 405. [CrossRef]
55. Singer, H.S.; Morris, C.M.; Williams, P.N.; Yoon, D.Y.; Hong, J.J.; Zimmerman, A.W. Antibrain antibodies in children with autism and their unaffected siblings. *J. Neuroimmunol.* **2006**, *178*, 149–155. [CrossRef]
56. Piras, I.S.; Haapanen, L.; Napolioni, V.; Sacco, R.; Van De Water, J.; Persico, A.M. Anti-brain antibodies are associated with more severe cognitive and behavioral profiles in Italian children with Autism Spectrum Disorder. *Brain Behav. Immun.* **2014**, *38*, 91–99. [CrossRef]
57. Nordahl, C.W.; Braunschweig, D.; Iosif, A.-M.; Lee, A.; Rogers, S.; Ashwood, P.; Amaral, D.G.; Van De Water, J. Maternal autoantibodies are associated with abnormal brain enlargement in a subgroup of children with autism spectrum disorder. *Brain Behav. Immun.* **2013**, *30*, 61–65. [CrossRef]
58. Kaufman, D.L.; Erlander, M.G.; Clare-Salzler, M.; Atkinson, M.A.; MacLaren, N.K.; Tobin, A.J. Autoimmunity to two forms of glutamate decarboxylase in insulin-dependent diabetes mellitus. *J. Clin. Investig.* **1992**, *89*, 283–292. [CrossRef]
59. Lancaster, E.; Dalmau, J. Neuronal autoantigens–pathogenesis, associated disorders and antibody testing. *Nat. Rev. Neurol.* **2012**, *8*, 380–390. [CrossRef]
60. Chen, M.-H.; Su, T.-P.; Chen, Y.-S.; Hsu, J.-W.; Huang, K.-L.; Chang, W.-H.; Chen, T.-J.; Bai, Y.-M. Comorbidity of allergic and autoimmune diseases in patients with autism spectrum disorder: A nationwide population-based study. *Res. Autism Spectr. Disord.* **2013**, *7*, 205–212. [CrossRef]
61. Comi, A.M.; Zimmerman, A.W.; Frye, V.H.; Law, P.A.; Peeden, J.N. Familial clustering of autoimmune disorders and evaluation of medical risk factors in autism. *J. Child Neurol.* **1999**, *14*, 388–394. [CrossRef]
62. Dahm, L.; Ott, C.; Steiner, J.; Stepniak, B.; Teegen, B.; Saschenbrecker, S.; Hammer, C.; Borowski, K.; Begemann, M.; Lemke, S.; et al. Seroprevalence of autoantibodies against brain antigens in health and disease. *Ann. Neurol.* **2014**, *76*, 82–94. [CrossRef]
63. Rolandsson, O.; Hägg, E.; Hampe, C.; Sullivan, E.P., Jr.; Nilsson, M.; Jansson, G.; Hallmans, G.; Lernmark, Å. Glutamate decarboxylase (GAD65) and tyrosine phosphatase-like protein (IA-2) autoantibodies index in a regional population is related to glucose intolerance and body mass index. *Diabetologia* **1999**, *42*, 555–559. [CrossRef]
64. Connery, K.; Tippett, M.; Delhey, L.M.; Rose, S.; Slattery, J.C.; Kahler, S.G.; Hahn, J.; Kruger, U.; Cunningham, M.W.; Shimasaki, C.; et al. Intravenous immunoglobulin for the treatment of autoimmune encephalopathy in children with autism. *Transl. Psychiatry* **2018**, *8*, 148. [CrossRef]

65. Rout, U.K.; Mungan, N.K.; Dhossche, D.M. Presence of GAD65 autoantibodies in the serum of children with autism or ADHD. *Eur. Child Adolesc. Psychiatry* **2012**, *21*, 141–147. [CrossRef]
66. Kalra, S.; Burbelo, P.D.; Bayat, A.; Ching, K.H.; Thurm, A.; Iadarola, M.J.; Swedo, S.E. No evidence of antibodies against GAD65 and other specific antigens in children with autism. *BBA Clin.* **2015**, *4*, 81–84. [CrossRef]
67. Ehrenreich, H. Autoantibodies against N-methyl-d-aspartate receptor 1 in health and disease. *Curr. Opin. Neurol.* **2018**, *31*, 306–312. [CrossRef]
68. Belbezier, A.; Joubert, B.; Montero-Martin, G.; Fernandez-Vina, M.; Fabien, N.; Rogemond, V.; Mignot, E.; Honnorat, J. Multiplex family with GAD65-Abs neurologic syndromes. *Neurol. Neuroimmunol. Neuroinflamm.* **2017**, *5*, e416. [CrossRef]
69. Yip, J.; Soghomonian, J.-J.; Blatt, G.J. Decreased GAD65 mRNA levels in select subpopulations of neurons in the cerebellar dentate nuclei in autism: An in situ hybridization study. *Autism Res.* **2009**, *2*, 50–59. [CrossRef]
70. Blatt, G.J.; Fatemi, S. Alterations in GABAergic Biomarkers in the Autism Brain: Research Findings and Clinical Implications. *Anat. Rec. Adv. Integr. Anat. Evol. Boil.* **2011**, *294*, 1646–1652. [CrossRef]
71. Chau, D.K.-F.; Choi, A.Y.-T.; Yang, W.; Leung, W.N.; Chan, C.W. Downregulation of glutamatergic and GABAergic proteins in valproric acid associated social impairment during adolescence in mice. *Behav. Brain Res.* **2017**, *316*, 255–260. [CrossRef]
72. Labouesse, M.A.; Dong, E.; Grayson, D.R.; Guidotti, A.; Meyer, U. Maternal immune activation induces GAD1 and GAD2 promoter remodeling in the offspring prefrontal cortex. *Epigenetics* **2015**, *10*, 1143–1155. [CrossRef]
73. Dalakas, M.C.; Li, M.; Fujii, M.; Jacobowitz, D.M. Stiff person syndrome: Quantification, specificity, and intrathecal synthesis of GAD65 antibodies. *Neurology* **2001**, *57*, 780–784. [CrossRef]
74. Hackert, J.K.; Müller, L.; Rohde, M.; Bien, C.G.; Bien, C.G.; Kirschstein, T. Anti-GAD65 Containing Cerebrospinal Fluid Does not Alter GABAergic Transmission. *Front. Cell. Neurosci.* **2016**, *10*, 923. [CrossRef]
75. Dalakas, M.C. Advances in the pathogenesis and treatment of patients with stiff person syndrome. *Curr. Neurol. Neurosci. Rep.* **2008**, *8*, 48–55. [CrossRef]
76. Stagg, C.J.; Lang, B.; Best, J.G.; McKnight, K.; Cavey, A.; Johansen-Berg, H.; Vincent, A.; Palace, J. Autoantibodies to glutamic acid decarboxylase in patients with epilepsy are associated with low cortical GABA levels. *Epilepsia* **2010**, *51*, 1898–1901. [CrossRef]
77. Widman, G.; Golombeck, K.; Hautzel, H.; Gross, C.C.; Quesada, C.M.; Witt, J.-A.; Rota-Kops, E.; Ermert, J.; Greschus, S.; Surges, R.; et al. Treating a GAD65 Antibody-Associated Limbic Encephalitis with Basiliximab: A Case Study. *Front. Neurol.* **2015**, *6*, 167. [CrossRef]
78. Daif, A.; Lukas, R.V.; Issa, N.P.; Javed, A.; VanHaerents, S.; Reder, A.T.; Tao, J.X.; Warnke, P.; Rose, S.; Towle, V.L.; et al. Antiglutamic acid decarboxylase 65 (GAD65) antibody-associated epilepsy. *Epilepsy Behav.* **2018**, *80*, 331–336. [CrossRef]
79. Blennow, K.; Fredman, P.; Wallin, A.; Gottfries, C.-G.; Långström, G.; Svennerholm, L. Protein Analyses in Cerebrospinal Fluid. *Eur. Neurol.* **1993**, *33*, 126–128. [CrossRef]
80. Brainin, M.; Barnes, M.P.; Gilhus, N.E. (Eds.) *European Handbook of Neurological Management: Volume 1*, 2nd ed.; Wiley-Blackwell: Chichester, West Sussex, UK, 2010.
81. Castellazzi, M.; Morotti, A.; Tamborino, C.; Alessi, F.; Pilotto, S.; Baldi, E.; Caniatti, L.M.; Trentini, A.; Casetta, I.; Granieri, E.; et al. Increased age and male sex are independently associated with higher frequency of blood–cerebrospinal fluid barrier dysfunction using the albumin quotient. *Fluids Barriers CNS* **2020**, *17*, 1–9. [CrossRef]
82. Zetterberg, H.; Jakobsson, J.; Redsäter, M.; Andreasson, U.; Pålsson, E.; Ekman, C.J.; Sellgren, C.M.; Johansson, A.G.; Blennow, K.; Landen, M. Blood–cerebrospinal fluid barrier dysfunction in patients with bipolar disorder in relation to antipsychotic treatment. *Psychiatry Res.* **2014**, *217*, 143–146. [CrossRef]
83. Kirch, D.G.; Kaufmann, C.A.; Papadopoulos, N.M.; Martin, B.; Weinberger, D.R. Abnormal cerebrospinal fluid protein indices in schizophrenia. *Boil. Psychiatry* **1985**, *20*, 1039–1046. [CrossRef]
84. Axelsson, R.; Martensson, E.; Alling, C. Impairment of the Blood-Brain Barrier as an Aetiological Factor in Paranoid Psychosis. *Br. J. Psychiatry* **1982**, *141*, 273–281. [CrossRef]

85. Bauer, K.; Kornhuber, J. Blood-cerebrospinal fluid barrier in schizophrenic patients. *Eur. Arch. Psychiatry Clin. Neurosci.* **1987**, *236*, 257–259. [CrossRef]
86. Pitts, A.F.; Carroll, B.T.; Gehris, T.L.; Kathol, R.G.; Samuelson, S.D. Elevated CSF protein in male patients with depression. *Boil. Psychiatry* **1990**, *28*, 629–637. [CrossRef]

13

A Study of Single Nucleotide Polymorphisms of the *SLC19A1/RFC1* Gene in Subjects with Autism Spectrum Disorder

Naila Al Mahmuda [1,*], Shigeru Yokoyama [1], Jian-Jun Huang [1], Li Liu [1], Toshio Munesue [1], Hideo Nakatani [2], Kenshi Hayashi [3], Kunimasa Yagi [4], Masakazu Yamagishi [3] and Haruhiro Higashida [1,*]

1 Research Center for Child Mental Development, Kanazawa University, Kanazawa 920-8640, Japan; shigeruy@med.kanazawa-u.ac.jp (S.Y.); jianjun453@163.com (J.-J.H.); liuli011258@sina.com (L.L.); munesue@med.kanazawa-u.ac.jp (T.M.)

2 Division of Neuroscience, Kanazawa University Graduate School of Medical Science, Kanazawa 920-8640, Japan; nak@yd5.so-net.ne.jp

3 Division of Cardiovascular Medicine, Kanazawa University Graduate School of Medical Science, Kanazawa 920-8640, Japan; kenshi@med.kanazawa-u.ac.jp (K.H.); myamagi@med.kanazawa-u.ac.jp (M.Y.)

4 Medical Education Research Center, Kanazawa University Graduate School of Medical Science, Kanazawa 920-8640, Japan; diabe@med.kanazawa-u.ac.jp

* Correspondence: nlmahmuda@gmail.com (N.A.M.); haruhiro@med.kanazawa-u.ac.jp (H.H.)

Academic Editor: Merlin G. Butler

Abstract: Autism Spectrum Disorder (ASD) is a group of neurodevelopmental disorders with complex genetic etiology. Recent studies have indicated that children with ASD may have altered folate or methionine metabolism, suggesting that the folate–methionine cycle may play a key role in the etiology of ASD. *SLC19A1*, also referred to as reduced folate carrier 1 (*RFC1*), is a member of the solute carrier group of transporters and is one of the key enzymes in the folate metabolism pathway. Findings from multiple genomic screens suggest the presence of an autism susceptibility locus on chromosome 21q22.3, which includes *SLC19A1*. Therefore, we performed a case-control study in a Japanese population. In this study, DNA samples obtained from 147 ASD patients at the Kanazawa University Hospital in Japan and 150 unrelated healthy Japanese volunteers were examined by the sequence-specific primer-polymerase chain reaction method pooled with fluorescence correlation spectroscopy. $p < 0.05$ was considered to represent a statistically significant outcome. Of 13 single nucleotide polymorphisms (SNPs) examined, a significant p-value was obtained for AA genotype of one SNP (*rs1023159*, OR = 0.39, 95% CI = 0.16–0.91, $p = 0.0394$; Fisher's exact test). Despite some conflicting results, our findings supported a role for the polymorphism *rs1023159* of the *SLC19A1* gene, alone or in combination, as a risk factor for ASD. However, the findings were not consistent after multiple testing corrections. In conclusion, although our results supported a role of the *SLC19A1* gene in the etiology of ASD, it was not a significant risk factor for the ASD samples analyzed in this study.

Keywords: autism spectrum disorder; reduced folate carrier; single nucleotide polymorphism

---

1. Introduction

Autism spectrum disorder (ASD) is a devastating neurodevelopmental disorder with a complex biological basis and is thought to involve multiple and variable gene–environment interactions. ASD is characterized by social impairments, communication problems, and restricted repetitive behaviors [1].

Most candidate genes currently implicated in ASD are involved in neurodevelopmental pathways, social-emotional behavior, or sex or neuropeptide hormonal signaling [2].

The *SLC19A1* gene on human chromosome 21q22.3 [3] encodes one of the key enzymes in the folate metabolism pathway. *SLC19A1*, also referred to as reduced folate carrier 1 (RFC1), functions as a bidirectional anion exchanger, accepting folate cofactors and exporting various organic anions. *SLC19A1* has five exons that contain the total open reading frame (ORF) [4–6]. The ORF of human *SLC19A1* cDNA encodes a protein with 12 transmembrane domains and a single *N*-glycosylation site [3,7–9]. *SLC19A1* mRNA is detectable in all human tissues [10].

Recent studies indicated that children with ASD may have changed folate or methionine metabolism, suggesting that the folate–methionine cycle may play an important role in the etiology of ASD [11]. Many important genes, including *SLC19A1*, are involved in the folate metabolism pathway and their roles in human diseases, such as gastric and esophageal cancers, have been studied in depth [12,13]. A marginal association with ASD was identified for a 19-bp deletion in the dihydrofolate reductase (*DHFR*) gene (odds ratio (OR): 2.69; 95% CI: 1.00–7.28; $p < 0.05$), which is involved in folate metabolism [14]. Common variants of the decreased folate carrier (*RFC*) and methylene tetrahydrofolate reductase (*MTHFR*) genes conferred increased susceptibility to ASD, suggesting a potential etiological role of impaired folate-dependent one-carbon metabolism in susceptibility to ASD [15].

However, the findings for genes involved in folate transport have been inconsistent between reports. Although the largest study to date found an important association between the *SLC19A1* gene and ASD [15], a subsequent study failed to replicate this finding [16]. Other studies have not identified any mutations in genes included in folate transport in ASD populations [17–19].

Here, we hypothesized that genetic variants in *SLC19A1* may play a role in the pathways that are altered in ASD and can therefore be considered candidate genes for testing in ASD patients. We performed a case-control study of 13 genetic variations to assess the involvement of *SLC19A1* in ASD. The study was performed in a Japanese population, in which genetic variants of *CD38* and *BST-1/CD157* were reported to be associated with increased risk of ASD [20,21].

2. Results

Thirteen SNPs were analyzed in this study, five of which (*rs914232*, *rs3788205*, *rs1023159*, *rs944423*, and *rs9979087*) were located in the *SLC19A1* gene region; these were subjected to statistical analysis. The eight other SNPs (*rs1888533*, *rs11700708*, *rs12627639*, *rs2838965*, *rs6518253*, *rs9974061*, *rs9980967*, and *rs2838968*) were located in the adjacent region. Two SNPs (*rs9980967*, *rs9979087*) were excluded due to insufficient genotyping data. However, there were no significant associations between any of these SNPs and ASD, with the exception of *rs1023159*. As the results suggested a role ($p = 0.0394$; Table 1) of this polymorphism alone or in combination with others as a risk factor for ASD, this SNP was subjected to further analysis. No association was found after multiple testing corrections. Tests of Hardy–Weinberg equilibrium deviations were performed for each marker in two groups of case and control individuals, and polymorphisms showed evidence of deviation from Hardy–Weinberg equilibrium. The genotyping rate was above 95%. LD analysis of these SNPs identified three haplotype blocks, one of which (Block 1; Figure 1) consisted of two SNPs including one (*rs1023159*) with the lowest *p*-value ($p = 0.0394$; Table 1) among those analyzed.

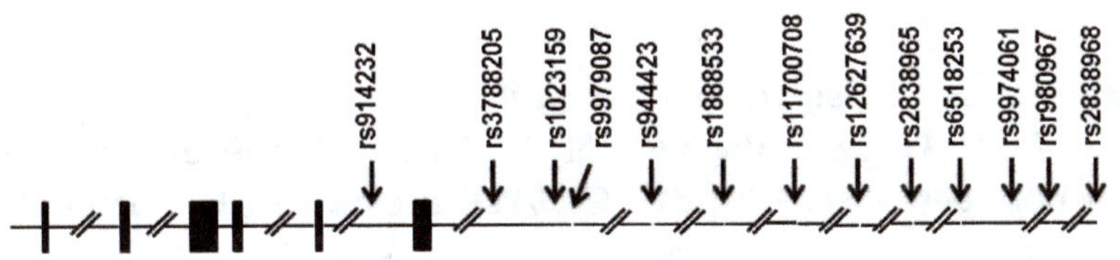

(A)

Figure 1. *Cont.*

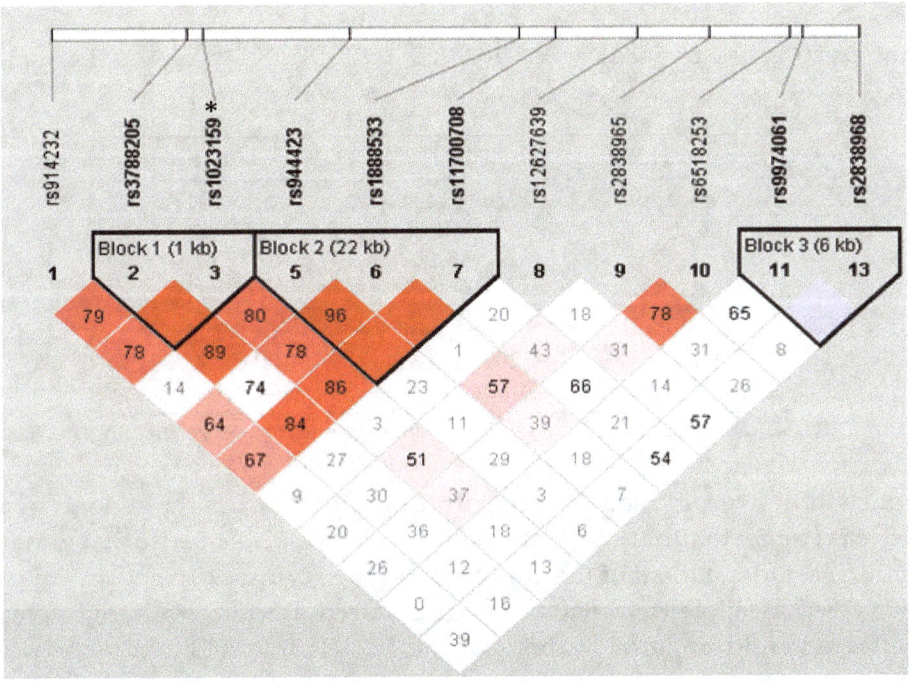

(B)

Figure 1. The genomic structure of *SLC19A1* (**A**). Bars, exons. Arrows, positions of single nucleotide polymorphisms (SNPs). Linkage disequilibrium plot of SNPs in the samples studied (**B**). Numbers in squares indicate D' values. Reference Number (rs) with asterisk indicates the SNP with $p < 0.05$. The blocks are defined following the four-gamete rule [22]. Explanation of color scheme: If $D' < 1$ and LOD (log of the likelihood odds ratio) <2, the cell color is white; if $D' = 1$ and LOD < 2, the cell color is blue; if $D' < 1$ and LOD $\geqslant 2$, the cell color is shades of pink/red; if $D' = 1$ and LOD $\geqslant 2$, the cell color is bright red.

Table 1. Genotype and allele frequencies of *rs1023159* at Kanazawa University Hospital for autism spectrum disorder (ASD).

rs1023159	Cases	Control	Odds Ratio (95% CI)	*p*
Genotype	(n = 144)	(n = 146)		
G/G	72 (50.0%)	62 (42.5%)	Reference	
A/G	63 (43.8%)	64 (43.8%)	0.85 (0.52–1.4)	0.5368
A/A	9 (6.3%)	20 (13.7%)	0.39 (**0.16–0.91**)	0.0394
Allele	(n = 288)	(n = 292)		
G	207 (71.9%)	188 (64.4%)	Reference	
A	81 (28.1%)	104 (35.6%)	0.71 (0.50–1.0)	0.0613

CI, confidence interval; *p*-values obtained by Fisher's exact test are given; $p < 0.05$ is indicated in bold.

3. Discussion

In this population-based case-control study, we investigated the relationship between polymorphisms in the *SLC19A1* gene and risk of ASD in a Japanese population. We identified no significant associations between SNPs of the *SLC19A1* gene and ASD, with the exception of one SNP, although the results eventually did not support a role of the SLC19A1 gene in the etiology of ASD in our sample.

We have also calculated the genotype and allele frequencies of *rs1023159* in Autism Genome Resources Exchange (AGRE) samples (Table 2). The frequency (15.5%) of the AA genotype in AGRE group of ASD cases, although with different ethnicity, was similar to the frequency (13.7%) observed in the group of Japanese controls.

Table 2. Genotype and allele frequencies of *rs1023159* in KU samples and AGRE samples for autism spectrum disorder (ASD).

rs1023159	KU	AGRE
Genotype	(n = 144)	(n = 191)
G/G	72 (50.0%)	63 (31.4%)
A/G	63 (43.8%)	104 (53.1%)
A/A	9 (6.3%)	30 (15.5%)
Allele	(n = 288)	(n = 394)
G	207 (71.9%)	230 (58.4%)
A	81 (28.1%)	164 (41.6%)

KU, Kanazawa University; AGRE, Autism Genome Resources Exchange.

Recent genetic studies recognized the contribution of the *SLC19A1* gene to neural tube defects (NTD) [23–28]. It was suggested that the maternal G allele may be a causative genetic risk factor for having a child with ASD independent of the child's genotype [29]. In case-control analysis, a significant increase in the *SLC19A1* G allele frequency was discovered among mothers of children with ASD, but not among affected children, and analysis of the *SLC19A1* A80G genotype within family trios discovered that the maternal G allele was allied with a significant increase in risk of ASD, whereas the inherited genotype of the children was not [29].

Evidence indicates that expression of *SLC19A1* in the intestine is subject to adaptive regulation in response to folate status [30]. Folic acid is the inactive, oxidized form of folate compounds that is important for many physiological systems of the body. Folate is the major one-carbon donor for *de novo* nucleotide synthesis for DNA replication and also for remethylation of homocysteine to methionine for essential methylation reactions [29]. The folate cycle interacts with the methionine cycle as well as the tetrahydrobiopterin construction and salvage pathways. Insufficiencies in folate can lead to anomalies in these pathways [31]. The methionine cycle is important for DNA methylation [15], a process that is important in regulating gene expression. Folate deficiency during various significant stages of fetal and infantile development upsets structural and functional alteration of the brain [32].

The reduced folate carrier is the principal mechanism by which folates and antifolates are delivered to mammalian cells and tissues [33]. As folate transport across cell membranes is mediated in part by the RFC, variants within this gene may affect the disease risk via an effect on folate and/or homocysteine levels [34]. Low levels of RFC could result in a number of pathophysiological states associated with folate deficiency, including cardiovascular disease, fetal anomalies, and neurological disorders [33]. Moretti *et al.* reported a 6-year-old girl with developmental delay, psychomotor regression, seizures, mental retardation, and autistic features associated with low cerebrospinal fluid (CSF) levels of 5-methyltetrahydrofolate, the biologically active form of folate in the CSF and blood [35]. Several studies reported considerably low CSF folate concentrations together with normal serum folate concentrations in children with autism [18,19,35–37].

SLC19A1 is situated on the CSF side of the choroid plexus, where it enables transport of concentrated folate into the CSF [11]. Taken together, variation in *SLC19A1* expression may involve both neuronal structures and metabolism in the Central Nervous System (CNS). Defective transport of folate into the CNS is related to cerebral folate deficiency (CFD), a neurological disorder that is important in diagnosis of children with unexplained neurodevelopmental symptoms, which suggests the possible involvement of the folate-methionine pathway in ASD [31]. Further, early-onset low-functioning autism with neurological deficits has been suggested as a characteristic of children with both autism and CFD [18,19,35,38].

The major limitation of this study was the small sample size, resulting in deviation from Hardy–Weinberg equilibrium and limited power (68%) to reliably detect the role of *SLC19A1* in ASD. We did not recognize any population stratification, admixture, and cryptic relation among the subjects in the present study, which may have contributed to the lack of association in this small sample. Another limitation was the lack of a replication cohort. Further studies with larger sample sizes and/or family-based association testing are needed to clarify the precise role of this gene in ASD. However, our findings were consistent with reports that *SLC19A1* may not contribute to genetic susceptibility to ASD in some populations.

4. Materials and Methods

4.1. Study Population

The study population consisted of 147 ASD subjects (113 males, 34 females; 15.6 $\pm$ 0.6 years old, mean $\pm$ s.e.m.) from the Outpatient Psychiatry Department of Kanazawa University Hospital, as described previously [20,39]. All subjects satisfied the Diagnostic and Statistical Mannual of Mental Disorders-IV (DSM-IV) criteria for pervasive developmental ailment and Childhood Autism Rating Scale. Two experienced child psychiatrists established the diagnosis of ASD in all patients based on semi-structured behavioral observations and conversations with the subjects and their parents. The interview structure and clinical records were described previously [20]. One of the following methods was used as an aid to evaluate the autism-specific behaviors and symptoms during interviews with parents: the Asperger Syndrome Diagnostic Interview [40], Autism Diagnostic Interview-Revised (ADI-R) [41], Pervasive Developmental Disorders Autism Society Japan Rating Scale [42], Diagnostic Interview for Social and Communication Disorders [43], or Tokyo Autistic Behavior Scale [44]. A total of 150 individuals were recruited as controls (115 males, 35 females; 23.8 $\pm$ 0.3 years old). All patients and controls were Japanese with no non-Japanese parents or grandparents. These controls were part of a stock used frequently for single nucleotide polymorphism (SNP) analysis of ion channels related to arrhythmia at Kanazawa University Heart Center. This study was approved by the ethics committee of Kanazawa University School of Medicine (July 2015), and all participants and/or their caregivers provided informed consent. The study protocol was performed in accordance with the Declaration of Helsinki.

4.2. Genotyping

Genomic DNA was extracted as described previously [39] from venous blood samples using a commercial kit (Wizard Genomic DNA Purification kit; Promega, Madison, WI, USA) or from nails using an ISOHAIR DNA extraction kit (Nippon Gene, Tokyo, Japan). The genomic DNA samples were subjected to whole-genome amplification, and SNPs were determined by the sequence-specific primer-polymerase chain reaction (SSP-PCR) method followed by fluorescence correlation spectroscopy as described by Bannai *et al.* [45]. We selected a set of tagging SNPs that capture common variations and linkage disequilibrium (LD) structures across the *SLC19A1* gene using the Tagger program incorporated with Haploview v4.2 software(Broad Institute of MIT and Harvard, Cambridge, MA, USA). The data source for tagging SNPs was the dbSNP database [46] and the HapMap genome browser, release 27 (operated by the National Institutes of Health (NIH), Bethesda, MD, USA) in the

JPT (Japanese individuals from Tokyo, Japan), CHB (Han Chinese individuals from Beijing, China), ASW (African ancestry in Southwest USA), and CEU (Utah residents of northern and western European ancestry) populations. Selection of tagging SNPs was based on pairwise tagging only and the minor allele frequency was ⩾5% in any one of the different ethnicities.

4.3. Statistical Analysis

Genotype and allele frequencies were examined using a contingency table and Fisher's exact test (GraphPad Prism 6; GraphPad Software, San Diego, CA, USA), and $p < 0.05$ was taken to indicate statistical significance. We also used the method of Nyholt [47], which estimates an "effective number" of independent tests and then adjusts the smallest observed p-value using simulation based on this number of tests. In our samples, the estimated effective number for independent tests was 9 and the p-value was 0.005. The observed genotype frequency distributions were compared with those expected from the Hardy–Weinberg equilibrium and analyzed by the chi "χ" squared test.

Statistical power was calculated using the Genetic Power Calculator [48,49] assuming a population prevalence of 0.015 for ASD [50], and a D' value of 1 between the marker and disease with a false positive rate of 5%.

5. Conclusions

This study showed no evidence supporting a role of the *SLC19A1* gene in the etiology of ASD. The ethnic and cultural background may have influenced the results of our study. However, these findings warrant additional discussion and confirmation in subsequent studies. Further cellular and molecular studies are required to elucidate the precise role of this gene in ASD.

Acknowledgments: We acknowledge financial support from the Strategic Research Program for Brain Sciences from the Japan Agency for Medical Research and Development and Grants-in-Aid for Scientific Research (24590375 and 25461335) from the Japan Society for Promotion of Sciences. We thank AGRE for their cooperation.

Author Contributions: Haruhiro Higashida, Shigeru Yokoyama, Jian-Jun Huang and Li Liu conceived and designed the research. Shigeru Yokoyama and Naila Al Mahmuda performed experiments and analyzed data. Toshio Munesue, Kenshi Hayashi, Kunimasa Yagi, Masakazu Yamagishi and Hideo Nakatani contributed participant recruitment, clinical assessment and sample collections. Naila Al Mahmuda prepared the initial draft; and Shigeru Yokoyama, Naila Al Mahmuda, and Haruhiro Higashida revised the manuscript. All authors reviewed the final manuscript and approved its publication.

References

1. American Psychiatric Association. *Diagnostic and Statistical Mannual of Mental Disorders (DSM-V)*, 5th ed.; American Psychiatric Pub.: Washington, DC, USA, 2013.
2. Chakrabarti, B.; Dudbridge, F.; Kent, L.; Wheelwright, S.; Hill-Cawthorne, G.; Allison, C.; Banerjee-Basu, S.; Baron-Cohen, S. Genes related to sex steroids, neural growth, and social–emotional behavior are associated with autistic traits, empathy, and Asperger syndrome. *Autism Res.* **2009**, *2*, 157–177. [CrossRef] [PubMed]
3. Moscow, J.A.; Gong, M.; He, R.; Sgagias, M.K.; Dixon, K.H.; Anzick, S.L.; Meltzer, P.S.; Cowan, K.H. Isolation of a gene encoding a human reduced folate carrier (RFC1) and analysis of its expression in transport-deficient, methotrexate-resistant human breast cancer cells. *Cancer Res.* **1995**, *55*, 3790–3794. [PubMed]
4. Tolner, B.; Roy, K.; Sirotnak, F.M. Structural analysis of the human RFC-1 gene encoding a folate transporter reveals multiple promoters and alternatively spliced transcripts with 5′ end heterogeneity. *Gene* **1998**, *211*, 331–341. [CrossRef]
5. Williams, F.M.; Flintoff, W.F. Structural organization of the human reduced folate carrier gene: Evidence for 5′ heterogeneity in lymphoblast mRNA. *Somat. Cell Mol. Genet.* **1998**, *24*, 143–156. [CrossRef] [PubMed]
6. Zhang, L.; Wong, S.C.; Matherly, L.H. Structure and organization of the human reduced folate carrier gene1. *Biochim. Biophys. Acta* **1998**, *1442*, 389–393. [CrossRef]
7. Prasad, P.D.; Ramamoorthy, S.; Leibach, F.H.; Ganapathy, V. Molecular Cloning of the Human Placental Folate Transporter. *Biochem. Biophys. Res. Commun.* **1995**, *206*, 681–687. [CrossRef] [PubMed]

8. Williams, F.M.R.; Flintoff, W.F. Isolation of a Human cDNA that Complements a Mutant Hamster Cell Defective in Methotrexate Uptake. *J. Biol. Chem.* **1995**, *270*, 2987–2992. [PubMed]
9. Wong, S.C.; Proefke, S.A.; Bhushan, A.; Matherly, L.H. Isolation of human cDNAs that restore methotrexate sensitivity and reduced folate carrier activity in methotrexate transport-defective Chinese Hamster ovary cells. *J. Biol. Chem.* **1995**, *270*, 17468–17475. [CrossRef] [PubMed]
10. Ganapathy, V.; Smith, S.; Prasad, P. SLC19: The folate/thiamine transporter family. *Pflugers Arch.* **2004**, *447*, 641–646. [CrossRef] [PubMed]
11. Main, P.A.; Angley, M.T.; Thomas, P.; O'Doherty, C.E.; Fenech, M. Folate and methionine metabolism in autism: A systematic review. *Am. J. Clin. Nutr.* **2010**, *91*, 1598–1620. [CrossRef] [PubMed]
12. Wang, L.; Chen, W.; Wang, J.; Tan, Y.; Zhou, Y.; Ding, W.; Hua, Z.; Shen, J.; Xu, Y.; Shen, H. Reduced folate carrier gene G80A polymorphism is associated with an increased risk of gastroesophageal cancers in a Chinese population. *Eur. J. Cancer* **2006**, *42*, 3206–3211. [CrossRef] [PubMed]
13. Zhang, Z.; Xu, Y.; Zhou, J.; Wang, X.; Wang, L.; Hu, X.; Guo, J.; Wei, Q.; Shen, H. Polymorphisms of thymidylate synthase in the 5′- and 3′-untranslated regions associated with risk of gastric cancer in South China: A case-control analysis. *Carcinogenesis* **2005**, *26*, 1764–1769. [CrossRef] [PubMed]
14. Adams, M.; Lucock, M.; Stuart, J.; Fardell, S.; Baker, K.; Ng, X. Preliminary evidence for involvement of the folate gene polymorphism 19 bp deletion-DHFR in occurrence of autism. *Neurosci. Lett.* **2007**, *422*, 24–29. [CrossRef] [PubMed]
15. James, S.J.; Melnyk, S.; Jernigan, S.; Cleves, M.A.; Halsted, C.H.; Wong, D.H.; Cutler, P.; Bock, K.; Boris, M.; Bradstreet, J.J.; *et al.* Metabolic endophenotype and related genotypes are associated with oxidative stress in children with autism. *Am. J. Med. Genet. B Neuropsychiatr. Genet.* **2006**, *141B*, 947–956. [CrossRef] [PubMed]
16. Paşca, S.P.; Nemeş, B.; Vlase, L.; Gagyi, C.E.; Dronca, E.; Miu, A.C.; Dronca, M. High levels of homocysteine and low serum paraoxonase 1 arylesterase activity in children with autism. *Life Sci.* **2006**, *78*, 2244–2248. [CrossRef] [PubMed]
17. Gordon, N. Cerebral folate deficiency. *Dev. Med. Child Neurol.* **2009**, *51*, 180–182. [CrossRef] [PubMed]
18. Moretti, P.; Peters, S.U.; del Gaudio, D.; Sahoo, T.; Hyland, K.; Bottiglieri, T.; Hopkin, R.J.; Peach, E.; Min, S.H.; Goldman, D.; *et al.* Brief Report: Autistic Symptoms, Developmental Regression, Mental Retardation, Epilepsy, and Dyskinesias in CNS Folate Deficiency. *J. Autism Dev. Disord.* **2008**, *38*, 1170–1177. [CrossRef] [PubMed]
19. Ramaekers, V.T.; Blau, N.; Sequeira, J.M.; Nassogne, M.C.; Quadros, E.V. Folate receptor autoimmunity and cerebral folate deficiency in low-functioning autism with neurological deficits. *Neuropediatrics* **2007**, *38*, 276–281. [CrossRef] [PubMed]
20. Munesue, T.; Yokoyama, S.; Nakamura, K.; Anitha, A.; Yamada, K.; Hayashi, K.; Asaka, T.; Liu, H.-X.; Jin, D.; Koizumi, K.; *et al.* Two genetic variants of CD38 in subjects with autism spectrum disorder and controls. *Neurosci. Res.* **2010**, *67*, 181–191. [CrossRef] [PubMed]
21. Yokoyama, S.; Al Mahmuda, N.; Munesue, T.; Hayashi, K.; Yagi, K.; Yamagishi, M.; Higashida, H. Association Study between the CD157/BST1 Gene and Autism Spectrum Disorders in a Japanese Population. *Brain Sci.* **2015**, *5*, 188–200. [CrossRef] [PubMed]
22. Wang, N.; Akey, J.M.; Zhang, K.; Chakraborty, R.; Jin, L. Distribution of recombination crossovers and the origin of haplotype blocks: The interplay of population history, recombination, and mutation. *Am. J. Hum. Genet.* **2002**, *71*, 1227–1234. [CrossRef] [PubMed]
23. O'Leary, V.B.; Pangilinan, F.; Cox, C.; Parle-McDermott, A.; Conley, M.; Molloy, A.M.; Kirke, P.N.; Mills, J.L.; Brody, L.C.; Scott, J.M. Reduced folate carrier polymorphisms and neural tube defect risk. *Mol. Genet. Metab.* **2006**, *87*, 364–369. [CrossRef] [PubMed]
24. Pei, L.J.; Li, Z.W.; Zhang, W.; Ren, A.G.; Zhu, H.P.; Hao, L.; Zhu, J.H.; Li, Z. Epidemiological study on reduced folate carrier gene (RFC1 A80G) polymorphism and other risk factors of neural tube defects. *J. Peking Univ. Health Sci.* **2005**, *37*, 341–345.
25. Pei, L.J.; Zhu, H.P.; Li, Z.W.; Zhang, W.; Ren, A.G.; Zhu, J.H.; Li, Z. Interaction between maternal periconceptional supplementation of folic acid and reduced folate carrier gene polymorphism of neural tube defects. *Chin. J. Med. Genet.* **2005**, *22*, 284–287.
26. Zhang, T.; Lou, J.; Zhong, R.; Wu, J.; Zou, L.; Sun, Y.; Lu, X.; Liu, L.; Miao, X.; Xiong, G. Genetic variants in the folate pathway and the risk of neural tube defects: A meta-analysis of the published literature. *PLoS ONE* **2013**, *8*, e59570. [CrossRef] [PubMed]

27. Shang, Y.; Zhao, H.; Niu, B.; Li, W.I.; Zhou, R.; Zhang, T.; Xie, J. Correlation of polymorphism of *MTHFRs* and *RFC-1* genes with neural tube defects in China. *Birth Defects Res. A Clin. Mol. Teratol.* **2008**, *82*, 3–7. [CrossRef] [PubMed]
28. De Marco, P.; Calevo, M.G.; Moroni, A.; Merello, E.; Raso, A.; Finnell, R.H.; Zhu, H.; Andreussi, L.; Cama, A.; Capra, V. Reduced folate carrier polymorphism (80A→G) and neural tube defects. *Eur. J. Hum. Genet.* **2003**, *11*, 245–252. [CrossRef] [PubMed]
29. James, S.J.; Melnyk, S.; Jernigan, S.; Lehman, S.; Seidel, L.; Gaylor, D.W.; Cleves, M.A. A functional polymorphism in the reduced folate carrier gene and DNA hypomethylation in mothers of children with autism. *Am. J. Med. Genet. B Neuropsychiatr. Genet.* **2010**, *153B*, 1209–1220. [CrossRef] [PubMed]
30. Said, H.M.; Chatterjee, N.; Haq, R.U.; Subramanian, V.S.; Ortiz, A.; Matherly, L.H.; Sirotnak, F.M.; Halsted, C.; Rubin, S.A. Adaptive regulation of intestinal folate uptake: Effect of dietary folate deficiency. *Am. J. Physiol. Cell Physiol.* **2000**, *279*, C1889–C1895. [PubMed]
31. Frye, R.E.; Rossignol, D.A. Cerebral Folate Deficiency in Autism Spectrum Disorders. *Autism Sci. Dig. J. Autsmone* **2011**. Available online: http://www.autismone.org/content/cerebral-folate-deficiency-autism-spectrum-disorders-richard-frye-md-phd-and-daniel-rossigno (accessed on 19 May 2016).
32. Ramaekers, V.; Sequeira, J.M.; Quadros, E.V. Clinical recognition and aspects of the cerebral folate deficiency syndromes. *Clin. Chem. Lab. Med.* **2013**, *51*, 497–511. [CrossRef] [PubMed]
33. Matherly, L.; Hou, Z.; Deng, Y. Human reduced folate carrier: Translation of basic biology to cancer etiology and therapy. *Cancer Metastasis Rev.* **2007**, *26*, 111–128. [CrossRef] [PubMed]
34. Stanislawska-Sachadyn, A.; Mitchell, L.E.; Woodside, J.V.; Buckley, P.T.; Kealey, C.; Young, I.S.; Scott, J.M.; Murray, L.; Boreham, C.A.; McNulty, H.; *et al.* The reduced folate carrier (*SLC19A1*) c.80G>A polymorphism is associated with red cell folate concentrations among women. *Ann. Hum. Genet.* **2009**, *73 Pt 5*, 484–491.[CrossRef] [PubMed]
35. Moretti, P.; Sahoo, T.; Hyland, K.; Bottiglieri, T.; Peters, S.; del Gaudio, D.; Roa, B.; Curry, S.; Zhu, H.; Finnell, R.H.; *et al.* Cerebral folate deficiency with developmental delay, autism, and response to folinic acid. *Neurology* **2005**, *64*, 1088–1090. [CrossRef] [PubMed]
36. Lowe, T.L.; Cohen, D.J.; Miller, S.; Young, J.G. Folic acid and B12 in autism and neuropsychiatric disturbances of childhood. *J. Am. Acad. Child Psychiatry* **1981**, *20*, 104–111. [CrossRef]
37. Ramaekers, V.T.; Rothenberg, S.P.; Sequeira, J.M.; Opladen, T.; Blau, N.; Quadros, E.V.; Selhub, J. Autoantibodies to folate receptors in the cerebral folate deficiency syndrome. *N. Eng. J. Med.* **2005**, *352*, 1985–1991. [CrossRef] [PubMed]
38. Ramaekers, V.T.; Sequeira, J.M.; Blau, N.; Quadros, E.V. A milk-free diet downregulates folate receptor autoimmunity in cerebral folate deficiency syndrome. *Dev. Med. Child Neurol.* **2008**, *50*, 346–352. [CrossRef] [PubMed]
39. Ma, W.-J.; Hashii, M.; Munesue, T.; Hayashi, K.; Yagi, K.; Yamagishi, M.; Higashida, H.; Yokoyama, S. Non-synonymous single-nucleotide variations of the human oxytocin receptor gene and autism spectrum disorders: A case-control study in a Japanese population and functional analysis. *Mol. Autism* **2013**, *4*, 22. [CrossRef] [PubMed]
40. Gillberg, C.; Gillberg, C.; Råstam, M.; Wentz, E. The Asperger Syndrome (and High-Functioning Autism) Diagnostic Interview (ASDI): A Preliminary Study of a New Structured Clinical Interview. *Autism* **2001**, *5*, 57–66. [CrossRef] [PubMed]
41. Lord, C.; Rutter, M.; le Couteur, A. Autism Diagnostic Interview-Revised: A revised version of a diagnostic interview for caregivers of individuals with possible pervasive developmental disorders. *J. Autism Dev. Disord.* **1994**, *24*, 659–685. [CrossRef] [PubMed]
42. Autism Society Japan. *Pervasive Developmental Disorders Autism Society Japan Rating Scale (PARS)*; Spectrum Publishing Company: Tokyo, Japan, 2006.
43. Wing, L.; Leekam, S.R.; Libby, S.J.; Gould, J.; Larcombe, M. The diagnostic interview for social and communication disorders: Background, inter-rater reliability and clinical use. *J. Child Psychol. Psychiatry* **2002**, *43*, 307–325. [CrossRef] [PubMed]
44. Kurita, H.; Miyake, Y. The Reliability and Validity of the Tokyo Autistic Behaviour Scale. *Psychiatry Clin. Neurosci.* **1990**, *44*, 25–32. [CrossRef]

45. Nishida, N.; Tanabe, T.; Takasu, M.; Suyama, A.; Tokunaga, K. Further development of multiplex single nucleotide polymorphism typing method, the DigiTag2 assay. *Anal. Biochem.* **2007**, *364*, 78–85. [CrossRef] [PubMed]
46. dbSNP: Short Genetic Variations. Available online: http://www.ncbi.nlm.nih.gov/SNP/ (accessed on 24 June 2015).
47. Nyholt, D.R. A simple correction for multiple testing for SNPs in linkage disequilibrium with each other. *Am. J. Hum. Genet.* **2004**, *74*, 765–769. [CrossRef] [PubMed]
48. Purcell, S.; Cherny, S.S.; Sham, P.C. Genetic power calculator: Design of linkage and association genetic mapping studies of complex traits. *Bioinformatics (Oxf. Engl.)* **2003**, *19*, 149–150. [CrossRef]
49. Genetic Power Calculator. Available online: http://pngu.mgh.harvard.edu/purcell/gpc/cc2.html (accessed on 27 June 2015).
50. Developmental Disabilities Monitoring Network Surveillance Year 2010 Principal Investigators; Centers for Disease Control and Prevention (CDC). Prevalence of autism spectrum disorder among children aged 8 years—Autism and developmental disabilities monitoring network, 11 sites, United States, 2010. *MMWR Surveill. Summ.* **2014**, *63*, 1–21.

14

Association between *IRS1* Gene Polymorphism and Autism Spectrum Disorder: A Pilot Case-Control Study in Korean Males

Hae Jeong Park [1], Su Kang Kim [1], Won Sub Kang [2], Jin Kyung Park [2], Young Jong Kim [2], Min Nam [3], Jong Woo Kim [2] and Joo-Ho Chung [1,*]

1 Kohwang Medical Research Institute, School of Medicine, Kyung Hee University, Seoul 02447, Korea; hjpark17@gmail.com (H.J.P.); skkim7@khu.ac.kr (S.K.K.)
2 Department of Neuropsychiatry, School of Medicine, Kyung Hee University, Seoul 02447, Korea; menuhin@hanmail.net (W.S.K.); parkdawit@naver.com (J.K.P.); jimmypage@nate.com (Y.J.K.); psyjong@gmail.com (J.W.K.)
3 Seoul Metropolitan Eunpyeong Hospital, Seoul 06801, Korea; passion17@hanmail.net
* Correspondence: jhchung@khu.ac.kr

Academic Editors: Merlin G. Butler and Katalin Prokai-Tatrai

Abstract: The insulin-like growth factor (IGF) pathway is thought to play an important role in brain development. Altered levels of IGFs and their signaling regulators have been shown in autism spectrum disorder (ASD) patients. In this study, we investigated whether coding region single-nucleotide polymorphisms (cSNPs) of the insulin receptor substrates (*IRS1* and *IRS2*), key mediators of the IGF pathway, were associated with ASD in Korean males. Two cSNPs (rs1801123 of *IRS1*, and rs4773092 of *IRS2*) were genotyped using direct sequencing in 180 male ASD patients and 147 male control subjects. A significant association between rs1801123 of *IRS1* and ASD was shown in additive ($p = 0.022$, odds ratio (OR) = 0.66, 95% confidence interval (CI) = 0.46–0.95) and dominant models ($p = 0.013$, OR = 0.57, 95% CI = 0.37–0.89). Allele frequency analysis also showed an association between rs1801123 and ASD ($p = 0.022$, OR = 0.66, 95% CI = 0.46–0.94). These results suggest that *IRS1* may contribute to the susceptibility of ASD in Korean males.

Keywords: autism spectrum disorder; insulin receptor substrate; single nucleotide polymorphism; insulin-like growth factor

1. Introduction

Autism spectrum disorder (ASD) is a neurodevelopmental disorder characterized by deficits in social communication, impaired reciprocal social interaction, and repetitive patterns of behaviors or interests [1]. ASD has been reported to occur in approximately six out of 1000 births, affecting males and females in a ratio of 4:1 [2]. ASD has been found throughout the world across all racial, ethnic and social backgrounds. Although the cause of ASD remains elusive, accumulating evidence suggests that genetic factors play a prominent role in this disease. Heritability is estimated to be above 90% [3]. Inherited copy number variations (CNVs) and chromosomal abnormalities have shown to contribute to genetic vulnerability to ASD [4,5]. In addition, recent multiple genome-wide association studies suggest several common single-nucleotide polymorphisms (SNPs) as markers of ASD [6–8].

Previous studies have revealed the importance of the insulin-like growth factor (IGF) pathway in the development and maintenance of the central nervous system (CNS). During both development and adulthood, increased IGF1 and IGF2 levels were associated with increased neuronal complexity and impaired learning, suggested that IGFs support the activity-dependent neuronal plasticity underlying cognitive processes [9,10]. Moreover, recent studies have highlighted a significant role for IGF1 in complex social interactions [11,12]. It has been reported that levels of IGF1, IGF2, and IGF binding protein 3 (IGFBP3) were significantly increased in patients with ASD [13]. Furthermore, both cross-sectional and longitudinal studies have reported that a subset of ASD patients show age-dependent brain overgrowth [14,15]. Brain overgrowth at an early age could be caused by conditional overexpression of IGF1 in the brain, which is responsible for significant increases in brain volume during the embryonic and early postnatal period [16]. Indeed, the significant correlation between head circumference and IGF1 levels was also shown in ASD patients, but not in the controls [13]. On the other hand, other studies reported lower IGF1 levels in the cerebrospinal fluid (CSF) of autistic patients [17,18]. In addition, it was proposed that a reduced peripartum level of IGF1 due to genetic, epigenetic, or environmental factors may be a sentinel biomarker of increased probability of the later development of autism [19].

Although little is known about the biological function of the IGF pathway molecules in ASD, given the previous reports, we speculated that IGFs and their signaling regulator genes might be candidate genes involved in ASD. However, to our knowledge, there have not been any studies on the possible genetic association of IGFs or IGF signaling regulator genes with ASD. In this study, we focused on key molecules of the IGF pathway, insulin receptor substrate 1 (*IRS1*) and *IRS2*, which are the major cytosolic substrates of the IGF receptors and mediators for the downstream pathway processes [20,21].

Insulin has been regarded as primarily a metabolic signal, while IGFs has been implicated as an important mitogen and cell differentiation factor [22,23]. The IRS family contains several members (IRS1-6), of which IRS1 and IRS2 have been most widely studied. IRS1 and IRS2 regulate body weight control and glucose homeostasis [24]. They could also control body growth and peripheral insulin action. Thus, they have been suggested as markers of an active IGF pathway within tumors [25,26], although they are involved in insulin signaling. Indeed, polymorphisms of *IRS1* and/or *IRS2* have shown the significant associations with diabetes, glucose levels [27], and obesity [28], as well as with cancers, along with IGF signaling regulator genes [29–31]. Herein, we investigated the association of the coding region single-nucleotide polymorphisms (cSNP) of *IRS1* and *IRS2*, active markers of the IGF pathway, with ASD in Korean males.

2. Results

Two cSNPs of *IRS1* and *IRS2* were polymorphic, and the genotype distributions of the SNPs were in Hardy-Weinberg equilibrium (HWE) ($p > 0.05$; data not shown). We calculated the power of the sample size to verify our data using a genetic power calculator [32]. Considering a two-fold genotype relative risk, the sample powers of the SNPs were 0.900 (rs1801123, number of effective samples for 80% power = 148) and 0.967 (rs4773092, $n = 110$), respectively ($\alpha = 0.05$). In addition, the sample powers of rs1801123 were 0.841 ($n = 175$) and 0.761 ($n = 213$) for a 1.9- and 1.8-fold relative risk, respectively. The sample powers of rs4773092 were 0.938 ($n = 128$) for a 1.9-fold relative risk, 0.889 ($n = 154$) for a 1.8-fold relative risk, and 0.889 ($n = 189$) for a 1.7-fold relative risk. Therefore, the results of our study had a significant power and sample size to detect the genotype relative risks up to 1.9-fold on rs1801123 and 1.8-fold on rs4773092.

As shown in Table 1, rs1801123 of *IRS1* was associated with ASD in additive (AG vs. GG vs. AA, $p = 0.022$, odds ratio (OR) = 0.66, 95% confidence interval (CI) = 0.46–0.95) and dominant models ($p = 0.013$, OR = 0.57, 95% CI = 0.37–0.89). The frequency of the genotypes containing the G allele (AG/GG, 36.7%) was decreased in the ASD patients compared to the control subjects (50.3%). In allele frequency analysis, we also found that rs1801123 was associated with ASD ($p = 0.022$, OR = 0.66, 95% CI = 0.46–0.94). The frequency of the G allele was lower in ASD patients (21.1%) than in control subjects (28.9%). This significance remained after the Bonferroni correction.

Interestingly, when we analyzed the differences between patients with autistic disorder and healthy individuals, rs1801123 of IRS1 showed a statistically more significant association (Table 2).

The association was revealed in the additive ($p = 0.0037$, OR = 0.56, 95% CI = 0.37–0.83) and dominant models ($p = 0.0041$, OR = 0.50, 95% CI = 0.31–0.81). Allele frequency analysis also revealed a stronger association between rs1801123 and autistic disorder ($p = 0.004$, OR = 0.56, 95% CI = 0.38–0.84). The frequencies of the AG/GG genotypes (33.6% and 50.3% in patients with autistic disorder and control subjects, respectively) and the G allele (18.6% and 28.9%) were more remarkably decreased in patients with autistic disorder compared to control subjects.

Table 1. Multiple logistic regression analysis of *IRS1* and *IRS2* polymorphisms in autism spectrum disorder (ASD) patients and control subjects.

SNP	Model/Allele	Genotype	Control	ASD	OR (95% CI)	*p*
			n (%)	*n* (%)		
rs1801123	Additive	AA	73 (49.7)	114 (63.3)	1	
Ala804Ala		AG	63 (42.9)	56 (31.1)		
IRS1		GG	11 (7.5)	10 (5.6)	0.66 (0.46–0.95)	**0.022**
	Dominant	AA	73 (49.7)	114 (63.3)	1	
		AG/GG	74 (50.3)	66 (36.7)	0.57 (0.37–0.89)	**0.013**
	Recessive	AA/AG	136 (92.5)	170 (94.4)	1	
		GG	11 (7.5)	10 (5.6)	0.73 (0.30–1.76)	0.48
	Allele	A	209 (71.1)	284 (78.9)	1	
		G	85 (28.9)	76 (21.1)	0.66 (0.46–0.94)	**0.022**
rs4773092	Additive	AA	41 (27.9)	51 (28.3)	1	
Cys816Cys		AG	76 (51.7)	95 (52.8)		
IRS2		GG	30 (20.4)	34 (18.9)	0.96 (0.70–1.32)	0.8
	Dominant	AA	41 (27.9)	51 (28.3)	1	
		AG/GG	106 (72.1)	129 (71.7)	0.98 (0.60–1.59)	0.93
	Recessive	AA/AG	117 (79.6)	146 (81.1)	1	
		GG	30 (20.4)	34 (18.9)	0.91 (0.53–1.57)	0.73
	Allele	A	158 (53.7)	197 (54.7)	1	
		G	136 (46.3)	163 (45.3)	0.96 (0.70–1.31)	0.8

Bold characters represent statistically significant values ($p < 0.025$). ASD, autism spectrum disorder. 1—It is a statistical reference in our genetic analysis.

Table 2. Multiple logistic regression analysis of *IRS1* and *IRS2* polymorphisms in patients with autistic disorder and control subjects.

SNP	Model/allele	Genotype	Control	Autistic Disorder	OR (95% CI)	*p*
			n (%)	*n* (%)		
rs1801123	Additive	AA	73 (49.7)	91 (66.4)	1	
Ala804Ala		AG	63 (42.9)	41 (29.9)		
IRS1		GG	11 (7.5)	5 (3.6)	0.56 (0.37–0.83)	**0.0037**
	Dominant	AA	73 (49.7)	91 (66.4)	1	
		AG/GG	74 (50.3)	46 (33.6)	0.50 (0.31–0.81)	**0.0041**
	Recessive	AA/AG	136 (92.5)	132 (96.3)	1	
		GG	11 (7.5)	5 (3.6)	0.47 (0.16–1.38)	0.16
	Allele	A	209 (71.1)	223 (81.4)	1	
		G	85 (28.9)	51 (18.6)	0.56 (0.38–0.84)	**0.004**
rs4773092	Additive	AA	41 (27.9)	36 (26.3)	1	
Cys816Cys		AG	76 (51.7)	70 (51.1)		
IRS2		GG	30 (20.4)	31 (22.6)	1.08 (0.77–1.51)	0.64
	Dominant	AA	41 (27.9)	36 (26.3)	1	0.76
		AG/GG	106 (72.1)	101 (73.7)	1.09 (0.64–1.83)	
	Recessive	AA/AG	117 (79.6)	106 (77.4)	1	0.65
		GG	30 (20.4)	31 (22.6)	1.14 (0.65–2.01)	
	Allele	A	158 (53.7)	142 (51.8)	1	
		G	136 (46.3)	132 (48.2)	0.96 (0.70–1.31)	0.8

Bold characters represent statistically significant values ($p < 0.025$). 1—It is a statistical reference in our genetic analysis.

3. Discussion

In our study, we found that rs1801123 of *IRS1* was significantly associated with ASD in Korean males. The G allele of rs1801123 contributed to a decreased risk of ASD and, particularly, the contribution was potently shown in patients with autistic disorder.

The IGF pathway plays an important role in regulating cell proliferation, differentiation and apoptosis, and, thus, IGFs and their signaling regulators have been studied in growth-, weight gain- , and obesity-related diseases [20,28,33–35]. IRS1 and IRS2 are key mediators of the IGF pathway [20,21]. Binding of IGFs to IGF receptors phosphorylates IRSs and triggers downstream cascades such as MAPK and PI3K/AKT signaling, which finally leads to cell proliferation and differentiation [20,21]. Thus, IRS1 and IRS2 together with IGFs and IGFRs have been involved in obesity, birth weight, diabetes mellitus, insulin sensitivity and cancer, showing the genetic associations of their polymorphisms [28–31,33,34].

In ASD patients, increased head growth, and particularly brain overgrowth in early life, has been reported with or without higher weights and body mass indexes (BMIs) Thus, several studies have suggested the involvement of growth-related hormones such as IGFs and their regulators, which lead to increased head growth and higher weights and BMIs, in the pathophysiology of autistic disorder/ASD [13,17,18]. Indeed, Mills et al. [13] reported increased levels of IGF1, IGF2, IGFBP3 and GHBP in the plasma of autistic disorder/ASD patients, and also showed a positive correlation between IGF1 level and head circumference in autistic disorder/ASD patients.

On the other hands, IGFs and their regulators have been also reported to play a role in growth retardation. Indeed, transgenic mice lacking *IRS1* showed prenatal and postnatal growth retardation [36, 37]. In mice lacking *IRS2*, growth retardation was also observed, although it was minimal compared to mice lacking *IRS1* [36]. Moreover, in the brain, IGFs and their regulators are essential factors for normal brain growth and development, as well as synaptogenesis and myelination [16,19,38]. They directly affect the rate that oligodendrocytes promote myelination, and thus factors which relatively reduce the production or availability of IGFs could retard normal nerve programming [19]. Indeed, in early laboratory embryos, the addition of IGF-receptor inhibitors blocked the normal formation of midbrain neurons [39]. *IGF1* knockout mice had defective neurologic development [40]. Moreover, other studies on the relationship between IGF1 level and autistic patients reported lower IGF1 levels in the cerebrospinal fluid (CSF) of autistic patients, although the IGF1 levels of patients were compared to abnormal controls instead of normal controls due to ethical reasons that do not allow researchers to obtain CSF from normal control subjects [17,18]. Thus, relatively low activities of IGF pathway molecules such as IGF1, IRS1 and IRS2 may play a role as risk factors in the pathophysiology of autistic disorder/ASD, leading to the growth and development retardation. Hence, it is controversial which one among excessive activations and reduced availabilities of IGF-related factors is involved in the pathology of autistic disorder/ASD.

In the present study, we found that rs1801123 of *IRS1* was associated with ASD, and the association was shown more strongly in patients with autistic disorder. In particular, our results showed that the frequency of the minor G allele of rs1801123 was decreased in patients with autistic disorder/ASD; thus, the G allele of rs1801123 may contribute to a decreased risk of autistic disorder/ASD as a protective factor. In a previous study, carriers of the minor allele of rs1801123 (TG/GG) were reported to be associated with higher fasting plasma glucose and insulin levels [27]. Furthermore, the G allele of rs1801123 was associated with an increased risk of breast cancer in women carrying the *BRCA1* mutation [30], although in a recent study of the same group using a large set of *BRCA1* and *BRCA2* mutation carriers, its lack of association was revealed [41]. Moreover, the G allele of rs1801123 was significantly associated with lymph node involvement in estrogen-receptor-positive primary invasive breast cancer patients, who were treated with surgery and tamoxifen [29]. These reports indicated that the minor allele of rs1801123 may be involved in the increased product and ability of the IGFs, along with the activation of the insulin-related signaling pathway. Therefore, the decreased frequency of the minor allele of rs1801123 in autistic disorder/ASD patients in our study may contribute to relatively low activation of the IGF pathway molecules. Taken together, we postulated that the activation of IGF pathway molecules may be reduced in autistic disorder/ASD patients, although it is controversial as mentioned above. Also, the G allele of rs1801123 may play a role as a protective factor against the decreased activity of the IGF pathway in autistic disorder/ASD. Further studies are needed to determine how rs1801123 and the IGF pathway affect the pathophysiology of autistic disorder/ASD.

Our study is the first pilot to report an association of the *IRS1* with autistic disorder/ASD. The limitation of our study is that only one SNP of each *IRS1* and *IRS2* was selected and analyzed. Replication studies are needed to determine the association between the *IRS1* and autistic disorder/ASD, as well as the lack of association of *IRS2*, analyzing more polymorphisms in addition to rs1801123 and rs4773092. Moreover, as shown in our sample power analysis, our results have statistical confidence, only assuming a genotype relative risk up to 1.9-fold on rs1801123. Thus, the relatively small sample size limits the generalizability of the findings from the present study. Our findings are preliminary and need to be validated in further studies with larger sample sizes. Our work provides evidence that the *IRS1* gene may play a role in the pathophysiology of ASD.

4. Experimental Section

4.1. Subjects

One hundred eighty male ASD patients (mean age ± standard deviation (SD), 15.5 ± 4.8 years) and 147 healthy male individuals (39.9 ± 5.8 years) were enrolled in this study. ASD patients were diagnosed with ASDs by well-trained psychiatrists, child and adolescent specialists according to Diagnostic and Statistical Manual of Mental Disorders, 4th ed (DSM-IV) criteria [42], using available historical information from interviews and clinical records. Each ASD patient was also evaluated using the Childhood Autism Rating Scale (CARS) [43], one of the most widely used instrument to evaluate the developmental degree of autism, applying cut-off score of 30. The average of CARS score was 38.6 ± 5.8 (mean ± SD). The ASD group consisted of 137 patients with autistic disorder, 11 patients with Asperger's disorder, and 32 patients with Pervasive Developmental Disorder-Not Otherwise Specified (PDD-NOS). A summary of clinical characteristics of ASD patients is provided in Table 3. The healthy adult controls were recruited from subjects who visited the hospital for routine health checkups. Controls were investigated to determine whether they or their first-degree relatives had psychiatric disturbances or previous psychiatric treatment through personal interviews. Only unaffected subjects with no psychiatric disorder or family history were included in this study.

Table 3. Clinical characteristics of ASD patients and control subjects.

Characteristics	ASDs	Control
Total no. of subject	180	147
Age (mean ± SD, years)	15.5 ± 4.8	39.9 ± 5.8
CARS score	38.6 ± 5.8	
Autistic disorder (*n* = 137)	41.1 ± 4.3	
Asperger's disorder (*n* = 11)	30.7 ± 0.4	
PDD-NOS (*n* = 32)	30.9 ± 1.0	

ASD, autism spectrum disorder; CARS, Childhood Autism Rating Scale; PDD-NOS, Pervasive Developmental Disorder-Not Otherwise Specified.

All the ASD patients and control subjects were of Korean background. The present study was conducted in accordance with the guidelines of the Helsinki Declaration and was approved by the Ethics Review Committee of Medical Research Institute, Kyung Hee University Medical Center on 15 September 2004 (2004-09-15). Written informed consents were obtained from the parents or guardians of ASD patients and control subjects.

4.2. Single-Nucleotide Polymorphism (SNP) Selection and Genotyping

Of SNPs in the *IRS1* and *IRS2*, cSNPs were targeted and selected from the National Center for Biotechnology Information SNP database [44]. Some cSNPs alter a functionally important amino acid residue, and these are of interest for their potential links with phenotype. Other cSNPs may prove useful for their potential links to functional cSNPs via linkage disequilibrium mapping [45,46]. We selected common SNPs with a minor allele frequency of >0.1 in Chinese and Japanese populations, excluding SNPs without data on genotype frequency. Finally, we selected two cSNP (rs1801123 (Ala804Ala) of *IRS1*, and rs4773092 (Cys816Cys) of *IRS2*).

Genomic DNA was extracted from the whole blood of each subject using the High Pure PCR Template Preparation kit (Roche, Mannheim, Germany) following the manufacturer's protocol. SNP genotyping was conducted with direct sequencing using the following primers for each SNP: rs1801123 in *IRS1* (sense, 5′-TCCTACTACTCATTGCCAAGATC-3′; antisense, 5′-CTATTGGTCTGA GCAGCTGTGT-3′), and rs4773092 in *IRS2* (sense, 5′-ATGTGGTGCGGTTCCAAGCTGT-3′; antisense, 5′-GCCAAAGTCGATGTTGATGTACT-3′). The PCR products were sequenced using the ABI PRISM 3730XL analyzer (PE Applied Biosystems, Foster City, CA, USA), and sequence data were then analyzed using SeqManII software (DNASTAR Inc., Madison, WI, USA).

4.3. Statistical Analysis

SNPStats [47] and SPSS 18.0 software (SPSS Inc., Chicago, IL, USA) were used to analyze the genetic data and the HWE. The association between SNP genotypes and ASD were estimated by computing the ORs and their 95% CIs with logistic regression analyses. In the logistic regression analysis for each SNP, the following models were used: codominant inheritance (that is, where the relative hazard differed between subjects with one minor allele and those with two minor alleles), dominant inheritance (subjects with one or two minor alleles had the same relative hazard for the disease), or recessive inheritance (subjects with two minor alleles were at increased risk of the disease). The chi-square test was used to compare allele frequencies between groups. To avoid chance findings due to multiple testing, a Bonferroni correction was applied by lowering the significance levels to $p = 0.025$ ($p = 0.05/2$) for two SNPs.

Acknowledgments: This work was supported by a grant from Kyung Hee University (Seoul, Korea) in 2012 (KHU-20121738).

Author Contributions: Joo-Ho Chung designed and directed the whole project. Won Sub Kang, Jin Kyung Park, Young Jong Kim, Min Nam and Jong Woo Kim collected the blood samples from ASD patients and control subjects. Hae Jeong Park and Su Kang Kim performed the experiments, collected the results, and analyzed the data. Joo-Ho Chung and Hae Jeong Park discussed and interpreted the data and results. Hae Jeong Park wrote the first draft of the manuscript. All authors contributed to and have approved the final manuscript.

References

1. Tanguay, P.E. Pervasive developmental disorders: A 10-year review. *J. Am. Acad. Child Adolesc. Psychiatry* **2000**, *39*, 1079–1095.
2. Nicholas, J.S.; Charles, J.M.; Carpenter, L.A.; King, L.B.; Jenner, W.; Spratt, E.G. Prevalence and characteristics of children with autism-spectrum disorders. *Ann. Epidemiol.* **2008**, *18*, 130–136.
3. Burmeister, M.; McInnis, M.G.; Zollner, S. Psychiatric genetics: Progress amid controversy. *Nat. Rev. Genet.* **2008**, *9*, 527–540.
4. Nowakowska, B.A.; de Leeuw, N.; Ruivenkamp, C.A.; Sikkema-Raddatz, B.; Crolla, J.A.; Thoelen, R.; Koopmans, M.; den Hollander, N.; van Haeringen, A.; van der Kevie-Kersemaekers, A.M.; et al. Parental insertional balanced translocations are an important cause of apparently de novo CNVs in patients with developmental anomalies. *Eur. J. Hum. Genet.* **2012**, *20*, 166–170.
5. Carter, M.T.; Nikkel, S.M.; Fernandez, B.A.; Marshall, C.R.; Noor, A.; Lionel, A.C.; Prasad, A.; Pinto, D.; Joseph-George, A.M.; Noakes, C.; et al. Hemizygous deletions on chromosome 1p21.3 involving the DPYD gene in individuals with autism spectrum disorder. *Clin. Genet.* **2011**, *80*, 435–443.
6. Anney, R.; Klei, L.; Pinto, D.; Regan, R.; Conroy, J.; Magalhaes, T.R.; Correia, C.; Abrahams, B.S.; Sykes, N.; Pagnamenta, A.T.; et al. A genome-wide scan for common alleles affecting risk for autism. *Hum. Mol. Genet.* **2010**, *19*, 4072–4082.

7. Weiss, L.A.; Arking, D.E. Gene Discovery Project of Johns Hopkins and the Autism Consortium. A genome-wide linkage and association scan reveals novel loci for autism. *Nature* **2009**, *461*, 802–808. [PubMed]
8. Wang, K.; Zhang, H.; Ma, D.; Bucan, M.; Glessner, J.T.; Abrahams, B.S.; Salyakina, D.; Imielinski, M.; Bradfield, J.P.; Sleiman, P.M.; et al. Common genetic variants on 5p14.1 associate with autism spectrum disorders. *Nature* **2009**, *459*, 528–533.
9. Chen, D.Y.; Stern, S.A.; Garcia-Osta, A.; Saunier-Rebori, B.; Pollonini, G.; Bambah-Mukku, D.; Blitzer, R.D.; Alberini, C.M. A critical role for IGF-II in memory consolidation and enhancement. *Nature* **2011**, *469*, 491–497.
10. O'Kusky, J.R.; Ye, P.; D'Ercole, A.J. Insulin-like growth factor-I promotes neurogenesis and synaptogenesis in the hippocampal dentate gyrus during postnatal development. *J. Neurosci.* **2000**, *20*, 8435–8442.
11. Schaevitz, L.R.; Moriuchi, J.M.; Nag, N.; Mellot, T.J.; Berger-Sweeney, J. Cognitive and social functions and growth factors in a mouse model of Rett syndrome. *Physiol. Behav.* **2010**, *100*, 255–263.
12. Moy, S.S.; Nadler, J.J.; Young, N.B.; Nonneman, R.J.; Grossman, A.W.; Murphy, D.L.; D'Ercole, A.J.; Crawley, J.N.; Magnuson, T.R.; Lauder, J.M. Social approach in genetically engineered mouse lines relevant to autism. *Genes Brain Behav.* **2009**, *8*, 129–142.
13. Mills, J.L.; Hediger, M.L.; Molloy, C.A.; Chrousos, G.P.; Manning-Courtney, P.; Yu, K.F.; Brasington, M.; England, L.J. Elevated levels of growth-related hormones in autism and autism spectrum disorder. *Clin. Endocrinol.* **2007**, *67*, 230–237.
14. Courchesne, E.; Carper, R.; Akshoomoff, N. Evidence of brain overgrowth in the first year of life in autism. *JAMA* **2003**, *290*, 337–344.
15. Courchesne, E.; Karns, C.M.; Davis, H.R.; Ziccardi, R.; Carper, R.A.; Tigue, Z.D.; Chisum, H.J.; Moses, P.; Pierce, K.; Lord, C.; et al. Unusual brain growth patterns in early life in patients with autistic disorder: An MRI study. *Neurology* **2001**, *57*, 245–254.
16. Popken, G.J.; Hodge, R.D.; Ye, P.; Zhang, J.; Ng, W.; O'Kusky, J.R.; D'Ercole, A.J. In vivo effects of insulin-like growth factor-I (IGF-I) on prenatal and early postnatal development of the central nervous system. *Eur. J. Neurosci.* **2004**, *19*, 2056–2068.
17. Riikonen, R. Neurotrophic factors in the pathogenesis of Rett syndrome. *J. Child Neurol.* **2003**, *18*, 693–697.
18. Vanhala, R.; Turpeinen, U.; Riikonen, R. Low levels of insulin-like growth factor-I in cerebrospinal fluid in children with autism. *Dev. Med. Child Neurol.* **2001**, *43*, 614–616.
19. Steinman, G.; Mankuta, D. Insulin-like growth factor and the etiology of autism. *Med. Hypotheses* **2013**, *80*, 475–480.
20. Laban, C.; Bustin, S.A.; Jenkins, P.J. The GH-IGF-I axis and breast cancer. *Trends Endocrinol. Metab.* **2003**, *14*, 28–34.
21. Jones, J.I.; Clemmons, D.R. Insulin-like growth factors and their binding proteins: Biological actions. *Endocr. Rev.* **1995**, *16*, 3–34.
22. White, M.F. Insulin signaling in health and disease. *Science* **2003**, *302*, 1710–1711.
23. Burks, D.J.; White, M.F. IRS proteins and β-cell function. *Diabetes* **2001**, *50*, S140–S145.
24. Withers, D.J.; Burks, D.J.; Towery, H.H.; Altamuro, S.L.; Flint, C.L.; White, M.F. IRS-2 coordinates IGF-1 receptor-mediated beta-cell development and peripheral insulin signalling. *Nat. Genet.* **1999**, *23*, 32–40.
25. Werner, H.; Le Roith, D. The insulin-like growth factor-I receptor signaling pathways are important for tumorigenesis and inhibition of apoptosis. *Crit. Rev. Oncog.* **1997**, *8*, 71–92.
26. Van Obberghen, E.; Baron, V.; Scimeca, J.C.; Kaliman, P. Insulin receptor: Receptor activation and signal transduction. *Adv. Second Messenger Phosphoprot. Res.* **1993**, *28*, 195–201.
27. Feng, X.; Tucker, K.L.; Parnell, L.D.; Shen, J.; Lee, Y.C.; Ordovas, J.M.; Ling, W.H.; Lai, C.Q. Insulin receptor substrate 1 (IRS1) variants confer risk of diabetes in the Boston Puerto Rican Health Study. *Asia Pac. J. Clin. Nutr.* **2013**, *22*, 150–159. [PubMed]
28. Lautier, C.; El Mkadem, S.A.; Renard, E.; Brun, J.F.; Gris, J.C.; Bringer, J.; Grigorescu, F. Complex haplotypes of *IRS2* gene are associated with severe obesity and reveal heterogeneity in the effect of Gly1057Asp mutation. *Hum. Genet.* **2003**, *113*, 34–43.
29. Winder, T.; Giamas, G.; Wilson, P.M.; Zhang, W.; Yang, D.; Bohanes, P.; Ning, Y.; Gerger, A.; Stebbing, J.; Lenz, H.J. Insulin-like growth factor receptor polymorphism defines clinical outcome in estrogen receptor-positive breast cancer patients treated with tamoxifen. *Pharmacogen. J.* **2014**, *14*, 28–34.

30. Neuhausen, S.L.; Brummel, S.; Ding, Y.C.; Singer, C.F.; Pfeiler, G.; Lynch, H.T.; Nathanson, K.L.; Rebbeck, T.R.; Garber, J.E.; Couch, F.; et al. Genetic variation in insulin-like growth factor signaling genes and breast cancer risk among BRCA1 and BRCA2 carriers. *Breast Cancer Res.* **2009**, *11*, R76.
31. Slattery, M.L.; Samowitz, W.; Curtin, K.; Ma, K.N.; Hoffman, M.; Caan, B.; Neuhausen, S. Associations among IRS1, IRS2, IGF1, and IGFBP3 genetic polymorphisms and colorectal cancer. *Cancer Epidemiol. Biomark. Prev.* **2004**, *13*, 1206–1214.
32. Genetic Power Calculator. Available online: http://pngu.mgh.harvard.edu/~purcell/gpc/cc2.html (accessed on 28 July 2016).
33. Rasmussen, S.K.; Urhammer, S.A.; Hansen, T.; Almind, K.; Moller, A.M.; Borch-Johnsen, K.; Pedersen, O. Variability of the insulin receptor substrate-1, hepatocyte nuclear factor-1α (*HNF-1α*), *HNF-4α*, and *HNF-6* genes and size at birth in a population-based sample of young Danish subjects. *J. Clin. Endocrinol. Metab.* **2000**, *85*, 2951–2953.
34. Almind, K.; Frederiksen, S.K.; Bernal, D.; Hansen, T.; Ambye, L.; Urhammer, S.; Ekstrom, C.T.; Berglund, L.; Reneland, R.; Lithell, H.; et al. Search for variants of the gene-promoter and the potential phosphotyrosine encoding sequence of the insulin receptor substrate-2 gene: Evaluation of their relation with alterations in insulin secretion and insulin sensitivity. *Diabetologia* **1999**, *42*, 1244–1249.
35. Almind, K.; Bjorbaek, C.; Vestergaard, H.; Hansen, T.; Echwald, S.; Pedersen, O. Aminoacid polymorphisms of insulin receptor substrate-1 in non-insulin-dependent diabetes mellitus. *Lancet* **1993**, *342*, 828–832.
36. Withers, D.J.; Gutierrez, J.S.; Towery, H.; Burks, D.J.; Ren, J.M.; Previs, S.; Zhang, Y.; Bernal, D.; Pons, S.; Shulman, G.I.; et al. Disruption of IRS-2 causes type 2 diabetes in mice. *Nature* **1998**, *391*, 900–904.
37. Tamemoto, H.; Kadowaki, T.; Tobe, K.; Yagi, T.; Sakura, H.; Hayakawa, T.; Terauchi, Y.; Ueki, K.; Kaburagi, Y.; Satoh, S.; et al. Insulin resistance and growth retardation in mice lacking insulin receptor substrate-1. *Nature* **1994**, *372*, 182–186.
38. Anlar, B.; Sullivan, K.A.; Feldman, E.L. Insulin-like growth factor-I and central nervous system development. *Horm. Metab. Res.* **1999**, *31*, 120–125.
39. Onuma, T.A.; Ding, Y.; Abraham, E.; Zohar, Y.; Ando, H.; Duan, C. Regulation of temporal and spatial organization of newborn GnRH neurons by IGF signaling in zebrafish. *J. Neurosci.* **2011**, *31*, 11814–11824.
40. Beck, K.D.; Powell-Braxton, L.; Widmer, H.R.; Valverde, J.; Hefti, F. Igf1 gene disruption results in reduced brain size, CNS hypomyelination, and loss of hippocampal granule and striatal parvalbumin-containing neurons. *Neuron* **1995**, *14*, 717–730.
41. Ding, Y.C.; McGuffog, L.; Healey, S.; Friedman, E.; Laitman, Y.; Paluch-Shimon, S.; Kaufman, B.; Swe, B.; Liljegren, A.; Lindblom, A.; et al. A nonsynonymous polymorphism in IRS1 modifies risk of developing breast and ovarian cancers in BRCA1 and ovarian cancer in BRCA2 mutation carriers. *Cancer Epidemiol. Biomark. Prev.* **2012**, *21*, 1362–1370.
42. Association Psychiatric Association. *Diagnostic and Statistical Manual of Mental Disorders*, 4th ed.; American Psychiatric Press: Washington, DC, USA, 1994.
43. Schopler, E.; Reichier, R.J.; Renner, B.R. *Childhood Autism Rating Scale*; Western Psychological Services: Los Angeles, CA, USA, 1988.
44. NCBI databases. Available online: http://www.ncbi.nlm.nih.gov/SNP (accessed on 28 July 2016).
45. Collins, F.S.; Guyer, M.S.; Chakravarti, A. Variations on a theme: Cataloging human DNA sequence variations. *Science* **1997**, *278*, 1580–1581.
46. Garg, K.; Green, P.; Nickerson, D.A. Identification of candidate coding region single nucleotide polymorphisms in 165 human genes using assembled expressed sequence tags. *Genome Res.* **1999**, *9*, 1087–1092.
47. ICO. Available online: http://bioinfo.iconcologia.net/index.php (accessed on 28 July 2016).

Novel Systems Modeling Methodology in Comparative Microbial Metabolomics: Identifying Key Enzymes and Metabolites Implicated in Autism Spectrum Disorders

Colin Heberling [1,2,*] and Prasad Dhurjati [2]

1 Department of Biotechnology, Johns Hopkins University, Rockville, MD 20850, USA
2 Department of Chemical and Biomolecular Engineering, University of Delaware, Newark, DE 19716, USA; dhurjati@udel.edu
* Author to whom correspondence should be addressed; cheb@udel.edu

Academic Editor: Merlin G. Butler

Abstract: Autism spectrum disorders are a group of mental illnesses highly correlated with gastrointestinal dysfunction. Recent studies have shown that there may be one or more microbial "fingerprints" in terms of the composition characterizing individuals with autism, which could be used for diagnostic purposes. This paper proposes a computational approach whereby metagenomes characteristic of "healthy" and autistic individuals are artificially constructed via genomic information, analyzed for the enzymes coded within, and then these enzymes are compared in detail. This is a text mining application. A custom-designed online application was built and used for the comparative metabolomics study and made publically available. Several of the enzyme-catalyzing reactions involved with the amino acid glutamate were curiously missing from the "autism" microbiome and were coded within almost every organism included in the "control" microbiome. Interestingly, there exists a leading hypothesis regarding autism and glutamate involving a neurological excitation/inhibition imbalance; but the association with this study is unclear. The results included data on the transsulfuration and transmethylation pathways, involved with oxidative stress, also of importance to autism. The results from this study are in alignment with leading hypotheses in the field, which is impressive, considering the purely *in silico* nature of this study. The present study provides new insight into the complex metabolic interactions underlying autism, and this novel methodology has potential to be useful for developing new hypotheses. However, limitations include sparse genome data availability and conflicting literature experimental data. We believe our software tool and methodology has potential for having great utility as data become more available, comprehensive and reliable.

Keywords: autism; metabolomics; comparative; microbial; computational; bioinformatics; biomarkers; gut; gastrointestinal; microbiome

1. Introduction

Autism spectrum disorders are a category of mental illnesses characterized by social cognitive impairments and stereotyped behaviors [1]. Autistic individuals often have trouble fitting into society and put a financial burden on their families, lifelong. Autism diagnosis has been steadily on the rise in the past decade or so, affecting one in every 88 children according to a source in 2012 [1] and one in every 68 children from current data (2015) from the Centers for Disease Control and Protection [2]. There are most likely many adults suffering from autism that have never been diagnosed. This is because there is as of yet no clear method to diagnose autism; diagnosis is purely based on making qualitative observations of an individual. This is why there is a pressing need to find reliable methods for autism diagnosis and for treatment, as well.

Recent research suggests that individuals with autism often suffer from gastrointestinal dysfunction, as well [3,4]. Rather than focusing on the illness by way of human genetics, many scientists are now exploring the impact of microbial genetics. There exists a full isolated ecosystem of microbial lifeforms that inhabit the human gastrointestinal tract. These microbes have a profound impact on the health and disease of the human host and in general have a symbiotic co-existence with the host [5]. Microbial species or strain composition is believed to largely contribute to homeostasis or abnormality in humans. While each person's microbial "fingerprint" is unique, there are specific patterns seen in those that are healthy and those that have specific illnesses [6,7]. Remarkably, autism has been correlated with the overgrowth of certain types of bacteria, such as certain species of *Clostridia* [8,9] and *Desulfovibrio* [9,10], and there is some preliminary evidence that *Sutterella* may be implicated, as well [11]. Data from the pyrosequencing study by Finegold *et al.* [9] suggested that several other organisms may be implicated in autism, as well, but these results were less significant than those implicating *Clostridia* and *Desulfovibrio*.

Nonetheless, one organism, *Akkermansia*, was chosen from among these organisms to be included in the study, to see how much of an impact these less significant organisms might have. *Akkermansia* is part of the *Verrucomicrobia* phylum. According to a study by Williams *et al.* [12] where live intestinal biopsies were taken to measure bacterial composition, *Verrucomicrobia* made up approximately 1% of the total bacterial composition in individuals with autism and only 0.5% in healthy age-matched controls. This was another leading factor for the decision to include *Akkermansia* in the present study.

As one might expect, as bacterial composition has an effect on health and disease, the molecular metabolites that these microbes produce are the "tools" that carry out these biological changes. For example, individuals with autism have been cited as having sulfur metabolic deficiencies, to suffer from elevated oxidative stress and to have trouble detoxifying xenobiotic compounds and heavy metals [13–15]. It is therefore important to analyze the metabolome of these individuals and that of healthy individuals (for control) in order to identify useful biomarkers and perhaps even gain a greater understanding of the disorder. Knowledge may be gained about other related illnesses, as well, such as others related to gastrointestinal dysfunction.

Metagenomics is the study of the genetic content contained in whole microbial ecosystems isolated from natural environments [16,17]. In contrast, the more traditional genomics is the study of only DNA from a single, isolated species or strain of organism. Metagenomics therefore brings with it new challenges in bioinformatics. This is because before regular genomics can be applied to each organism, the key organisms need to be identified by aligning sample DNA reads to reference sequences contained in curated databases [18]. Of course, the environment that this study focuses on is the human gut microbiome. This study does not use the conventional methods of metagenomics, but rather simplifies the problem by constructing artificial metagenomes based on genomes of organisms already known to be contained in the target environment. There are numerous pieces of literature already describing the composition of microbes contained in autistic individuals and "healthy" individuals. The present study constructs a metagenomics "model", rather than conducting a pure metagenomics study.

2. Methods

The literature suggests that there are distinct microbiomes characteristic of a "healthy" individual and that of an autistic individual [4]. Therefore, the first step was to choose the microorganisms to represent these microbiomes. It was the intended goal to be as comprehensive as possible with this step, so that all possible enzymes and metabolites that are possible to exist in urinary or stool samples are covered. Choosing the correct microorganisms can be tricky, as sometimes there are conflicting data or interpretations of data in different literature [19]. Another quandary is whether to include the more common organisms in both microbiomes studied or to only include the "problem" organisms; that is, the microorganisms thought to cause the main differences between the two microbiomes. In the latter case, the autistic microbiome could be represented with just a few species of microbe. The end goal is to find the key enzymes and metabolites expressed that are entirely different in the autistic individual. Of course, autism is a complex disorder with multiple different pathways for pathogenesis, so the autistic microbiome chosen will try to represent all cases of autism arising from gut microbiological origin.

Only those microorganisms thought to be represented in significantly higher amounts (proportionally) in the guts of autistic individuals were chosen for the autistic microbiome, with the core microorganisms representative of a healthy human gut for the control microbiome. However, there is still no consensus on what defines a typical "healthy" gut microbiome, so the "control" microbiome was chosen based on a few key steps. First, those microbes that have been reported to be in decreased quantities in autism were included in the "control" microbiome [9,12,20]. Next, those reported to have no change in composition were included. Finally, other organisms that are normally found in the human gut, but that had very little discussion in related autism literature were included in the "control" microbiome. To facilitate this final step, we have unpublished work where the MEtaGenome Analyzer (MEGAN software) [21,22] was used to analyze three sets of metagenomic data from the Human Microbiome Project's collection of human stool samples [6,23]. These design criteria may seem confusing at first if we take into consideration that those microorganisms that are decreased in autism are nonetheless still implicated in autism, just like those organisms that are found in increased amounts. However, our design considerations are predicated on the assumption that those organisms that are found in decreased numbers in autism are in fact usually beneficial for the host in otherwise "healthy" microbiomes. There is at least some evidence for two such cases: *Lactobacillus* species and *Bifidobacterium* species [24]. We can therefore justify stratifying gut microbes into two groupings based on a simple binary distinction: those microbes that are found in increased numbers in autism and those microbes that are not found in increased numbers in autism. Comparing these two groups should reveal key differences in expressed enzymes. Thus, finding enzymes that are expressed in the "autism" group and not in the "control" group may identify metabolites indicative only of our "problem" organisms and thus may serve as potential biomarkers for autism. On the other hand, finding enzymes that are expressed by the "control" group and not the "autism" group may also identify key biomarkers, except in this case, clinicians may be able to look for decreased quantities of such molecules instead.

Enzyme Commission (EC) numbers were used for the comparative analysis. EC numbers are a standardized way to identify enzymes, much like CAS numbers (Chemical Abstracts Service) for common chemicals. GenBank files for each microbe were downloaded from the National Center for Biotechnology Information (NCBI) [25]. The limitations of this study occurred at this stage. Not all microbes known have a completely sequenced genome uploaded to NCBI, and even less still have their protein products annotated with EC numbers. This greatly limited which organisms could be used in the study. The following list organizes microorganisms into three categories: those included in the first software query, those additional organisms that were able to be included in Query 2 after *de novo* EC number annotations were made (more detail later) and those organisms that were desired to be included, but in the end were not.

The usual approach for metagenomics presents significant bottlenecks for analysis and data storage. This is why the idea came about that there may be another approach that is more efficient in very specific circumstances. Instead of using metagenomic data, this study attempts to construct an artificial metagenome by carefully choosing the microorganisms to include in the model and using the curated database of GenBank files to analyze the full spectra of enzymes coded in the genomic DNA of these organisms. This study is differentiated from a proteomics study, because we are only interested in proteins that have been assigned a standardized Enzyme Commission (EC) number, so that there is no ambiguity between gene products. Two enzymes from two different organisms may have the same EC number, but slightly different amino acid sequences or slightly different protein names in the GenBank annotation files. Using EC numbers will allow automated programs to match identical enzymes correctly. The enzymes are correlated with their associated chemical reactions and the implicated metabolites. This method of intentionally leaving out some information and looking at the bigger picture on more of a systems level could be classified as systems biology [26].

A personal computer was used for all programming and analysis. A simple, personally-designed online application was used for all analysis. This software can be found at the web link [27]. Full instructions on how to use the software can be found in a link to the readme file on the main program interface linked above. The software utilizes a relational database system using MySQL to store and query information from the GenBank annotation files from NCBI and information from an EC number database [28]. The EC number data file was parsed for inserting data into a personally-designed database table. The following example (Figure 1) shows the type of information contained in the data file that was parsed for EC numbers.

```
ID    1.8.1.19
DE    Sulfide dehydrogenase.
CA    Hydrogen sulfide + (sulfide)(n) + NADP(+) = (sulfide)(n+1) + NADPH.
CF    Flavoprotein; Iron-sulfur.
CC    -!- In the archaeon Pyrococcus furiosus the enzyme is involved in the
CC        oxidation of NADPH which is produced in peptide degradation.
CC    -!- The enzyme also catalyzes the reduction of sulfur with lower
CC        activity.
DR    Q8U195, SUDHA_PYRFU;  Q8U194, SUDHB_PYRFU;
//
```

Figure 1. Example data extracted from The ENZYME Database in 2000, Bairoch [28].

The web application allows its user to choose two groups of microbiomes for metabolomics comparison. The program was designed with the intent to be used for any microbial metabolomics study between two microbiomes, two small alterations of the same microbiome or even simply between two single organisms. The application allows the user to upload a new genome file in GenBank format. Initially, the application could only accept GenBank files with EC number annotations present, but now, there does not need to be any EC number annotations in the original file. However, inserting EC number annotations with automation has certain limitations. Database queries fall into three categories for each comparison: no matches, one unique match or more than one match. In the event that there is more than one match, manual curation will be necessary. In the meantime, the program instead prints the first three matches to the GenBank file and makes a designation within the file and within the associated database that says that the information may be less reliable than unique matches or the data that was already annotated in the original file.

The application returns output directly to the screen within the web browser. The output consists of a data table, where each row contains columns showing the GI accession number (from NCBI) of the organism that the data come from, the organism's common name, an EC number, the predominant name associated with that EC number, the associated biochemistry, a "reliability factor" and a keyword describing which microbiome the data are associated with (default "Microbiome 1" and "Microbiome 2", or custom names supplied by the user on the form page). The table is broken up into three major sections: those enzymes that are identical between the two microbiomes and those enzymes that are unique for each microbiome. For this study (and likely others that might benefit from this software package), the sub-tables showing the unique results are most useful. An example partial result (Figure 2) might be as follows.

In Figure 2, GI accession is the unique identifier for that GenBank record within NCBI, and the reliability column differentiates between new annotations with multiple EC number matches (reliability = 0) and new annotations with unique matches and old annotations (reliability = 1).

Organisms in Microbiome1:

187426706 Akkermansia muciniphila ATCC BAA-835

Organisms in Microbiome2:

149935097 Bacteroides vulgatus ATCC 8482
291526581 Eubacterium rectale DSM 17629

Received search term query ''.

Similar coded enzymes: 619 match(es).

GI Accession	Organism Name	EC_number	Enzyme Name	Biochemistry	Reliability	Microbiome Name
187426706	Akkermansia muciniphila ATCC BAA-835	1.3.1.12	Prephenate dehydrogenase.	Prephenate + NAD(+) = 4-hydroxyphenylpyruvate + CO(2) + NADH.	0	Microbiome1
291526581	Eubacterium rectale DSM 17629	1.3.1.12	Prephenate dehydrogenase.	Prephenate + NAD(+) = 4-hydroxyphenylpyruvate + CO(2) + NADH.	1	Microbiome2
187426706	Akkermansia muciniphila ATCC BAA-835	6.5.1.2	DNA ligase (NAD(+)).	NAD(+) + (deoxyribonucleotide)(n) + (deoxyribonucleotide)(m) = AMP + beta-nicotinamide D-ribonucleotide + (deoxyribonucleotide)(n+m).	1	Microbiome1
291526581	Eubacterium rectale DSM 17629	6.5.1.2	DNA ligase (NAD(+)).	NAD(+) + (deoxyribonucleotide)(n) + (deoxyribonucleotide)(m) = AMP + beta-nicotinamide D-ribonucleotide + (deoxyribonucleotide)(n+m).	1	Microbiome2

Figure 2. Example extract from the original software results page.

Three queries total were made with the web application. The first involved the organisms from the top section of Table 1. The second added the five organisms from the middle section of Table 1. In the third query, we tried to filter our results to just the organisms that are thought to be most important in each microbiome. These microbiomes consisted of those in Table 2. Table 1 is also available in the Supplemental Material as Table S1.

Table 1. Microorganisms chosen for the comparative metabolomics study. Organisms included in Query 2 had *de novo* Enzyme Commission (EC) number annotations.

Query	"Healthy" Microbiome	"Autism" Microbiome
Included in Query 1	Bacteroides fragilis Bifidobacterium longum Ruminococcus bromii Roseburia intestinalis Faecalibacterium prausnitzii Eubacterium rectale Alistipes putredinis Alistipes shahii Weissella koreensis Prevotella ruminicola Odoribacter splanchnicus Methanobrevibacter smithii Clostridium leptum Lactobacillus acidophilus	Desulfovibrio desulfuricans Clostridium perfringens Clostridium difficile Akkermansia muciniphila

Table 1. *Cont.*

Query	"Healthy" Microbiome	"Autism" Microbiome
Additional organisms includedin Query 2	Bacteroides thetaiotaomicron Bacteroides caccae	Sutterella wadsworthensis Clostridium bolteae Bacteroides vulgatus
Desired, but not included	Bacteroides finegoldii Bacteroides ovatus Bacteroides uniformis Bifidobacterium adolescentis Bifidobacterium pseudolongum Eubacterium siraeum Dorea Veillonella Turicibacter Barnesiella intestinihominis Odoribacter laneus Dialister invisus	Desulfovibrio piger Desulfovibrio intestinalis Clostridium butyricum Clostridium paraputrificum Clostridium subterminale Clostridium tertium Clostridium bifermentans Clostridium glycolicum Bacteroides stercoris Parabacteroides distasonis Parabacteroides merdae Paraprevotella xylaniphila Eubacterium eligens Prevotella oulorum

Table 2. Selected organisms for Query 3 of the Metabolomics Software.

	Organisms in Control:
392623967	Bacteroides caccae CL03T12C61
60495220	Bacteroides fragilis ATCC 25285 = NCTC 93
29342100	Bacteroides thetaiotaomicron VPI-5482
666001751	Bifidobacterium longum BXY01
488447870	Lactobacillus acidophilus La-14
148552872	Methanobrevibacter smithii ATCC 35061; PS; DSMZ
	Organisms in Autism:
149935097	Bacteroides vulgatus ATCC 8482
480704622	Clostridium bolteae 90A9
110676061	Clostridium perfringens ATCC 13124
219869941	Desulfovibrio desulfuricans ATCC 27774
115252745	Peptoclostridium difficile 630
512689910	Sutterella wadsworthensis HGA0223

The organisms chosen for each query were input into the program and the results copied and pasted into an Excel file (available as the Supplemental Material, Tables S2–S7: each query is separated into two worksheets, one for complete raw data, and one for filtered data of interest). The "unique" results were looked through manually and considered on a case by case basis, with literature data in mind. Special attention was paid to those enzymes and metabolites found in the methionine and cysteine metabolic pathways and those involved with oxidative stress [13] and amino acid metabolism [29–31].

3. Results

The full results will not be reproduced here, but can easily be reproduced using the online software and the methods detailed above. The full results for each query are available as the Supplemental Material, Tables S2, S4, and S6. Additionally, the full results have been filtered for the most meaningful results and pasted within the Supplemental Material, Tables S3, S5, and S7. The first query resulted in the most meaningful results. It had 19,959 identical enzyme matches between the two microbiomes tested, 834 unique enzymes for the "control" microbiome and 161 unique enzymes for the "autism" microbiome. Gene copies are included in this count, so these numbers are a bit inflated. The identical enzymes are meaningless for this study, so we direct our attention to the tables of "unique" enzymes. Any meaningful results must be found manually. Table 3 below shows the differences in match statistics between each query. The majority of the results found with Query 1 were also found in Queries 2 and 3, with possibly a few minor differences. Judging by the quantity of the results, these minor differences were assumed to be near negligible. Therefore, when comparing Queries 1 and 2, we can come up with an approximate difference in the number of unique results by subtracting the statistics. Therefore, for instance, Query 2 only had 19 new results unique to the "control" microbiome and 34 new results unique to the "autism" microbiome, compared to the results of Query 1. Thus, one can see that Queries 2 and 3 would have less novel results overall than Query 1, given that Query 1 was conducted first.

Table 3. Comparing match statistics between web application queries.

Query	Similar Enzymes	Control Unique	Autism Unique
1	19,959	834	161
2	41,035	853	195
3	14,451	356	387

From an experimental study on metabolic biomarkers in autistic individuals [29], we know that many amino acids are found in significantly lower abundance *vs.* controls, including glycine, serine, threonine, alanine, histidine, glutamine, glutamate and the organic acid, taurine. Antioxidants (especially glutathione) are also in much lower abundance. Another study [30] cites reduced glutathione as being in much lower abundance and another type of antioxidant, thioredoxins, as being in much higher abundance. James *et al.* [13] claims that there is a metabolic bottleneck in many autistic individuals, where the conversion of methionine to cysteine is inhibited, leading to diminished glutathione formation. This information was kept in mind when analyzing the data. The relevance of these findings will be discussed in more detail in the Discussion Section.

In Tables 4–11 we present the most meaningful results obtained from the data mining. The majority of the results come from the first web application query. First, for the enzymes unique to the "control" microbiome, we present enzymes indicative of glutamate metabolism. Some of the entries below contain notation, such as "×3" after an organism name. This denotes that that organism has that number of gene copies coding for that particular enzyme (the first table with this notation is Table 6 below).

Table 4. Acetylornithine transaminase expression ("control" unique).

2.6.1.11	**Acetylornithine Transaminase**	***N*(2)-Acetyl-L-ornithine + 2-Oxoglutarate = *N*-Acetyl-L-glutamate5-semialdehyde + L-Glutamate**
Expressed by the following organisms:		
291516108	Alistipes shahii WAL 8301	
291516108	Alistipes shahii WAL 8301	
60495220	Bacteroides fragilis ATCC 25285 = NCTC 93	
291526581	Eubacterium rectale DSM 17629	
291526581	Eubacterium rectale DSM 17629	
295102938	Faecalibacterium prausnitzii L2/6	
148552872	Methanobrevibacter smithii ATCC 35061; PS; DSMZ	
324314063	Odoribacter splanchnicus DSM 220712	
294473972	Prevotella ruminicola Bryant 23	
291541371	Roseburia intestinalis XB6B4	

Table 5. Phosphoserine transaminase expression ("control" unique).

2.6.1.52	**Phosphoserine Transaminase**	**(1) *O*-Phospho-L-serine + 2-Oxoglutarate = 3-Phosphonooxypyruvate + L-Glutamate (2) 4-Phosphonooxy-L-threonine + 2-Oxoglutarate = (3*R*)-3-Hydroxy-2-oxo-4-phosphonooxybutanoate + L-Glutamate**
Expressed by the following organisms:		
167660682	Alistipes putredinis DSM 17216	
291516108	Alistipes shahii WAL 8301	
60495220	Bacteroides fragilis ATCC 25285 = NCTC 93	
295102938	Faecalibacterium prausnitzii L2/6	
324314063	Odoribacter splanchnicus DSM 220712	
294473972	Prevotella ruminicola Bryant 23	
291541371	Roseburia intestinalis XB6B4	
291543183	Ruminococcus bromii L2-63	

Table 6. 2-oxoglutarate synthase expression ("control" unique).

1.2.7.3	**2-Oxoglutarate Synthase**	**2-Oxoglutarate + CoA + 2 Oxidized Ferredoxin = Succinyl-CoA + CO(2) +2 Reduced Ferredoxin + 2 H(+)**
Expressed by the following organisms (multiple gene copies present):		
291516108	Alistipes shahii WAL 8301 (×5)	
148552872	Methanobrevibacter smithii ATCC 35061; PS; DSMZ (×5)	
324314063	Odoribacter splanchnicus DSM 220712 (×3)	

Table 7. Glutamate synthase expression ("control" unique).

1.4.1.14	**Glutamate Synthase (NADH)**	**2 L-Glutamate + NAD(+) = L-Glutamine + 2-Oxoglutarate + NADH**
Expressed by the following organisms:		
291526581	Eubacterium rectale DSM 17629 (×3)	
295102938	Faecalibacterium prausnitzii L2/6 (×4)	
291541371	Roseburia intestinalis XB6B4 (×3)	
291543183	Ruminococcus bromii L2-63 (×3)	

There were several enzymes of interest coded by *Lactobacillus acidophilus* alone, many involving methionine and cysteine metabolism. Arginase produces ornithine from arginine, a precursor to glutamate. Mercury (II) reductase is included, because sulfur metabolism is involved with detoxifying toxic heavy metals, such as mercury. NADH peroxidase is an antioxidant, and the enzymes associated with methionine metabolism are ultimately associated with glutathione formation, another antioxidant. See Table 8 for these results.

Table 8. Enzymes of interest coded by Lactobacillus acidophilus: Query 1.

2.1.1.10	Homocysteine *S*-methyltransferase.	*S*-methyl-L-methionine + L-homocysteine = 2 L-methionine.
2.1.1.14	5-methyltetrahydropteroyltriglutamate homocysteine *S*-methyltransferase.	5-methyltetrahydropteroyltri-L-glutamate + L-homocysteine = tetrahydropteroyltri-L-glutamate + L-methionine.
3.5.3.1	Arginase.	L-arginine + H_2O = L-ornithine + urea.
4.2.1.22	Cystathionine beta-synthase.	L-serine + L-homocysteine = L-cystathionine + H_2O.
4.4.1.1	Cystathionine gamma-lyase.	L-cystathionine + H_2O = L-cysteine + NH_3 + 2-oxobutanoate.
1.16.1.1	Mercury(II) reductase.	$Hg + NADP^+ + H^+ = Hg^{2+} + NADPH$.
2.1.1.176	16S rRNA (cytosine(967)-C(5))-methyltransferase.	*S*-adenosyl-L-methionine + cytosine(967) in 16S rRNA = *S*-adenosyl-L-homocysteine + 5-methylcytosine(967) in 16S rRNA.
1.11.1.1	NADH peroxidase.	$NADH + H_2O_2 = NAD^+ + 2\,H_2O$.

Other enzymes of interest were antioxidants superoxide reductase (1.15.1.2), coded by *Faecalibacterium prausnitzii*, and glutathione peroxidase (1.11.1.9), coded by *Prevotella ruminicola*. Several others exhibited metabolic pathways associated with glutamate, cysteine and methionine and a few for some amino acids of less interest, such as serine or histidine.

The following (Table 9) are some enzymes of interest from the "autism" microbiome. Interestingly, *Clostridium perfringens* is the only organism studied (among both microbiomes) that codes for glutamate: cysteine ligase and glutathione synthase, the two enzymes needed for glutathione formation.

Table 9. Enzymes of interest coded by the "autism" microbiome; Query 1.

110676061	Clostridium perfringens ATCC 13124	4.1.1.50	Adenosylmethionine decarboxylase.	S-adenosyl-L-methionine = S-adenosyl 3-(methylthio)propylamine + CO_2.
115252745	Peptoclostridium difficile 630	4.1.1.50	Adenosylmethionine decarboxylase.	S-adenosyl-L-methionine = S-adenosyl 3-(methylthio)propylamine + CO_2.
110676061	Clostridium perfringens ATCC 13124	4.1.1.22	Histidine decarboxylase.	L-histidine = histamine + CO_2.
110676061	Clostridium perfringens ATCC 13124	6.3.2.2	Glutamate–cysteine ligase.	ATP + L-glutamate + L-cysteine = ADP + phosphate + gamma-L-glutamyl-L-cysteine.
110676061	Clostridium perfringens ATCC 13124	6.3.2.3	Glutathione synthase.	ATP + gamma-L-glutamyl-L-cysteine + glycine = ADP + phosphate +glutathione.
219869941	Desulfovibrio desulfuricans ATCC 27774	2.6.1.44	Alanine–glyoxylate transaminase.	L-alanine + glyoxylate = pyruvate + glycine.
219869941	Desulfovibrio desulfuricans ATCC 27774	1.8.99.3	Hydrogen sulfite reductase.	$(O_3S.S.SO_3)^{2-}$ + acceptor + 2 H_2O + OH^- = 3 HSO_3^- + reduced acceptor.
115252745	Peptoclostridium difficile 630	4.4.1.11	Methionine gamma-lyase.	L-methionine + H_2O = methanethiol + NH_3 + 2-oxobutanoate.
115252745	Peptoclostridium difficile 630	1.8.1.2	Sulfite reductase (NADPH).	H_2S + 3 $NADP^+$ + 3 H_2O = sulfite + 3 NADPH.
115252745	Peptoclostridium difficile 630	5.4.3.5	D-ornithine 4,5-aminomutase.	D-ornithine = (2*R*,4*S*)-2,4-diaminopentanoate.
115252745	Peptoclostridium difficile 630	5.1.1.12	Ornithine racemase.	L-ornithine = D-ornithine.

It was found that *Desulfovibrio desulfuricans* and *Clostridium difficile* uniquely coded for enzymes that involved the use of thioredoxins, including sarcosine reductase, betaine reductase and glycine reductase.

Queries 2 and 3 had much less novel results in comparison. We will look at these results first, then take a look at why adding new EC number annotations to the files did not change much in terms of the overall results.

Query 2 only resulted in one new meaningful result (Table 10): the conversion of *S*-adenosyl-methionine to *S*-adenosyl-homocysteine, part of the transsulfuration pathways.

Table 10. SAM (*S*-adenosyl-methionine) conversion to SAH (*S*-adenosyl-homocysteine).

219869941	Desulfovibrio desulfuricans ATCC 27774	2.1.1.77	Protein-L-isoaspartate (D-aspartate) *O*-methyltransferase	*S*-adenosyl-L-methionine + protein L-isoaspartate = *S*-adenosyl-L-homocysteine + protein L-isoaspartate α-methyl ester.

Query 3 also resulted in only one major meaningful result, as well as two more that are at least noteworthy, involved with cyanide metabolism (Table 11). Of course, cyanide is highly toxic to humans, so the fact that *Clostridium difficile* is the only organism studied that can metabolize it is interesting, but its relevance to the present study is inconclusive. Also of note was that *Bifidobacterium* and *Lactobacillus* of the control microbiome uniquely coded for 2-haloacid dehalogenase, and *Lactobacillus* uniquely coded for haloalkane dehalogenase. Again, upon searching the literature in regards to these results, the interpretation is inconclusive. The relevance to the present study cannot be determined.

Table 11. Enzymes of interest coded by the "autism" microbiome in Query 3.

115252745	Peptoclostridium difficile 630	2.8.1.2	3-mercaptopyruvate sulfurtransferase.	3-mercaptopyruvate + cyanide = pyruvate + thiocyanate.
115252745	Peptoclostridium difficile 630	2.8.1.1	Thiosulfate sulfurtransferase.	Thiosulfate + cyanide = sulfite + thiocyanate.
115252745	Peptoclostridium difficile 630	4.4.1.8	Cystathionine beta-lyase.	L-cystathionine + H_2O = L-homocysteine + NH_3 + pyruvate.
666001751	Bifidobacterium longum BXY01	3.8.1.9	(*R*)-2-haloacid dehalogenase.	(*R*)-2-haloacid + H_2O = (*S*)-2-hydroxyacid + halide.
666001751	Bifidobacterium longum BXY01	3.8.1.2	(*S*)-2-haloacid dehalogenase.	(*S*)-2-haloacid + H_2O = (*R*)-2-hydroxyacid + halide.
666001751	Bifidobacterium longum BXY01	3.8.1.10	2-haloacid dehalogenase (configuration-inverting).	(1) (*S*)-2-haloacid + H_2O = (*R*)-2-hydroxyacid + halide. (2) (*R*)-2-haloacid + H_2O = (*S*)-2-hydroxyacid + halide.
488447870	Lactobacillus acidophilus La-14	3.8.1.2	(*S*)-2-haloacid dehalogenase.	(*S*)-2-haloacid + H_2O = (*R*)-2-hydroxyacid + halide.
488447870	Lactobacillus acidophilus La-14	3.8.1.5	Haloalkane dehalogenase.	1-haloalkane + H_2O = a primary alcohol + halide.

In order to analyze why some organisms provided more information than others, we compared the number of EC number annotations within each GenBank file to the total CDSs (coding sequences) within each file. For the new organisms added for Queries 2 and 3, we can see that very few annotations were actually added compared to the total CDSs. "Good" coverage seems to lie between 12% and 25% when taking the ratio of EC number annotations to total CDSs, and all five of the newly annotated files fall well short of this mark. However, Bifidobacterium had greatly improved coverage after updating EC number annotations, rising from <4% to >25%. Despite this, very few new results were obtained. Table 12 shows these statistics. This table is included in the Supplemental Material as Table S8 as well. It may seem strange at first that there are so few EC number annotations compared to the number of annotated CDSs, but keep in mind that enzymes are only a fraction of the organisms' proteome (e.g., non-catalytic proteins, such as inter-membrane proteins), and some of the organisms' genes code for non-translated RNA transcripts, such as tRNAs. There also seems to be a dearth in annotation of EC numbers in general.

Table 12. GenBank file statistic comparisons between the number of EC number annotations and coding sequences (CDSs).

	Original File			Updated EC Annotations				
Organism Name	**Total CDSs**	**Total EC Numbers**	**%**	**Total EC Numbers**	**Total "Multi-EC" Designations**	**Actual EC Total**	**%**	**% Increase**
Akkermansia muciniphila	2138	286	13.38	401	34	367	17.17	28.32
Alistipes putredinis	659	92	13.96	110	6	104	15.78	13.04
Alistipes shahii	2563	548	21.38	603	17	586	22.86	6.93
Bacillus subtilis	4140	912	22.03	941	8	933	22.54	2.30
Bacteroides fragilis	4406	366	8.31	377	5	372	8.443	1.64
Bifidobacterium longum	1903	68	3.57	672	189	483	25.38	610.29
Clostridium difficile	3902	1015	26.01	1,035	6	1029	26.37	1.38
Clostridium leptum	602	100	16.61	114	4	110	18.27	10.00
Clostridium perfringens	2878	504	17.51	539	10	529	18.38	4.96
Desulfovibrio desulfuricans	2356	292	12.39	392	32	360	15.28	23.29
Escherichia coli	4967	612	12.32	1542	285	1257	25.31	105.39
Eubacterium rectale	2898	636	21.95	696	16	680	23.46	6.92
Faecalibacterium prausnitzii	2756	586	21.26	641	17	624	22.64	6.48
Lactobacillus acidophilus	1876	486	25.91	585	31	554	29.53	13.99

Table 12. *Cont.*

Organism Name	Original File			Updated EC Annotations				% Increase
	Total CDSs	Total EC Numbers	%	Total EC Numbers	Total "Multi-EC" Designations	Actual EC Total	%	
Methanobrevibacter smithii	1795	414	23.06	454	12	442	24.62	6.76
Odoribacter splanchnicus	3498	515	14.72	603	27	576	16.47	11.84
Prevotella ruminicola	2791	480	17.20	519	12	507	18.17	5.62
Roseburia intestinalis	3630	709	19.53	793	17	776	21.38	9.45
Ruminococcus bromii	1811	467	25.79	496	9	487	26.89	4.28
Weissella koreensis	1335	93	6.97	288	61	227	17	144.09
Bacteroides caccae	3441	0	0.00	76	19	57	1.656	
Bacteroides thetaiotaomicron	4787	0	0.00	413	125	288	6.016	
Bacteroides vulgatus	4065	0	0.00	267	80	187	4.6	
clostridium bolteae	5830	0	0.00	737	227	510	8.748	
Sutterella wadsworthensis	2433	0	0.00	136	39	97	3.987	

4. Discussion

The present study successfully identified several key enzymes associated with autism spectrum disorders using a bioinformatics data mining approach, by comparing the metabolomes of two distinct microbiomes. We must compare the results to published experimental data in order to evaluate the impact of this study, such as those found in [29–33].

We expected to find key biomarkers unique to *Desulfovibrio* and *Clostridia* species indicative of autism, but instead, the key was based on identifying enzymes that were missing from these organisms; hence, a decreased abundance of such enzymes could be used as diagnostic biomarkers for autism. Several different amino acids have previously been reported to be in lower abundance in autistic individuals, but in this study, the amino acid that stood out the most was glutamate. Several organisms in the "control" microbiome coded for enzymes associated with glutamate metabolism, but were curiously missing from the "autism" microbiome. Glutamate is an integral part of glutathione, a tripeptide made of glutamate, cysteine and glycine. It was known before that glutathione was down-regulated in autism, but researchers focused their attention on an inhibition of cysteine metabolism to be the culprit.

Upon closer inspection of glutamate's association with autism, we find that there is a hypothesis that does not involve oxidative stress at all. Glutamate is the human body's major excitatory neurotransmitter, which works in opposition to gamma-aminobutyric acid (GABA) [34,35]. Contrary to the Ming *et al.* study [29], these studies, as well as Adams *et al.* [31] reported higher quantities of glutamate *vs.* neurotypical controls. Tevarst van Elst *et al.* [34] actually reviewed two different hypotheses: that a hypoglutamatergic condition is related to autism and also that a hyperglutamatergic condition is related to autism. Regardless of which one it is, the authors theorize that an imbalance in the neurological excitation/inhibition chemical signaling in the central nervous system is thought to be associated with autism. Furthermore, glutamate decarboxylase is the enzyme responsible for converting glutamate into GABA. Loss of the gene coding for GABA in host neurons has been shown to lead to symptoms characteristic of autism [36]. Going back to the results of our software (*i.e.*, Query 2), we found that glutamate decarboxylase is expressed by organisms from both the control and autism groups. Therefore, what then is the association of our research to the hypotheses on glutamate and autism? That remains to be determined, but we must not ignore the fact that we might not have heard of this field of research had not our software pointed in that direction. Even with limited data availability, it seems that our software can be useful in developing new hypotheses and revealing literature that was previously unknown to us.

After completing our analysis, we came across another study where *Akkermansia muciniphila* was found in decreased amounts in individuals with autism [37]. According to the authors, *Akkermansia* is integral to the host's gut health; the gut mucus layer is reduced as *Akkermansia* composition within the gut is depleted. This contradicts the Finegold *et al.* pyrosequencing study. In light of these two conflicting studies, it seems that we may have been correct in assuming that the involvement of *Akkermansia* in autism is questionable at best. We still included it in the study, because theoretically, it should serve as a basis for comparison. If we think that certain *Clostridia* species and sulfate reducers are indicative of autism, then we may be biased towards results that agree with that assumption. If we include a questionable case, such as *Akkermansia*,in the "autism" group analysis, then we may better be able to rule out false positives. Regarding this inclusion, no significant results were found in Queries 1 or 2, leading to the exclusion of *Akkermansia* from Query 3. Query 3 had quite similar results as Queries 1 and 2, which lends credence to the idea that those organisms still included in the "autism" group for Query 3 are more likely to be involved in autism pathogenesis.

Hydrogen sulfide has been cited as a toxic metabolite produced by *Desulfovibrio* species [10], but data on this metabolite were inconclusive. It was found that *Desulfovibrio* is not the only organism (in either microbiome) that can metabolize hydrogen sulfide. What we did notice is that *Clostridium difficile* codes for enzymes that metabolize alternative pathways for ornithine and methionine, precursors to glutamate and cysteine, respectively, with the enzymes ornithine racemase, D-ornithine 4,5-aminomutase, adenosylmethionine decarboxylase and methionine gamma-lyase. Nearly every organism studied codes for enzymes using ferredoxins and thioredoxins, alternative antioxidants to glutathione, which also use a sulfhydryl electron acceptor for reducing power. It is possible that thioredoxins were found in much higher abundance in autistic individuals [28], because thioredoxins had to take over from glutathione as the body's dominant antioxidant. However, if glutathione is usually dominant, then there must be something not as chemically favorable associated with ferredoxins and thioredoxins or perhaps they are just not sufficient to fill in the antioxidative gap that glutathione usually fills. That *Clostridium difficile* can uniquely use ornithine and methionine for other purposes other than glutathione formation provides evidence for this hypothesis. Interestingly, the final two catalytic steps in glutathione formation are uniquely coded by *Clostridium perfringens*, part of the "autism" microbiome. However, many of the precursor steps are uniquely coded by *Lactobacillus acidophilus*, part of the "control" microbiome. Glutathione is still existent in autistic individuals, so perhaps *Clostridium perfringens* allows for some extra utility in glutathione formation; or maybe this is just coincidence.

Quite remarkable was the fact that nearly every reaction of the transsulfuration and transmethylation metabolic pathways was coded by the organisms studied, but that each microbiome ("control" and "autism") could not express the pathways in their entirety alone. This suggests some sort of interdependence between the two microbiomes on completing these pathways. The control microbiome supplies glutamate metabolism, and cysteine and glutathione formation is split between the two groups of organisms. Based on this information, it seems that organisms, such as abnormal *Clostridia* species and *Desulfovibrio*, may be products of the sulfur metabolic deficiency found in so many autistic individuals and, therefore, may be essential in filling a unique metabolic niche. However, because of the known toxic byproducts of these organisms, they may still be causing gastrointestinal inflammation and subsequent neuro-inflammation associated with "leaky gut syndrome", leading to regressive autism [15,31]. Therefore, even though these organisms may be causing some major ill effects, the matter becomes complicated by the necessity of their presence in the host. The sulfur metabolic deficiencies and lack of proper anti-oxidation therefore seem to lie at the heart of the problems that lead to regressive autism. If treatment is possible, it would therefore be more likely to entail dietary supplements that restore the metabolic deficiencies to normal conditions [13], rather than eradicating the proposed offending organisms from the host's gut. James *et al.* [13] reported some improvements in symptoms with specific dietary supplements, and a study by Adams *et al.* [38] provides some more evidence of this. The Adams *et al.* study included adult subjects with autism, as well.

It is important to note that there were some crucial limitations to this study. Besides the obvious, that this study is purely computational, the dependence on having annotation data for EC numbers greatly limits the scope of the study. When the first query to the web application was completed and analyzed, it was thought that including more organisms of interest (with newly annotated EC numbers) would greatly strengthen the study. This, in fact, hardly had any impact at all on the initial study. These files had so few annotations, that they did not give good representations of the metabolome of these organisms. Thus, we can only surmise that there may be other more meaningful results possible with better data. It is possible that this study could be improved by creating new gene annotations altogether by using the publically available BLAST tool for sequence alignment of microbial genomic DNA and then annotating these genes with translated gene products and EC numbers. Also of note is that the two *Clostridium* species studied most deeply in this context (*C. perfringens* and *C. difficile*) have not, to our knowledge, been specified as part of the "autism" microbiome, but they happened to be two of the most widely available and comprehensive genomes of *Clostridia* that could appear in the human gut. Therefore, they were chosen as "representatives" of the *Clostridium* genus, and thus, associated results should be interpreted with scrutiny. It appears that this type of study has not been attempted previously, yielding mixed results. This provides substantial evidence that the present approach is novel and may be a step in a new, potentially useful direction, but its novelty severely limits its impact, because of a lack of resources. It is surmised that as data on microbial genomics and data on gut bacteria associated with autism patients improves, so too will the utility of our novel software and our comparative modeling approach. Future work could include full *de novo* genomic sequencing of gut microbes and validation through next-generation sequencing devices, followed by comprehensive annotation with accurate EC numbers. On NCBI's server, there is a noted difference in genomic comprehensiveness between microorganisms, where key gut microbes are covered definitively less than model organisms, such as *Escherichia coli* or *Bacillus subtilis*. We need to be able to have more studies on gut microbes in their natural habitat and their interactions with host cells in order to have more experimental data to fine-tune our metabolomics model. It also remains to be determined what would be the best way of evaluating data significance from this type of study.

Nevertheless, we still believe that substantial results came about from this study. We have not seen this type of comparative analysis conducted with autism in mind before, and we are proud to say that our computational approach was successful, given some of its parallels to previous experimental studies. Some experimental studies were not able to be validated with this approach, which is to be expected. As stated earlier, this software was designed with the intent to be used for many other applications, besides autism, hence making the software publically available online. Many other human illnesses and conditions are thought to be associated with the human gut microbiome [5], and we believe that these applications might benefit from our approach, as well. Microbiomes in other environments may also benefit; much potential could be lost if the software's use were limited to only the human gut.

Acknowledgments: Colin Heberling would like to acknowledge Thomas Koval and the Johns Hopkins Advanced Academic Programs (AAP) graduate program for guidance and for the opportunity to work on this project, as well as Joshua Orvis for instruction in web development as applied to bioinformatics and for his guidance on an early prototype of the online software.

Author Contributions: Prasad Dhurjati provided a mentoring and supervisory role throughout this project and contributed to its conceptual design. Colin Heberling had a large part in the project's conceptual design and contributed fully to its execution and analysis.

References

1. Baio, J. Prevalence of Autism Spectrum Disorders. In *Autism and Developmental Disabilities Monitoring Network, 14 Sites, United States, 2008*; Centers for Disease Control and Prevention, Surveillance Summaries: Atlanta, GA, USA, 2012; Volume 61, SS03, pp. 1–19.
2. CDC Features—Ten Things to Know About New Autism Data. Available online: http://www.cdc.gov/Features/dsAutismData/ (accessed on 25 February 2015).
3. Parracho, H.M.R.T.; Bingham, M.O.; Gibson, G.R.; McCartney, A.L. Differences between the gut microflora of children with autistic spectrum disorders and that of healthy children. *J. Med. Microbiol.* **2005**, *54*, 987–991. [CrossRef] [PubMed]
4. Adams, J.B.; Johansen, L.J.; Powell, L.D.; Quig, D.; Rubin, R.A. Gastrointestinal flora and gastrointestinal status in children with autism—Comparisons to typical children and correlation with autism severity. *BMC Gastroenterol.* **2011**, *11*, 22. [CrossRef] [PubMed]

5. Kranich, J.; Maslowski, K.M.; Mackay, C.R. Commensal flora and the regulation of inflammatory and autoimmune responses. *Semin. Immunol.* **2011**, *23*, 139–145. [CrossRef] [PubMed]
6. Human Microbiome Project Consortium. Structure, function and diversity of the healthy human microbiome. *Nature* **2012**, *486*, 207–214.
7. Turnbaugh, P.J.; Hamady, M.; Yatsunenko, T.; Cantarel, B.L.; Duncan, A.; Ley, R.E.; Sogin, M.L.; Jones, W.J.; Roe, B.A.; Affourtit, J.P.; *et al.* A core gut microbiome in obese and lean twins. *Nature* **2009**, *457*, 480–485. [CrossRef]
8. Finegold, S.M.; Downes, J.; Summanen, P.H. Microbiology of regressive autism. *Anaerobe* **2012**, *18*, 260–262. [CrossRef] [PubMed]
9. Finegold, S.M.; Dowd, S.E.; Contcharova, V.; Liu, C.; Henley, K.E.; Wolcott, R.D.; Youn, E.; Summanen, P.H.; Granpeesheh, D.; Dixon, D.; *et al.* Pyrosequencing study of fecal microflora of autistic and control children. *Anaerobe* **2010**, *16*, 444–453. [CrossRef]
10. Finegold, S. Desulfovibrio species are potentially important in regressive autism. *Med. Hypotheses* **2011**, *77*, 270–274. [CrossRef] [PubMed]
11. Wang, L.; Christophersen, C.T.; Sorich, M.J.; Gerber, J.P.; Angley, M.T.; Conlon, M.A. Increased abundance of *Sutterlla* spp. and *Ruminococcus torques* in feces of children with autism spectrum disorder. *Mol. Autism* **2013**, *4*, 42. [CrossRef] [PubMed]
12. Williams, B.L.; Hornig, M.; Buie, T.; Bauman, M.L.; Paik, M.C.; Wick, I.; Bennett, A.; Jabado, O.; Hirschberg, D.L.; Lipkin, W.I. Impaired carbohydrate digestion and transport and mucosal dysbiosis in the intestines of children with autism and gastrointestinal disturbances. *PLoS ONE* **2011**, *6*. [CrossRef] [PubMed]
13. James, S.J.; Cutler, P.; Melnyk, S.; Jernigan, S.; Janak, L.; Gaylor, D.W.; Neubrander, J.A. Metabolic biomarkers of increased oxidative stress and impaired methylation capacity in children with autism. *Am. J. Clin. Nutr.* **2004**, *80*, 1611–1617. [PubMed]
14. Alberti, A.; Pirrone, P.; Elia, M.; Waring, R.H.; Romano, C. Sulphation deficit in "Low-Functioning" autistic children: A pilot study. *Biol. Psychiatry* **1999**, *46*, 420–424. [CrossRef] [PubMed]
15. Heberling, C.A.; Dhurjati, P.S.; Sasser, M. Hypothesis for a systems connectivity model of autism spectrum disorder pathogenesis: Links to gut bacteria, oxidative stress, and intestinal permeability. *Med. Hypotheses* **2013**, *80*, 264–270. [CrossRef] [PubMed]
16. Nealson, K.; Venter, J.C. Metagenomics and the global ocean survey: What's in it for us, and why should we care? *ISME J.* **2007**, *1*, 185–190. [CrossRef] [PubMed]
17. Rusch, D.B.; Halpern, A.L.; Sutton, G.; Heidelberg, K.B.; Williamson, S.; Yooseph, S.; Wu, D.; Eisen, J.A.; Hoffman, J.M.; Remington, K.; *et al.* The Sorcerer II Global Ocean sampling expedition: Northwest Atlantic through Eastern Tropical Pacific. *PLoS Biol.* **2007**, *5*. [CrossRef]
18. The Human Microbiome Jumpstart Reference Strains Consortium. A catalog of reference genomes from the human microbiome. *Science* **2010**, *328*. [CrossRef]
19. Fernell, E.; Fagerburg, U.L.; Hellström, P.M. No evidence for a clear link between active intestinal inflammation and autism based on analyses faecal calprotectin and rectal nitric oxide. *Acta Paediatr.* **2007**, *96*, 1076–1079. [CrossRef] [PubMed]
20. Finegold, S.M.; Molitoris, D.; Song, Y.; Liu, C.; Vaisanen, M.L.; Bolte, E.; McTeague, M.; Sandler, R.; Wexler, H.; Marlowe, E.M.; *et al.* Gastrointestinal microflora studies in late-onset autism. *Clin. Infect. Dis.* **2002**, *35* (Suppl. 1), S6–S16. [CrossRef]
21. Heberling, C. Human gut microbiome functional analysis—Exploring the capabilities of the MEGAN Software. April 2013; unpublished.
22. Huson, D.H.; Auch, A.F.; Qi, J.; Schuster, S.C. MEGAN analysis of metagenomic data. *Genome Res.* **2007**, *17*, 377–386. [CrossRef] [PubMed]
23. Human Microbiome Project Consortium. A framework for human microbiome research. *Nature* **2012**, *486*, 215–221.
24. Lin, M.Y.; Chang, F.J. Antioxidative effect of intestinal bacteria *Bifidobacterium longum* ATCC 15708 and *Lactobacillus acidophilus* ATCC 4356. *Dig. Dis. Sci.* **2000**, *45*, 1617–1622. [CrossRef] [PubMed]
25. *The National Center for Biotechnology Information*; U.S. National Library of Medicine: 8600 Rockville Pike, Bethesda, MD, USA, 2014. Available online: http://www.ncbi.nlm.nih.gov/ (accessed on 25 September 2014).

26. Dhurjati, P.; Mayadevan, R. Systems biology: The synergistic interplay between biology and mathematics. *Can. J. Chem. Eng.* **2008**, *86*, 127–141. [CrossRef]
27. Heberling, C. Comparative Microbial Metabolomics. Available online: http://cheberling-homepc.com/comparative_microbial_metabolomics/gene_search_form.cgi (accessed on 12 October 2014).
28. Bairoch, A. The ENZYME database in 2000. *Nucleic Acids Res.* **2000**, *28*, 304–305. [CrossRef] [PubMed]
29. Ming, X.; Stein, T.P.; Barnes, V.; Rhodes, N.; Guo, L. Metabolic perturbance in autism spectrum disorders: A metabolomics study. *J. Proteome Res.* **2012**, *11*, 5856–5862. [PubMed]
30. Al-Yafee, Y.A.; Al-Ayadhi, L.Y.; Haq, S.H.; El-Ansary, A.E. Novel metabolic biomarkers related to sulfurdependent detoxification pathways in autistic patients of Saudi Arabia. *BMC Neurol.* **2011**, *11*, 139. [CrossRef] [PubMed]
31. Adams, J.B.; Audhya, T.; McDonough-Means, S.; Rubin, R.A.; Quig, D.; Geis, E.; Gehn, E.; Loresto, M.; Mitchell, J.; Atwood, S.; *et al.* Nutritional and metabolic status of children with autism *vs.* neurotypical children, and the association with autism severity. *Nutr. Metab.* **2011**, *8*, 34. [CrossRef]
32. Yap, I.K.S.; Angley, M.; Veselkov, K.A.; Holmes, E.; Lindon, J.C.; Nicholson, J.K. Urinary metabolic phenotyping differentiates children with autism from their unaffected siblings and age-matched controls. *J. Proteome Res.* **2010**, *9*, 2996–3004. [CrossRef] [PubMed]
33. Wang, L.; Angley, M.T.; Gerber, J.P.; Sorich, M.J. A review of candidate urinary biomarkers for autism spectrum disorder. *Biomarkers* **2011**, *16*, 537–552. [CrossRef] [PubMed]
34. Van Tebartz, E.L.; Maier, S.; Fangmeier, T.; Endres, D.; Mueller, G.T.; Nickel, K. Disturbed cingulate glutamate metabolism in adults with high-functioning autism spectrum disorder: Evidence in support of the excitatory/inhibitory imbalance hypothesis. *Mol. Psychiatry* **2014**, *19*, 1314–1325. [CrossRef] [PubMed]
35. El-Ansary, A.; Al-Ayadhi, L. GABAergic/glutamatergic imbalance relative to excessive neuroinflammation in autism spectrum disorders. *J. Neuroinflamm.* **2014**, *11*. [CrossRef]
36. Zhang, K.; Hill, K.; Labak, S.; Blatt, G.J.; Soghomonian, J.-J. Loss of glutamic acid decarboxylase (Gad67) in Gpr88-expressing neurons induces learning and social behavior deficits in mice. *Neuroscience* **2014**, *275*, 238–247. [CrossRef] [PubMed]
37. Wang, L.; Christophersen, C.T.; Sorich, M.J.; Gerber, J.P.; Angley, M.T.; Conlon, M.A. Low relative abundances of the mucolytic bacterium *Akkermansia muciniphila* and *Bifidobacterium* spp. in feces of children with autism. *Appl. Environ. Microbiol.* **2011**, *77*, 6718–6721. [CrossRef] [PubMed]
38. Adams, J.B.; Audhya, T.; McDonough-Means, S.; Rubin, R.A.; Quig, D.; Geis, E.; Gehn, E.; Loresto, M.; Mitchell, J.; Atwood, S.; *et al.* Effect of a vitamin/mineral supplement on children and adults with autism. *BMC Pediatr.* **2011**, *11*, 111. [CrossRef]

Permissions

All chapters in this book were first published by MDPI; hereby published with permission under the Creative Commons Attribution License or equivalent. Every chapter published in this book has been scrutinized by our experts. Their significance has been extensively debated. The topics covered herein carry significant findings which will fuel the growth of the discipline. They may even be implemented as practical applications or may be referred to as a beginning point for another development.

The contributors of this book come from diverse backgrounds, making this book a truly international effort. This book will bring forth new frontiers with its revolutionizing research information and detailed analysis of the nascent developments around the world.

We would like to thank all the contributing authors for lending their expertise to make the book truly unique. They have played a crucial role in the development of this book. Without their invaluable contributions this book wouldn't have been possible. They have made vital efforts to compile up to date information on the varied aspects of this subject to make this book a valuable addition to the collection of many professionals and students.

This book was conceptualized with the vision of imparting up-to-date information and advanced data in this field. To ensure the same, a matchless editorial board was set up. Every individual on the board went through rigorous rounds of assessment to prove their worth. After which they invested a large part of their time researching and compiling the most relevant data for our readers.

The editorial board has been involved in producing this book since its inception. They have spent rigorous hours researching and exploring the diverse topics which have resulted in the successful publishing of this book. They have passed on their knowledge of decades through this book. To expedite this challenging task, the publisher supported the team at every step. A small team of assistant editors was also appointed to further simplify the editing procedure and attain best results for the readers.

Apart from the editorial board, the designing team has also invested a significant amount of their time in understanding the subject and creating the most relevant covers. They scrutinized every image to scout for the most suitable representation of the subject and create an appropriate cover for the book.

The publishing team has been an ardent support to the editorial, designing and production team. Their endless efforts to recruit the best for this project, has resulted in the accomplishment of this book. They are a veteran in the field of academics and their pool of knowledge is as vast as their experience in printing. Their expertise and guidance has proved useful at every step. Their uncompromising quality standards have made this book an exceptional effort. Their encouragement from time to time has been an inspiration for everyone.

The publisher and the editorial board hope that this book will prove to be a valuable piece of knowledge for researchers, students, practitioners and scholars across the globe.

List of Contributors

Elena Masini, Eleonora Loi, Ana Florencia Vega-Benedetti and Patrizia Zavattari
Department of Biomedical Sciences, Unit of Biology and Genetics, University of Cagliari, 09042 Cagliari, Italy

Marinella Carta
Center for Pervasive Developmental Disorders, Azienda Ospedaliera Brotzu, 09121 Cagliari, Italy

Giuseppe Doneddu
Centro per l'Autismo e Disturbi correlati (CADc), Nuovo Centro Fisioterapico Sardo, 09131 Cagliari, Italy

Roberta Fadda
Department of Pedagogy, Psychology, Philosophy, University of Cagliari, 09123 Cagliari, Italy

Teri Smith, Susan Sharp, Ann M. Manzardo and Merlin G. Butler
Department of Psychiatry and Behavioral Sciences, University of Kansas Medical Center, 3901 Rainbow Boulevard, Kansas City, Kansas 66160, USA

Marco Colizzi
Section of Psychiatry, Department of Neurosciences, Biomedicine and Movement Sciences, University of Verona, 37134 Verona, Italy
Department of Psychosis Studies, Institute of Psychiatry, Psychology and Neuroscience, King's College London, London SE5 8AF, UK
Child and Adolescent Neuropsychiatry Unit, Maternal-Child Integrated Care Department, Integrated University Hospital of Verona, 37126 Verona, Italy

Elena Sironi, Federico Antonini, Marco Luigi Ciceri and Leonardo Zoccante
Child and Adolescent Neuropsychiatry Unit, Maternal-Child Integrated Care Department, Integrated University Hospital of Verona, 37126 Verona, Italy

Chiara Bovo
Medical Direction, Integrated University Hospital of Verona, 37126 Verona, Italy

Jessie M. Cameron and Valeriy Levandovskiy
Genetics and Genome Biology, Peter Gilgan Center for Research and Learning, Toronto, ON M5G 0A4, Canada

Wendy Roberts and Evdokia Anagnostou
Department of Paediatrics, University of Toronto, Toronto, ON M5S 1A1, Canada
Holland Bloorview Kids Rehabilitation Hospital, 150 Kigour Rd, Toronto, ON M4G 1R8, Canada

Stephen Scherer
Genetics and Genome Biology, Peter Gilgan Center for Research and Learning, Toronto, ON M5G 0A4, Canada
The Centre for Applied Genomics and Genetics and Genome Biology, the Hospital for Sick Children, Toronto, ON M5G 1X8, Canada
McLaughlin Centre and Department of Molecular Genetics, 686 Bay Street, 13th Floor, Peter Gilgan Center for Research and Learning, Toronto, ON M5G 0A4, Canada

Alvin Loh
Department of Paediatrics, University of Toronto, Toronto, ON M5S 1A1, Canada
Surrey Place Center, 2 Surrey Place, Toronto, ON M5S 2C2, Canada

Andreas Schulze
Genetics and Genome Biology, Peter Gilgan Center for Research and Learning, Toronto, ON M5G 0A4, Canada
Department of Paediatrics, University of Toronto, Toronto, ON M5S 1A1, Canada
Department of Biochemistry, University of Toronto, Toronto, ON M5S 1A8, Canada

Mariangela Gulisano, Rita Barone, Lara Cirnigliaro, Selena Di Silvestre, Serena Martellino, Nicoletta Maugeri, Maria Chiara Milana, Miriam Scerbo and Renata Rizzo
Child and Adolescent Psychiatric Section, Department of Clinical and Experimental Medicine, Catania University, Via Santa Sofia 78, 95123 Catania, Italy

Salvatore Alaimo, Alfredo Ferro and Alfredo Pulvirenti
Bioinformatics Unit, Department of Clinical and Experimental Medicine, Catania University, Viale Andrea Doria 6, 95125 Catania, Italy

In Hyang Kim and Jong-Eun Park
Department of Psychiatry, Seoul National University Hospital, Seongnam, Gyeonggi 463-707, Korea

Hee Jeong Yoo
Department of Psychiatry, Seoul National University Hospital, Seongnam, Gyeonggi 463-707, Korea
Department of Psychiatry, Seoul National University, College of Medicine, Seoul 110-744, Korea

Namshin Kim
Epigenomics Research Center, Genome Institute, Korea Research Institute of Bioscience and Biotechnology, Daejeon 305-806, Korea

Kyung Kim
Epigenomics Research Center, Genome Institute, Korea Research Institute of Bioscience and Biotechnology, Daejeon 305-806, Korea
Department of Biomedical Informatics, Ajou University, School of Medicine, Suwon 443-749, Korea
Department of Biomedical Science, Ajou University Graduate School of Medicine, Suwon 443-749, Korea

Seong-Hwan Rho
Simulacre Modeling Group, Seoul 140-897, Korea

Soon Ae Kim
Department of Pharmacology, Eulji University College of Medicine, Daejeon 301-746, Korea

Ki Young Lee
Department of Biomedical Informatics, Ajou University, School of Medicine, Suwon 443-749, Korea
Department of Biomedical Science, Ajou University Graduate School of Medicine, Suwon 443-749, Korea

Byung Yoon Choi
Department of Psychiatry, Seoul National University, College of Medicine, Seoul 110-744, Korea
Department of Otolaryngology, Seoul National University Hospital, Seongnam, Gyeonggi 463-707, Korea

Sanae Tanaka
Division of Integrated Art and Sciences and Local Community Support, Research Center for Child Mental Development, Kanazawa University, Kanazawa 920-8640, Japan

Aiko Komagome and Oko Arai
The COI Site, Tokyo University of the Arts Tokyo 110-8714, Japan

Aya Iguchi-Sherry
Artlink Central, Scotland FK8 1EA, UK

Akiko Nagasaka
Department of Childhood Care and Education, Faculty of Social Work, Kinjo University, Hakusan 924-8511, Japan

Chiharu Tsuji, Teruko Yuhi and Haruhiro Higashida
Department of Basic Research on Social Recognition, Research Center for Child Mental Development, Kanazawa University, Kanazawa 920-8640, Japan

Maki Rooksby
Adverse Childhood Experiences (ACE) Lab, Institute of Health and Wellbeing, University of Glasgow, Glasgow G12 8RZ, UK
Social Brain in Action Lab, Institute of Neuroscience and Psychology, University of Glasgow, Glasgow G12 8QB, UK

Mitsuru Kikuchi
Department of Psychiatry and Neurobiology, Graduate School of Medical Science, Kanazawa University, Kanazawa 920-8640, Japan

Takahiro Tsuji
Department of Basic Research on Social Recognition, Research Center for Child Mental Development, Kanazawa University, Kanazawa 920-8640, Japan
Department of Ophthalmology, Faculty of Medical Sciences, University of Fukui, Fukui 910-1193, Japan

Kana Minami
Department of Basic Research on Social Recognition, Research Center for Child Mental Development, Kanazawa University, Kanazawa 920-8640, Japan
Department of Health Development Nursing, Institute of Medical, Pharmaceutical and Health Sciences, Kanazawa University, Kanazawa 920-0942, Japan

Ole A. Andreassen
NORMENT, KG Jebsen Centre for Psychosis Research, University of Oslo, Oslo 0424, Norway
Division of Mental Health and Addiction, Oslo University Hospital, Oslo 0315, Norway

Arvid Heiberg
Department of Medical Genetics, Oslo University Hospital, Oslo 0424, Norway

Terje Nærland
NORMENT, KG Jebsen Centre for Psychosis Research, University of Oslo, Oslo 0424, Norway
NevSom, Department of Rare Disorders and Disabilities, Oslo University Hospital, Oslo 0424, Norway

Jarle Johannessen
NORMENT, KG Jebsen Centre for Psychosis Research, University of Oslo, Oslo 0424, Norway
Autism Society Norway, Oslo 0609, Norway

Sigrun Hope
NORMENT, KG Jebsen Centre for Psychosis Research, University of Oslo, Oslo 0424, Norway
Department of Neurohabilitation, Oslo University Hospital, Oslo 0424, Norway

Anne Lise Høyland
Regional Centre for Child and Youth Mental Health and Child Welfare, Department of Mental Health, Faculty of Medicine and Health Sciences, Norwegian University of Science and Technology, Trondheim 7491, Norway
Department of Pediatrics, St. Olavs Hospital, Trondheim University Hospital, Trondheim 7006, Norway

Jana Strohmaier and Marcella Rietschel
Department of Genetic Epidemiology in Psychiatry, Central Institute of Mental Health, Medical Faculty Mannheim, University of Heidelberg, Mannheim 68159, Germany

Tonje Torske
Division of Mental Health and Addiction, Vestre Viken Hospital Trust, Drammen 3004, Norway

Srdjan Djurovic
NORMENT, KG Jebsen Centre for Psychosis Research, University of Oslo, Oslo 0424, Norway
Department of Medical Genetics, Oslo University Hospital, Oslo 0424, Norway
Department of Clinical Science, University of Bergen, Bergen 5021, Norway

Simonetta Panerai, Raffaele Ferri, Valentina Catania, Marinella Zingale, Donatella Gelardi and Maurizio Elia
Oasi Research Institute-IRCCS, 94018 Troina, Italy

Daniela Ruccella
Psychoeducational Service for Children with Autism and Intellectual Disability, Società Cooperativa Sociale "I Corrieri dell'Oasi" (CdO), 94100 Enna, Italy

Daniela Fasciana
Center for Diagnosis and Early Intensive Treatment of Autism Spectrum Disorder, 93100 ASP Caltanissetta, Italy

Costas Koufaris and Carolina Sismani
Department of Cytogenetics and Genomics, the Cyprus Institute of Neurology and Genetics, Nicosia 1683, Cyprus

Zheng Wang, MinHyuk Kwon, Lauren M. Schmitt and Matthew W. Mosconi
Schiefelbusch Institute for Life Span Studies, University of Kansas, 1000 Sunnyside Ave., Lawrence, KS 66045, USA
Clinical Child Psychology Program, University of Kansas, 1000 Sunnyside Ave., Lawrence, KS 66045, USA
Kansas Center for Autism Research and Training (K-CART), University of Kansas Medical School, Overland Park, KS 66213, USA

Suman Mohanty and Stormi P. White
Center for Autism and Developmental Disabilities, University of Texas Southwestern Medical Center, Dallas, TX 75390, USA

Evangelos A. Christou
Department of Applied Physiology and Kinesiology, University of Florida, Gainesville, FL 32611, USA

Kimon Runge, Ludger Tebartz van Elst, Simon Maier, Kathrin Nickel, Dominik Denzel, Miriam Matysik, Hanna Kuzior and Dominique Endres
Section for Experimental Neuropsychiatry, Department of Psychiatry and Psychotherapy, Medical Center, Faculty of Medicine, University of Freiburg, Freiburg im Breisgau, Germany
Department of Psychiatry and Psychotherapy, Medical Center, Faculty of Medicine, University of Freiburg, Freiburg im Breisgau, Germany

Tilman Robinson and Rick Dersch
Department of Neurology, Medical Center, Faculty of Medicine, University of Freiburg, Freiburg im Breisgau, Germany

Thomas Blank
Institute of Neuropathology, Medical Center, Faculty of Medicine, University of Freiburg, Freiburg im Breisgau, Germany

Katharina Domschke
Department of Psychiatry and Psychotherapy, Medical Center, Faculty of Medicine, University of Freiburg, Freiburg im Breisgau, Germany
Center for Basics in Neuromodulation, Faculty of Medicine, University of Freiburg, Freiburg im Breisgau, Germany

Naila Al Mahmuda, Shigeru Yokoyama, Jian-Jun Huang, Li Liu and Toshio Munesue
Research Center for Child Mental Development, Kanazawa University, Kanazawa 920-8640, Japan

Hideo Nakatani
Division of Neuroscience, Kanazawa University Graduate School of Medical Science, Kanazawa 920-8640, Japan

Kenshi Hayashi and Masakazu Yamagishi
Division of Cardiovascular Medicine, Kanazawa University Graduate School of Medical Science, Kanazawa 920-8640, Japan

Kunimasa Yagi
Medical Education Research Center, Kanazawa University Graduate School of Medical Science, Kanazawa 920-8640, Japan

Hae Jeong Park, Su Kang Kim and Joo-Ho Chung
Kohwang Medical Research Institute, School of Medicine, Kyung Hee University, Seoul 02447, Korea

Won Sub Kang, Jin Kyung Park, Young Jong Kim and Jong Woo Kim
Department of Neuropsychiatry, School of Medicine, Kyung Hee University, Seoul 02447, Korea

Min Nam
Seoul Metropolitan Eunpyeong Hospital, Seoul 06801, Korea

Colin Heberling
Department of Biotechnology, Johns Hopkins University, Rockville, MD 20850, USA
Department of Chemical and Biomolecular Engineering, University of Delaware, Newark, DE 19716, USA

Prasad Dhurjati
Department of Chemical and Biomolecular Engineering, University of Delaware, Newark, DE 19716, USA

Index

www.ingramcontent.com/pod-product-compliance
Lightning Source LLC
LaVergne TN
LVHW060059220926
848484LV00008BA/2295